The U.S. Invasion
of Grenada

The U.S. Invasion
of Grenada

Legacy of a Flawed Victory

PHILIP KUKIELSKI

McFarland & Company, Inc., Publishers
Jefferson, North Carolina

LIBRARY OF CONGRESS CATALOGUING-IN-PUBLICATION DATA

Names: Kukielski, Philip, 1948– author.
Title: The U.S. Invasion of Grenada : Legacy of a Flawed
Victory / Philip Kukielski.
Other titles: Legacy of a flawed victory
Description: Jefferson, North Carolina : McFarland & Company, Inc.,
Publishers, 2020 | Includes bibliographical references and index.
Identifiers: LCCN 2019043665 | ISBN 9781476678795
(paperback : acid free paper) ∞ |
ISBN 9781476638324 (ebook)
Subjects: LCSH: Grenada—History—American Invasion, 1983. |
United States—Armed Forces—Grenada.
Classification: LCC F2056.8 .K84 2020 | DDC 972.9845—dc23
LC record available at https://lccn.loc.gov/2019043665

BRITISH LIBRARY CATALOGUING DATA ARE AVAILABLE

ISBN (print) 978-1-4766-7879-5
ISBN (ebook) 978-1-4766-3832-4

Front cover: A U.S. Army UH-60 Black Hawk helicopter in Grenada
during Operation Urgent Fury on October 25, 1983 (Department of Defense)

Printed in the United States of America

*McFarland & Company, Inc., Publishers
Box 611, Jefferson, North Carolina 28640
www.mcfarlandpub.com*

For Elisa, editor-in-chief
of my life and work

Table of Contents

Preface

The secret invasion of Grenada in the fall of 1983 took me, and most Americans, totally by surprise. Like most of my countrymen, on that day, I could not have successfully pointed to the island on a world map. Nonetheless, I had chosen a profession that routinely required me to write about subjects starting from scratch. On the morning of Oct. 25, I was a local news reporter assigned to the city desk of the *Providence Journal* in Rhode Island. My boss sought a local angle on the invasion to supplement the sparse wire service reports on the invasion then emanating from Washington and the Caribbean. I was dispatched to the suburban home of a ham radio hobbyist, who was monitoring shortwave broadcasts from the embattled island.

My D-Day vantage proved better than most—even though it was 2,141 miles away from the fighting. I spent the afternoon and early evening listening to tension-filled shortwave broadcasts from American civilians on Grenada. I was surprised to discover that the squawky reports I heard on the public airwaves were also being closely monitored at the top levels in Washington. These real-time, eyewitness accounts turned out to be the most reliable information that anyone stateside was getting that day about what was happening to U.S. civilians on the island. The principal conversation I overheard was between an American medical school student on the island, who had a generator-powered ham radio in his dorm room, and an American hobbyist, who had a rig at his New Jersey home. The student ham reported on the movements of Grenadian soldiers, who had surrounded his beachfront campus, and the U.S. soldiers and airmen, who had been sent to evacuate him and his American classmates at St. George's University Medical School. The student's stateside interlocutor asked questions that came from the State Department. At one point, I heard another ham interrupt the conversation to say he had a White House military attaché on the line. This ad hoc, radio-relay link struck me as a most curious way to manage a supposedly secret, multi-national rescue mission.

This mystifying D-Day experience was the start of a long personal quest. The story that follows here is the product of a decades-long journalistic inquiry into why, and how, the world's greatest superpower waged an impromptu, one-week war with a Caribbean microstate—and to what enduring effect. My initial zeal for this subject was fueled by soon-to-follow sad news. One of the 19 Americans killed during the invasion was Lt. Jeffrey Scharver, a Marine helicopter pilot from Barrington, Rhode Island. His Cobra attack helicopter was shot down when he was providing covering fire for the rescue of another downed Marine pilot. I was assigned to write an in-depth story on the circumstance of his death for the statewide paper's Sunday magazine. As I interviewed the Marines who served with Scharver, it became apparent that his final flight was a risky and unexpected mission. His two-man Cobra was called upon to perform heroic actions in order to set right a cascade of events that had gone wrong for Navy SEALs in the first hours of the fighting.

Extracting the full story of Operation Urgent Fury from the web of secrecy that encased it did not prove to be an easy journalistic assignment. Reporters were barred from the battlefield for the first three days of the operation. By the time they were allowed to set foot on the island, the fighting was essentially over. The after-action reporting by journalists never quite caught up with all that happened prior to the press corps' arrival. By the end of 1983, order had been restored on Grenada. American combat troops and foreign reporters came home. The southernmost Windward Island, a nation the size of Atlanta, again faded into insignificance on the world stage.

But the military flaws of Urgent Fury were like the fabled peas under the mattress for the Pentagon. The American Goliath did not rest easy on this preordained victory. As time went on, details of the operation's many snafus leaked out in various public forums. The Grenada experience got inexorably drawn into a then-simmering Washington debate over Pentagon organizational reform. In 1988, I wrote a fifth anniversary piece on the invasion's unexpected afterlife as a catalyst for change. I interviewed many of the key military players in the invasion, including the late Vice Adm. Joseph P. Metcalf III, the on-scene invasion commander, who had recently retired. My understanding of the operation was further advanced by two working vacations I subsequently spent in Grenada in the next few years. I toured battlegrounds and wrote about the island's nascent efforts to convert to a tourist-driven, free enterprise economy.

For many years, even decades, the best independent, unclassified history of the invasion was Mark Adkin's *Urgent Fury: The Battle for Grenada*, published in 1989. In 1983 Adkin was a British infantry officer serving on the staff of the Barbados Defence Force, a principal contributor to the multinational invasion coalition. Adkin had first-hand knowledge of the role played by all the Caribbean parties, including the Cubans and Grenadians. But Adkin was not privy to portions of the invasion story that played out in Washington and on military bases in the continental United States. Details from these sources, and others, dribbled out after 1989 in subsequently declassified military monographs, scholarly books, academic journals, military studies and memoir accounts.

This updated narrative of the invasion and its aftermath was assembled from shards of public information scattered across more than three decades. Putting the story together into a coherent chronological account has been akin to assembling a mosaic from thousands of pieces of irregularly shaped and variably colored glass. The central problem with telling the full story of the invasion, even now, is that virtually all the U.S. government–created information about the operation was initially classified top secret or higher. That classification stuck like a birthmark to the source material long after there was any compelling national security reason for keeping most of the information secret.

As a practical matter, I found that the principal way that initially classified information regarding Urgent Fury subsequently became public was if someone in authority who was privy to the information saw a particular benefit in having select material reviewed for release. This was typically done so that a particular document could be broadly shared with a larger audience to serve a training, policy or public relations purpose. Other formerly classified information was revealed in memoir accounts written by, or for, former Reagan administration policymakers or special operations veterans. This insider-driven declassification system was supposed to have changed under an executive order issued in 2009 by President Obama. That revision of the classification system was aimed at expediting targeted declassification requests filed by the general public, principally historians and journalists. The 2009 order also raised the bar that agencies had to meet to still keep historical information classified after 25 years. That quarter-century benchmark was passed in 2008 by Urgent Fury. Regrettably, in my research, I found scant evidence of substantive declassification of Urgent Fury historical records on the 25-year mark by the military on its own initiative.

This book is based in significant part on Freedom of Information Act (FOIA) filings and Mandatory Declassification Review (MDR) requests that I and other civilian researchers have submitted for Urgent Fury documents over the years. (Most classified documents are exempted from release under the FOIA law. The separate MDR process is used for still-classified documents.) One of my principal research interests was a Washington, D.C., collection of more than 300 mostly classified oral history interviews with key Urgent Fury participants that were conducted by military historians between 1983 and the 1990s. Sixty-one of these interviews were made available to me in audio tape or transcript form after declassification by the Army. I believe I am the first civilian without a security clearance to review most of these interviews. Other classified interviews in this collection that I also requested in 2016 contained content that required sign-off by government agencies other than the Army. That process, regarded as the "black hole" of MDR requests, is still underway and could take still more years to complete.

The oral histories I reviewed are part of a huge, mostly classified Urgent Fury collection archived at the U.S. Army Center of Military History at Fort McNair in Washington, D.C. That collection was used by Edgar Raines, Jr., a staff historian at the center, to write an authoritative history of Urgent Fury, titled *The Rucksack War*, which was published by his Army agency in 2010. As the title suggests, Raines focused primarily on the formidable logistical challenges that the affected Army units faced in attempting to execute a hastily planned airborne operation on short notice.

Beyond the classification barrier, I also found the Urgent Fury historical record to be a muddled one. Because the historical record of Urgent Fury special forces operations remains classified, many inaccurate, thinly sourced accounts of Navy SEAL and Delta Force operations have been published over the years. I hope my version will be closer to the currently documentable truth.

As an unaffiliated outsider, I bring an all-agencies, multi-national approach to this historical inquiry. I hope that my journalistic telling will make for an easy and engaging read, especially suitable for civilian readers with no prior background with the military or this subject. I use a narrative, rather than an analytic form, to spool out my account of the invasion in digestible doses. This chronological approach instructs mostly by showing, rather than telling. The narrative establishes a time-specific context for events and also allows for amplifying digressions at relevant points. Key players can be presented as multi-faceted characters in an unfolding drama, as opposed to pop-up proper names in a postgraduate-level history lecture.

My aim has been to compile the most accurate, readable account of the invasion possible, based on the now-available evidence. To do that I have relied most heavily on the published memoirs of the participants and for-the-record interviews conducted by me or other journalists and historians. The late H. Norman Schwarzkopf is a recurring voice, sharing his view of the action as the Army's principal advisor to the invasion task force commander. Schwarzkopf, then a two-star general, later became an American hero for leading an international coalition to victory over Iraq in the 1990–91 Persian Gulf War. He died in 2012, but he left behind a copious record of his Urgent Fury experiences in an autobiography and three extensive declassified oral history interviews I reviewed. I have also had the benefit of personally interviewing many participants presented here. Some of the interviews were conducted by me in the course of reporting Grenada-related stories over the years for newspaper publication. Those interviews are generally cited here by the date of publication for the by-lined stories in which the interviewees were quoted. Other interviews were conducted more recently by me specifically for this book to fill in gaps in the narrative not covered by oral histories, memoirs or documents.

My central thesis is that Grenada was a flawed victory that, in the long run, was more noteworthy for the shortcomings it exposed than for the battles that were won against a mismatched adversary. The Pentagon ultimately deserves institutional accolades for systematically documenting its battlefield inadequacies and then embracing necessary remedial reform. The Urgent Fury-induced changes wrought in the military in the mid and late 1980s prepared the uniformed services to wage the two Gulf Wars and the War on Terror. By Oct. 25, 1983, the case for Pentagon reform had already achieved critical mass based on the failed Iranian hostage rescue, the Beirut barracks terrorist bombing and other post–World War II military misadventures. Urgent Fury's snafus were not sufficiently egregious to have been solely the cause of reform, but they were uniquely suited to serve as an accelerating agent for organizational change.

In terms of scope, this telling makes necessary omissions in the service of producing a manageable-length popular history for a North American audience. I give short shrift to the intense diplomatic discussions that took place in the capital cities of the Caribbean and elsewhere during the final run-up to the invasion. That aspect of Urgent Fury was most comprehensively and recently told by Gary Williams, a British foreign policy scholar, in *U.S.–Grenada Relations: Revolution and Intervention in the Backyard* published in 2007. Similarly, the final chapter offers a mostly American-centric view of the invasion aftermath. I leave the Caribbean post-war view to others better positioned by location and experience. Bernard Coard, the putative Grenadian villain of Urgent Fury, is now joining the historical discussion after serving 26 years in prison for ordering the political executions that precipitated the invasion. Coard began telling his version of 1983 events in Grenada with the 2017 publication of *The Grenada Revolution: What Really Happened*, the first of several volumes on the subject. I have attempted to put his revealing assertions into an objective context.

Resolving conflicting memories of events by otherwise credible sources has been difficult, especially when describing the chaos of firefights. I have eschewed barracks gossip, unattributed quotes and speculation. All my cited sources are named and independently verifiable. The story of special forces operations in Grenada has been the most difficult to obtain. Virtually all those official records are still classified and participants say they are still bound by non-disclosure agreements they signed before leaving the service. In making my judgments about whose facts to embrace, I confess certain prejudices. As for the precise chronology of combat, I have relied mostly on two Air Force-connected works: *Grenada Grinder: The Complete Story of AC-130H Spectre Gunships in Operation Urgent Fury* by Michael J. Couvillon and *Urgent Fury: The United States Air Force and the Grenada Operation* by Dean C. Kallander and James K. Matthews. In expressing time, I have used the 24-hour clock when dealing with military matters, and a.m. and p.m. in sections when civilians dominate the story (and the time-referenced quotes). I have used Associated Press style for expressing military ranks and identified Spanish-surnamed figures on subsequent reference by their second (father's) surname. I found that Adkin's *Urgent Fury* gives the best account of the Grenadian and Cuban intentions and capabilities. Raines' *Rucksack War* is the most thoroughly researched from the U.S. military side. I relied on Raines for guidance when other accounts diverged or conflicted.

I am indebted to many who helped me along the way on this long journey. Joel Rawson and Carol Young were editors at the *Providence Journal* who indulged and supported my interest in the subject in the 1980s. Later, after leaving the *Journal's* employ, two editors at the *Boston Globe*, Chris Rowland and Stephen Heuser, saw merit in my pitch of a 30th anniversary look back at Urgent Fury. Stephen F. Knott and Richard J. Norton, professors at the Naval War College in Newport, helped me research and focus a story for the *Globe's* Sunday Ideas section in September 2013 that led to a proposal for this book.

Fred Allison and Ashleigh Simmons of the History Division at Marine Corps University at Quantico, Virginia, jump-started my book research by sharing 29 unclassified Urgent Fury oral history interviews conducted by Marine historians. Mary Curry guided me through the extensive published and unpublished Urgent Fury FOIA collection at the National Security Archive Reading Room at George Washington University. Nate Jones of that non-profit organization gave me some expert coaching on making FOIA and MDR requests. Lisette Matano was my guide to the Booth Family Center Special Collections at Georgetown University that contains a well-organized Grenada document collection. This collection was donated by Gregory W. Sandford, a State Department diplomat, who co-authored *Grenada: The Untold Story*, published in 1984. My Georgetown research brought me in contact with Jose Perez Reisler, a faculty member at the University of Madrid who was working on his Ph.D. thesis, a socio-political analysis of the Grenadian version of Marxism. Reisler was helpful in guiding me to scholarly research on the island's revolutionary era. Robert L. Jordan, a dean and anatomy professor at the St. George's Medical School, was most generous in sharing his irreplaceable first-hand knowledge of the invasion, the medical school and the island. Anne Lucas, the daughter of a valiant Army helicopter pilot killed on D-Day, was an ambassador to other Urgent Fury Gold Star families. Frank R. Shirer was my principal contact at the U.S. Army Center of Military History (CMH) until his retirement in 2018. He supervised my by-appointment access to freshly declassified oral history interviews. I also found valuable Grenada documents at CMH's sister library at the U.S. Army Heritage and Education Center in Carlisle, Pennsylvania. Rich Baker, a retired Air Force master sergeant, gave me basic training on the use of their public-friendly military library. I completed my grand tour of Grenada archives in D.C. area with visits to the Library of Congress. I found small-press books and pamphlets there that were not on the shelves anywhere else. I also found valuable oral history interviews with U.S. government officials archived online in the library's "Frontline Diplomacy" collection and, separately, on the website for the Miller Center (of public affairs) affiliated with University of Virginia. Dr. Robert L. Pfaltzgraff, Jr., the Shelby Cullom Davis Professor of International Security Studies at the Fletcher School, Tufts University, generously shared two revealing interviews he conducted in the late 1980s with two top Reagan-era national security figures.

As for official government records, the CIA and the State Department both separately maintain virtual FOIA Reading Rooms that include Urgent Fury documents. These websites allow public searches and download of records that have been declassified as a result of previous FOIA or MDR requests. I also found other Grenada-related declassified documents from various federal agencies online in the proprietary database: U.S. Declassified Documents Online. The online version of the Ronald Reagan Library had valuable White House documents, including official presidential appointment diaries and texts of speeches. The online version of the Margaret Thatcher Foundation Archive contains many cables that document London's pique with the American-led intervention into a Commonwealth country. I found most of the Congressional records I needed in the Federal Depository Library collection in the Fenwick Library at George Mason University in Fairfax, Virginia. I must also offer a hometown shout-out to my anonymous partners in this project on the staff of the Fairfax County Public Library system. Their research librarians tracked down obscure books and articles for me through their excellent web-based interlibrary loan program. Finally, thanks to two college classmates, William J. "Bill" Hughes and Warren Junium, both former Navy officers, who, respectively, applied the eye of an aviator and a mariner to draft chapters of my manuscript.

Introduction

Nineteen eighty-three was a year in American history when the domestic outlook brightened and technology leaped forward—but hidden dangers lurked abroad. On the plus side, the domestic economy was emerging from the recession of the early 1980s. Interest rates were still in the double digits, but inflation was abating and job creation were starting to pick up. The American workplace was in the early stages of an epic migration from the office into the home and into the Ethernet. Jan. 1, 1983, is commonly regarded as the day the Internet was born. On that day, an experimental computer network called ARPANET converted to the file-sharing protocols that later came to define the Internet. In the spring, IBM introduced the PC XT, its first personal computer with a hard drive. Microsoft released a word processing software called Word in the fall.

These cyber innovations proved a boon to American productivity, but they were viewed with existential alarm in the Kremlin. Computers were becoming so ubiquitous in the United States that children played with them, but, in Moscow, not even every office in the Defense Ministry had one, a top Russian military lamented to an American journalist. The KGB did a sophisticated secret analysis of the fundamental strength of the two countries in the early 1980s and concluded that Moscow was losing the Cold War. The Soviet economy was stagnant. Its leader, Yuri Andropov, was also ailing, suffering from fatal kidney disease. For good reason, the Soviets felt vulnerable.

President Reagan, then in the third of his eight years in office, exacerbated Soviet anxiety. He authorized provocative military exercises, derided the Soviet Union as an "evil empire" and proposed a "Star Wars" plan to wage a new arms race in space. Andropov privately believed that America was planning a surprise nuclear attack that would decapitate the Kremlin leadership. French president François Mitterand compared U.S.–Soviet relations in 1983 to the 1962 Cuban missile crisis and the 1948 Berlin blockade.

This was the toxic geopolitical environment that prevailed in the early fall of 1983 when a prosaic leadership struggle developed in Grenada. Two like-minded men who had been friends since boyhood vied for control of the Marxist-inspired microstate in the West Indies. The dispute had Cold War ramifications. Grenada had legacy governmental ties to the United Kingdom, and extensive social ties to the United States, but had recently come under the ideological sway of both Havana and Moscow. Further complicating the picture, the power struggle was occurring in a section of the world that America had historically considered its "backyard," and on an island that Reagan considered a Communist colony in the making.

This narrative begins on Oct. 17, 1983, when the leadership struggle had turned hostile, but not yet murderous. My conceit in telling the story of the subsequent American invasion is to only share with the reader the background knowledge that was generally available to the military line officers who were called on to plan and execute the impromptu operation. That approach, I found, goes a long way in explaining why the operation was fought as it was. Everyone was acting on limited information, no sleep, short notice, strict secrecy rules and exacting deadlines. Seemingly inexplicable mishaps, like bombing a mental hospital, become understandable if the reader marches along in cadence with what the combat commanders knew and experienced in this "come-as-you-are" operation. I also found that Grenada's regrettable snafus were invariably counterbalanced by inspiring, little-known heroics.

The initial chapters advance generally chronologically, but the content is presented thematically. The priority concern of the invasion commanders kept changing as battlefield surprises altered their objectives. The focus is on what went wrong because the Grenada battlefield was defined by its accidents, snafus and equipment limitations. This may strike some as picking at a healed wound, but my redemptive purpose is made clear in the concluding chapters. The invasion backstory is told in the penultimate chapter, The Route to Intervention, rather than at the beginning, because I believe the provocations for the invasion are more accurately weighed if you know the result. Readers who come to this telling with prior knowledge of the invasion from other sources may opt to read Chapter 11 first.

1

39 Hours to "Go"

The Marines who were first to fight on the Caribbean island of Grenada on Oct. 25, 1983, left American soil on Navy ships a week earlier with another destination and mission in mind. They thought they were bound for peacekeeping duty in Lebanon, by way of an amphibious training exercise off the Iberian Peninsula. So, if you mentioned Grenada (grih-NAY-duh) to the Marine officers before they shipped out, they would have been nonplussed. They might have assumed you were mispronouncing Granada, the Moorish-influenced province in Spain with the similarly spelled name. Grenada (with an e), a Windward Island microstate just off the coast of Venezuela, was a continent away from where they headed—and totally outside their current world-view. Most of the Leather-necks, like most Americans, didn't even know that the newly independent nation even existed. On Oct. 17–18, this self-sufficient Marine expeditionary force of 1,700 from Camp Lejeune in North Carolina trundled aboard five Navy ships, loaded their supplies and equipment, and set sail for the Mediterranean. The embarked Marines constituted the 22nd Marine Amphibious Unit (MAU), a reinforced infantry battalion supported by a squadron of helicopters, a platoon of tanks and a battery of artillery.

The flagship of Amphibious Squadron Four was the USS *Guam*, a 603-foot amphibious assault ship. Within NATO, this type of ship was known as an LPH, an acronym for "Landing Platform Helicopter." Landlubbers would call them aircraft carriers for helicopters. Instead of fixed-wing aircraft, this 18-year-old warship carried 22 transport and attack helicopters on its crowded flight deck. The *Guam's* four associated transport ships—the USS *Trenton*, the USS *Fort Snelling*, the USS *Manitowoc* and the USS *Barnstable County*—carried the MAU's support personnel and equipment, including amphibious vehicles, tanks and jeeps.[1]

Most of the Marines embarked at Morehead City, North Carolina, but some assigned to berths on the *Guam* had to travel to Norfolk, Virginia, because the aging flagship had a last-minute problem.[2] The amphibious group left the East Coast on a transatlantic crossing under a cloud-dappled autumn sky with gentle winds and swells. The 22nd MAU was ultimately bound to relieve brother Marines in the 24th MAU who had been performing peacekeeping duty in Lebanon since the previous May. The Marine Corps had been first dispatched to Beirut by the Reagan administration in August 1982. They deployed as part of a multinational effort to quell civilian bloodshed in a long-running civil war that also came to involve Israeli and Syria forces. Sectarian fighting had ravaged and divided a beautiful port city once regarded as the Paris of the Middle East. The 22nd MAU was bound for a second six-month tour of duty in Beirut that was becoming more perilous with each passing day.

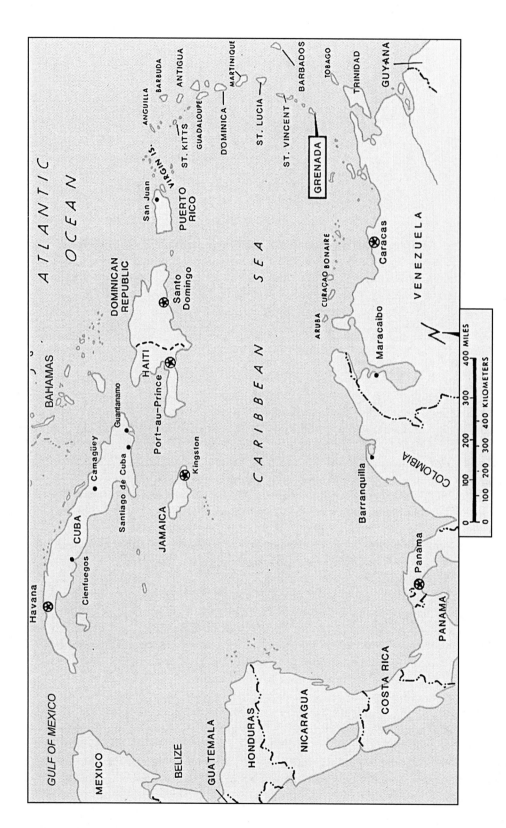

Caribbean islands. This map positions Grenada in the Caribbean Basin, at the southern end of the Windward Islands in the Eastern Caribbean. The Windwards constitute a subdivision of a longer arc of volcanic islands known as the Lesser Antilles. The Lesser Antilles, combined with the Greater Antilles and the Bahama Archipelago, constitute the West Indies (courtesy U.S. Military Academy, Department of History).

After the third day at sea, just after the five ships passed Bermuda, the amphibious squadron received unexpected orders.[3] At 2030 on Thursday, Oct. 20, the group's commodore, Navy captain Carl R. Erie, was directed by the Pentagon to turn south and take up a holding station east of Puerto Rico.[4] Some of the Marines, resting in their bunks below decks, no doubt noticed the alteration in course and the increase in speed to 16 knots.[5] However, they assigned no particular significance to the changes, because no immediate announcement was made as to the reason. At around the same time on Oct. 20 that the *Guam* group made its turn south, a similar course change was being made about 150 miles further north in the Atlantic by an affiliated Mediterranean-bound naval group.[6] A six-warship, Norfolk-based Carrier Battle Group, led by the aircraft carrier USS *Independence*, was ordered to take a holding position in the vicinity of the island of Dominica.[7]

In all, an 11-ship task force was being assembled by the Pentagon in the Caribbean for a potential mission, yet to be precisely defined. The *Independence* group, under the command of Rear Adm. Richard C. Berry, was 72 hours away from Grenadian waters. The *Guam* group under Erie was 96 hours away.[8] Both commanders were told to proceed separately to their respective holding positions to await further instructions. All the warships were ordered to proceed stealthily under strict electronic emission control conditions (EMCON) that restricted their use of radar and prohibited outbound radio transmissions. They had their orders, but couldn't ask questions.

Marine colonel James P. Faulkner, the 22nd MAU commander, got his first word of the diversion at 0430 on Friday, Oct. 21, eight hours after the *Guam* group changed course.[9] He immediately guessed that the detour was related to recent radio reports of a bloody coup that had occurred on Grenada on the day they set sail. (Some aboard had personal radios that could pick up news broadcasts by the Voice of America and the BBC.) The Grenadian coup was the violent denouement to a months-long power struggle on the island. Two rival leaders were vying for control of the Communist-inspired, nominally socialist government which had ruled the island nation since 1979. A doctrinaire faction within the ruling Marxist-Leninist party pressured the populist prime minister, Maurice Bishop, to share power with his erstwhile friend and rival, Bernard Coard, the deputy prime minister. Bishop initially agreed, but soon balked. The Coard-led hardliners, backed by the Grenadian military, then assumed total control of the one-party government on Oct. 12, 1983. Bishop was put under house arrest until he relented.

A week later, on Wednesday, Oct. 19, thousands of Bishop loyalists marched to his home and set him free. Bishop moved immediately to reassert his power by taking control of a colonial-era fort in the capital that served as headquarters for the Grenadian military. The hardliners responded by dispatching Grenadian soldiers in armored vehicles to disperse the crowd, regain the fort and recapture Bishop. The soldiers were met at the fort by Bishop supporters who had armed themselves with seized weapons. Shooting started and blood was shed on both sides. The soldiers quickly prevailed over the civilians. Bishop and seven of his supporters, including three cabinet ministers, were taken prisoner. The eight captives were led away to an interior courtyard at the fort and executed by a military firing squad on the orders of the coup leaders. The cold-blooded assassinations were a shocking event in the normally laid-back, English-speaking Caribbean. A new military-led, interim regime quickly emerged. They sought to restore order by announcing a four-day, shoot-on-sight, round-the-clock curfew on all residents.

Faulkner correctly guessed that the unexplained course change was saber-rattling by Washington to ensure the safety of Americans on the island, particularly the 600-odd U.S. citizens who were students at St. George's University Medical School. At most, Faulkner thought his Marine force might be called on to evacuate American civilians.[10] His suspicions were publicly corroborated on Friday, Oct. 21, when the CBS Evening News led its nightly broadcast with a story on the secret naval diversions toward Grenada. David C. Martin, the network's Pentagon correspondent, reported that the Lebanon-bound task force had been detoured south in the event that American citizens on Grenada needed to be extricated. Martin's report made no suggestion that any other purpose might be involved in the diversion, but he added that there was concern that the arrival of an American carrier in Grenadian waters might be "misinterpreted" by the new regime. (Martin later said that he had no idea at the time that the military mission was anything more than a possible evacuation.)[11] The CBS report was picked up by the Associated Press and confirmed by an unnamed "Defense Department official" at a Pentagon press briefing that evening. The ship diversion, amplified by additional reporting from Grenada, ran on the front pages of both the New York Times and the Washington Post on Oct. 22. At that point, policy makers in Washington, and in capitals around the world, were alerted that U.S. Marines were on the way to Grenada. Given the 20th century history of multiple Marine-led interventions in the Caribbean, strategic surprise was effectively lost—if it ever was realistically achievable under the crisis conditions then prevailing in the Eastern Caribbean. Though secrecy was now compromised, no corresponding adjustment to the rigid security rules governing the operation was made by the Pentagon. This effectively straight-jacketed the American military to questionable benefit just as it was preparing to flex its muscles for the first time since Vietnam.

At sea, Marine officers, billeted on different ships in the Guam group, found it most efficient to communicate among themselves by using blinker lights to send Morse-code messages from bridge to bridge.[12] This old-technology, work-around solution was a portent of communication limitations that would plague the impending operation for days to come. Faulkner and his MAU staff assembled on the Guam to begin planning for an evacuation of American citizens from the island, but intelligence information was scant. The Guam's only nautical chart of the Grenadian waters was last updated in 1936.[13] The land map of the island the Marine planners reportedly used was taken from a tourist brochure that happened to be in the Guam's ship's library.[14]

Fortunately for the planners, two officers on board had some personal familiarity with their likely destination. One Navy staff officer, Cmdr. Richard A. Butler, was an amateur yachtsman who had sailed the Windward Islands on vacation six years earlier. Also, one of Faulkner's staff intelligence officers had recently stopped off on the island on his honeymoon. He was able to offer a first-hand description of the island's only operating commercial airport at Pearls. By another fortuitous circumstance, Lt. Col. Ray L. Smith, the Marine battalion commander, had recently written a study for the Armed Forces Staff College on a hypothetical landing on the island.[15] (Grenada had been a declared foreign policy concern for the Reagan administration for the previous two years.)

A shipboard plan was drafted on speculation for a combined amphibious and airborne incursion to evacuate civilians. It called for a company of 22nd MAU Marines to land by helicopter at Point Salines (pronounced SAY-leans) on the southwestern tip of the island to seize control of a 9,000-foot runway being constructed there by Cuban and Grenadian workers. Simultaneously, other 22nd MAU Marines would stage an amphibious landing at Grand Anse Beach on the western coast of the island. These

Marines would then move inland from the beachhead to sever the road from St. George's, the capital city, to the new airport. The degree of force used to accomplish the air evacuation of American civilians would be determined by the amount of resistance the Marines encountered. Though the mission to divert to Grenada came as a surprise to the 22nd MAU, it was a task the unit was well prepared to undertake. As part of their pre-deployment training, the MAU helicopter squadron had conducted extensive night operations. The unit as a whole had recently participated in a 48-hour exercise built around a theoretical diversion from a transatlantic transit to seize the fictional island of "Andros" in the Caribbean. The training exercise was similar to the real-life mission they were drafting, but not precisely the same.[16]

At this stage, the Marines were expecting that the incursion, if it happened at all, would be a humanitarian extraction, by force if necessary, but not a military takeover. The Marine officers reviewed standard operating procedures for conducting a "non-combatant evacuation operation," an "NEO" in military-speak. But, absent more specifics on the when, why and how of the mission, the planning was more conceptual than concrete. None of the Marine officers thought that they'd actually be ordered to execute the operation they were discussing. "It is doubtful that we will be called on to carry out the mission," Faulkner, the MAU commander, wrote in his journal.[17]

The next few days, however, brought an inexorable evolution in Washington toward a more aggressive "regime-change" invasion. This mid–October weekend in the third year of President Ronald Reagan's first term was supposed to have been an opportunity for a long-planned presidential getaway with friends at the Augusta National Golf Club. Reagan and his wife, Nancy, were hosted at the Georgia resort by Secretary of State George P. Shultz and former New Jersey senator Nicholas F. Brady and their wives. Donald T. Regan, the secretary of the treasury, and his wife were also invited. The husbands planned to play a foursome round at the then male-only golf course. White House staffers referred to it as the "George Shultz Invitational." Instead of fraternal relaxation, the weekend brought what presidential scholars now consider the biggest foreign policy crises of Reagan's first term. The president was well aware of the storm clouds rising over Grenada as his scheduled Friday-night departure approached. Before leaving Washington, he personally affirmed the 11-ship diversion toward Grenada by approving National Security Decision Directive 110. That presidential order, drafted by the National Security Council staff, directed that "all prudent measures" be taken to protect the safety of American citizens on the troubled island. It further directed U.S. government agencies to "also be prepared to participate in a multi-lateral effort to restore order on Grenada and prevent further Cuban/Soviet intervention/involvement on the island."[18] The Pentagon was specifically authorized to secretly move American military forces to "reduce response time for the conduct of non-combatant evacuation operations (NEO) on Grenada." Simultaneously, the secretary of state was directed to contact NATO allies and friendly Caribbean Basin governments to sound them out on their willingness to participate in a Grenada intervention force.

Reagan had considered canceling the Augusta trip, but decided to go ahead rather than encourage speculation that some American action in the Caribbean was imminent. Just in case this turned out to be a working weekend, Robert C. "Bud" McFarlane, the newly named national security advisor, came along as a last-minute addition to the presidential entourage. The president had just checked into the Eisenhower Cottage at the Augusta resort and gone to sleep when the first Grenada decision point of the weekend arose. At 0245 on Saturday, Oct. 22, Shultz was awakened by a phone call informing him that the State Department had just received a diplomatic cable that warranted an immediate presidential response.[19] The Organization of Eastern Caribbean States (OECS), a regional group, was asking the United States to lead an intervention to restore order and democracy on Grenada. The news was significant, but not unexpected. Shultz and McFarlane conferred and decided to wake the president. At about 5 a.m. the three men gathered on the lower-level sitting room of the six-bedroom cottage.[20] The American response to the military intervention proposed by Grenada's Caribbean neighbors animated the pre-dawn conversations. Shultz was an advocate for military action. "The entire Grenada operation was driven by the State Department," he later unabashedly declared in his Washington memoir.[21] Shultz was concerned that the murderous political turmoil on the island created conditions that were ripe for Americans on the island to be taken hostage. He didn't want a repeat of the humiliation America suffered in 1979 when 66 hostages were taken from the embassy in Teheran, Iran, and held for 444 days. Reagan's election in 1980 was due in no small part to the public's perception that President Jimmy Carter's one-term administration had failed to adequately respond to that provocation. A conference call was organized involving key Washington players, including Vice President George H.W. Bush and Caspar W. Weinberger, the secretary of defense. Reagan joined the secure call, still dressed in his slippers and pajamas.[22] Shultz urged action while Weinberger

President Ronald Reagan, in his pajamas, conferred with Secretary of State George P. Shultz (also on the sofa) and National Security Advisor Robert C. McFarlane in the Eisenhower Cottage at the Augusta Golf Club at around 5 a.m. on Saturday, October 22, 1983. Reagan was awakened on a get-away weekend to discuss the Grenada intervention request, received earlier that night in Washington from the Organization of Eastern Caribbean States (courtesy Ronald Reagan Library [c17822-15]).

advised delay to gather more information, a reversal of their stereotypic policy roles. The two cabinet members were united in their loyalty to the president, but they differed on how readily to use military force as an instrument of American policy. The clash of personality and principle between the two strong-willed men was not unusual. "You never had a day when the secretary of state and the secretary of defense weren't at each other's throats," James A. Baker III, then Reagan's chief of staff, ruefully confided years later to a presidential historian.[23] In this instance, the vice president sided with Weinberger. Bush, a former CIA director under President Ford, supported a delay to attempt to enlist Venezuela or some other Spanish-speaking country to join the English-speaking OECS coalition.[24] Shultz found Reagan to be "decisive" and "ready to go" in the conversation, but the president stopped short of issuing any orders. As soon as the call ended, Shultz urged Reagan to call back to ask what size of force the Pentagon had in mind for the operation. Regardless of the answer, Shultz coached the president to say that he wanted the number doubled. Shultz wanted Reagan to signal to the military that the Oval Office was inclined to decisively intervene.[25]

The conference call was followed by a 9 a.m. emergency weekend meeting of the National Security Council's Special Situations Group, chaired by Bush.[26] Attendees were advised to arrive by different entrances to shield this multi-agency meeting from the White House press corps. The venue was moved from the cramped Situation Room in the White House subbasement to a newer and bigger meeting room in Room 208 in the Old Executive Office Building next door.[27] The purpose of this two-and-a-half-hour meeting was to review the latest diplomatic and military information on the Grenada crisis and then to decide on appropriate next steps based on the president's strong inclination to intervene.

The Caribbean request now broadened the proposed Pentagon role beyond evacuating Americans and subduing any opposition to their extraction to also include "restoring orderly government to Grenada." The State Department presented an inch-thick "total action plan" to invade Grenada no later than dawn on Tuesday, Oct. 25.[28] Reagan participated in the meeting by secure phone for five minutes at 9:31 a.m. from the golf course in Georgia. Bush summarized the preceding discussion and sought Reagan's view of the intervention's ultimate objective. Reagan responded: "Well, if we've got to go in there, we might as well do all that needs to be done."[29] The key take-away action from this meeting was the final preparation of a second, superseding presidential order. National Security Decision Directive 110A authorized an invasion with regime change, instead of a mere rescue, as its objective. Rear Adm. John Poindexter, the deputy NSC director, got Reagan's authorization on Saturday afternoon and sent copies to the Pentagon, the State Department and the CIA.[30]

"I've OK'd an outright invasion in response to a request by 6 other Caribbean nations including Jamaica & Barbados," Reagan wrote in his personal diary.[31] But, despite the unequivocal language of that handwritten Oct. 22 entry, Reagan's directive was, in fact, not yet a final order. One commentator later aptly described it as a "75%" decision.[32] It was still possible that a deal could be reached with the Grenadian coup leaders to peaceably evacuate American civilians from the island by ship or plane. Also, Reagan wanted to be sure that the Caribbean states that were calling for the intervention would unflinchingly stand behind the United States if shooting started. Ambassador Francis J. (Frank) McNeil, a senior State Department diplomat, was dispatched from Washington to Barbados to gauge the Caribbean coalition's mettle for combat, should it come to that.

Reagan, meanwhile, attempted to maintain an illusion of normalcy by playing a Saturday morning round of golf as planned. The desired deception was not easily accomplished. Shultz conspicuously kept contact with the State Department using a radio telephone on the back of the golf cart. While they were on the links, Les Janka, a deputy press secretary, interrupted them to report that the White House press corps was asking if the ships headed to Grenada were an invasion force. The golfers responsible for the task force diversion acted like they didn't have any idea what Janka was talking about.[33] The deputy press secretary, in turn, denied the rumors to the press in an act that cost him his professional credibility and later led to his forced resignation. The headline over the resulting story in the Sunday *Washington Post* said: "US Says Situation Still Unclear as Naval Force Nears Grenada." The story quoted "two aides travelling with President Reagan" as saying the ships were just a show of force and no invasion was planned.[34] The truth was the first casualty of the coming military action on Grenada.

More hazards lay ahead on the golf course. The foursome made it as far as the 16th hole when Secret Services agents suddenly surrounded the president's party and whisked them away in armored White House limousines. A deranged man with a .38-caliber pistol had smashed his pickup truck through a gate to the golf club. He took seven hostages, including two White House staffers, and held them in the nearby pro shop demanding to speak to the president. Reagan unsuccessfully attempted to appease the gunman by talking to him by phone from his limousine. The president called five times, but the gunman hung up each time he called.[35] Eventually the man released the hostages and was arrested. The Reagan party called it a day in mid-afternoon without completing their round of golf. They remained in Augusta, however, to maintain the image of calm they were trying so hard to project to the world, but they were having difficulty achieving in reality.

The invasion was a go, but a still-evolving, tentative one. On the military front, the Joint Chiefs had been working with Adm. Wesley L. McDonald, the commander-in-chief of Atlantic Command (CINCLANT), since Friday, Oct. 14, even before Bishop's assassination, to plan an intervention to protect Americans if the order came from the president. But, in the ensuing days, the case for intervention advanced unexpectedly from a routine "what if?" inquiry to a "get ready!" imperative. On Thursday evening, Oct. 20, Gen. John W. Vessey, Jr., chairman of the Joint Chiefs of Staff, also contacted Army major general Richard A. Scholtes, the commander of the new Joint Special Operations Command (JSOC) to ask how he would envision a military intervention.[36]

By Saturday, Oct. 22, there were two draft invasion plans under consideration. The Atlantic Command's plan assigned the assault to the Marines of the 22nd MAU, supported by the Navy jets from the carrier *Independence*. The alternate JSOC plan gave the job to Army Rangers based in the continental United States, with help from shore-based Navy SEALs and Army Delta Force commandoes.[37] Both approaches would involve about the same number of troops: 1,800. Either way, the initial assault would be closely followed by paratroopers from the Army's 82nd Airborne Division who would serve as a mop-up and occupation force.

Neither approach satisfied the defense secretary when he met with the Joint Chiefs at the Pentagon on Saturday to review the progress of planning. Though Weinberger had his reservations about the wisdom of the intervention, he, like Shultz, pressed for the Joint Chiefs to double the force. "I always had in mind that one of the major problems with our attempt to rescue our hostages in Iran in 1979 was that we sent too few helicopters," Weinberger later wrote in his Pentagon memoir.[38] The chairman of the Joint Chiefs had his own concerns that he wanted addressed. Whatever the final plan, Vessey did not want a large group of high-ranking American officers to be visibly present on the ground in Grenada. He apparently was concerned that the United States would appear to be overreacting to the military threat posed to it by a poor Caribbean country of about 90,000 people. To limit the Army brass involved, he directed that only two battalions of the 82nd Airborne be involved, effectively cutting them away from their parent command, the XVIII Airborne Corps.[39] The corps controlled such specialized support functions as military police, construction engineers and long-range communication. This decision to cut out the corps level would have major implications later as the 82nd Airborne tried to keep its combat troops supplied and supported when they arrived on Grenada by airlift. "In retrospect, General Vessey's decision to exclude the XVIII Airborne Corps from the chain of command

Top: Adm. Wesley L. McDonald, USN, commander-in-chief of Atlantic Command (CINCLANT), 1983 (National Archives [330-CFD-DN-ST-85-10949]). *Bottom, left:* Gen. John W. Vessey, Jr., USA, chairman of the Joint Chiefs of Staff, undated (Joint Chiefs of Staff). *Right:* Maj. Gen. Richard A. Scholtes, USA, commanding officer, Joint Special Operations Command, 1982 (National Archives [330-CFD-DA-SC-87-10831]).

was the single most important cause of problems in Urgent Fury.... The arbitrary elimination of the corps level of command and staff from Urgent Fury made the accomplishment of that mission infinitely more difficult," concluded the author of one subsequent Army historical study.[40]

At around the same time on Saturday that Reagan was conferring by phone with his national security advisers in Washington, McDonald was holding a staff-level planning meeting at his headquarters in Norfolk. The strict secrecy rules imposed on the impending operation by the Joint Chiefs prohibited printed messages. Virtually all the pre-invasion coordination planning by units of different services had to take place in conversations in person or on secure phones.[41] The Norfolk session had an incongruously casual ambiance despite the gravity of the matters at hand. McDonald was dressed in a track suit and many of other participants were dressed in weekend attire.[42] McDonald's footwear selection for that day was not recorded, but his backstory called for him to be a "brown shoe" sailor. Naval regulations allowed for aviation officers and senior enlisted to wear brown shoes with their khaki uniforms, while surface ship sailors were restricted to black shoes. The shoe hue was more than a matter of conformity to uniform regulations; it also colored the wearer's view of the Navy, the military and the world.

McDonald was accustomed by training and experience to view combat from the air. He was a 1946 graduate of the U.S. Naval Academy who trained as a jet fighter pilot. He established his bona fides as a warrior by leading the first retaliatory air strike against North Vietnam on Aug. 5, 1964, after the Gulf of Tonkin incident.[43] He went on to take command of an aircraft carrier and then a carrier group. He was promoted to rear admiral before the Vietnam War ended and, by 1983, he wore four stars on his shoulders. He simultaneously commanded three organizations: the U.S. Atlantic Command, the U.S. Atlantic Fleet and NATO's Allied Atlantic Command. In short, he was at the pinnacle of a distinguished naval career that spanned the entire post–World War II era. He knew a lot about how the Navy and Marines then operated, less about the Air Force and Army, and much less about the newly constituted, hush-hush Joint Special Forces Command (JSOC), which included Navy, Army and Air Force commandoes and aviators.

There was tension in the air as McDonald convened a morning meeting at his headquarters in Norfolk of his Pentagon pickup team. Representatives from other service branches were invited, but key players didn't know each other well, and were not particularly inclined to like each other. Marine brigadier general Walter D. Fillmore, the deputy chief of staff for the Navy's Atlantic Command, bristled at the sight of officers from the 82nd Airborne. He thought that the Marines of the 22nd MAU, already in route to the island, were more than a sufficient force for the mission.[44] The 82nd Airborne representatives, in turn, were surprised to learn that their Army boss, Lt. Gen. Jack V. Mackmull, the commander of the XVIII Airborne Corps, was not in the planning loop for Grenada. Brig. Gen. Robert B. Patterson, representing the Air Force's Military Airlift Command (MAC), was not invited to Norfolk in time for him to attend, though some MAC staff officers were present.[45] Air Force transport aircraft would be needed to fly Army and JSOC units from their bases in the United States. The Marine amphibious force at sea was not personally represented at all.

McDonald opened the meeting by reviewing the two available options and inviting discussion.[46] The Army representatives predictably pressed for "the Army position": JSOC troops as an assault force with the 82nd Airborne Division as follow-on occupation soldiers. It was also possible under this option for the 82nd Airborne to lead the way. Lt.

Col. Frank H. Akers, the operations officer for the 82nd, impressed McDonald with his declaration that the 82nd would be ready to go to war within 18 hours, sooner than any other unit representative could promise. McDonald was swayed by the Army option as the safer choice because it offered the knock-out punch of the 82nd Airborne if the initial assault ran into trouble. The conferees reached an informal consensus on an H-Hour of 0230 so that the assault force would arrive in total darkness. Trained and equipped to fight in the dark, the JSOC assault troops were counting on surprise and stealth to overwhelm Grenada's defenses before dawn. After the meeting, McDonald called Vessey at the Pentagon on a secure phone to compare notes. The issue of what forces to use was still not finalized. Vessey brought McDonald up to date on the morning's developments in Washington and McDonald shared his latest thinking about the draft invasion plan.

Vessey's opinion on combat matters carried authority far beyond the rank he wore on his shoulder boards. He was regarded as "the wise old man" of the American military. At 61, the four-star general had been serving on active duty in the Army for 44 years, longer than almost anyone then in uniform in any branch of the armed services. He was viewed in the ranks as a GI's general because of his Audie Murphy–like, movie-script life story. Vessey enlisted in the Minnesota National Guard in 1939 at the age of 16 by lying about his age. His artillery unit was part of the 34th Infantry Division, the Army unit credited with landing the first soldiers to fight in the European Theater. By the time he turned 21, he had seen combat in North Africa and had risen through the enlisted ranks to serve as a first sergeant of his battery. (Vessey would later tell a newspaper interviewer that combat service as first sergeant was the most difficult job he ever had in the Army, but also the best.)

He won a battlefield commission as an officer in May 1944 on the bloody beachhead at Anzio, Italy. He was immediately sent forward to direct artillery fire. Two other sergeants promoted at the same time became casualties, but Vessey survived the war without debilitation and made a career of the military. It took a while for his paper credentials to match up to his battlefield experience. He earned his bachelor's degree at age 41 by taking classes at night and by correspondence. He learned to fly an Army helicopter when he was 48. In between, in Vietnam, at age 45, Vessey won the Distinguished Service Cross, the U.S. Army's second highest honor. In March 1967, then a lieutenant colonel, Vessey was ordered to establish a fire support base at Suoi Tre, deep in Viet Cong–controlled territory.[47] His 300-man artillery battalion was attacked by a reinforced regiment of Vietnamese and partially overrun. Vessey and his men fired their howitzers at point-blank range to inflict heavy losses on the attackers and eventually beat off the six-hour assault. At one critical point in the fierce battle, Vessey grabbed a grenade launcher and personally knocked out a group of enemy rocket launchers which were inflicting heavy casualties on his men.[48]

So, when Vessey and McDonald spoke about Grenada, the conversation was mud-splatted soldier to salt-stained sailor. Vessey had just come from the Saturday morning White House meeting at which Reagan authorized the operation to proceed. Vessey endorsed McDonald's inclination for an all-services, joint invasion force supported by the 82nd Airborne. Vessey knew this overwhelming-force option would be favored by his boss, Secretary Weinberger. This plan also involved the Rangers, a specialized, light infantry parachute force that Vessey played a key role in fostering after World War II.

At 1654 on Saturday, Oct. 22, on the basis of Reagan's "75%" decision, the JCS issued an execute order to CINCLANT (McDonald) and the other affected service commands. The order directed them to launch a multi-national, multi-service operation on Grenada to restore order, neutralize Grenadian and Cuban forces and protect American civilians "no later than dawn on Tuesday, Oct. 25."[49] The order set H-Hour just two and a half days away. At around 2200 Saturday night, the *Guam* amphibious group received three separate messages from Norfolk. One directed the group to turn toward Grenada, but another advised the commodore that the U.S. Army intended to assault Grenada with paratroopers.[50] No mention was made of a Marine role. Faulkner, the 22nd MAU commander, initially took this to mean that his Marines were to be held in reserve in case the Army needed help. He wasn't much impressed with the paratrooper-led assault plan. Faulkner consulted military meteorologists and learned that the Windward Islands had been aptly named by the first European explorers. The island's trade winds averaged 15 miles per hour with gusts up to 25. A parachute drop in a moderate-to-strong tropical breeze risked scattering troopers all over a drop zone, and many casualties if they were also under fire. He wrote "poor decision" in his notes and underlined it.[51] Faulkner held out hope that his Pentagon superiors would eventually come to the same conclusion and turn back to his Marines at the last minute as a better alternative. Later Saturday, McDonald departed Norfolk to fly to Washington for a final face-to-face planning with Vessey and others at the Pentagon on Sunday morning.

Everyone's world changed overnight. Just after midnight Eastern time on Sunday, Oct. 23, the four-story, steel and concrete Marine headquarters in Beirut was blown up by a suicide truck bomb. The building collapsed, killing 220 Marines, 18 sailors and three soldiers. FBI experts later estimated that the explosion was the largest non-nuclear blast ever measured, equivalent to 6,000 tons of TNT. President Reagan was informed of the Beirut attack in another wake-up phone call from McFarlane at 0227 Sunday, Oct. 23.[52] He spent more than two hours discussing the situation in person with Shultz and McFarlane and by phone with Marine Corps commandant general Paul X. Kelley. At around 0630, Reagan's motorcade left the star-crossed golf outing to return to Washington on Air Force One. Reagan arrived at the White House from Andrews Air Force Base by helicopter in a driving rain. As he entered the Situation Room in the West Wing basement at 0900, he greeted Weinberger by declaring: "Remind me never to go away again. Look what happens."[53]

A full day of National Security Council meetings on the two foreign policy crises lay ahead for the president and his top advisers. A 103-minute morning session was followed by a three-hour afternoon session, beginning at 4 p.m.[54] The final decision to intervene in Grenada hung on the threat the new military regime posed to the Americans on the island. In the Situation Room, Reagan was handed a State Department cable reporting that efforts to facilitate an evacuation of Americans by ship or plane had faltered. An American-British diplomatic delegation from Barbados flew to Grenada on Saturday to check on the condition of their respective citizens. They also explored the practicalities of an organized exodus of foreign citizens with a Grenadian army major representing the coup leaders. The conversations got complicated, in part, because Grenada's Caribbean neighbors had imposed a transportation embargo on the island in revulsion over the bloody end of the Bishop regime. The embargo effectively barred the arrival of regularly scheduled airlines or passenger vessels. The American diplomatic emissaries discussed using charter air or sea transportation instead, but they were unable to reach agreement with their Grenadian counterpart on an immediate evacuation plan that would satisfy their respective security concerns.

The British, however, read the situation on Grenada as a glass half full. The Foreign

President Reagan conferred with his senior national security advisory team in the cramped Situation Room in the White House basement on Sunday, October 23, 1983. The U.S. response to the situations in both Grenada and Lebanon was the subject of back-to-back policy meetings all day. Seated around the table (clockwise from Reagan) are George P. Shultz, the secretary of state; John McMahon, deputy director of the Central Intelligence Agency; James A. Baker III, Reagan's chief of staff; Robert C. McFarlane, the national security advisor; Edwin Meese III, counselor to the president; Gen. John W. Vessey, Jr., chairman of the Joint Chiefs, Caspar W. Weinberger, secretary of defense and Vice President George H.W. Bush (courtesy Ronald Reagan Library [c17840-20a]).

Office in London was assuaged that the coup leaders had untaken actions to protect the lives and property of foreign nationals. They saw no reason for either the British or the Americans to believe that their citizens on the island were in any danger.[55] The American delegation read the situation as a glass half empty and reported to Washington that the Grenadians were not serious about letting the Americans go. The students were not hostages per se, but they were being played by the Grenadians as diplomatic pawns. After the Tehran experience, the White House and the State Department were looking for iron-clad guarantees that Americans on the island were safe. "We kept turning over every stone to get 100% assurance, but could not get it," a top State Department official later explained. "That is when the decision to take action was made."[56]

An intelligence report filed by a CIA case officer operating undercover in the American delegation reported that medical students on the island were frightened and wanted out. The officer's assessment was personally delivered to Reagan at a Grenada meeting in the Situation Room on Sunday afternoon.[57] Reagan noticed that not everyone in the room was on the distribution list for the message. He read it aloud for all to hear. Reagan was persuaded that the medical students were in imminent danger and the United States needed to intervene to secure their safety. It was time for a presidential decision.

Christopher M. Lehman, a special assistant for national security affairs, later recalled what happened next. "I had the good fortune to be in the room when Reagan simply said: 'There are Americans there and they are in danger. We are going!'"[58] With that declaration, the president committed American troops to overt combat for the first time since direct U.S. military involvement in the Vietnam War ended in 1973. At one point, Vessey asked for a private meeting with Reagan and the top-ranking representatives of each present government agency.[59] The room was culled to six individuals so that Vessey could discuss the high risks the operation would pose for the SEALs and other special operations forces which would be involved. There was also "frank discussion" of the political risks for the president if the operation failed.

Across the Potomac River, the Pentagon was also unusually busy at the highest levels that Sunday. McDonald arrived from Norfolk to brief the Joint Chiefs on the latest version of the Grenada plan, accompanied by Scholtes, the JSOC commander. Their draft plan was a shared creation of the two commands, but Scholtes, a two-star, was subordinate to McDonald. McDonald briefed the uniformed service chiefs in a flag-draped, secure conference room at the Pentagon known as "The Tank." His plan called for the invasion force to simultaneously seize Grenada's two airports: one at Pearls on the east coast and the new, not-yet-operational facility still under construction at Point Salines on the southwestern tip of the island. A combined force of Marines and special forces operators would attack and seize Pearls Airport while a similar mixed force of Army Rangers and special forces commandos would seize the unfinished runway at Point Salines.[60] The chiefs were OK with the basic concept of the simultaneous airport seizure but, beyond that, the plan was not well received. "I think everyone was concerned about the complexity of the plan," Vessey later recalled. The chairman was particularly troubled by the command and control problems associated with using mixed-service forces that were not familiar with each other, operating under separate commands in an unrehearsed scenario. Vessey did not want the JSOC forces split up. Vessey also had a lot of confidence in JSOC's capabilities and in Scholtes as a leader. (Scholtes had been Vessey's chief of staff when he commanded the 4th Infantry Division in Germany a decade before.)[61]

Much of the Sunday morning discussion was on how to simplify the draft invasion plan. For a start, the chiefs, including Vessey, strongly suggested the seizure of the airport at Pearls be assigned just to the Marines and the runway at Point Salines just to the Rangers. The chiefs were also concerned about the latest intelligence reports which (erroneously) estimated the island might be defended by a force of close to 4,500, composed of 1,500 regular Grenadian soldiers, 2,000 Grenadian reservists and 1,000 Cuban advisers and armed construction workers.[62] Marine Corps commandant Kelley insisted that Marines play more than a supporting role in the invasion force. "The Marines must land on the island of Grenada or you will have destroyed the Marine Corps," he declared.[63] The loss of life in Beirut was the worst single-day total for the Marines since Iwo Jima. Vessey wanted a sharp geographic division between the area of operation for the Marines and the Army. Vessey used his finger to draw an east-west line across the center of the mango-shaped island. The northern half would belong to the Marines, while the southern half, including the capital of St. George's, would belong to the Army and JSOC. Vessey intended the map line as a suggestion, but it was clearly something more.

Kelley's anguished plea and Vessey's finger across the map later gave rise to the widespread view that the Tank session was a pie-dividing session by top Pentagon commanders, each looking to carve out a slice of the action for their service. However, Lt. Gen.

Richard Prillaman, then director of operations for the Joint Chiefs, later asserted that there was strong justification for involving all services in the Grenada plan. The Air Force and Navy offered airlift and/or air cover. JSOC continuously trained for hostage rescues. The Army had the combat-ready paratroopers. The Marines were already nearby and well trained for both helicopter and amphibious assaults. "But the basic idea that when you run one of these things, everybody wants a piece of the pie—that's essentially true. It just happens that, in this case, there was a need for them," Prillaman later told a military historian.[64]

McDonald worked frantically for two hours with the JCS staff on a revision of the plan. The enhanced involvement of the Marines, while expanding and segregating the assault troops by service, also injected a new level of complexity into the already tangled command and control provisions of the invasion plan. Scholtes was surprised by the Marine objection at this late stage of planning and stunned that it was immediately supported by Vessey. (The Beltway rap on Vessey as chairman was his reluctance to interpose himself between feuding Pentagon factions.)[65] Including Marine infantry in the plan now meant that all four Pentagon armed–service branches would be participants in the D-Day firefights. Even the U.S. Coast Guard, then a uniformed agency under the Department of Transportation, got in on the first day action by dispatching an aircraft and a cutter for search and rescue duty.[66] But the strict secrecy rules imposed on the operation prevented dissemination of the invasion plan to all the commands and agencies that would be called on to assist the operation. Many key supporting players were out of the planning loop, up through and including the Pentagon's service secretaries.

One lingering question to be resolved was who would be the ground commander of the vanguard operation if shooting started. The two obvious choices were of disparate rank: Faulkner, the Marine colonel who commanded the 22nd MAU, and Scholtes, the two-star Army general who commanded the Ranger and special operations troops. Vessey sought to finesse this issue by directing McDonald to "find a three-star" who would command the joint task force from out at sea and outrank all the other on-scene commanders. McDonald was also told that he needed to have an Army general assigned to the task force staff as his ground force adviser.[67]

The expanded role of the Marines also affected the timing of the attack. McDonald was concerned that the Marines were not prepared to conduct helicopter operations in the dark. He proposed delaying H-Hour until 0500, just half an hour before dawn.[68] Scholtes objected to the change because it would rob his special forces of their night-fighting advantage. They initially compromised on a plan for the special forces to attack at 0400, one hour before the 0500 H-Hour for all the conventional forces. In the event, no unit could achieve its deadline. McDonald flew back to Norfolk, while the JSC staff at the Pentagon briefed the revised invasion plan back to the service chiefs. This time it played well and the amended plan was quickly passed up the chain of command to the secretary of defense and then to the president. The Reagan administration and the Pentagon were now challenged with dealing with simultaneous national security threats in the Middle East and in the Eastern Caribbean. Lebanon and Grenada were fused into a single time-compressed crisis for Washington decision-makers.

While all this stressful high-level activity was going on in Washington on Sunday morning, Army major general H. Norman Schwarzkopf was bass fishing near his quarters at Fort Stewart in Georgia. Schwarzkopf was in his kitchen at 1800 on Sunday evening prepping the catch for a family dinner when the phone rang. Schwarzkopf recalled the subsequent events in his 1992 autobiography.[69] The voice on the other end was Maj. Gen. Dick Graves, the operations chief at Forces Command at Fort McPherson, Georgia. Graves wanted to know if Schwarzkopf had any pressing plans in the next few weeks. Schwarzkopf said he didn't, but that was an entirely relative answer. When the call came, the two-star general's day job was running an Army armored division, the 24th Mechanized Infantry. Graves said he would call back. Schwarzkopf's first thought was that the call was related to the tragic news from Lebanon. He gulped down his fish fry and anxiously waited for Graves to call a second time.

Mrs. Brenda Schwarzkopf picks up a three-star rank insignia from a case offered by Chief Warrant Officer 3 John L. Drummond, left, as she and General Maxwell R. Thurman, second from left, vice chief of staff, U.S. Army, prepare to pin the stars on the shoulders of Lieutenant General H. Norman Schwarzkopf during his promotion ceremony at the Pentagon. This photograph was taken in 1986, three years after Urgent Fury. Schwarzkopf was a two-star during Grenada (National Archives photograph [330-CFD-DA-SC-91-09549]).

"How quickly can you get up here to Atlanta?" Graves asked, but it was actually a command. "You're going on a military operation. You'll be away for about three weeks." Schwarzkopf hurriedly started to pack. He laid out his summer and winter uniforms on the bed. Which to bring? He drove to his office where he could make a secure follow-up phone call to Graves. That's when he first learned his destination was Grenada. Only the summer uniforms went into the travel bag. The general then flew by Army aircraft to Charlie Brown Field, a general aviation airport serving Atlanta, for a private, face-to-face meeting with Graves at a military terminal just before midnight. Graves told him he was to be the Army's liaison to a Navy-led invasion of the island. "A lot of Army forces are going to be involved—the 82nd Airborne and Special Operations units and the 1st Ranger Battalion—and Washington wants to make sure the Navy uses them correctly. That's where you come in," Graves said.

"Hold it," Schwarzkopf interrupted. "It doesn't sound as if I'm exactly going to be welcome."

"As a matter of fact, you're not. The Navy doesn't like the fact that you're being sent."

Schwarzkopf surmised that he had been selected because his rank and experience were a good fit for the advisory job. As the commander of a rapid-deployment division he had knowledge of how the Rangers operated. He also knew how a Navy command operated on the basis of two years he spent in Hawaii as a one-star general on the strategy and plans staff of Pacific Command.[70] Schwarzkopf got back on his plane at midnight to fly north to Virginia to meet his new Navy boss. It suddenly hit him that he would have been hard pressed to find Grenada on a Caribbean map.

A few hours before Schwarzkopf got his surprise phone call in his kitchen, Vice Adm. Joseph P. Metcalf III, the three-star commander of the Navy's Atlantic's Second Fleet, had an unexpected visitor appear at 1430 behind his home on Naval Station Norfolk. The visitor was McDonald's deputy who said his boss had been calling all over looking for him. "You better get yourself over to the compound because you're it," the visitor advised Metcalf.[71] He had been selected to lead the all-service task force that would invade Grenada in 39 hours. Metcalf's combat assignment did not come as quite the same surprise to him that it was to Schwarzkopf. He and McDonald knew each other well; Metcalf served under McDonald's command and the two admirals were also Norfolk neighbors.

Metcalf got the call, in part, because he fit the bill. The Second Fleet's area responsibility was the western Atlantic from the North Pole to the Caribbean. One of Metcalf's Second Fleet roles was to also serve as the commander of an established multi-service unit known as Joint Task Force 120 that could be activated in times of crisis to execute

Vice Adm. Joseph P. Metcalf III, commander, Joint Task Force 120, 1983 (National Archives [330-CFD-DF-SN-84-10812]).

contingency missions. Metcalf's fleet staff had been monitoring Grenada's political turmoil for a week. He was aware that McDonald's command was working on a secret intervention plan. Metcalf was not yet personally involved, though he could have been. "My
rationale was that I wanted to avoid being wedded to, or emotionally identified with, the
development of a particular plan," he later wrote in chapter for a textbook on military
decision-making.[72]

In choosing Metcalf for the invasion assignment, McDonald bypassed another command, U.S. Forces Caribbean at Key West, which, on paper, had the role of conducting
joint operations in the West Indies. In fact, a first-draft Grenada invasion plan, OPLAN
2360, already existed. But what was on paper was not what won wars. This relatively new
command had no component combat forces permanently attached to it and consisted
mainly of a one-star admiral and headquarters staff of 87.[73] Vessey didn't have a high
opinion of the unit. "I had visited that headquarters, and you talk about an extra tit on
a hog, that's what it was. It had no capability to carry out the operation," Vessey later told
a military historian.[74]

Metcalf, on the other hand, was well suited by position, experience and personality
to lead a "come as you are" Caribbean invasion that was set to begin less than two days.
Metcalf was the son of a prosperous wool manufacturing family in Holyoke, Massachusetts, a New England mill town.[75] As a teenager, the call of the sea lured him than more
than a career in the textile trade. He joined the Navy in 1946 as a seaman at the age of
19. After a serving a year as a white hat swabbie, he won an appointment to the U.S.
Naval Academy at Annapolis. He was commissioned an ensign in 1951 as the Korean War
was settling into a stalemate. He rose to command positions spanning nearly a decade
during the Vietnam War. His wartime resume ranged from commanding an LST during
the first amphibious landing of the war in 1966 to commanding the Navy forces which
covered the chaos of Saigon in 1975 when South Vietnam fell to the North. A Navy peer
described him as a "rock-hard, salt-stained, dyed-in the-wool Surface Warrior."[76]

As a student of naval history, he was known to sentence untutored subordinates to
remedial sessions at the Pentagon library. But he was also forward thinking about the
impact of technology on the battlefield. He loved gadgets and was an early advocate of
computer-assisted naval combat. He was credited with being involved with the Pentagon's
first experiment with e-mail. He eagerly embraced being boss. His personal credo was
"When you are in command, COMMAND!"[77] He did not suffer fools, but he could also
be witty and wise. The warrior in him also didn't take well to being pushed around.
During one stint at the Pentagon, he chaffed under the thumb of a nit-picking superior.
He developed a novel defense. He deliberately added misspelled words to his reports up
the chain of command. He figured his over-zealous boss would be so busy fixing his
booby-trapped grammar that he'd leave the content alone. It worked. Similarly, oppressed
subordinates at the Pentagon learned of this ruse through scuttlebutt and were inspired.[78]

On Sunday, Oct. 23, Metcalf got his orders to take command of Task Force 120 and
invade Grenada by dawn the next Tuesday. He got a quick briefing on the invasion plan
from Atlantic Command. In general, he liked what he heard about the Marines being
involved and the Marines and the Army having clearly defined areas of operation. He
was much less enthusiastic about the involvement of special forces, but he accepted that
was a decision that had been made at the Joint Chiefs level. His overriding concern, however, was time. He had 39 hours to prepare for war.

Metcalf next headed to Pier 25 on the Norfolk Naval Station where his amphibious command ship, the *Mount Whitney*, was moored. On paper, the activation of Task Force 120 called for a command staff of 88 from a variety of uniformed services, but there was no time to assemble such a large number—and no space for all of them on the already-deployed *Guam* in any case.[79] Instead, Metcalf gathered his fleet staff of 40 and selected 17 to fly away to battle with him. He picked that figure because that was the maximum number of passengers that could fit in one Navy helicopter.[80] He was thousands of miles from the scene of impending action. He and his staff would have to travel fast and light to get there before the shooting started. Metcalf well understood he was about to enter a maelstrom that would test his endurance, his skills and command all his attention for the indefinite future. He was also well aware that managing his bosses in Washington would be every bit as taxing as fighting the enemy in the Caribbean. That was a lesson he had learned during the agonizing, and politically fraught, evacuation of Saigon. "What I observed was a classic example of what I term 'the six-thousand-mile screwdriver'— the minute direction of the day-to-day operations of a field commander by a higher and remote authority," he later wrote.[81]

When he got his Grenada assignment, eight years after the fall of Saigon, he was determined to manage up as well as down. "I organized my staff to influence the Joint Chiefs of Staff and the commander-in-chief, Atlantic Command. I wanted to explicitly influence what they were telling me to do," he wrote. One of his first decisions was to assign one of the select 17, Capt. Robert T. Reading, an operations officer, to be his full-time representative to higher commands stateside. Reading's job was to crank out regular situation reports (SITREPs in military-speak) with the help of three others. "I don't care if we are talking about hangnails—we will put out two SITREPS an hour," he ordered. Reading also served as the sole "voice of Urgent Fury" in secure communication lines back to the United States. (His D-Day stint at the microphone lasted 17 hours with an average of three SITREPS per hour.) In short, Reading was "the officer in charge of keeping them off my back," Metcalf later quipped to a reporter.

But allocating four of his 17 slots to managing his bosses left Metcalf critically short of staff to coordinate such vital combat functions as communications, logistics and fire control.[82] His staff was also top heavy with Navy officers and short of representatives of the other services in key positions. "Admiral Metcalf did not have the kind of staff that is necessary to run a joint operation," Prillaman, the Pentagon director of operations, later confided to a military historian. "He had nobody to advise him on ground operations. He had no air component or any adviser on air operations. He had essentially an administrative staff that is capable of moving boats around, but not capable to run a tactical operation." The Pentagon recognized Metcalf's staff deficiency right from the start. The JCS tried to get him the specialized help he was lacking, but the catch-up efforts were outstripped by the operational necessities of the fast-moving crisis.

Back in Washington, on Sunday evening at 6:55 p.m.,[83] President Reagan signed National Security Directive 110A calling for the landing of "U.S. and allied Caribbean military forces in order to take control of Grenada, no later than dawn Tuesday, Oct. 25." The directive set three objectives for the operation: assuring the safety of U.S. citizens, restoration of democratic government on the island and "the elimination of current, and the prevention of further, Cuban intervention in Grenada."[84] In essence, this affirmed and formalized the execute order that the Pentagon had issued 24 hours earlier.

At 2200 on Sunday, two liaison officers from McDonald's headquarters arrived by helicopter on the *Guam* with a draft operations order for a multi-service surprise assault on the island.[85] The Marines role was to conduct an assault landing that would secure the northern half of the island including Pearls Airport and the nearby coastal town of Grenville on the east coast. Butler, the Navy amphibious force chief of staff, was flabbergasted by the news. Based on the civilian radio broadcasts they had heard, the threat to Americans on Grenada, never firmly established, seemed to be winding down. Marine officers greeted the order with excitement. "It's on! Midnight. It's on," exulted Smith, the 22nd MAU infantry battalion commander, recording his reaction in a tiny notebook he carried. His Marines would be on the point of the spear, rather than waiting in reserve.

In fact, at that moment, unbeknownst to Smith, the first hostile act of the invasion was already underway—and had already gone tragically wrong. Just after nightfall on Sunday, 16 Navy SEAL Team Six commandoes approached Grenadian waters in two Air Force C-130 transport planes after flying eight hours non-stop from Pope Air Force Base in North Carolina.[86] The SEALs prepared to parachute into dark, wind-swept seas about 40 miles off the island's coast. The SEALs were making an at-sea rendezvous with the USS *Clifton Sprague*, one of the consort ships in the *Independence* group. Waiting on the guided-missile frigate was their SEAL team leader, Lt. Pat Twohey, and five other SEALs who had rendezvoused with the *Sprague* at around noon in St. Vincent. Also boarding there was a four-man U.S. Air Force combat control team, which would accompany the SEALs on a clandestine reconnaissance of Point Salines. Their joint mission was to determine whether the Point Salines runway had been obstructed, how it was defended and whether the unfinished surface would support the weight of military transports. Rangers, elite paratroopers who specialized in airport seizure operations, preferred to land in their planes rather than jump, if defenses allowed. The air controllers were to set up radio navigation beacons near the runway that would guide the final approach of Air Force transport planes carrying the Rangers. The controllers would also direct whatever air strikes might be necessary to support the assault on the unfinished airport. The two C-130 transports carried two specially modified Boston Whalers, rigged for parachute drop. The SEALs would use the open fiberglass boats to navigate to the Grenadian shore in the dark once they picked up their team leader and the Air Force controllers from the frigate.

Lt. Col. John T. Carney, Jr., the commander of the newly formed 21-man Air Force special operations detachment of air combat controllers, was also among those waiting on the *Sprague*. The senior officer on the mission, Carney, was a former Air Force Academy football assistant coach and an expert in clandestine reconnaissance forays. Three years earlier he had personally selected the remote spot in the Iranian desert that was used as a helicopter refueling point for the aborted attempt to rescue 53 Americans then being held hostage in Teheran. Carney's new unit was initially designated as "Det 1 MACOS—Detachment One, Military Airlift Command Operations Staff"—subsequently changed in 1983 to "Det. 4. NAFCOS."[87] In either incarnation, their official name was an inscrutable, bureaucratic mouthful. They preferred to go by their self-conferred nickname: Brand X. Carney offered the most detailed and credible of several diverging accounts of what happened next in his memoir published in 2002.[88]

As the SEALs aloft prepared to jump, the Sprague deployed sailors in its own Boston Whaler to pluck the parachutists from the water. The original plan was for the jump to occur in daylight at 1600 local time. Later, the drop time was delayed until 1800 to allow the planes to take a longer route to the drop zone to avoid detection by Cuban electronic surveillance. But the Air Force planners made a fatal miscalculation in amending the exacting timetable for the operation. Grenada is one time zone ahead of the Eastern United States. Based on the rotation of the earth, the sun immutably rises and sets in Grenada about an hour before it does in the Eastern United States. But, during Daylight Saving Time, America "springs ahead" and Grenada doesn't. Thus, from spring to autumn, the East Coast and Grenada are nominally operating on the same time as displayed on the clock, but celestial dawn and dusk still arrives one hour earlier in St. George's than in Washington. Military plans are typically drafted on ZULU time (Greenwich Mean Time), rather than local time, to avoid time zone confusion, but the Grenada incursion was an exception. The drop at 1800 "local" time happened half an hour after sunset on a moonless Eastern Caribbean night, instead of half an hour before dusk on the East Coast. This greatly complicated the jump for all the airmen, sailors and parachutists involved. Worse, a sudden squall enveloped the C-130s in a shroud of rain, throwing off the close coordination of the two planes.

Master Chief Johnny Walker was the jump master in the lead plane. He was surprised at what he saw when the rear-facing cargo ramp opened.[89] He had been briefed to expect a daylight drop into calm seas and light winds. What he witnessed was total darkness, six- to eight-foot seas and 20-knot winds. He grabbed a flashlight from a C-130 crewman and tried to attach it to his plane's Whaler, cognizant he was applying a band aid solution to a serious problem. Then he led his team off the end of the ramp and into a rain storm. Walker and the rest of the SEALs jumped in full combat gear which included ammunition, canteens and, in most cases, weapons. The jump was supposed to have been at 1,500 feet, but it seemed much lower to Walker. He hit the water hard and immediately was stripped of this swim fins. The stiff winds kept his parachute inflated and it started to pull him through the waves facedown. Walker found himself swallowing sea water, instead of air, until he managed to collapse the chute. He then cut himself free and started swimming toward where he thought his Whaler had landed. Walker didn't know it yet, but the Whaler from his plane had sunk into the waves.

Both C-130s ejected the men and their 18-foot boats at the same time, but much farther apart than planned.[90] The *Sprague's* recovery boat and the frigate needed to maneuver to retrieve the distressed jumpers. Unable to find his boat or his teammates, Walker decided to swim to the *Sprague*, which he saw had rigged a cargo net on it bow. As he neared the ship, he heard three shots ring out, which he assumed had been fired by another desperate SEAL. He swam briefly toward the shots before exhaustion forced him to turn to the safety of the ship. Just before reaching the ship, Walker encountered another swimming SEAL. The two men finally climbed the cargo net to learn that they were the last to be pulled from the water. Other jumpers had swum to the frigate or a Whaler, but four were missing.

All the lost were experienced frogmen who had official Navy rates that had nothing to do with their actual clandestine work: Hull Technician 1st Class Stephen L. Morris, 31, of South Plainfield, New Jersey; Senior Chief Engineman Robert R. Schamberger, 42, of Oakland, New Jersey; Machinist Mate 1st Class Kenneth J. Butcher, 31, of West Islip, New York; and Quartermaster 1st Class Kevin E. Lundberg, 32, of Kodiak, Alaska. The surviving SEALs searched for their lost brothers until they were ordered to break off to complete their pre-invasion mission. Others continued the search the next morning on the sea and from the air for three more days. Capt. Robert A. Gormly, the SEAL Team Six commander, monitored the drop by radio from the United States. He never learned exactly what went wrong. "I can only surmise that the four men couldn't get rid of their [parachute] canopies, were dragged through the water facedown and drowned," he wrote in his 1998 autobiography.[91]

Gormly placed much of the blame on the arrival time mix-up. "In all my years with the SEALs, Urgent Fury was the only occasion on which I saw the standard military procedure of using Zulu time violated. Doing that had caused us to jump in the dark instead of daylight as we had planned," he later wrote.[92] But, besides the darkness and the bad weather, inadequate training and equipment were also factors in the drownings. None of the Air Force or Navy participants was fully trained for what they were being asked to do under these weather conditions in the dark of night, and the SEALs' open boats proved insufficiently seaworthy. It was an ignominious start for SEAL Team Six in its first combat action since being constituted as a clandestine antiterrorism unit in October 1980.

The surviving SEALs, joined by the combat controllers, set off from the frigate in the *Sprague*'s Boston Whaler for the long, rough, sea journey to Grenada.[93] The Whaler towed a 15-foot, inflatable-hulled Zodiac for use when they got close to shore, but it was not deployed. When the reconnaissance team was still about 30 miles away from Grenada, they encountered a ship panning a searchlight that they believed to be a Grenadian patrol craft.[94] When the Whaler slowed to evade the craft, the open boat lost one engine and started to take on water. After all the delays and mishaps, it became evident that they would not be able to reach the shore before daylight, raising the risk that they would be detected. The mission was postponed a day and the exhausted recon party returned to the *Sprague*. (On the return trip they encountered the USS *Caron*, a Navy destroyer collecting signals intelligence. Gormly later learned this may have been the ship with the searchlight the SEALs thought was the Grenadian patrol boat.[95])

Another attempt to survey the airport at Point Salines was made on the night before the invasion.[96] A second Whaler was airdropped to replace the one that was lost, so that two boats were available to perform the mission as originally planned. The *Sprague* moved to a new position closer to shore. The recon party again set off from the *Sprague* in two Whalers with a Zodiac in tow. Again, they encountered a craft they believed to be a Grenadian patrol boat and abruptly cut their engines. The boats took on water in the heavy seas, swamping the outboard engines and their satellite radio. The frustrated SEALs were unable to restart their flooded motors. Eventually, with H-Hour approaching, the mission was aborted. The 20-man reconnaissance team drifted in the disabled boats until they could be picked up by the *Caron* at around dawn on D-Day.[97]

At around the same time that the first SEAL mission was ending in frustrating failure, Metcalf and Schwarzkopf met for the first time. That encounter didn't go well either. The meeting came Monday, Oct. 24, at a 0730 at a flag officer briefing in Norfolk called by McDonald to bring all the principal players in the invasion together for the first time. Metcalf was a believer in Vice Admiral Horatio Nelson's admonition: know your subordinate commanders.[98] He also welcomed the opportunity to look them in the eye and let them know who was in charge. As he feared, Schwarzkopf got a reception that made him feel "about a welcome as a case of the mumps."[99] It didn't help that he and Metcalf made for a mismatched pair at first meeting. At six-foot-three and more than 230 pounds, the general nicknamed "The Bear" towered over his shorter and leaner boss. Metcalf sought to knock Schwarzkopf down to size by turning their initial conversation into a cross-examination. Metcalf pummeled Schwarzkopf with pointed questions about what he expected to contribute to the operation. Then, just to be sure he got the message, McDonald took Schwarzkopf aside for a preemptive attitude adjustment. "Now for Chrissakes, try and be helpful, would you?" McDonald admonished. "We're got a tough job to do and we don't need the Army giving us a hard time." Scholtes, the JSOC commander, also go off to a rocky start in his first meeting with his new Navy boss.[100] Metcalf was angry that the Army general had not responded to an attempt by Metcalf to contact him. Scholtes had never gotten the message and suspected that the reason had something to do with the incompatibility between Navy and JSOC secure communication equipment. But he irked Metcalf by reminding him that military etiquette put the burden of establishing communications on the senior headquarters, not the subordinate.

The Norfolk meeting room glittered with stars. Besides McDonald, Metcalf, Scholtes and Schwarzkopf, Maj. Gen. Edward L. Trobaugh, commander of the 82nd Airborne Division, was also in the room. Patterson, a one-star, represented the Air Force command that would supply the transport aircraft for the invasion. A State Department delegation was led by L. Craig Johnstone, the deputy assistant secretary of state for Inter-American Affairs, a flag-rank-equivalent position.[101] Notable by their absence, however, were any representatives of the Navy or Marine forces at sea who were poised to join the battle. Metcalf, however, was unconcerned. "I knew how they operated," he later explained.[102]

McDonald opened the session by dialing down the expectations. "Before we get into the operational plan, everyone should bear in mind the strong possibility that we won't have to carry it out. The crisis is still being handled through diplomatic channels, and we are told it is likely that the rebels will back down," he said.[103] McDonald's final battle plan called for the island to be taken with a textbook tactic known as a *coup de main*.

Brigadier General Robert B. Patterson, left, speaks with a U.S. Navy officer and a member of the Eastern Caribbean Defense Force during the multiservice, multinational Operation Urgent Fury (National Archives [330-CFD-DF-SN-84-10921]).

(The term is a French epigram for a swift, sudden blow.) In this application, the *coup de main* called for Americans to use their superior firepower and technology to overwhelm Grenada's defenders in a simultaneous, surprise attack. The Navy would cordon off the island while the Marines from the *Guam* landed by helicopter on the northeastern coast to seize Pearls Airport and the port town of Grenville. Meanwhile, Army Ranger paratroopers, flying directly from bases in the United States, would land from the air at Point Salines on the southwest coast. They would seize the airfield there and then link up with American medical students at the True Blue campus, located in a hollow just 75 meters off the eastern edge of the east-west airfield.

While the Rangers and Marines subdued any organized military resistance to the American incursion, a separate force of special forces commandoes would be stealthily at work protecting the island's political future. Just prior to the arrival of the main invasion force, a task force of Navy SEALs, Delta Force operators and Army Rangers would arrive by helicopter to undertake three politically-sensitive secret missions in and around St. George's. They were tasked with freeing political prisoners being held at Richmond Hill Prison on a ridge overlooking St. George's, capturing Radio Free Grenada's 50-kilowatt transmitter station north of St. George's and securing the governor general at his official residence. Sir Paul Scoon was regarded as the geopolitical linchpin of the entire operation. He possessed vestigial powers under the suspended Grenadian constitution to form a new government friendly to American interests.

Resistance was now expected to be weak to non-existent. The Grenadian military numbered just 500–600 regular soldiers, supplemented by 2,000 or so unsalaried, unmotivated militia. It was generally considered to be poorly trained and equipped. The island had no defensive missiles and no combat ships or planes. The defenders' most formidable weapons were visually aimed anti-aircraft guns and Soviet-made, armored personnel carriers. The Grenadian military was backed by 43 Cuban military advisers. There were no Cuban soldiers on the island, per se, but the 636 Cuban construction workers at Point Salines lived in military-style barracks that were equipped with AK-47 gun racks. The average age of the workers was 38 it was later learned, but most had some prior military training. They were believed to be more akin to a Navy Seabee construction battalion than a civilian airport construction crew, but they didn't wear military uniforms.

Metcalf later recalled hearing very optimistic intelligence estimates predicting that mission was a "piece of cake" that would be opposed by a "rag-tag outfit" of Cubans and a Grenadian army that would "cut and run."[104] He also found his own commanders to be "extremely confident" and exuding "a distinct air of bravado." But Metcalf privately had his own doubts about what he heard, as did other battle-tested commanders. Trobaugh, the 82nd Airborne commander, was discomforted by the session for multiple reasons.[105] To begin with, he came expecting to get a formal briefing that would involve presentations by staff officers on intelligence, logistics and other command functions. Instead he found himself at a conference table participating in a "freewheeling discussion" of the topic. Further, his infantryman instincts told him the plan as outlined by McDonald was too ambitious given the size of the spearhead forces, the short deadline and limited amount of inter-service coordination that had been done. However, the principal concern voiced around the conference table at the meeting was what to do about the failed SEAL reconnaissance mission at Point Salines.[106] The Air Force needed to know if their transport aircraft would be able to safely land on the partially completed runway. Scholtes appealed for the invasion to be delayed by a day so that more intelligence could be gathered by his SEALs and other assets.[107] Schwarzkopf and Patterson thought Scholtes' plea was going to carry the day, but he ran into resistance. According to Patterson, a State Department representative (apparently Johnstone) said, in essence: "You mean that the world's strongest military power is about to take on the world's weakest and you have got to have 24 more hours? We have a coalition of nations down there waiting to do this; we wanted to do it Saturday. Here it is Monday. We cannot delay it."[108] Trobaugh found the civilian's call to the colors to be offensive. "I knew damn well he wasn't going to be the guy that was there on the ground getting shot at," he later confided to a military historian.[109]

But McDonald, reflecting the signals he was getting from Washington, also pushed back on postponement. "You're kidding me. You want to delay this 24 hours?… Well, I'll have to go back to the Chairman of the JCS [Vessey], go back to the President, and tell him we can't do this," Patterson later recalled McDonald saying.[110] McDonald affirmed the date as planned. Still protesting, Scholtes appealed for a delay in his pre-invasion arrival time to allow his SEALs to make a second try at a Salines recon before the conventional forces arrived.[111] McDonald agreed. This further delay ended up setting 0500 for the simultaneous arrival of the Rangers, Marines and JSOC forces. This shared H-Hour was perilously close to dawn when the tactical advantage would shift abruptly from invader to defender.[112]

The revised start time was the start of a slippery slope. The mission was too often amended, the operation too hurriedly planned, secrecy too tight, the fighting units too geographically disbursed, and the transit distances too long, for everything to come off precisely on time. As it was, the operation was already running late. While McDonald's four-hour morning meeting was still going on, Metcalf got up to leave for the Caribbean. Patterson caught Metcalf just long enough to introduce the admiral to his Air Force liaison officer (Col. Jon Vilensons) for the first time. "He's your Air Force guy," Patterson said, but he suspected that in the rush Metcalf didn't understand that he was just the operation's airlift representative on the *Guam*.[113] Patterson oversaw the D-Day airlift from Barbados. Another Air Force one-star general, Richard L. Meyer, separately commanded aircraft in Puerto Rico that were making sure that Cuba did not intervene.[114] Patterson didn't learn that Meyer was also the AFFOR (commander of all the forward Air Force aircraft) until the third day of the operation. "To this very day I have never seen a piece of paper from CINCLANT [McDonald] or anyone saying how the command relationships were going to be," Patterson later remarked.[115]

The Patterson-assigned Air Force liaison officer joined Schwarzkopf and two other Army staff officers as late additions to Metcalf's hand-picked, mostly Navy, staff of 17. Metcalf and his ad hoc entourage left Norfolk before noon on a Navy C-9 passenger jet bound for Barbados. From there, they were scheduled to fly by helicopter to their combat posts aboard the *Guam*. Because of their mid-meeting departure, the Metcalf party left thinking the invasion was set for 0400.[116] Schwarzkopf used the flight down to introduce himself to the other staff members and learn more about the invasion plan, especially the ground operation. Still, even at this advanced stage, he believed the whole operation would be called off before any shots were fired. On arrival on Barbados, the general was disconcerted to see reporters swarming the tarmac at Grantley Adams Airport. The secret invasion got to be much less of a surprise the closer they got to the scene of battle. Reporters in the English-speaking Caribbean were abundantly aware from belligerent statements being made by their local leaders that some sort of military action was contemplated.

On Grenada, the coup leaders also had a surprisingly clear picture of what was happening outside its borders, despite their lack of a formal off-island intelligence apparatus. Grenadians were monitoring news reports of developments in Washington and Barbados even more attentively than Washington was monitoring news coming from the Windwards. At 1750 on Sunday, Oct. 23, the government-run Radio Free Grenada accurately reported that troops from the Caribbean islands and other "foreign forces" were then gathering on Barbados for an armed intervention of Grenada. A warship had been detected inside Grenadian waters only seven and a half miles from shore. Militia were ordered to report to their posts immediately.[117] The broadcast said an invasion was expected "tonight," but was a day and a half early on the timing.

Metcalf's plane landed at Grantley Adams civilian airport outside of Bridgetown, Barbados, at mid-afternoon on Monday, Oct. 24. During a brief stopover to change aircraft, Metcalf was supposed to link up with the Caribbean coalition's military commander, Brig. Gen. Rudyard "Rudy" Lewis, the chief of staff of the Barbados Defence Force. Lewis was detained and Metcalf decided he couldn't wait 45 minutes for him to arrive.[118] Metcalf's staff stayed incommunicado aboard the Navy jet on the tarmac until Marine helicopters arrived to take them to the *Guam*. Metcalf's one-helicopter staff had grown to three. The extra helicopters were required for the additional representatives who had been added from the Pentagon's other uniformed services, the CIA and the State Department. The 1700 departure of about 50 "Marines" on three helicopters from the civilian airport in Bridgetown was witnessed and was immediately, if imprecisely, reported by the Associated Press. A story that ran at the bottom of the front page of the *New York Times* the next morning quoted a named spokesman for the U.S. embassy in Bridgetown as saying the departing uniformed personnel "could be used as part 1 of the options to effect a departure of the Americans waiting on Grenada and to insure their safety."[119]

At around the same time Monday afternoon that Metcalf's staff was arriving in Barbados, the Joint Chiefs were meeting with the president in the Cabinet Room of the White House, along with Weinberger. Reagan polled each of the service chiefs separately on the intervention plan. Each asserted the plan would work, though all expressed concern about the lack of adequate intelligence and an opportunity to rehearse. The intervention endorsement by the chiefs was a qualified one by Vessey's telling. "Generally, their views were, 'Okay, we would prefer that the students came out some other way than to engage in a military operation, but if we have to engage in a military operation, we are prepared to support the military operation and we have a plan that we believe will work,'" he later recalled.[120] With this final affirmation, at around 1700 Reagan handed Weinberger a signed copy of National Security Decision Directive 110A, instructing the military to proceed with the intervention at dawn on Tuesday, Oct. 25.[121] The invasion authority was now literally out of the president's hands—but not yet too late to be recalled.

Metcalf's helicopter landed on the *Guam* at 1745, just in time for dinner. The new arrivals supped on a white tablecloth at a long table in the admiral's mess. They had just finished the soup course and were starting on the turkey when Capt. Conrad J. Ward, Metcalf's chief of staff, interrupted the repast. He reported that President Reagan had signed the final invasion order. "It's a go!" Ward declared. There was stunned silence. "We're going," Ward repeated for the dumbstruck. "H-hour has been bumped back one hour. It's a go at 0500."[122] No one seated at the table assigned much significance to the additional one-hour delay until the fatal consequences of a near-dawn start began to manifest themselves. By then it would be too late. Why the extra hour was added is still murky decades later. In a 1987 military oral history interview, Schwarzkopf speculated that time was added to allow for analysis of 11th hour intelligence to be gathered by air and sea.[123] Metcalf, however, offered a different version to an academic interviewer in 1988. Metcalf said that McDonald slipped H-Hour to near dawn because he believed that the Marines not adequately prepared to land and fight at night.[124] Perhaps both versions are true.

On the *Guam*, the assembled officers drifted off to attend to final preparations. Metcalf took a nap at Ward's urging. Schwarzkopf took seasickness pills at his stomach's insistence. The seas were getting rough, but he was also feeling another source of queasiness as he looked out into the black night from the darkened bridge of the *Guam*. "I realized that by this time tomorrow, we'd be at war. I had misgiving about whether we should be sending troops to Grenada. Were we being committed to another war that the American public wouldn't support?"[125] That same question was also very much on the mind of President Reagan back in Washington. He had summoned five top congressional leaders from both sides of the aisle to a secret evening meeting at the White House to brief them on the impending invasion. Fearful of leaks, the attendees were gathered personally by the White House chief of staff. Baker drove up to Capitol Hill with a top legislative aide to call the select aside. The invitees were instructed not even to tell their wives where they were going. The summoned legislators entered the White House living chambers through an underground passageway and up back stairs from the basement.[126]

The two-hour session began just before 8 p.m. in the Yellow Oval Room on the second floor of White House. The attendees sat opposite a burning fireplace on an antique sofa with matching chairs. On the south side, three large windows offered a view of the South Lawn, with the Ellipse and the Washington Monument in the distance. It was another historic meeting in a room that had been a stage for presidential history since John Adams. Franklin D. Roosevelt was working here on Dec. 7, 1941, when he got word of the Japanese surprise attack on Pearl Harbor. This time, the Americans were staging the surprise attack.

"I have a national security decision that I want to share with you," Reagan said to begin the somber meeting. The president offered a summary of recent events including the plea for intervention by Grenada's Caribbean neighbors. "I feel we have absolutely no alternative but to comply with this request," Reagan said. "I think the risks of not moving are far greater than the risks of taking the action we have planned."[127] McFarlane, his national security advisor, later recalled that, at this point, only one of the five present legislative leaders offered his support for the decision: Sen. Howard H. Baker, Jr., a Tennessee Republican, then the Senate majority leader. "He [Baker] said you are going to take a lot of heat here, and I stress that because it shows I think how secondary the notion of a national perspective is among Congressmen," McFarlane later recalled.[128] "I don't think it was partisanship, I think it was just the nature of the political animal, that political animals in Congress are much more attuned to what they see as a sentiment of their people who vote for them, and much less to any concept of the national interest."

As Reagan spoke, Edwin Meese III, the president's top-ranking political adviser and a former district attorney, scanned the faces of the assembled congressional jury. He especially watched the reaction Thomas P. "Tip" O'Neill, Jr., then the Speaker of the House.[129] O'Neill was Reagan's principal Democratic counterweight, but he was also Reagan's after-hours friend. His response was key to the invasion garnering bipartisan support. "Well, Mr. President, it's your show," Meese heard O'Neill declare. Meese took this remark to mean Reagan would solely own political responsibility for the military action, for good or ill.

The president then turned the presentation over to Vessey, McFarlane and Weinberger who reviewed the military details of the operation using flip charts. Reagan left the meeting at 8:47 p.m. to take a call in the adjoining Trophy Room from British prime minister Margaret Thatcher. She had just been advised of the decision to intervene in the second of two "Dear Margaret" official letters from Reagan that day. The "Iron Lady" of the United Kingdom was irate. She urged Reagan to call off the action, reminding him that Grenada was a member of the British Commonwealth.

Sen. Howard Baker later recalled Reagan's end of the conversation as he overheard it though a closed door. "He said, 'Margaret,' long pause. 'But Margaret,' and he went through that about three times and he came back sort of sheepish and said, 'Mrs. Thatcher has some reservations about this.'" The Southern senator concluded that Thatcher was the only person who could intimidate Ronald Reagan.[130] Reagan was distressed by Thatcher's reaction, but he held firm. The invasion would go ahead as scheduled, whatever the international or domestic consequences. Asked later by a member of the British Parliament why he didn't get Thatcher's opinion ahead of time, Reagan quipped: "Because I didn't want her to say no."[131]

O'Neill also had grave doubts about the wisdom of the American intervention, but he kept his opinion under wraps until the fighting was essentially over. "The invasion was already underway, so even if we opposed it there was nothing we could do," O'Neill later related in his memoirs.[132] Under the terms of the 1973 War Powers Resolution, the president is required in every possible instance to consult with Congress before introducing American armed forces into hostilities. Since Reagan had turned over his signed presidential order for the invasion three hours before the meeting began, this session didn't meet the letter of the law in O'Neill's view.

James A. Baker III, Reagan's chief of staff, remembers O'Neill standing up to leave after the briefing and declaring: "Well, Mr. President, this isn't consultation. This is notification. Good luck."[133] Baker thought O'Neill left the meeting upset, but other Reagan staffers in the room detected a more empathetic response from the Boston-reared politician who was second in the line of succession to the president after the vice president. O'Neill was observed reaching over to touch Reagan's arm several times during the briefing. At the end of the meeting, O'Neill shook hands with the Reagan and said: "God bless you, Mr. President."[134]

After the congressional leaders departed at around 10 a.m., Reagan was left in his living quarters with Vessey, a man whom he had handpicked for the chairman's post. Among other kinships, the two men shared a common belief that the best way to preserve the peace is to always be ready for the next war. Reagan asked Vessey to review his decision timeline. Vessey later recalled responding: "Now is the time, you have to say go ahead now or we can't make it tomorrow morning." He added, however, that the operation could still be cancelled as late as a few hours before the scheduled landings. The president, again, said go—for the last time.[135]

At that point, Vessey recalled that McFarlane told Reagan that the White House Situation Room would be open all night and would be prepared to brief him at any time. Reagan turned to Vessey. "General, what are you going to do?" he asked. "Mr. President, as soon as I send the message to the Pentagon to go ahead, I'm going home and go[ing] to bed.... I'll get up early in the morning and come over to the Pentagon after the landing has been made and wait for the first reports to come in," Vessey replied. "Thank you, and I'm going to do the same thing," the president said. Vessey then called the Pentagon with a prearranged execute message and both president and chairman retired to their respective beds.

This anecdote reveals the human component of momentous presidential decision-making. It is also historically remarkable because none of Vessey's direct dealings with the president or the operational commanders was strictly in his job description as chairman of the Joint Chiefs. Despite its four-star luster, the chairman's job, by Vessey's reading of the federal statutes, was a servile one. Vessey told an oral historian in 1986, near end of his four-year tenure, that he saw himself essentially as the servant of three masters.[136] His primary master was the National Command Authority (the president and the secretary of defense) who were the civilian national security decision makers. His second master was the Joint Chiefs as a body. He served as a member and chairman of that committee. His de facto role was to coax, not compel, them toward consensus. Finally, and most loosely, he was the servant of the commanders of the nine unified military commands which had responsibility for waging war, either in a defined geographic area of the globe or through some specialized military function. The chairman of the Joint Chiefs was not by statute in the chain of command and had no forces directly under his personal control. In the case of Urgent Fury, he served as the overlord of the American military forces only because Weinberger opted to delegate his full statutory power to him.[137]

While these high-level power dramas were unfolding in Washington, the Marines at sea had retired to their berthing spaces on the invasion eve to watch a war movie. The scheduled showing for that day on the *Guam* was preempted for a special screening of *The Sands of Iwo Jima* starring John Wayne. After victory was valiantly secured by the Duke in the Western Pacific, the men were sent to their bunks to sleep. Few, if any, did. Most would be facing combat in the morning for the first time. They knew the real version had no relation to what they had just seen depicted on the silver screen. They packed their field gear and cleaned their weapons one last time. Many Marines had the jitters. "A lot didn't want to go," recalled Master Sgt. George T. Curtis, the maintenance chief for the helicopter squadron. Nobody was eager to die fighting for an ill-defined cause in a place they persisted in calling "Granada." Curtis sought to buttress the resolve of the younger helicopter crew members by sprinkling at least one Vietnam combat vet among the crew of every flight of three transports.[138]

As the Marines struggled with their fears, the 11-ship task force crept closer to Grenada's shores. Six frogmen from SEAL Team 4 who were part of the MAU's shipboard underwater demolition detachment departed the *Fort Snelling* on a night reconnaissance mission. A beach at the eastern end of the Pearls runway had been identified as the preferred amphibious landing site. The SEALs were under the command of Lt. Michael J. Walsh, a 17-year Navy veteran, who heard the news of the Beirut bombing just as he was leaving the amphibious assault ship. His SEAL platoon traveled 20 miles through rough seas in a SeaFox, a 36-foot, fiberglass-hulled craft, and a smaller Zodiac boat. As they neared shore, they encountered boats they took to be patrol craft and took evasive action to avoid detection.[139] The delay thwarted their initial plan to recon the length of the beach by land as a platoon. Instead, Walsh split his men into two groups. Two SEALs were dispatched to swim up to the intended landing beach. The remaining frogmen performed a reconnaissance of the approaches to the beach from the sea on the Zodiac. The two swimmers who crawled onto the beach discovered soldiers digging foxholes. The SEALs hid themselves to avoid being detected. The soldiers came close before a rain squall sent them looking for shelter away from the shore. The SEALs completed their interrupted reconnaissance, radioed a recall signal and were joined on the beach by the other members of the platoon. The entire SEAL team then took up temporary residence in the abandoned foxholes to await the dawn and the Marine invasion.

Meanwhile, back on the *Guam*, all 57 pilots of Marine Medium Helicopter Squadron 261 gathered in the briefing room for their final instructions. Maj. Frank L. Brewer, the executive officer of the helicopter squadron, later remembered the palpable tension in the room and the apprehension he read on all the faces.[140] Of the group, only he and the squadron's commanding officer, Lt. Col. Granville R. Amos, had ever witnessed live-fire combat, let alone being personally shot at. The disastrous aircraft collisions in the Iranian desert in 1980 which had doomed the attempted rescue of the American hostages were on every pilot's mind. Nearly all of the squadron's pilots had been trained by Marine veterans of that failed mission. The desert debacle had involved RH-53D Navy Sea Stallion helicopters similar to the CH-53 variant the Marine squadron was about to fly into battle.

As the 22nd MAU pilots attended their briefing, reveille sounded at 0100 though the amphibious group summoning the Marines of Echo, Fox and Golf companies to also prepare for combat. A predawn breakfast was served in the wardrooms and on the mess decks. Marine infantrymen drew live ammunition. Echo Company loaded aboard CH-46 helicopters on the *Guam*, while Fox Company remained on the ship as a ready reserve. Golf Company loaded aboard their amphibious landing vehicles (amtracs) on the *Manitowoc*. Tanks, jeeps and the reconnaissance platoon were simultaneously loaded on three LCUs in the well deck of the *Fort Snelling*.[141]

Port-side view of the USS *Guam* (LPH-9), an amphibious assault ship, which served as Vice Adm. Joseph P. Metcalf III's command ship during Operation Urgent Fury. Metcalf and his 50-member staff were crammed into the flag plot compartment inside the "island" superstructure on the flight deck. This 1983 photograph was taken off Lebanon a month after the invasion (National Archives [330-CFD-DM-ST-84-07375]).

By 0300, Walsh had radioed his beach reconnaissance report: "Walk Track Shoes," the code phrase for marginal landing conditions. The beach itself was suitable for landing craft, but the SEALs found the approach passed through a coral reef with plunging surf.[142] The news was disappointing, but the MAU invasion plan had made provisions for this eventuality. The amphibious operation was now temporarily shelved. The initial assault force of two rifle companies would land by helicopter in two separate movements. Echo Company would land first near Pearls at the appointed H-Hour. Fox Company would follow about an hour later at the port town of Grenville, two miles away. Golf Company, now loading in their 14 amtracs on the *Manitowoc*, replaced Fox Company as the reserve unit. Tanks and jeeps loaded onto three LCUs (landing craft) in the well deck of the *Fort Snelling*. This armored amphibious force would land only if a suitable alternative beach was found after daylight.[143]

On the *Guam*, Navy captain Garret Ogle, head of ship's surgical team, made final preparations for receiving casualties. Triage stations were set up in three positions on the hanger deck for initial assessment of the wounded. Four operating tables were readied in the ship's main operating room. The first battle-related casualties would be arriving soon, and in far greater numbers than expected.[144] The *Guam* treated 76 wounded or injured over the next six days; two surgeons conducted 16 shipboard operations.[145]

Meanwhile, Metcalf and his command team of nearly 50 officers crowded into the flag plot on the *Guam*, a control center designed to serve one quarter that number. Normally, Metcalf took his staff to sea on the *Mount Whitney*, a *Blue Ridge*–class command ship, but this flagship vessel could not be deployed in time from Norfolk. The *Mount Whitney*'s sophisticated command, control and communications capabilities would much be missed by the officers who stood shoulder-to-shoulder for hours in the *Guam*'s command workspace. The staff's hold over its multi-service command was tenuous. The Marines, Ranger and JSOC forces assigned to the spear point of the attack would fight independently under their respective commanders in the critical first hours of the coming battle.

2

Everyone Goes Late

The first Marine helicopter lifted off the darkened deck of the *Guam* in a driving rain at 0315 on Oct. 25. The night was moonless. The air crews recalled it was like flying through an inkwell. All the aircraft were equipped with night-vision goggles, but not all the pilots were yet qualified in their use.[1] Radio silence rules prevented communication among the launched aircraft or with the ship. Assembling the spearhead assault force was further complicated by the fuel capacity of the CH-46 transports. They needed to take off, assemble into formation and then land again to pick up their troops and top-off on fuel.[2] It took until almost 0500, the designated H-Hour, to get all the 21 helicopters loaded and on their way toward the island about 10 miles away.

The landing was set for LZ Buzzard, less than a kilometer south of Pearls Airport. The selected spot was marked on their maps as a disused racecourse. As the first-wave transports started to land, pilots were startled to see shadowy, green-tinged images in their night-vision glasses. Palm trees, some 60 feet tall, loomed everywhere. "It almost looked like you were landing in front of the Palm Springs Inn," recalled Maj. Melvin W. DeMars, Jr., one of the CH-53 pilots.[3] Grazing cows the size of water buffalos also came into view. Amos, the helicopter squadron commander, ordered his pilots to shift to a less-obstructed section of the LZ. The first helicopter touched down at 0520, 20 minutes later than planned[4]—but still ahead of the Rangers and special forces who were landing elsewhere, and even further behind schedule.

The first Marines to set foot on Grenadian soil were unopposed. The first shots fired came when the following waves of helicopters arrived and dawn illuminated their landing. Two 12.7 mm anti-aircraft guns located on a hill about a kilometer north of the runway briefly came to life.[5] The two guns were promptly silenced by cannon and rocket fire from the escorting Marine AH-1T Sea Cobra gunships. Still, the shooting spooked the arriving Marines. The later waves dropped their passengers and were airborne again in less than 15 seconds. One Marine broke an arm after getting shoved off the back of a departing helicopter. Hasty unloading of vehicles from the heavy-lift helicopters led to mishaps. The first jeep off sank in the marshy ground and turned over.[6] Two other jeeps became entangled on a ramp while being disgorged from a CH-53.[7] One Marine broke a leg in the 30-minute struggle to free the vehicles.

There was also very nearly a friendly fire incident—an early omen of misfortunes to befall other units later in the fighting. One of Marine Cobras happened to catch the SEAL reconnaissance team commander out in the open while he was scouting an enemy beach position that he feared threatened his hidden men.[8] Walsh raised his weapon over

40

his head in non-threatening gesture and trusted the pilot to identify him as an American. Walsh saw a Cobra take aim on him with its three-barrel turret cannon, but it held fire as it passed over. Then a new threat developed as the Cobra dueled with one of the anti-aircraft guns. Spent rounds from the 12.7 mm machine guns fell to earth very close to where the rest of the SEAL team was dug in. Walsh later learned that the assaulting Marines had not been informed that his frogmen were still on the beach.

The opening exchange of fire at Pearls produced no reported casualties by fire on either side, but it established, de facto, the start of hostilities. (None of the involved nations had declared war on any of the others—or ever did.) The Americans, absent their Caribbean partners, were the first to step foot on Grenadian soil, but the Grenadian militia were the first to open fire with their anti-aircraft guns. The Americans were ostensibly there to rescue American civilians, but the medical students were all located 20-odd miles away on the other side of island. Marines would not play any role in attempts to reach the students on the first day. There were no Cuban military personnel assigned to defend Pearls or Grenville on D-Day. At this initial point, the fighting was just between the Grenadian militia and the Marines of the 22nd MAU.

Two platoons from Echo Company moved from the landing zone to the nearby Pearls airfield, arriving as dawn was brightening into sunrise. The Marines breached a chain-link fence around the terminal, triggering some small arms fire from defenders who fled to the west.[9] One platoon was then ordered north to secure Hill 275, the source of the short-lived anti-aircraft fire. By then the Grenadian gunners had returned to their positions but, unaccountably, they did not fire their crew-served weapons on the advancing American infantry. As the Marines neared the crest of the hill, the Grenadian militiamen ran off, dressed in T-shirts and shorts. Meanwhile, other Echo Company Marines secured the airport. Pearls was a rundown regional civil aviation facility consisting of a 5,151-foot runway, a small fuel storage facility and a terminal/operations building. A British journalist described the cinderblock structure as a "squalid leftover from colonial days which looks for all the world like a Victorian railway station transported to the tropics." The biggest commercial plane Pearls could safely handle was a turbo-prop carrying fewer than 50 passengers. The airfield had no landing lights or modern electronic navigational aids. It closed down at night and in bad weather.[10]

The Marines captured two planes they found parked at the field, both Soviet-made. One was an AN-2R biplane, a newly arrived gift to Grenada from the Soviet government, which still carried Aeroflot civilian markings. Ostensibly this single-engine utility transport was intended to be used to spray bananas with pesticide, but it could also be used for variety of other purposes. The Marines found its cargo cabin rigged for parachute drops. The other aircraft was an AN-26 Cubana Airlines twin-engine turboprop. This civilian transport had arrived at midday on Oct. 24 from Havana carrying a two-man Cuban crisis management team. The late-arriving Cuban officials were Col. Pedro Tortoló Comas, a career military officer who had been in charge of the Cuban military mission to Grenada until six months earlier, and Carlos Andrés Diaz Larranaga, a Cuban diplomat who was Cuba's Caribbean section chief and reported to the Central Committee. On landing, the two emissaries immediately departed for the capital city, but they left their 12-man civilian aircrew behind at the airport. The Echo Company Marines took the Cuban flight crew into custody.

At this early point there were no documented wounded from hostile fire from any nationality. The Marines didn't know it yet, but Fidel Castro had made it clear to Cubans

Top: Aerial view of Pearls Airport on Grenada's northeastern coast on October 28, 1983, three days after it was secured by the 22nd MAU Marines. An Air Force C-130 is shown on the runway and two Marine CH-46 helicopters are in front of the terminal. A Cuban and a Grenadian plane are parked on the grass. This 5,151-foot runway was too short to land long-haul jets (National Archives [330-CFD-DF-ST-84-09783]). *Bottom:* This Polish-made AN-2R Colt biplane, captured by Marines at Pearls Airport, was Grenada's only government-owned aircraft at the time of the invasion. It was a recent gift from the Soviet Union and still bears Soviet civilian markings. It was ostensibly intended for banana spraying, but could have been used for a variety of civilian and military purposes (National Archives [330-CFD-DA-ST-86-04153]).

on the island, and to Grenada's new rulers, that Havana's support for the coup was arm's length at best. In a written message delivered to both groups two days earlier, Castro declared: "If the U.S. intervenes, we must vigorously defend ourselves as if we were in Cuba, in our camp sites, in our workplaces close by, but only if we are directly attacked. I repeat: only if we are directly attacked. We would thus be defending ourselves, not the Government or it deeds. If the Yankees land on the [Point Salines] runway section near the University or its surroundings to evacuate their citizens, fully refrain from interfering."[11] The two emissaries had been dispatched by Castro to execute his "stand-off, unless attacked" command. This difficult defensive assignment ended the careers of both. Diaz was killed in climatic fighting that was to occur at Point Salines on the second day of the invasion. Tortoló survived the Cuban last stand, but was court-martialed for his military performance.

At around the same time Echo Company reached the Pearls terminal, Fox Company landed two miles away at the port town of Grenville. Again, the pre-selected landing zone, designated LZ Oriole, looked more accommodating on the map and aerial photos that it did close up. Amos again quickly selected an alternate: a soccer field in the center of town that was surrounded by a high brick wall. Amos saw people on the ground waving to him in apparent welcome. He took a warrior's gamble that the second wave touchdown would again be unopposed. His reading of the situation proved correct. The Marines at Grenville were greeted as liberators by local civilians who were displeased by the military regime in the capital city. They helped the arriving Americans identify Grenadian soldiers who had shed their uniforms for civilian clothes and locate hidden arms caches.[12] The locals also loaned the Americans civilian vehicles to transport the captured military arms. The Marine commanders adjusted their military mindset accordingly; they would ask questions first and shoot later. The 400 Marines were discovering that resistance to the invasion of the island varied according to location, and also to the political loyalties of whomever was holding the gun that was opposing them.

The professional soldiers of Grenada's People's Revolutionary Army (PRA) were Soviet-equipped, Cuban-trained and beholden to the hardline Marxist faction that had seized control of the government. On paper, the PRA consisted of 906 full-time soldiers and paramilitary guards. However, only 463, about half the permanent personnel, answered the mobilization call.[13] The regular PRA soldiers who reported were assigned to key anti-aircraft guns positions and elite mobile infantry units built around armored personnel carriers. They were prepared, trained and equipped to defend their homeland. But the island had more strategic points than it had professional soldiers. The PRA relied on the militia volunteers to man the remaining defensive positions. The unpaid and ill-prepared militia, never a combat-ready force, was further dispirited by the shocking assassination of Prime Minister Bishop, a beloved populist leader. Only 257 militia members, about one out of 10, heeded the call to report to their posts. Fewer still put up more than token resistance to the invaders. The airport and the port city on the eastern side of the island were declared secure by 0730.[14] A handmade sign was hung above the "PEARLS" sign on the terminal entrance unofficially renaming it Marine Corps Air Station Douglas in memory of a revered sergeant major who was among the Marines killed in the Lebanon barracks bombing.

The military scene playing out to the west at Point Salines was not nearly so sanguine; it was more like Beirut than the Grenville reception. Ranger paratroopers were greeted by anti-aircraft and small arms fire that turned their landing plans into turmoil. Only Air

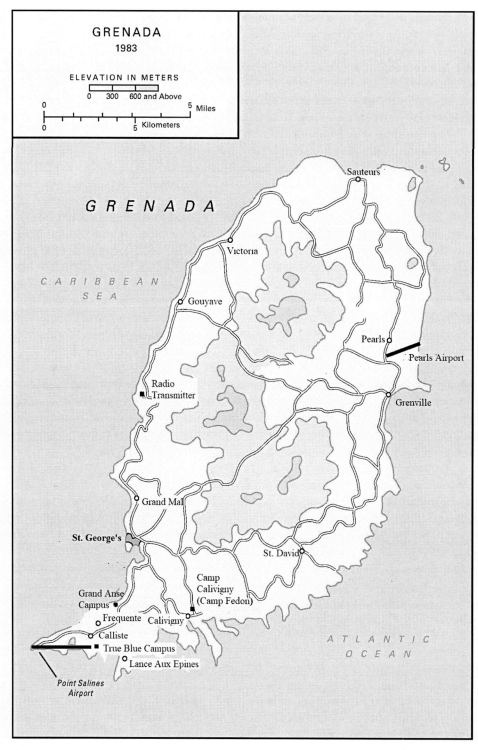

This map shows the major communities on the mainland of Grenada and the relative position of the two airfields, which were principal D-Day targets (adapted from base map, courtesy U.S. Army Center of Military History).

Force suppressing fire, Castro's order restricting Cuban resistance, and an in-flight tactical adjustment by the officer leading the Ranger assault prevented a massacre of the Army's elite light infantry force. Smith, the Marine infantry commander, heard the excited calls coming from the Army sector over his unit's all-services satellite radio. "They sounded like they had just fallen into World War II all over again," he later recalled.[15]

The Rangers received their first alert to the come-as-you-are invasion at 0300 on Friday, Oct. 21, when a phone call awakened Lt. Col. Wesley B. Taylor, Jr., at his home at Hunter Army Airfield in Savannah, Georgia. The caller told the commander of the 1st Ranger Battalion that that his presence was "required" at Fort Bragg in North Carolina. The summons was urgent, but only moderately so. He dressed quickly, but he chose to drive the five hours to Fayetteville in his truck, rather than fly.[16] That precisely calibrated response was characteristic of Taylor. He impressed everyone with his ability to combine calmness with action; as a military leader he was described as intelligent, deliberate, confident and unflappable. As a first lieutenant, he had earned a Silver Star for valor for "conspicuous gallantry and intrepidity" while serving as airborne advisor from 1967–68 in Vietnam. His similarly valorous actions in Grenada would earn him a Legion of Merit.[17]

In 1983 Fort Bragg served as the host installation for the headquarters of a shadowy military organization called the U.S. Joint Special Operations Command (JSOC). This classified unit was created three years earlier by the Pentagon, in the wake of the failed Iranian hostage rescue, in order to control future operations that involved special forces from more than one service. The administrative headquarters was located in a nine-acre, fenced-off area in the sprawling Army post that had previously served as the stockade.[18] The cell blocks were converted into spaces for classes, sleeping and storage. The jailhouse chapel became a conference room. Entry to the command center technically required security clearance above top secret.[19] When Taylor arrived at JSOC at mid-morning, he was told to start thinking about how he would seize the airport under construction on Point Salines. But, at that point, Taylor thought the probability was low that the Rangers would be given the execute order. He had been through these planning exercises many times before. The Rangers had been activated in their current elite light infantry form in 1974, but never yet used in combat.[20] (Post-Vietnam Rangers earned their elite status by volunteering four times: first for the post-draft Army, second for a grueling four-week Ranger indoctrination program, third for parachute training and finally two months at Ranger School.)

As Friday progressed, the momentum steadily increased toward execution. Taylor called his executive officer, Maj. John Nix, back in Georgia and told him to start gathering a leadership team to work on an airport seizure plan. Initially, Taylor thought that only his 1st Battalion would be involved in the mission. But, on Friday afternoon, the 1st Battalion's brother battalion on the West Coast was also included into the discussions. Lt. Col. Ralph Hagler, the commanding officer of the 2nd Ranger Battalion, was contacted at his office at Fort Lewis, Washington, near Tacoma. He was ordered to report to Fort Bragg the next morning to prepare for imminent action on Grenada. While Hagler was in the air to North Carolina on a commercial flight, his battalion received orders from the Pentagon for an unscheduled "exercise" deployment. The 2nd Rangers reported to McChord Air Force Base adjoining their home base in Washington and prepared for a red-eye flight on Air Force C-141Bs to Hunter Army Airfield.

Hagler and Taylor and their respective battle staffs linked up at Fort Bragg at a 1700 meeting on Saturday, Oct. 22. The Ranger officers were now told to plan to simultaneously seize and secure the airfields at Point Salines and Pearls. Taylor's 1st Battalion would have primary responsibility for seizing Salines; Hagler's 2nd Battalion would seize Pearls.[21] The commanders were advised that the mission would be limited to a total of 700 of their best men. That was the maximum number that could be airlifted from the United States with the available, fully trained Air Force C-130 transport air crews. The Ranger participation was envisioned as a one-day mission. After the first day, the 22nd MAU Marines would land to relieve them. The officers were given a room with a chalkboard, pencils and paper. They were told to prepare a briefing to be delivered the next morning to Scholtes and his JSOC staff.[22]

Taylor's team evaluated four or five alternative courses of action. The most desirable was for a small initial assault team to drop by parachute and clear the runway. Following planes would then land and unload the remaining force in a rapid and controlled manner. The officers weren't sure about the condition of the runway or the degree of opposition they would encounter. The planners concluded that they needed to be prepared to deliver the entire force by parachute, if "airland" wasn't possible. H-Hour was then set for 0230 local time, the dark of night. Intelligence was limited as to the enemy's numbers, disposition and readiness to fight. Maps were especially deficient. Instead of the standard 1:25,000-scale maps preferred for military planning, the Rangers were handed 1:50,000-scale, British-made tourism maps that contained limited information on terrain, road markings and longitude and latitude.[23] Their key objective, the airport under construction at Point Salines, was drawn in by hand.[24]

After about four hours of work, Rangers were called into another conference room for an update meeting. The JSOC staff shared the latest intelligence information about the turmoil on the island, but the real news came from Scholtes. "You will be on the ground [in Grenada] Tuesday morning," Scholtes said.[25] That unequivocal statement instantly dispelled the suspicion that this all-nighter would be turn out to be another drill that went nowhere. At around midnight, the 1st Battalion's executive officer called back to Hunter on a secure line to tell subordinates to start a recall of the entire battalion to an assembly at 0500 on Sunday, Oct. 23. Nix wanted to be sure that the unit's weekend deer hunters would be in uniform and on base, not wearing an orange vest in a hunting blind.

The Ranger officers then returned to their planning labors with newfound zeal. When Sunday morning came, the officers had a draft briefing plan ready, but they lost their principal audience. Scholtes, the JSOC commander, was away, attending the Pentagon wash-up of the invasion plan in "the Tank" (literally and figuratively) with McDonald. The Ranger-drafted briefing was delivered instead to Lt. Col. Richard A. Pack, Scholtes' J-3 operations officer. "I guess it was approved, although no one ever really, as far as I could tell, stood up and said, 'Yes, that's a good plan, great plan, or it's okay.' Just silence was consent, I guess, in this case, and we drove on," Nix later recalled.[26] Blessed or not, the officers hustled back to their commands in Georgia to put their chalkboard plans into action. But the mission kept changing as they were proceeding. The eleventh-hour alterations in the plan that were made at the Pentagon on Sunday now filtered down to the men who would actually do the fighting.

The first big change came at about 1400 on Sunday afternoon when the word reached Nix that the Marines had been assigned the primary responsibility for securing Pearls Airport instead of 2nd Battalion. This relegated 2nd Battalion to assisting the 1st Battalion in seizing the airfield at Point Salines. Once the airport was secure, the 2nd Battalion would race by jeep to seize their principal D-Day objective: Camp Calivigny, a military training compound on a peninsula about seven and a half miles east of the Salines airport. Later Sunday, Nix got word of yet another change. One of Taylor's three rifle companies, Charlie Company, had been detached to support the Delta Force assault on Richmond Hill Prison. Among other things, that loss of 100 men meant that Taylor could take all his other readily available men, and still stay within his assigned airlift limit. It also meant that Charlie Company would immediately have to be transported the 250 air miles from Hunter Army Airfield to Pope Air Force Base to link up with Delta Force. Charlie Company departed for North Carolina at dawn on Monday, Oct. 24, aboard Air Force C-141s.[27]

By Monday afternoon, the ever-evolving invasion plan called for the bulk of the two Ranger battalions to fly non-stop from Hunter to Grenada in 16 four-engine, turboprop C-130 Air Force transports. Five planes would be MC-130E "Combat Talon" models specially equipped with precision navigation gear. The planes could pinpoint their drop zones while flying in the dark and at low altitude to avoid detection. The other 11 planes would be standard, cargo-carrying C-130Hs crammed full of men, ammunition, motorcycles, jeeps.[28] The plan called for the 16 transports to arrive in three phases. The lead phase of seven planes would carry the 1st Ranger Battalion from Hunter. The 2nd Battalion would fly immediately behind in a second phase of five planes, also from Hunter. A third phase of four C-130 transports would depart later from Pope with Charlie Company, the 1st Battalion unit which had been detached to support the JSOC secret commando missions. These four planes would also carry a total of eight small special operations "Little Bird" helicopters in their cargo bays. Six were MH-6 utility transports and two were AH-6 light attack helicopters. The plan was for the Charlie Company Rangers to ride the MH-6 transports into battle escorted by the AH-6 gunships once the Point Salines runway was secure.[29]

These 16 MC-130/C-130 transports were augmented by two EC-130 ABCCC command planes from Keesler Air Force Base in Mississippi. These two planes (known as "A, B, triple Cs") carried the trail bosses for this flying wagon train. The cargo bay of this C-130 variant was modified to carry a 40-foot, self-contained, command capsule. The interior was outfitted with work stations and seating for a battle staff of up to 15, as well as a galley and a latrine.[30] On the outside, these planes had air conditioning pods protruding from the forward fuselage that looked like Mickey Mouse ears. These distinguished them from the smooth skin, standard version called a "slick" C-130. Scholtes, the Task Force 123 commander, flew in one of the mouse-eared EC-130s; his deputy, Col. Bill Palmer, flew in the other.[31] Together they would provide airborne command and control over the Ranger air assault.

Three AC-130H Spectre gunships were assigned to ride shotgun for the 18 unarmed transports. The Spectres carried no paratroopers, but they bristled with three types of large-caliber guns on the left side of their fuselage. Two rapid fire 20 mm Vulcan cannons were mounted forward of the wing. Two heavier guns were located just aft of the wing: a 40 mm Bofors cannon and, behind that, a 105 mm howitzer. In layman's terms, the 20 mm was fired like a shotgun, the 40 mm like a rifle and the 105 mm like a cannon.[32] These three AC-130 gunships were based at yet a third airfield, Hurlburt Field on Florida's panhandle.

Finally, three larger Air Force C-5A transport planes were separately assigned to carry special forces troops and nine Black Hawk helicopters from North Carolina to a civilian airport in Barbados. There the helicopters the C-5s carried in their bellies would be off-loaded in total darkness and readied for flight. The Black Hawks would then take aboard about 100 SEALs and Delta commandos to attack three designated political objectives on Grenada before the main force of Marines and Ranger arrived. So, in summary, an air armada of 24 transport and escort aircraft was assembled for a complex, multiphased assault on Grenada departing from four different military airfields in the United States. The fixed-wing aircraft included 21 C-130s of various types, plus 3 larger C-5s. An additional 17 rotary-wing aircraft (nine Black Hawk helicopters and eight Little Birds) were carried into battle in the cargo holds of seven of the transports.

At mid-afternoon on Monday, Oct. 23, the Rangers from 1st Battalion gathered in Hanger 850 at Hunter Army Airfield for final departure preparations. Military trucks hauled in parachutes, rations, water and live ammunition for distribution to the paratroopers. At around 1500, the 1st Battalion's executive officer got word from his Air Force support team that their H-Hour had been pushed back by two and a half hours from 0230 to 0500. The Ranger leadership was told this meant that their takeoff time, and all the associated pre-flight prep and loading activities, had also been pushed back by about two hours. Nix saw opportunity in the unexpected delay. He ordered the mess hall to started cooking the men a hot meal before they departed. When Scholtes personally confirmed the change in the H-Hour, Taylor, the battalion commander, passed the word to his company commanders to get their men to lie down and get some rest.[33]

The delay also gave Taylor time to personally address his men on what was to come. Taylor spoke for about 15 minutes from a podium placed on a truck flatbed. "This is not an exercise," he declared with calculated understatement. "You're trained, you're ready and you have a mission. You're American Rangers."[34] Taylor was just finishing his speech when Nix learned that the Rangers and the Air Force had different interpretations of the H-Hour delay. The C-130s were taxing toward the hanger, expecting to immediately board the Rangers. The Air Force was aiming to have their transports fully loaded at the time originally planned, despite the "time over target" delay.

Pandemonium ensued as a two-hour load-and-prep was compressed into less than half that time. Taylor watched one of his units march at double-time onto one plane and then realize they had boarded the wrong aircraft. They immediately marched back off and onto the right one, just as smartly. The first MC-130 "Combat Talon" left Georgia soil at 2115 on Oct. 24 for the 2,300-mile trip, seven-and-a-half-hour flight. The departure was 45 minutes late by the Air Force schedule, but they still had a cushion at the other end because of H-Hour delay until 0500. All the C-130s refueled in flight twice in route to holding positions 70 nautical miles off the coast of Grenada.[35]

The complex airlift plan suffered its first equipment failure almost immediately. One of the AC-130s from Hurlburt had an engine fire, forcing the crew to return to base to switch planes. The mishap, however, later proved beneficial. The delay caused this gunship air crew to arrive over Grenada later than the other two gunships, further extending the period of overhead fire support on the first day. (All three gunships already carried extra crew to allow pilots and other control operators to take in-flight breaks and permit missions up to twice as long as the Vietnam War standard.[36])

The preferred plan at this point called for the Rangers in the first three aircraft to parachute onto the airfield at Point Salines, clear it of any obstacles and suppress any enemy resistance. If successful, this would allow the remaining Rangers to land on the secured field in their planes and then race off in their vehicles. This roll-off tactic was modeled on the daring 1976 Israeli commando raid that rescued hijacked airline passengers being held by terrorists at Entebbe Airport in Uganda. The landing situation was still fluid when the transports took off because it was still unclear what reception the Rangers would receive at the end of their journey. As a worst-case precaution, all the aircraft were rigged for all the passengers to jump, if necessary. In his final briefing, Taylor had warned his paratroopers that they might drop from as low as 500 feet to minimize the exposure to enemy fire and maximize the likelihood that they would land directly on the runway.[37]

The flight to Grenada was long, loud, tense and uncomfortable for the most of the Rangers. Each plane carried about three dozen soldiers, plus the Air Force aircrew. Most of the paratroopers sat shoulder-to-shoulder on red nylon seats with their backs to the fuselage,[38] but at least two MC-130s were outfitted with mattresses instead of seats. Most cargo bays were jammed full of jeeps. Those who could slept, but the roar of the four turboprop engines was hardly soporific. The planes flew low, 500 feet, to avoid radar detection, but that altitude made for a bumpy ride. Some Rangers got air sick and puked into military-issue barf bags. The dank cabin air reeked of vomit and sweat.[39]

The Ranger officers busied themselves in-flight with final details. Taylor was especially engaged. At around 2200, half an hour after takeoff, the 1st Battalion commander got word that the latest examination of aerial photographs of Point Salines showed that the runways were obstructed. Taylor was counting on the second reconnaissance by SEAL Team Six to provide definitive word on the type and extent of the obstructions, as well as details on the airport defenses. If the SEALs found the runway to be undefended, it might still have been possible for the first planes to clear the runway in time for the rest of the initial phase to land. At around 0030 Taylor got more bad news. The second SEAL recon had failed, leaving the precise situation on the ground still uncertain.[40]

By default, it fell to the Air Force to make the visual reconnaissance of the runway that had so tragically frustrated the SEALs. At around 0330, an AC-130H Specter piloted by Maj. Michael J. Couvillon made a stealthy 90-second pass over the runway, flying at 9,000 feet, just below the cloud level, so as not to be seen or heard from the ground. "Our intent was not to wake anybody up," Couvillon recalled.[41] From the air, the runway was dimly outlined by low-intensity "bean bag" lights, but the tarmac surface was invisible to the pilot's eye. The aircraft's low-light television cameras and infrared detectors, however, revealed an unwelcoming scene. The runway was blocked by three construction vehicles parked in the center of the runway and several more blocking the runway at the west.[42] The tarmac was also further obstructed by randomly scattered, smaller obstacles, which were later found to include 55-gallon barrels filled with coral, spikes, concertina wire and carts.[43]

Couvillon's gunship radioed his disappointing news to the commanders in the C-130 armada, using a one-word code name that is lost in his memory. At 0400, just an hour before H-Hour, Taylor reluctantly concluded that all of 1st Battalion should drop from an altitude of just 500 feet, less than the height of the Washington Monument. The minimum jump altitude in peacetime was then 1,200 feet. A low-altitude jump increased the chances of landing injuries, but limited hang time to just 12 seconds—too little time for reserve chutes to open if the main chute failed. It was a bold, wartime decision. The level of difficulty was compounded by stiff surface winds of 20 knots, gusting to 25. The safety limit for peacetime drops was 13 knots.[44]

Taylor's drop decision was affirmed by Air Force Maj. Gen. William J. Mall, Jr., the

This aerial photograph of the unfinished runway at Point Salines looks from west to east. It illustrates the narrowness of the Ranger drop zone and the proximity of water hazards (National Archives [330-CFD-DA-ST-85-02198]).

MAC mission commander, who was flying with Taylor in his MC-130, and by Scholtes flying in his EC-130E.[45] The planes in the first phase assembled themselves about a minute apart for a low-level approach to the airfield. The Grenadians knew Point Salines would be a prime invasion target, but they were expecting an amphibious assault, not a parachute drop. They had fortified the beach to the south of the east-west runway. Aircraft guns were positioned on the hills north of the runway, but were expecting to engage aircraft flying above 600 feet.[46]

The medical school campus was in a hollow just past the eastern end of the tarmac. The American invaders wisely chose to approach from the west where the runway opened to the sea. The two lead aircraft, carrying the runway clearing teams, separated themselves from the others, hoping to complete their work in time for all the others to land.[47] The MC-130s encountered thunderstorms and rain showers as they approached the island's coast from the northwest just before 0500. In the final minutes, about 20 miles out, the MC-130E that was supposed to lead the way had a navigational equipment malfunction.[48] The computer failure left the pilot unable to make the necessary air drop calculations based on the wind conditions. The release point needed to be precise because the drop zone had water on both sides. At 0454, Capt. John P. Abizaid, the Alpha Company commander flying with his airport seizure specialists, got the unwelcome news. In the darkened cabin, he saw the aircraft's jumpmaster make a hand motion across his throat to signal "no jump."[49]

The pilot of the lead MC-130E recommended against switching places with the second for safety reasons. They were flying low, in the dark, in the rain without running lights. Based on that report, Air Force colonel Bruce Fister, the Air Component Commander (ACC), flying with Scholtes, directed the third plane, also a MC-130, to lead the assault.[50] Scholtes reluctantly authorized a 30-minute delay in H-Hour to 0530 to reorganize the drop sequence. The delay worsened the tactical picture for the Rangers, who would now land after the Marines, and just after first light. Moreover, the Ranger attack would be made with the hilt of their sword, instead of the point. In the reordered drop, Taylor and his headquarters staff in the third MC-130 would be the first Rangers on the ground, instead of landing after the airport clearance specialists in the first two planes, Taylor had hoped that his plane would be the first to land on the cleared runway. Instead, about 50 miles from the target, his plane got the word to prepare to be the first to the fight.

The 40-odd parachutists on Taylor's plane fell into two groups. Two dozen were the 1st platoon of Bravo Company in Taylor's battalion. The others constituted the Tactical Operations Center (TOC) for the battalion: the officers in charge of communications, intelligence and supporting fire, supported by Air Force combat air controllers. The TOC team constituted the brains of the battalion. The brawn of the assault force was on the first two planes which had aborted their drop. As they approached landfall, the two Air Force jumpmasters on Taylor's plane inspected each man's parachute and then made their way to the two rear exit doors. They took position near a light that was glowing red. "Stand up!" the jumpmasters barked. Taylor and his men struggled to gain their footing under enormous loads of weapons and gear. Each Ranger had two parachutes, a main and reserve, that together weighed about 35 pounds. They also carried ammunition and water strapped to their bodies in pouches and belts that added another 25 pounds. But the heaviest weight of all was in their rucksacks, crammed with more battle gear.[51] One jumper compared staggering toward the doors of the plane to moving along a passageway of a ship in a stormy sea.

When the jumpmasters opened the doors, gusts of humid tropical air entered the cargo bay. Debris swirled up inside the fuselage. "Hook up," the jumpmasters barked. The Rangers attached the static lines of their parachutes to an overhead cable that ran the length of the cargo bay. The jumpmasters then led the stooped Rangers through a final check of their equipment. "Drop zone coming up," the jumpmasters warned. In the pilot's seat of the MC-130E, Air Force lieutenant colonel James L. Hobson peered through his night vision glasses, looking for land. About six miles out, Hobson saw the outline of the runway emerge from the greenish gloom. About a mile out, he was momentarily blinded by a searchlight that swept across the aircraft's canopy and then locked onto the cockpit. Because the anti-aircraft guns defending the airfield were not radar-equipped, searchlights were needed to illuminate targets in the dark. Hobson's co-pilot, Capt. P.R. Helm, spoke what was on both their minds. "Jim, I don't think this is going to be a big surprise," Helm said.[52] The first Ranger in line on both sides of the cargo bay stood in the open doorway poised to jump into the nascent dawn and evident danger. "Green light!" called Maj. Don James, the plane's navigator, as the indicator light changed color at 0536. "Go, go, go!" the jumpmasters urged as the Rangers hurtled through the door in "shotgun" fashion that propelled four men into the air every second. Green parachutes blossomed in the morning sky as tracer bullets from anti-aircraft machine guns and small arms made a lattice-work of the sky around them. Maj. John J. Maher III, the 1st Battalion's operations officer, looked down and saw glowing red and green rounds passing just below his boots. He looked up and saw still more tracer bullets passing above his parachute canopy and through the suspension lines.[53] He watched as the plane he had just exited banked right and dove toward the open ocean chased by fire from Grenadian 23 mm anti-aircraft guns, leveling off below 100 feet. Those golf ball-size rounds exploded in telltale airbursts of red, yellow and orange. The pilot of the next plane later compared the scene to the annual Fourth of July fireworks display in Washington, D.C.[54]

The following MC-130 twice attempted to drop its Rangers, but was driven away by ground fire, taking three hits from small arms. Hobson radioed for the rest of the first wave to break off its approach. The aborted drop required another reshuffling of the planned drop sequence. For the next 15 minutes Taylor and his plane-load of men were alone on a hostile shore. The arrival of the Rangers over the target was no surprise. The first Rangers set foot on the asphalt at Point Salines at 0537, 17 minutes after the first Marines landed at Pearls. Amazingly, all landed without injury or casualty, though six of them had holes in their parachutes.[55] This miracle can be fairly credited to two factors: the decision to drop at low altitude and Castro's order to the Cubans on the island not to fire unless they were attacked. The two Grenadian-manned 23 mm anti-aircraft guns positioned on a hill near the village of Frequente, northeast of the runway, were unable to depress their barrels low enough to target the plane.[56] The extent to which Cubans heeded Castro's order is contested, but there is no question that the Cuban response to the paratroopers was initially restrained.

The Rangers didn't learn until later that they were opposed at Point Salines by two independent forces, one Cuban and one Grenadian, which were operating under different leadership, rules of engagement and areas of operation. Castro's order not to obstruct American attempts to extract the medical students was interpreted by the Cubans on the island as an order to remain in their two camps in the vicinity of the airport. The Cubans alone controlled the ground defensive positions for the central and eastern end of the airport.[57] Grenadian soldiers were barred from entering the Cuban-controlled zone. Tortoló, the Cuban commander, had pulled Cuban military advisers away from the Grenadian army so that they could serve as small unit leaders for the civilian Cuban construction workers. The airport workers all had some prior military training and could be activated as a reserve military battalion. They were organized into three provisional companies and their small arms were supplemented by mortars and recoilless rifles from the Grenadian army stores.[58]

In a speech after the shooting stopped on Grenada, Castro declared that Havana's relations with the coup leaders who had ordered Prime Minister Bishop killed "was actually cold and tense, so that, at the time of the criminal Yankee aggression, there was no coordination whatsoever between the Grenadian army and the Cuban construction workers and other cooperation personnel."[59] This assertion later got left-handed corroboration from a CIA intelligence assessment. The all-sources report declared that "we have not been able to confirm that armed Cubans defended other than their own positions or were involved in coordinating a defense with Grenadian forces."[60] The anti-aircraft fire the Air Force planes encountered came primarily, if not exclusively, from Grenadian gunners. The AK-47 fire came primarily from the Cuban construction workers. Castro later maintained that, on his orders, "Cubans were sleeping and their weapons were stored at the time of the airdrop" and did not fire on American troops until they "advanced toward the Cubans in a belligerent way."[61] Some captured Cubans later told U.S. interrogators that they disobeyed orders and joined the fight alongside Grenadians earlier than the start time cited by Castro.[62] Either way, the point remains that the airport resistance, though unexpected and terrifying in its intensity, was not nearly as deadly or as effective as it could have been. "That was the invaders weakest moment. If the Cubans had fired first, they would have killed or wounded dozens—perhaps hundreds—of U.S. soldiers in those early hours," Castro later asserted in a Nov. 14, 1983, speech in Havana.

3

Nine Chalks to Chaos

The most secret aspect of the secret invasion of Grenada turned out, fatefully, to be the most heralded. The U.S. military's elite special operation anti-terrorism units, Navy Seal Team Six swimmers and Army Delta Force operators, did not arrive over Grenada in their Black Hawk helicopters until after Marine and Ranger assault troops had landed. By then, the island was illuminated by daylight and its defenders were fully alerted. The lightly-armed American commandos had been stripped of their two biggest tactical advantages: stealth and surprise. The result was a near disaster that has been shrouded in official secrecy ever since.

The special forces units were late-comers to the intervention planning. Circumstances outside their control conspired to keep them from ever catching up. The Atlantic Command had been working on an intervention plan for nearly a week, when on Thursday night, Oct. 20, Scholtes, the JSOC commander, got his first call about the operation from the Pentagon. (See Chapter 1.) Scholtes and the officers of Seal Team Six and Delta Force worked through the weekend on what they might add to a Navy-led operation. It wasn't until Sunday that it was firmly decided that in Washington that regime change was the ultimate goal of the intervention, not merely rescuing American citizens. Rangers and the Marines were assigned the job of quickly subduing any organized Grenadian or Cuban military resistance. Meanwhile, the SEALs and Delta Force fighters would take on three politically sensitive missions in and near the capital city aimed at protecting Grenadians who could help restore parliamentary democracy on the island.

The key to executing all three missions was getting the commandoes to their targets by airlift before dawn. That task was assigned to a new, secret Army aviation unit designated the 160th Special Operations Aviation Regiment (Airborne), or Task Force 160 for short. This special command had been formed two years earlier, in the aftermath of the failed 1980 rescue of American embassy hostages being held in Tehran, Iran. That high-risk clandestine mission was aborted when two aircraft collided in a fireball at a desert staging area, killing eight. Task Force 160 rose like a phoenix from the ashes of the Operation Eagle Claw debacle. Its mission was to provide a reliable, stealthy means of inserting commandoes into hostile environments on foreign soil by helicopter. The unit founders dubbed themselves "the Night Stalkers" because the aircrews trained to fly and fight in the dark. Pilots flew specially equipped helicopters very low and very fast while wearing night-vision goggles. It was a dangerous job, even in peacetime. In 1983 alone, four aircraft were lost and 16 men were killed in training accidents.[1] The future existence of the task force was in question. Grenada was to be the troubled unit's first combat test—and an occasion for organizational redemption or extinction.

Urgent Fury was also to be the first combat test for the first-generation UH-60A Black Hawk manufactured by the Sikorsky Aircraft Division of United Technologies Corporation. The Black Hawk was designed to be the successor to the UH-1 Huey, the workhorse utility helicopter of the Vietnam War.[2] The Army wanted a replacement that would be harder to disable by ground fire and better able to transport a full 11-man squad of troops in high altitude and/or high temperature conditions. The new helicopter also needed to be easy to airlift and fit in the belly of an Air Force C-130 with its rotor blades folded. For improved combat survivability, the aircraft was built with redundant flight controls, self-sealing fuel tanks and armored seats. It was designed with the view that its primary threat would be the Soviet ZSU-23, a 23 mm anti-aircraft gun which turned out to be Grenada's principal air defense weapon. All these key design features would be put to a severe real-world test in Urgent Fury.

The invasion plan called for nine UH-60 Black Hawks and their Task Force 160 aircrews to be loaded aboard three Air Force C-5A Galaxy transport planes at the unit's base in Fort Campbell, Kentucky.[3] The giant C-5As would then fly to Pope Air Force Base in North Carolina, 575 miles away, to pick up about 100 special forces commandoes from Fort Bragg. Some Night Stalker aircrew members, who were away for the weekend, missed the C-5As at Fort Campbell and had to race to Fort Bragg in a rented car to catch up.[4]

All three C-5s were fully loaded and airborne for the Caribbean by late evening on Oct. 24.[5] The nearly five-hour flight to Barbados gave the officers of the various services aboard a much-needed opportunity to compare notes. The Air Force airlift general, Patterson, flew on the C-5 that was also carrying Lt. Col. Terry Henry, the Army commander of Task Force 160. Patterson shared the unwelcome news that the entire invasion planned had been slipped by an hour until 0500, just before daylight.[6] The C-5s actually pulled back on power so that they wouldn't land earlier than their revised arrival time of 0250. All three transports were on the ground at Grantley Adams by 0330.[7] The Air Force had estimated that it would take about an hour to reassemble the helicopters and get them on their way to Grenada. That proved unrealistically optimistic. There were unexpected delays in unloading the Black Hawks at night at the blacked-out airport and preparing them for flight and combat. By the time the helicopters departed at 0530, they were significantly behind schedule.[8]

Each Black Hawk carried a crew of five and 12 or more passengers. The flight crews ran deep in pilots who were all eager for the combat experience, though some of older men had seen fighting in Vietnam. Thirty-six pilots where assigned to the nine helicopters. Eighteen sat in the pilot or copilot seats. Nine more functioned as navigators and another nine served as door gunners.[9] Each aircraft also carried a SEAL or Delta-led assault team that was designated Chalk One through Nine. Delta operators constituted the first six chalks and SEALs the last three. (A chalk is a military term used to refer to an airborne unit or load assigned to a particular aircraft. It derives from the World War II practice of prominently marking airplanes or helicopters with chalk-written numbers prior to an assault so that their passengers could readily identify their designated aircraft.)

The helicopters traversed the 156 miles of open water between the two islands flying below 500 feet to avoid radar. But, by the time they sighted Grenada's verdant, volcanic hills, dawn had broken. Viewed from land, the dark green helicopters were starkly silhouetted against a rising sun and a clearing tropical morning sky. Pilots monitoring the Radio Free Grenada commercial radio frequency heard a chilling broadcast. "At 5:30 this morning, foreign troops began landing in our country. Our armed forces are engaging them," the female announcer declared. The broadcast urged Grenadians to grab weapons and shoot down any American aircraft they saw overhead. The Black Hawk aircrews test-fired their side-mounted M60 machine guns and prepared for a hostile reception.

The nine Black Hawks crossed Grenadian coast from the east after about an 80-minute flight.[10] Marines waved at them from the freshly secured Pearls Airfield. The aircraft then flew along the southern coast to the western side of the island where they turned north toward the capital of St. George's. When they passed over Point Salines on the southwestern tip of the island, they saw Army Rangers engaged in a firefight on the unfinished runway. It was now apparent to all on the Black Hawks that any hope of a surprise assault on their targets was lost.

Chalk 9, the last helicopter in line, spilt away from the group and headed toward Radio Free Grenada's transmitter at Beausejour, about seven kilometers north of the capital.[11] Lt. Donald K. (Kim) Erskine, the leader of the SEAL team in Chalk 9, remembers feeling very apprehensive about what was about to happen. He was a veteran of a dozen years with the Navy frogman teams and had seen combat before as an 18-year-old enlisted man in Vietnam. So far, this mission had violated just about everything he had been taught about planning and rehearsing a surprise assault.[12]

He considered the intelligence he had been supplied to be comically inadequate: an aerial photograph of the radio station and a tourist map of the island. Three of his 11 men were last-minute additions to his eight-man boat crew. They were the remaining members of the Blue Team, the unit that had been tasked with the ill-fated reconnaissance of Point Salines. Erskine didn't even know all their names. The first shot had not been fired and he was already exhausted and exasperated. He had been awake for two days continuously revising his assault plan as the SEAL mission was refined and modified by decisions made in Washington and Norfolk. Under an early version of the plan, Erskine's team was to have flown with the Army Rangers to Point Salines to secure the American medical students. However, as the strategic objective expanded from rescue to regime change, his SEAL team was relegated to an "after-thought" mission to secure the island's government-owned, long distance radio transmitter.

On the dawn of D-Day, Erskine found himself on his feet in an over-crowded, open-door helicopter, bathed in sunlight and stinking of aviation fuel. During the flight from Barbados to Grenada, a fitting on a rubber bladder inside the cabin had sprung loose, spewing high-octane fuel. The helicopter crew chief managed to repair the rupture, but explosively flammable liquid was still sloshing around the floor. One spark and the passengers would be ablaze. Fortunately, they didn't have much farther to go in their final approach on their target from the southwest. Their Black Hawk flew over a mountain, down a canyon and found the radio relay station in an open field at the coastal village of Beausejour. Farm equipment blocked the planned landing zone in front of the station so the Black Hawk put down in the meadow behind and to the west. The aircraft started taking small fire from the station's defenders as it banked to land. The Black Hawk's door gunner provided 45 seconds of suppressing machine gun fire. That was all the cover the team needed to close 50 meters from their landing zone to the cinder-block building. The SEALs quickly cleared the facility's eight rooms. The Grenadians who were shooting at them on their arrival took off in a truck.

Aerial view of Radio Free Grenada's long-distance transmitter station, which was a Navy SEAL target on D-Day. The facility is at the center bottom. The 50 KW transmitter tower is at the small white building to the left. Embattled SEALs fled the building under fire and swam out to sea from Beauséjour Bay shown at the top (National Archives [330-CFD-DA-ST-85-02254]).

Erskine prepared to defend the stand-alone facility by sending men out on the left and right flank. Some set up an ambush position on the north-south road outside the radio station that ran along the rugged coastline to the capital. As a further precaution, Erskine mapped out an emergency escape route for his team that took them over three fences toward a beach on the island's western shore. Erskine knew the SEALs would find safety by swimming out to sea where Air Force planes and Navy ships would be patrolling.

Erskine's orders were to briefly hold the station until CIA operatives arrived from St. George's by helicopter with the governor general. Scoon who would then broadcast an appeal for his countrymen to lay down their arms. That plan quickly unraveled. The first surprise was that the SEALs' arrival had no immediate impact on the government-run station's ability to broadcast. Radio Free Grenada continued to transmit its pro-coup propaganda message until 0745 from its main studio near Grand Anse Beach south of St. George's using a backup 10-killowatt transmitter.[13] Erskine also soon discovered that he was unable to make contact with his superiors. The encrypted satellite radio the SEALs carried wasn't working as expected. The frequencies and codes had unexpectedly changed overnight and they didn't know the new settings. Erskine could hear other calls on his backup field radio, but was unable to successfully transmit his situation because of its limited range. Erskine recognized that he would have to rely entirely on his own wits and judgment to deal with what came next.

SEALs assigned to guard the road stopped a station wagon carrying civilians: a mother, father, three children and a dog. Erskine ordered his men to take the family prisoner to prevent them from spreading word of the SEALs presence. At around 9 a.m., about a dozen uniformed Grenadian militia approached the radio station riding in a Soviet-made, GAZ truck and civilian vehicles. Erskine hailed the caravan to halt. Following the rules of engagement he had been issued, he identified himself and demanded that the soldiers throw down their weapons. A brief standoff ensued until one of the Grenadians slipped behind a tractor and opened fire. The SEALs responded with a fusillade that lasted only 15 seconds, but left all the soldiers either killed or wounded. The truck was a smoking wreck, sending a tell-tale plume of smoke into the air. Erskine ordered his two medical corpsmen to tend to the 10 wounded survivors while other SEALs separated out the dead soldiers.[14] The radio station was turned into a field hospital. The concrete floor was thick with blood. Everyone was screaming; the wounded soldiers in pain and the family in fear. Erskine decided to let the civilians go. The American presence at the station was hardly a secret any longer. The SEAL ambush site on the heavily traveled coast road turned into a checkpoint. A truck equipped with a searchlight came by headed for Point Salines. Three more men, believed to be Cubans, were taken prisoner by the SEALs.

What was planned as a temporary seizure was now devolving into a holding operation. An old Grenadian man, drawn by the action, brazenly walked up to the station to claim a front row seat. News of the fall of the radio transmitter site reached the Grenadian military leadership at Fort Frederick outside of the capital by around 8 a.m.[15] Lt. Cecil Prime, the deputy chief of operations for the People's Revolutionary Army, was ordered to collect a detachment from the PRA's elite mobile unit and launch a counterattack on the SEALs.

Prime was a professional soldier and committed member of the military clique that had assumed control of the island following the assassination of Prime Minister Bishop and seven of this close supporters. Prime already had blood on his hands from his supporting role in those murders.[16] Prime assembled an armored personnel carrier, a platoon of soldiers, a mortar crew and some civilian vehicles and set off north from the capital. The convoy stopped on a ridge 500 yards short of the station where Prime planned his counter attack.[17] He set up the mortar crew next to a nearby school to supply covering fire. The eight-wheeled BTR-60 closed on the station along the road from the southeast. Meanwhile, the PRA platoon dismounted their civilian vehicles and approached the station through a field from the south and southwest in a pincer movement.

Erskine was on the roof of the station trying to get his backup radio to work when one of his men called up to him. "Get down here. Guys are coming from everywhere!" Erskine found himself in a firefight in which he was outnumbered, outgunned and unable to call for help. His team had nothing to match the firepower of the BTR-60's 14.5 mm heavy machine gun. "I'm dead. There's no way out of this," Erskine remembers thinking. Erskine ordered his men to retreat inside the station, but the masonry walls were being blown apart by the armored vehicle in front of his eyes. One of the SEALs on the roof, Larry Barrett, fired a rocket-propelled grenade from his rifle. The softball-sized explosive hit the APC with a glancing blast, jamming the gun turret and giving the SEALs momentary reprieve. Erskine ordered his men to abandon the building. One by one they dove out the door. Bullets were everywhere. Erskine remembers hearing the distinctive "snap" sound the rounds made as they whizzed past at supersonic speed. The SEALs followed their escape route to the sea. The immediate challenge was crossing the open field where they had landed, a football-field-long meadow that ended in a chain-link fence. They proceeded in leapfrog fashion, as they had been trained. One SEAL squad got up and ran about 30 yards while the other laid down covering fire. Then it was the other squad's turn. Erskine remembers being knocked from his feet several times by bullets. The first bullet shattered his canteen, another sliced the heel off his boot. The third time he felt tremendous pain. A bullet mangled his right elbow and blasted a pistol from his hand. Erskine converted one of his knee pads into a crude bandage and pressed on. Somehow all the SEALs survived the perilous passage over open ground until they reached a high fence topped by coiled barbed wire. Erskine pulled wire cutters from his pocket and another SEAL cut a hole in the fence. Yet another team member held their pursuers at bay by lobbing grenades at them with a rifle-mounted M203 grenade launcher. Erskine used the pause to count his men; one short. Erskine looked back and saw Danny Knoft, their radio operator, still in the open. He was wounded and dragging the unit's satellite radio. "Danny! Shoot the radio and run," Erskine shouted. The SEAL dispatched the radio's classified electronic components with a round from his 9 mm pistol and joined the others. Another enlisted SEAL, Van Hall, was also wounded in the mad dash, hit in the leg by an AK-47 ricochet.

Fortunately for the SEALs, the Grenadian soldiers were stalking them cautiously. They had suffered their own casualties in the running firefight. Once through the chain-link fence, the SEALs entered dense jungle-like vegetation. The SEALs crossed a neck-deep, fast-running river and followed a path that led to a beach on Beausejour Bay. The SEALs shed their shoulder-held weapons and most of their equipment before entering the surf. The team swam in pairs parallel to shore for a short way to cover their tracks, then exited the water to climb the steep cliffs that faced the bay. Erskine was in great pain, but managed to stabilize his smashed elbow by stemming the bleeding and splinting his arm between two rods.

At this point, the team was effectively split into two groups. The SEALs watched from concealed positions in jungle growth as Grenadian soldiers looked for them. Their pursuers came as close as 10 feet before they suspended their active search at dusk. As darkness fell, Erskine authorized three SEALs to swim toward a fishing village and attempt to steal boats and return for the others. Failing that, they would swim out to sea and try to contact Navy ships offshore or U.S. aircraft flying overhead. At one point a Task Force 160 "Little Bird" helicopter flew so close to the other SEALs they could have jumped on its skids as it passed the cliff edge. Later a new threat emerged as Navy A-7 jets strafed the radio station and vicinity in an attempt to cover their escape. The cannon fire nearly took out the hidden SEALs on one pass. A SEAL petty officer turned to Erskine and said: "Sir, maybe it's time to get the hell out of here." Erskine led his group of eight to a rock outcropping where they could jump directly from the cliffs to the bay below. They then swam several miles out to sea. Staying together was difficult in the dark and swells. The team of 12 SEALs ended up swimming in three separate groups. The first group to be recovered was the trio which had been sent to steal fishing boats. The three swimmers found an unattended boat offshore. They climbed aboard and cut the anchor line with a knife. They tried to row away, but to no evident effect. It took them about an hour to realize the boat was held to the bottom by two anchors, not just one. Just after 2100 the USS *Caron*, patrolling offshore, spotted their strobe lights in the water and turned to investigate.[18] A whale boat was launched by the destroyer to retrieve the exhausted trio in the commandeered boat. All were rescued by Navy boat or Army helicopter. Most were immediately taken aboard the *Caron*, a destroyer in the *Independence* group. Shortly after, Erskine and the SEALs swimming with him also approached the vicinity of the *Caron*. They heard an aircraft overhead and fired red flares. A search and rescue aircraft saw the distress signal and dropped a high intensity parachute flare to illuminate the SEALs position. The *Caron* saw the exchange of flares and again launched its motor whale boat to retrieve Erskine's group. A total of 10 SEALs were safely aboard the *Caron* when the ship learned of a third group of two swimmers close to shore. Because of proximity to the beach and the depth of the water, an Army helicopter was directed to extricate the pair and fly them to Point Salines. Metcalf reported the radio station recovery complete at 0135 on Oct. 26.[19] Erskine was transferred from the *Caron* to the *Guam* for emergency surgery and then flown on to Bethesda Naval Hospital in Maryland. Military doctors were able to save his arm and he remained on active duty. He was awarded a Silver Star for his "daring actions, dynamic leadership and steadfast valor."[20]

As nightmarish as the assault on the radio station turned out to be, the attack on the Richmond Hill prison turned out to be even worse. Eight aircraft arrived over St. George's in full daylight at about 0615, more than an hour late.[21] As the Black Hawks dashed over red-tiled rooftops in the picturesque port city, an interlocking network of Grenadian-manned anti-aircraft guns opened fire.[22] Orange, red and green tracer rounds laced the air, visible to all the passengers because the doors had been removed for quick exit. The unescorted transport helicopters had only side-mounted machine guns for self-defense. The Delta fighters were expecting little resistance to their raid and they arrived lightly armed and protected. They carried carbine rifles and pistols, but had dispensed with both helmets and Kevlar vests because of the tropical heat.[23] No other aircraft had been tasked to support the prison raid. Marine Cobra helicopters and Air Force AC-130 gunships were otherwise engaged supporting the landings at Pearls and Point Salines. Navy jets from the *Independence* had not yet been cleared to attack targets in St. George's, which was in the Army's designated zone.[24]

This view of Richmond Hill Prison was taken on October 28, 1983, the day after the hilltop prison was secured by advancing Marines on the second day of fighting. The high walls, steeply sloping terrain and guard towers greatly complicated the daylight Delta Force attack on D-Day (National Archives [330-CFD-DN-SN-85-02127]).

The original plan was for the helicopters to fly to a traffic circle in the center of the capital city where they would break off into two groups to complete their individual missions. However, because of the heavy and unexpected anti-aircraft fire, the turning point was missed.[25] The first attempt to assault the prison was driven away by the intense fire. In Chalk 4, the pilot, Capt. Keith J. Lucas, was hit in the right arm. Sp4c. Loren Richards, a door gunner, was hit in the leg.[26] All eight aircraft flew off to sea to regroup and try again. On the second approach Chalks 7 and 8 found the traffic circle and belatedly headed for the governor general's mansion.[27] The remaining six helicopters flew though a valley toward Richmond Hill Prison, located atop a north-south ridge line southeast of the city core. As the prison came into view, the leading aircraft were raked by fire coming from four anti-aircraft guns that had been positioned to defend nearby Fort Frederick, the de facto Grenadian military headquarters.[28] If the attacks had occurred in darkness as originally planned, these visually-aimed, World War II–era guns would have been firing at specters. But, in daylight, the Cuban-trained, Grenadian anti-aircraft gun crews put up a witheringly effective grid of fire. Two four-barrel 12.7 mm guns and two twin-barrel 23 mm guns were firing at point blank range at the helicopters as they closed on the hilltop prison. Forty or so Grenadian soldiers stationed at the prison also fired their AK-47s at them.[29] Black Hawk door gunners hammered back with their M60 machine guns. Delta operators joined the fight with their M-4 carbines, targeting the AAA gun crews. Maj. Larry Sloan, the prison air assault commander, directing the attack from the navigator's jump seat of his Black Hawk, was hit in the shoulder.[30] The pilot of his aircraft, Chief Warrant Officer Dave Bramel, took a round in his leg. Still, the Black Hawks swooped low over the prison to disgorge their Delta B Squadron teams. The plan called for two helicopters to hover over the prison courtyard so their passengers could "fast rope" to the ground.[31] Eric L. Haney, one of the Delta operators aboard Sloan's helicopter, looked down and was amazed by what he saw. "The damn place was abandoned! The main gate to the prison was wide open and so were all the doors we could see," Haney recalled in his memoir.[32] One of Haney's Delta team members held a 90-foot rope on his lap and got ready to toss it out the door. "Do not! Do not! Don't! Don't," Haney yelled. "Let's get out of here," said his team leader. The radios squawked with agreement from Delta team leaders in other helicopters. "The whole ordeal had lasted no more than 10 minutes, but it seemed like several lifetimes," Haney wrote. "Even now, I shudder on the inside just to think about it."

As the Black Hawks flew off, Lucas, the wounded pilot in the fourth helicopter, was killed instantly when an anti-aircraft round exploded in his cockpit. Chief Warrant Officer 2 Paul Price, the copilot, though grazed by the blast, took over the controls. The aircraft belched black smoke and flew south, away from the prison toward Point Salines, where there was a runway and Rangers were on the ground. The crippled aircraft struggled to maintain air speed and altitude as it passed over a Grenadian military compound at Frequente where it took more hits from ground fire. The helicopter inverted and crashed at Amber Belair, a coastal plateau about five kilometers south of the capital. The impact of the landing was so severe that it ripped the tail rotor off the aircraft and sent the four main rotor blades flying. The Black Hawk rolled over twice and caught fire. Nearly everyone on board was wounded, either by the prior enemy fire or the crash impact.[33]

The lead Black Hawk in the flight was also badly mauled in the firefight over the prison. One 12.7 mm round went through the floor of the Chalk 1 and into a PRC-66 radio carried by Maj. William G. "Jerry" Boykin in his rucksack. (Boykin was Delta's operations officer, a key staff position, but he cajoled his bosses into letting him join the combat

Visually aimed anti-aircraft weapons formed the backbone of the Grenadian air defenses. Anti-aircraft fire shot down three helicopters and damaged at least six others on D-Day. This Soviet-made ZU-23 was a twin-barrel, 23 mm gun that was typically crewed by five soldiers. It offered a high rate of fire and was considered easy to operate (National Archives [330-CFD-DF-ST-84-09745]).

A DShKM-4, a four-barrel, 12.7 mm anti-aircraft gun, was the Soviet equivalent of a quad 50-caliber machine gun (National Archives [330-CFD-DF-ST-85-03399]).

mission.[34]) When the round hit the radio, shards of debris blasted through Boykin's armpit and into his chest and shoulder, just missing a major artery. The long bone in Boykin's left arm was also severed. One of the Delta fighters in Boykin's helicopter slapped a bandage on his chest. Another teammate plunged a syringe of morphine into his thigh. The round that incapacitated Boykin was just one of 54 that were later found to have pierced the skin of the aircraft. Two other Delta operators onboard the aircraft were also wounded, as was the pilot, Chief Warrant Officer 3 Bill Flannery.

Flannery banked away from the prison to fly out to sea in search for a Navy ship that would accept him and his injured. Four other Black Hawks, also with wounded aboard, followed suit. The Army pilots were not trained or cleared for landing on Navy ships, but did so anyway. The Black Hawk flown by Bramel circled the *Guam* and ignored frantic attempts by the crew to wave off him off their flight deck.[35] A furious *Guam* "air boss" raced out to the copter to protest the unauthorized arrival. He instantly adjusted his attitude when he saw the condition of the crippled copter and its battle-wounded pilot. That paved the way for other Black Hawks to also land in turn with their wounded. Some Black Hawks opted to land on the deck of the USS *Moosbrugger*, a destroyer in the aircraft carrier task group that was the designated primary search and rescue ship.[36] Their wounded were offloaded and assembled in an improvised aid station in the hanger bay. Haney remembers there were eight wounded on his helicopter alone. Boykin was among the seriously wounded who were shuttled by Marine helicopter from the *Moosbrugger* to the *Guam* for emergency surgery.

The nightmare wasn't over. The surviving members of the prison assault who were

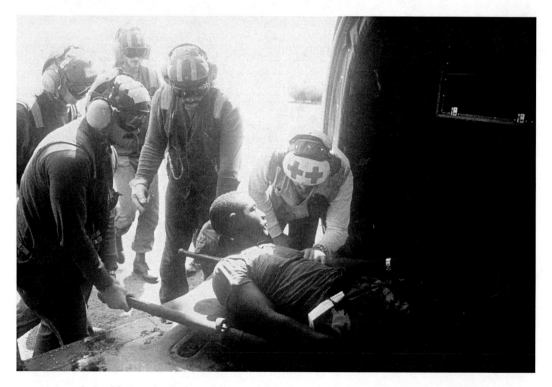

A wounded soldier is checked out by a Navy corpsman. The *Guam*'s two surgeons performed 16 shipboard operations during the fighting (National Archives [330-CFD-DA-ST-85-02210]).

A Task Force 160 OH-6A "Little Bird" helicopter ferried a wounded American serviceman to the USS *Guam* on the second day of the invasion (National Archives [330-CFD-DF-SN-84-10848]).

still ambulatory got back onboard their Black Hawks to complete the second part of their purported pre-invasion mission. They flew to Point Salines, just a mile away, to seize the high ground north of the airfield in support of the Ranger parachute assault. The Delta fighters were supposed to have arrived before the Rangers, but the airdrop was already underway by the time Haney's team arrived during one of the pauses between drops. Delta witnessed the delayed arrival of the main body and the completion of largest combat parachute operation since World War II.

Meanwhile, the crash scene on Amber Belair Hill east of Point Salines was more gruesome than inspiring. Lucas was dead at his controls as flames enveloped the cockpit. Except for Chief Warrant Officer 1 Jon Ecker, a spare pilot-navigator, most, if not all, the other 11 passengers were wounded.[37] According to Haney, the door gunner had been hit in the foot by a round that left it hanging by skin and sinew. Others had been blinded by hydraulic fluid that sprayed from the severed lines. One of the Delta operators had been shot in the leg before the crash crushed his pelvis and pinned underneath the wreckage. Three of the wounded lifted the fuselage high enough to extricate him. The wreckage was atop of a plateau with steep sides that sloped down to the island's irregular southern coast. The terrain offered no suitable place for the Army Black Hawks to land. Men from the surviving helicopters fast-roped to the ground to form a defensive perimeter around the crash site.[38] PRA soldiers approached from the north, but were held at bay by the Delta fighters on the ground and a Spectre AC-130 gunship overhead.[39] A mayday call went out that was heard by Navy destroyers on picket duty offshore. A Navy SH-3H Sea King from the *Independence*, detached to operate with the destroyer squadron, was instructed to search for the downed Army copter.[40] It wasn't hard to find. An angry black plume of smoke marked the crash site in jungle growth about a kilometer east of the contested runway.

The Sea King pilots, Cmdr. Harvey G. Fielding and Lt. Cmdr. Gerald Joseph Carroll, Jr., flew an aircraft that was not designed to execute a contested combat rescue. Their Sikorsky-built helicopter was a cousin to the "Marine One" variant used to transport the president and the "Jolly Green Giant" version flown by the Air Force on rescue missions. The Navy version was painted bright white and was used primarily for antisubmarine warfare patrols. Pilots affectionately compared it to a flying pickup truck or recreational vehicle. This variant lacked the armor and self-sealing fuel tanks of its green Air Force cousin, but it was commonly used as a "plane guard" during naval air operations at sea. In this case, the Sea King compensated for its design limitations by having two experienced flyers at its controls. Fielding, the pilot, was the commander of Helicopter Antisubmarine Squadron 15, a six-aircraft Sea King unit based on the *Independence*. He assigned himself to fly the first shift of search and rescue duty on D-Day because none of his subordinate pilots had combat rescue training. Fielding selected Carroll, a Vietnam-era combat veteran and seasoned aviator, to be his co-pilot. He also hand-picked two Navy enlisted volunteers for his cabin crew. M-16 rifles carried by two Marine volunteers from the *Independence*'s complement were the helicopter's only weapons.[41]

Fielding was nominally tasked with conducting combat search and rescue over open ocean, but he stretched that boundary a bit by making a quick reconnaissance pass over the coastal crash site. Fielding and Carroll never spotted the wreckage, but they did see two camouflaged fighters emerge from the jungle growth. Then the pilots heard a radio call for help on Guard UHF, an ultrahigh frequency reserved around the world exclusively for military aircraft emergency calls.[42] The caller said that there were five or six wounded crash survivors who needed evacuation. Fielding and the caller improvised a plan for the survivors to make their way down to a bay at the base of the plateau where the extraction would be sheltered from crew-served anti-aircraft guns. The amphibious Sea King would meet them at the shoreline.

Fielding then flew out to sea so as not to attract attention to the impending rendezvous. While he loitered offshore, Fielding was instructed by the destroyer squadron commander not to fly any closer than 3,000 yards (1.7 miles) from the island. No amplification was offered, but, at this point, the *Independence* had not been cleared to conduct air operations over the Army zone.[43] After 35 to 40 minutes, Fielding heard another radio call on the Guard UHF frequency. The crash survivors had made it down to the bay, but one needed immediate evacuation. Fielding relayed this dire news to the destroyer squadron. "If I can't go in, you need to get somebody else," Fielding added. "We'll lose this guy otherwise. I know where they are. I've already been in there." The logic of that argument prompted a reconsideration by his shipborne handlers. "OK, cleared to go," Fielding was told. Just to make sure everyone monitoring the emergency frequency heard the approved plan, Fielding asked for the call to be repeated.

Multiple factors inhibited Task Force 160 from mounting their own rescue of the downed Black Hawk survivors. All the surviving Black Hawks had suffered battle damage. The crash site was in jungle growth and exposed to direct enemy fire. Also, Fielding and Carroll were trained to land on Navy ships, while the Army pilots were not. Fielding's plan for a water rescue appeared to be the best of the available bad options. The SH-3H was built with a waterproof hull that would allow it to float in emergencies for short periods. The selected shoreline landing zone was topographically sheltered from opposing heavy weapons fire, but marginal in other respects. The beach was constricted by boulders. There was just five feet of clearance on either side of the 60-foot-diameter of the main rotor blades. Moreover, the Sea King would have to make a difficult downwind approach in order to land with its cabin door facing the shore.

On landing, the helicopter bobbed in three feet of water with one landing wheel on the beach and the other in the surf. The Delta fighters waded into chest-deep surf to reach the aircraft door. The Sea King cabin crew jumped into the water to help lift the wounded into the helicopter. It took about 10 minutes to load the passengers and their equipment onto an aircraft that already carried an air crew of six. The survivors and their gear added about a ton of additional weight. Per protocol, a crewman began to call out a report on the condition of each of the passengers. Impatient to take off, Fielding cut the recitation short before learning that 11 had been taken aboard instead of the six he was expecting. The aircraft struggled to get airborne with its heavy load. The hot, humid air further degraded its lift aerodynamics. The extraction was also complicated by the wind direction which dictated a sharp left turn to exit the cove. Fielding compensated by water-taxing from the beach until he could get enough forward speed to get airborne. Carroll dumped some fuel to lighten their load, but that was a slow process. Barely flying above the wave tops, the aircraft struggled to gain altitude. At one point, Fielding warned the passengers to be prepared for reentry into the water. In desperation, he tried "milking the throttle." This counter-intuitive maneuver involved lowering the aircraft's "collective" control to briefly trade altitude for the RPMs needed for sustained lift. It worked. About then a call came over the radio: "You're on fire!" Fielding was alarmed, but skeptical. He quickly concluded the warning was a false alarm. Water droplets were being pulled up from the surface of the ocean by the rotor wash. When the beads of sea water reached the heat of the engines, they turned to steam that was mistaken for smoke.

Fielding headed toward his temporary roost on the *Moosbrugger*, but he was turned away. The destroyer's limited medical facilities were overwhelmed by the unscheduled arrival of Army Black Hawks with their wounded. Fielding was directed to fly to the *Guam* instead, but he didn't know exactly where it was. He managed to locate the flagship by tagging along behind a *Guam*-bound Marine helicopter for the 30-minute flight. His overloaded Sea King made a "mushy" no-hover landing on the *Guam's* flight deck. Only then did Fielding learn how many men he had actually rescued. Two of the wounded Delta fighters were so seriously injured that they were later medically retired.[44] After the last of the passengers had been unloaded, Fielding turned to his co-pilot and remarked: "Gerry, that was pretty significant. We earned our money today." The Navy concurred with that understated assessment. Both pilots were hailed as heroes and awarded the Distinguished Flying Cross for "superb airmanship, brilliant judgment, calm demeanor and selfless devotion to duty."[45] (Lucas, the Army pilot of the downed Blackhawk, was also posthumous awarded the same aviation medal for valor.[46])

4

SEALs Besieged

The debacles at the prison and the radio station left only the mission to reach Governor General Paul Scoon with a chance for success. The secret invasion came as no surprise to Scoon. He was learning of the impending invasion through multiple back channels in the days just before the fighting began.

When Prime Minister Maurice Bishop was assassinated on Oct. 19, Grenada was thrown into chaos. The Grenadian military took over, declared martial law and dissolved the Bishop government. Gen. Hudson Austin, the head of the Grenadian military, was in nominal control, but Bishop's ambitious deputy, Bernard Coard, orchestrated the coup. He was pulling the strings of power from behind the scenes. Scoon survived the government turmoil because, both before and after the coup, was considered strictly a figurehead. Scoon's continued presence in office presented a useful illusion of normalcy and continuity to the outside world as the socialist regime tilted ever more toward dogmatic Communist ideology.

Scoon lived and worked in a three-story mansion, officially known as Government House, majestically located on a hill overlooking the tiled-roofed capital. Its creole-style architecture consisted of a Georgian main building spiced up by the later addition of a two-story Italianate gallery, which was topped by a covered veranda. A British-appointed governor/administrator had been in residence here for two centuries, but, after independence in 1974, the executive powers of the holder of that office were considerably diminished. The title was changed to governor general and the official role reduced to mostly ceremonial duties, as opposed to true governing. The hand-me-down mansion also suffered from official indifference. Scoon regularly sparred with the Bishop's government for more funds for roof repairs and interior renovations.[1]

Scoon's resume made him a logical choice for the head-of-state position at a time when the island was still molting from dependency into statehood. Scoon was a native of the island, the son of a butcher and a food vendor who grew up in a fishing village.[2] His mother urged him to pursue an education, which eventually led him to leave home for post-secondary study in London and Toronto. He returned to take a job as a teacher of English literature and economics at the government-run Grenada Boys Secondary School from 1953 to 1967.[3] He was a don of the Queen's English and fond of quoting Shakespeare and Chaucer. His pedagogical emphasis was on fostering integrity and decorum in his male students. In addition to his classroom duties, he also served as the master for boarding students from outlying islands and villages during the school year. He taught the boarders to arrive promptly for meals and which spoon to use for what purpose. An

This is a view of St. George's, the capital of Grenada, looking northeast from Fort Rupert, as it appeared in 1989. The arrow marks the approximate (obscured) location of the governor general's mansion, also known as Government House (photograph by the author).

This mansion known as Government House housed the residence and offices of Sir Paul Scoon, Grenada's governor general. Securing Scoon's safety was a critical D-Day mission for Navy SEALs (National Archives [330-CFD-DF-ST-84-09780]).

observant Catholic, he also made sure his charges attended religious services on Sundays.[4] Scoon became Grenada's chief education officer in 1967, the equivalent of being the island's school superintendent. From there, he soon moved on to other government posts: the number-two man in the Ministry of Education and then secretary to the cabinet, the head of Grenada's civil service. He was lured back to London in 1973 to take a job as the deputy director of the Commonwealth Foundation, a non-profit organization dedicated to supporting the growth of learned professions and the advancement of civil society in the former territories of the British Empire.

After gaining independence in 1974, Grenada followed a pattern typical of former British colonies by organizing as a constitutional monarchy with a Westminster-style parliamentary government. Elizabeth II was nominally queen of Grenada, as well as queen of England, but on Grenada, and many other Commonwealth nations, she delegated her royal role to a local governor general. This allowed Grenada to put a black face on their resident head-of-state. The post-colonial governor was still beholden to the queen, but did not take direction from either Buckingham Palace or the government of Great Britain.

Scoon was the second Grenadian to hold the reconstituted post. He was selected for the job in 1978 by Eric Gairy, the charismatic, but despotic, labor activist who had led his county to independence and became its first elected prime minister. Five months after Scoon took office, the Gairy government was overthrown in a coup led by Bishop, the leader of the socialist New JEWEL Movement Party. Bishop suspended the constitution after taking power, but asked Scoon to stay on in a diminished figurehead role. It was a role fraught with traditions, ambiguities and contradictions. Scoon played the role with dignity, discretion and aplomb even as the job became immensely more complicated during his tenure.

Bishop moved into an official residence next door to Scoon. The neighbors played early morning tennis together on the Scoon's backyard court. They were friendly, but poles apart ideologically. Scoon was a queen's man in a country run by Bishop, who looked to Marx, Lenin and Castro for inspiration. Scoon was knighted by the queen in 1979, a customary honor for post-colonial governors, and assumed the additional title of "Sir Paul." When Scoon and Bishop appeared together, the British national anthem was played in full to mark Scoon's presence and the first half of the Grenadian national anthem was played on Bishop's arrival.[5]

The subsequent assassination of Bishop on Oct. 19, 1983, was the second time during Scoon's first five years in office that the Grenadian government had changed hands at the point of a gun. The latest coup leaders kept him close, but they also curried his favor. The army-led Revolutionary Military Council (RMC) wanted his cooperation in forming a new cabinet. In a post-invasion interview, Scoon characterized his brief relationship with the RMC as "very good." Scoon said that coup leaders "came to me soon after they assumed power and told me what their plans were. They kept me in the picture as to what they were doing. As to whether or not I approved of the things they wanted to do is a different matter."[6]

Sir Paul Scoon, the governor general of Grenada, was a Grenadian appointee who served as the island's head of state and link to the British crown, 1983 (National Archives [330-CFD-DN-SN-84-12013]).

In the U.S., American government officials publicly described Scoon's post-coup status as under "house arrest," but that phase implied far more restraint than was actually applied. When a "shoot on sight" curfew was imposed on the island on Oct. 20, Scoon's staff were issued passes that gave them freedom of movement. A lone police guard was stationed at the gate to Government House, but Scoon was allowed to use his phone and receive visitors. Scoon was very selective in the calls he accepted and also very guarded in what he said on the phone. He knew that all calls he originated were recorded and scrutinized for counter-revolutionary content. Just before dawn on Saturday morning, Oct. 22, Scoon took a transatlantic call from the queen's assistant private secretary, Robert Fellowes. Scoon assured Fellowes that he and his wife, Esmai, were under no threat and were both in "good form."[7] Scoon also authorized Fellowes to share his comments with Washington, which Fellowes did through the British Foreign Office.

Scoon's form, however salutary at the time, was about to change. That Saturday marked the beginning of Scoon's unexpected evolution from accommodation to activism. This sea change was precipitated by the arrival of a charter plane carrying three envoys from the British and American embassies on Barbados. The two Americans were Kenneth A. Kurze, the counselor for political and economic affairs, and Linda C. Flohr, a third secretary who was also a covert CIA case officer.[8] The British were represented by David Montgomery, a deputy high commissioner, the Foreign Office equivalent of a deputy ambassador. The trio's stated purpose was to check on the well-being of U.S. and British citizens on the island under the martial law curfew, and to discuss evacuation options with representatives of the medical school. In Flohr's case, her mission also included gathering military intelligence for a possible U.S.–led invasion.

Given the tense political situation on the island, the visitors were given extraordinary freedom of movement by the island's military junta, including escorted access to Point Salines airfield. Montgomery was able to speak with a number of long-time British residents. He found them to be angry with the new regime for the assassinations of Bishop and bitter about the havoc the leadership crisis had wrought on the island. Montgomery reported to London that one of two outcomes was likely: the revolutionary government would succumb to fractional bickering and then anarchy or Bishop's surviving supporters would ally themselves with other dissidents to confront the fledgling government in a general strike. The fate of the islands was "in the hands of a clutch of inexperienced political opportunists dressed up as soldiers," he reported to the Foreign Office.[9]

For her part, Flohr, the CIA officer operating under diplomatic cover, was more focused on military capabilities of the pretenders than their governing skills. She was able to collect first-hand information about the location of gun positions around the airfield and the nearby medical school campus which she transmitted back to Barbados by letter and telephone. She also attempted to transmit intelligence information to a CIA pleasure yacht offshore using a hand-held radio. However, it is unclear how much of this battlefield information actually reached military planners in the United States at this late stage.[10]

The next day, Sunday morning, Oct. 23, Scoon had a pivotal meeting at his official residence with Montgomery, the newly arrived British diplomat. Scoon directed him not to sign the visitor's book and spoke with him on a bench in the garden. Montgomery briefed Scoon on what he knew about the high-level discussion that Grenada's Caribbean anxious neighbors were having among themselves and with Britain and the United States. He also relayed press speculation that the United States might be preparing to intervene militarily and asked if Scoon was prepared to support it, say, by making a broadcast to his nation.[11] Scoon's response was equivocal. He told Montgomery he feared for his life if he "directly challenged" the military council's authority by asking for "outside help," but he said that he would do "whatever was required of him," if an intervention came without his explicit invitation. In his memoir, Scoon described his diplomatic posture in this left-handed way: "if a military operation to achieve (law and order) were to be undertaken by our sister states—if necessary, with assistance of the United States, I would give such an initiative my fullest support."[12]

Flohr, the CIA case officer, also pressed for a one-on-one meeting with Scoon. In his memoir, Scoon makes no acknowledgment that he was aware of Flohr's covert CIA affiliation. He describes her as a "junior officer" who was an emissary of the American ambassador to Barbados. He wrote that he was chary of the contact because the United States and Grenada had been at loggerheads for years over an official exchange of ambassadors. However, he eventually relented and granted Flohr a pre-invasion meeting.[13]

Scoon didn't state what was discussed, but it is likely he learned from Flohr that an American intervention was planned for Tuesday. Flohr had been told the assault date at this point and also had been instructed to be at Government House on the morning of Oct. 25 so that she could be evacuated with the Scoon party.[14] (A post-invasion inquiry by the British House of Commons' Foreign Affairs Committee learned that Scoon received confirmation of the American invasion the Sunday before from an unnamed emissary.)[15]

Flohr also used the occasion of the invasion-eve meeting with Scoon to observe the Grenadian defenses in the vicinity of the mansion and to report back to Barbados by telephone. There was a Grenadian army security unit stationed in the neighborhood to protect the now vacant residence of the martyred prime minister and the neighboring home of Coard, Bishop's deputy who was now the island's country's unpopular leader. The permanent Grenadian guard force had been recently reinforced by armored personnel carriers. Also towed anti-aircraft guns were positioned on nearby high points. After completing her survey, Flohr took refuge in the home of John Kelly, the resident British diplomat on the island.[16] His house was located on high ground and had a view of Point Salines and half of the island.

At the same time Scoon was conversing with visiting diplomats and a CIA spy, the governor general was also communicating with Gen. Austin, the former prison guard who was the public face of the provisional military government. On the evening before the invasion, Scoon received a courtesy call from Austin advising him that American ships had been sighted offshore and an invasion was imminent. Austin also told him that the Grenadians had been previously warned of the impending invasion by President Forbes Burnham of Guyana, who had learned the news through Caribbean diplomatic channels.[17]

Scoon woke on Oct. 25 to the sound of a stray goat bleating in his garden and the roar of American aircraft overhead. He went to his balcony and saw a helicopter hovering and taking opposing fire. His phone rang. His stepson called to report the news that Marines had landed at Pearls Airport on the eastern side of the island. Scoon directed everyone in the house to seek safety in the basement. That group of 11 included his wife, his household staff and two policemen. One was a young policeman who was regarded as a suspected spy for the coup leaders. The other was the frightened guard who was supposed to be on duty at the main entrance.[18]

The two helicopters assigned to secure the Governor General were led by Maj. Robert Lee Johnson, the air mission commander of the nine-helicopter flight and a company commander with Task Force 160. The two Black Hawks flared into a hover over Scoon's residence and prepared to unload their SEALs by rope. Johnson watched from of one Black Hawks as the SEALs in the other helicopter slid 60 feet to mansion's front garden. Two of the SEALs carried chain saws as well as their weapons. They planned to cut down two banana trees so that Johnson's helicopter could land three civilian passengers who were not "fast rope" trained.

Besides SEALs, Johnson's aircraft carried the CIA's Caribbean branch chief, a CIA radio operator who had a portable broadcast transmitter, and Lawrence G. Rossin, a State Department political officer. The civilians carried a draft letter for Scoon to sign that would formally request the intervention they were already actively conducting.[19] Rossin had been dispatched from a desk in Washington as a last-minute addition to the rescue team because he had gotten to know Scoon while stationed in Barbados from 1980 to 1982. The portable transmitter would allow Scoon to make a broadcast to his nation as soon as they reached him.[20] Rossin was dressed in his best safari suit in optimistic anticipation of an unopposed arrival followed by a photo op with Scoon.[21]

Also onboard Johnston's copter was Gormly, the SEAL Team Six commander. He was attired in jungle-camouflaged fatigues and prepared for combat. "Go! Go! Go!" Gormly ordered his men as the 90-pound coils were dropped over the mansion's rear.[22] Nine SEALs dove out the helicopter's open door. Just then, Johnston's helicopter was raked by shots from an AK-47. The helicopter maneuvered out of the line of fire. That repositioning exposed the helicopter to anti-aircraft fire coming from the vicinity of Fort Frederick, the Grenadian military operational headquarters located on a hill about a mile away. The helicopter turned sideways, using its armored belly as a shield against the exploding shells. The remaining passengers clung to handholds inside the cabin to keep from being pitched out the open door. Then the copter came under further attack from anti-aircraft guns located at Fort Rupert, an 18th century fortification which guarded the entrance to St. George's harbor.

One of the rounds ripped up through the cockpit floor. It tore a softball-sized chunk of flesh out of Johnston's left leg and knocked him unconscious. Chief Warrant Officer 3 David Rosengrant, the copilot who was flying the copter, looked wide-eyed at the gaping wound. The crew chief reached over Johnson's inert body and grabbed the control for the rear flap. Rosengrant managed to level out the helicopter out just feet above the capital's harbor. Rosengrant then headed out to sea, despite Gormly's demand that they return to the mansion. Instead, Rosengrant flew to the *Guam*, 10 miles offshore, to get immediate medical attention for Johnson's spurting artery. The cockpit radio was shot up in the assault so Rosengrant arrived without conversation with the ship. Struggling to control the damaged copter, he landed hard and bounced once before coming to rest on the busy flight deck.

The helicopter's controls were so damaged that the engines would not shut down. The engines were screaming and the blades continued to rotate like spinning scythes. Deck crews used fire hoses to subdue the runaway turbines by drowning them with seawater. A later examination found 48 bullet holes in the fuselage including one in the main gear box. Rosengrant's Black Hawk just one of several Army helicopters to unceremoniously land on the *Guam*'s flight deck that morning with wounded Delta and SEAL fighters aboard.

In the midst of the chaotic scene playing out on the flight deck of his flagship, Metcalf received an urgent message from the Navy's comptroller at the Pentagon. The message warned that the Army helicopters should not be refueled until a funds transfer arraignment had been worked out between the two services. Metcalf's chief of staff handed his boss the missive. He handed it back. "This is bullshit," Metcalf declared. "Give them the fuel."[23]

Of the nine Task Force 160 Black Hawks that flew from Barbados that morning, one had crashed on the island and another had crash landed on the deck of the *Guam*. Five more had suffered battle damage over the prison.[24] Only two were considered ready for immediate further combat action. The human toll was equally grim. The Black Hawk headcount included 77 special forces personnel and 45 helicopter air crew members and three government-agency civilians.[25] Of these 100-plus personnel carried into combat as passengers or crew on the Black Hawks, at least a quarter ended up as casualties. One (Lucas) was killed and at least 32 were combat wounded.[26] Lucas' death was eventually acknowledged by the Pentagon, but none of the Delta, SEAL or Task Force 160 wounded

A Navy firefighting crew on the USS *Guam* hosed down an Army Task Force 160 Black Hawk helicopter that crash-landed on its deck in the opening hours of the invasion. This Black Hawk was one of two UH-60s sent to the governor general's mansion. This aircraft was hit by ground fire 48 times and had a severely wounded Army major aboard. Its controls were so badly shot up that the engines would not shut down until they were drowned by seawater (National Archives [330-CFD-DN-SN-85-02069]).

are included in the official list of 125 "reportable" Urgent Fury wounded later compiled by each service's Office of Casualty Affairs.[27] Years after the fighting stopped, it appears a decision was made to acknowledge only the special unit combatants killed on Grenada (Lucas and the four drowned SEALs), but not the number or names of the special unit wounded.

The Pentagon's official blind eye to these 32 or more wounded has not kept others from noting the true toll of Urgent Fury for the historical record. One credible combat memoir lists 11 Task Force 160 members as having been wounded in Urgent Fury.[28] Indeed, a consolidated list of Grenada casualties dated Nov. 4, 1983, that was released by the Pentagon to the news media named six Task Force 160 members among the then-acknowledged wounded. But by 1988, all six of the previously named Task Force 160 casualties disappeared from an Army Personnel Agency listing of all Army personnel wounded in military action on Grenada.[29] The six who were statistically "unwounded" (author's term) between 1983 and 1988 were majors Robert Johnson, Jr., and Larry R. Sloan; staff sergeants John Hulgeruo and Gary W. Minerve; and Sp4cs. Ronald McCall and Larry (Loren) R. Richards.

Similarly, the names of three Navy SEALs wounded on Grenada also disappeared from official Navy lists during the spring of 1988. In March 1988, the Naval Military Personnel Command listed three SEAL Team Six members based in Norfolk as having been wounded in the invasion of Grenada.[30] The three were: Erskine and Hall, shot during the radio station raid, and Richard Donovan Hansen, wounded in the Government House fight. But by June 1988 the names of all three were dropped from the list of "reportable wounded in action" reported by the Navy Office of Casualty Affairs.[31]

The elite Delta Force proportionately suffered the most of any unit involved in Urgent Fury because of the disastrous daylight attack on the prison. Eighteen Delta operators were wounded in the prison assault, according to an 25th anniversary accounting attributed to retired lieutenant colonel Lewis H. Burruss, who was the Delta deputy commander during Urgent Fury.[32] However, none of the Delta Force wounded ever appeared on any publicly released Pentagon list of Urgent Fury casualties. That's apparently because of a bureaucratic slight-of-hand designed to keep the U.S. Army's 1st Special Forces Operational Detachment—Delta (1stSFOD-D), a top-secret "black" organization.

Delta Force, as it came to be known, was activated on Nov. 19, 1977, as the Army's elite counterterrorism force, with hostage rescue as its principal mission.[33] The unit was the brainchild of Col. Charlie A. Beckwith, a decorated Green Beret and 101st Airborne commander in Vietnam. Based his experience in previous assignments in London and Southeast Asia. He proposed that the Army create a highly selective, unorthodoxly organized, clandestine commando unit modeled on the British Special Air Service (SAS). At that time, international terrorism was just beginning to be recognized at the Pentagon and the White House as a national security threat that would require a structural response by the military. The unit that Beckwith created over the ensuing two years was selected from among experienced soldiers of above-average intelligence, who could pass a rigorous background screening. Those who satisfied the credentials check were then subject to a grueling qualification program designed to weed out far more applicants than were accepted. Upon assignment to Delta, its new members disappeared from the regular military personnel rolls and became "operators" within a secret system known as the Department of Army Security Roster (DASR).[34] This designation allowed them to operate undercover in regions of the world where it would be politically untoward to acknowledge them as U.S. soldiers. They were intended to be breed apart from both spies and regular soldiers. Delta operators were allowed to grow their hair long and have beards. They rarely wore a uniform and commonly called their officers by their first name.

Multiple books on Urgent Fury have asserted over the years that there were more Delta operators or Delta-detached Rangers killed in Urgent Fury than were acknowledged by the Pentagon.[35] However, this writer has uncovered no trail leading to the name of an unacknowledged Urgent Fury combat KIA. Two Delta Urgent Fury veterans (Haney and Boykin) have written battlefield memoirs that collectively name most of the unacknowledged Delta wounded in the prison attack, but neither make any mention of Delta fighters killed in action on Grenada. Nonetheless, the unofficial toll of Urgent Fury combat wounded (157 or more) substantially exceeds the official "reportable" number of 125. Since all the unreported wounded were members of JSOC, the Pentagon's official accounting distorts the historical record of the first combat by this newly created joint command.[36]

5

Rangers Seize Salines

Once on the ground, the first planeload of 1st Battalion Rangers divided into two groups. The 1st platoon of Bravo Company, under the leadership of 1st Lt. Patrick Stackpole, set up a defensive position on high ground, north of the runway and west of the control tower.[1] Further to the east, Taylor and his TOC staff established a command post on high ground south of the runway.

The north side of the runway was primarily defended by Cuban construction workers. They were armed with AK-47s, machine guns, recoilless rifles and mortars drawn from Grenadian stores, and under the leadership of the Cuban military advisors assigned to the island. On Oct. 22,[2] Castro ordered his island personnel to prepare defense positions around their work and living areas on the Point Salines peninsula. He instructed them only to fire if fired upon, and not to impede American attempts to evacuate its citizens. But, if attacked, he directed them to "vigorously defend" their ground as if it was Cuban soil. Castro wanted to demonstrate to Americans how fiercely Cubans would fight to defend their homeland, according to a top Havana diplomat.[3]

As a practical matter, that directive meant that the Cubans were positioned inside a cylindrical-shaped swath of land that ran northeast from the middle of the runway to an area south of Grand Anse Bay. The area was bounded by a barracks compound immediately north of the airport terminal known as the Old Camp and a newer headquarters compound still under construction to the northeast, near the village of Calliste. The Americans referred to the new compound as Little Havana. The Cuban workers were in their beds, rather than in their defensive trenches, when the first planes arrived, according to public assertions by Castro that were later independently corroborated.[4]

The anti-aircraft guns in the vicinity of the airport were manned by Grenadians, including a four-barrel 12.7 anti-aircraft gun on a hill near the Old Camp.[5] Other PRA soldiers were guarding the gates around the True Blue Campus of the medical school at the eastern end of the runway, or stationed at the Great House, a plantation-era building west of the terminal that was also used for offices by the Cuban engineers. The Grenadians at Point Salines opened fire as soon as they saw American planes over the airport, but the Cubans were initially restrained by their leaders. The principal initial anti-aircraft opposition came from two Grenadian-manned ZU-23 guns positioned near the Grenadian Army supply depot at Frequente to the northeast of the eastern end of the runway.

"We have a fight here. I have targets," radioed Maj. Jim Roper, the Air Force air liaison officer (ALO) who jumped with the Army Rangers.[6] Roper's call for help was transmitted at 0538, just as dawn was illuminating objects on the ground. Roper was initially

Top: **This photograph shows the unfinished airport terminal buildings and the cluttered loading apron on the second day of the operation (National Archives [330-CFD-DF-SN-84-10856]).** *Bottom:* **This photograph shows the so-called Old Cuban Camp that was located on a hill immediately behind the new terminal buildings (National Archives [330-CFD-DF-SN-84-10856]).**

separated from Taylor, the Ranger commander. He opted to call for immediate suppressing fire, acting solely on his own, admittedly questionable, authority.[7] The call was heard by an AC-130 gunship circling overhead piloted by Maj. Clement Twiford. Roper directed Twiford's toward fire coming from a trench at the base of the control tower about one hundred meters away. Given the twilight and the distance it was impossible for the Americas to discern if this fire was coming from Grenadians or Cubans.

The Bravo Company platoon led by Stackpole took cover from the opposing fire in a drainage ditch on the north side of the runway.[8] Stackpole moved his men through the ditch to a predetermined assembly area and then up a hill to establish a 360-degree defensive position. There they awaited the arrival of the rest of their company before beginning their D-Day mission: clearing the Cuban work camp. Taylor meanwhile, established his command center about a mile to the east in a roofless concrete building on the south side of the runway.[9] With opposition subdued by the presence of Twiford's Spectre, Taylor ordered the men with him to begin clearing the runway. Breaking into two-man teams, they started to remove parked vehicles, barrels, wire fences and other obstructions from the asphalt. Less than 10 minutes into the clearing operation, the 105 mm gun on Twiford's Spectre misfired. This required his plane to fly over water until the round could be manually cleared from the disabled gun.[10] Another Spectre circling nearby, piloted by Maj. Couvillon, heard the radio report of a gun problem and joined the fight for the runway. When Couvillon neared the runway, he saw a 23 mm anti-aircraft gun firing on Twiford from Frequente, northeast of the runway. He engaged the Grenadian-manned gun and silenced it with two quick bursts of cannon fire.[11] The ZU-23s had a maximum effective range against air targets of one and a half miles. The orbiting Spectres could engage the ground artillery defenses at the limit of their capabilities with airborne guns that were aimed by computers.[12]

The presence of the anti-aircraft guns at Salines came as unwelcome surprise to the invaders. "They weren't supposed to be there," Taylor later said. "The information we had when we left was: no antiaircraft."[13] The intelligence briefing that the airborne forces had received before departure was based on a Defense Intelligence Agency analysis of satellite pictures taken of the runway on Oct. 16, nine days before the fighting. The analysis noted that Grenadians had 24 mobile AA guns in their inventory, but none were then deployed from their garrison.[14] But, by the morning of the invasion, most of the wheeled guns had been moved by trucks at night and strategically placed around the island. The presence of guns around the airport had been clandestinely reported to the Washington by Flohr, the CIA undercover officer, but that information, inexplicably, never reached the Ranger commanders.[15]

Despite the brief lull in opposing fire, Taylor's position was extremely precarious. The first Rangers on the ground were outnumbered more than 15–1 by armed Cubans and Grenadians at that point. The Marines were 15 miles away on the other side of the island. Reinforcements were on the way, but slow to arrive. A second C-130 transport conducted its drop at 0552, 22 minutes after Taylor's plane.[16] From the ground, one Ranger officer judged the anti-aircraft fire to be twice as intense as the initial drop. Three immediately following planes aborted their runs, driven off by the anti-aircraft and small arms fire. At 0600, a half hour into the fight for the runway, there were just two planeloads of Rangers on the ground, about 80 men. Schwarzkopf watched the initial Ranger drops with awe and apprehension from the bridge of the *Guam* offshore. "You have to visualize literally a cone of red and green tracer fire, coming up in to the air, C-130 aircraft flying in directly underneath this cone of tracer fire, paratroopers dropping in the air and then being shot at, in the air, from all sides on the ground. I can't recall any combat operation that the United States has ever been involved in that could have been more intense than that," he later recalled.[17] (The Air Force term for the anti-aircraft display that Schwarzkopf described was "Blue Christmas coming up.")

Within a half an hour after the second drop, the orbiting Spectres had silenced about three quarters of the hundred or so small arms that Roper saw firing on the first two planes.[18] By then, Twiford and Couvillon had also knocked out five anti-aircraft gun positions in the vicinity of the airport. This was no small achievement as the slow-moving Spectres were not ordinarily employed to take on anti-aircraft guns. But in this case, the anti-aircraft fire was not radar-controlled and not all the destroyed guns may have been manned. The Grenadian defensive plan for the island called for a battery of six more ZU-23 militia-manned guns to be positioned around the Point Salines runway. Fortuitously for the Americans these guns were not deployed because the militia gunners did not report for duty.[19]

The obstructed runways and the opposition encountered by the first two aircraft made it imperative that all the following planes be ready to jump their paratroopers, rather than air-land as preferred. Most of the Ranger officers on those planes received their orders to jump directly from Taylor over their satellite radios. But at least three of the following C-130s were not equipped with the special hatch-mounted antennas necessary to receive satellite transmissions. Taylor's only means of communicating with them in flight was by passing a message to his pilot, which would then be relayed to the pilots of the unequipped C-130s. In the event, due to the missing antennas, radio malfunction or human misunderstanding, or some combination of the three, the order received by the Rangers in those planes was "airland" instead of the intended "all jump" order.[20]

Taylor's executive officer, Maj. Nix, was flying in one of planes that lacked the hatch antenna, the fifth plane in the line of 12. Nix had spent the entire flight sitting on the steps to the cockpit waiting for update messages from his commanding officer that never reached him. Nix's C-130 carried 42 Rangers along with two jeeps and two motorcycles. Nix and eight other soldiers formed the back-up tactical operations center (TOC) that would take over if Taylor's command unit was knocked out of action.[21] About 20 minutes before H-Hour, Nix and his Rangers were all hooked up ready to jump. The aircraft's loadmaster yelled: "It's an airland!" That unexpected news created bedlam in the belly of their aircraft as the Rangers shed their parachutes, buoyance vests and everything else that was associated with a jump. These now-unnecessary items were hastily tossed toward the front of the aircraft to get them out of the way. Fifteen minutes later, the molting of the paratroopers was complete; they were ready to step onto asphalt instead of jumping into sky.

At that point, the Air Force loadmaster turned to Nix and asked: "How long will it take you to get ready to jump?" Nix was stunned by the question, realizing it was prelude to an unwelcome reversal. He turned to a nearby Ranger sergeant who advised him that it would take a minimum of an hour for the men to put all their jump gear back on and perform the minimum safety checks. As that answer was being passed back to the pilot, the battalion's first sergeant turned to Nix with another option. He advised that, if necessary, most of the Rangers could jump without their rucksacks and, instead, carry what supplies they could in their pockets. At that point, the loadmaster informed Nix that the plane only had 30 minutes of fuel left. If Nix wanted to join this fight, he and his Rangers would have to jump—and soon. More bedlam ensued as the men retrieved their just-discarded parachutes and only the most essential elements of their equipment. Many of their rucksacks and several of their radios were left behind. Only the most cursory of safety checks were made.

The remaining 10 transport planes finally arrived over the still-contested runway an hour after Taylor landed. The airdrop resumed at 0634 and continued until 0710.[22] Green parachute canopies now blossomed in the clearing morning sky over the airport. Their arrival was met with opposition that Roper, the Air Force controller, now rated as "minor," but others described more dramatically. "Rangers, be hard. We'll be taking some ground-to-air fire," Hagler, the 2nd Battalion commander, said just before leading his plane of Rangers out the door.[23] The 2nd Battalion paratroopers also dropped at 500 feet, but, on Hagler's orders, they jumped without their reserve chutes. There wasn't enough hang time to deploy them at this altitude. The C-130 pilots took evasive action as soon as they unloaded their paratroopers. They rolled hard right and ejected bundles of chaff and flares to confuse any radar-controlled, or infrared-seeking anti-aircraft missiles that might be on the ground. That proved to be unnecessary because the Grenadian defenders had no missiles in their arsenal.

The principal drama of the final jump was provided by a hapless paratrooper whose static line got snagged as he exited the plane. The 20-year-old Ranger, Sp4c. William Fedak, swung wildly below the fuselage, still tethered to the plane.[24] Other Rangers watched from the runway as the plane's jumpmaster, Air Force Technical Sergeant Charles Tisby, reeled Fedak back to safety. (Taylor attributed this malfunction to the lack of safety checks on the hastily re-rigged planes.)[25] There were other minor mishaps. One jumper, Sp4c. Harold E. Hagen, broke a leg.[26] Another jumper landed in the ocean, but was wearing his water wings and made it safely to shore.[27] One 1st Battalion fire support officer broke four bones in his foot, but soldiered on.[28] Many others shrugged off sprains, scrapes and bruises suffered in landing or when they were dragged by their chutes. There were also newly arrived physical obstacles. In the middle of the mass jump, Task Force 160 Black Hawks from the aborted prison raid unexpectedly landed at the runway. They gathered in a western section of the drop zone where the surrounding high ground sheltered them from anti-aircraft guns. Some newly arriving Rangers landed almost on top of the shut-down copters as aircrew members were already working on repairs.[29]

More confusion ensued as Rangers from two different battalions found themselves side by side, unsure where they were supposed to go. Due to the in-flight reshuffling that occurred when the first planes turned away, the planes carrying the remainder of Taylor's 1st Battalion Rangers were now intermingled with the second element of five planes carrying Hagler's 2nd Battalion. In the reshuffle, Hagler's plane actually jumped ahead of the C-130 carrying Nix, Taylor's 1st Battalion executive officer. One of the intermingled jumpers was Capt. Jose G. Ventura, the S-4 (logistics) officer for the 2nd Battalion. Adrenalin was surging though his body as he jumped at low attitude, without a reserve chute and under sporadic anti-aircraft and small arms fire. He managed to land on his feet and then immediately sat down to keep his chute from dragging him in a stiff 20-knot wind.[30] He looked around and saw Rangers everywhere standing and gathering up their chutes, as if on a training exercise. Ventura grabbed at the nearest Rangers, throwing them to the ground. "What the hell are you doing!" he shouted. "Leave that stuff. Get down. Can't you see they are firing?" He ordered the men to move off the runway toward berms that would offer them cover while they assessed the situation. Ventura saw Cubans with AK-47s scurrying around the high ground, but he told his men to only fire if fired upon. He also noticed some Rangers he didn't recognize. "What unit?" he asked. "1–75," they responded. "God damn it, get your ass over to the far [eastern] end [of the runway]. That's where you're supposed to be." He was stunned when seven other 1st Battalion Rangers nearest to him rose up and also moved away. "I realized: 'Oh my God, you know, we're intermingled here.'" Nix, the 1st Battalion executive officer, spent his first hour on the ground playing "traffic cop" directing individual Rangers where to go.[31]

When the full parachute force of 497 Rangers sorted themselves out, the two Ranger Battalions set about the job of securing the area surrounding all sides of the runway. Under the original battle plan, Taylor's 1st Battalion was assigned to an area of operations around the eastern half of the airport roughly from a lagoon to the True Blue medical campus. Hagler's 2nd Battalion would secure the western end, from the lagoon to the ocean, including the control tower and the high ground north of the runway.[32] The first task for Rangers of both battalions was to finish the job of clearing the runway of obstructions that was begun by Taylor's men. The Rangers were joined in this effort by last-minute recruits from the 82nd Airborne: two heavy equipment operators plucked from the ready rooms of their combat engineer company. One of the enlisted men, Sp4c. William R. Richardson, had just gotten his jump wings and was making his first-ever jump as a member of a unit. The two were supposed to have driven an airdropped Army bulldozer, but that drop was aborted. Instead, the engineers commandeered eight Cuban construction vehicles and drove them off the runway. One Ranger, driving an asphalt roller for the first time, flattened the steel rods that the Cubans had driven into the runway about 50 feet apart and strung with barbed wire.[33]

By 0725, 15 minutes after the mass air drop, the runway was officially, if optimistically, declared to be secure.[34] The first fixed-wing aircraft were cleared to land on the eastern end of the unfinished runway beginning at 0737. Among the first transports to arrive were the four C-130s that had departed separately from Pope Air Force Base. They carried Delta Force's A Squadron and Charlie Company of the Ranger 1st Battalion, which had been detached to support the Delta raiders. These four aircraft also carried eight OH-6 light helicopters that were outfitted either as mini-gunships (AH-6) or troop carriers (MH-6).[35] Their rotors were quickly unfolded and the two AH-6s set off for a belated attack on Fort Rupert, the permanent Grenadian military headquarters in St. George's. The "Little Birds" found air defenses around the capital to be too formidable and they returned to Salines within 10 minutes.[36] (This action appears to have given rise to later erroneous reports that an attack helicopter was shot down over Salines on D-Day in addition to Lucas' transport.)[37] The assault on Fort Rupert (also known as Fort George) was cancelled. None of these diminutive aircraft were listed in the public inventory of U.S. military at the time.[38] Their existence was publicly revealed for the first time in photographs and film footage taken by civilians during the first days of the fighting on Grenada. It is also significant to note that this repulsed attack was launched on another "dry hole" D-Day target because of faulty intelligence.[39] After the bloodshed at Fort Rupert on Oct. 19, the Coard faction moved their operational headquarters to Fort Frederick, outside the city, and remained there through the first 24 hours of the invasion. Little Birds and Charlie Company Rangers also conducted a search and rescue mission to the Lucas crash site, but found no recoverable remains in the hot ash.[40]

The landing of Delta's four C-130s at Point Salines was accompanied by the arrival of Scholtes, the JSOC commander, in his command EC-130. Scholtes set up a ground headquarters at the airport terminal at the center of the runway to oversee the still-unfolding missions involving the governor general and the radio station. He also had many Delta Force casualties who needed urgent medical attention. One of Scholtes' first orders on reaching Grenadian soil was to cancel the 2nd Ranger Battalion's planned secondary attack on the Calivigny training complex, 12 kilometers from the runway. That D-Day mission was a bridge too far for his engaged Rangers. A secondary, on-order, SEAL mission to seize and control Grenada's diesel-powered electric plan was also scrapped.

As the runway was being cleared, other Rangers moved into the northern hills behind the terminal buildings where the so-called Old Cuban Camp was located. The camp consisted of 22 prefabricated, wood-frame, 40-man barracks that housed most of the foreign airport construction laborers.[41] A three-man team led by First Sgt. Richard Clayton of Bravo Company of the 1st Battalion assaulted defensive positions in the camp, killing two and taking 28 prisoners.[42] According to Castro, it wasn't until this point, at about 0700, "when U.S. troops advanced toward the Cubans in a belligerent way" that sanctioned combat commenced between the two nations."[43] The 1st platoon of Bravo Company under Stackpole followed a trail from the runway to the compound and then moved through the camp from west to east.[44] Snipers and machine gunners covered their advance. The military skills of the Cuban workers were no match for the elite Rangers. The Cubans realized that giving up was much safer than resisting. Construction workers poured from the barracks to surrender, leaving behind their weapons and military gear. Soon they had collected about 275 prisoners who were eventually turned over to the 2nd Battalion.

The captured Cubans were immediately interrogated in Spanish by Capt. Ventura, a 2nd Battalion staff officer. Ventura learned that a majority of them had been working on the island for about 14 months, but there were also some new arrivals.[45] The more-veteran workers had received some rifle instruction from Cuban military advisers, but some Cubans did not know how to operate their weapons. Also, many of the AK-47s were brand new and had not been test-fired to adjust their aiming sights. The Cubans told Ventura that they had received a garbled message from Havana two days before, instructing them not to fire unless fire upon. "If you are not supposed to fire, why are you firing?" Ventura asked. "Well, we have our problems too," one worker responded. "We've got those guys who are gung-ho, more or less, who want to kill Americans and we couldn't control them. They were running and shooting."

In the fight around the runway it was often unclear if the source of the fire on Americans was from Grenadians or Cubans. The Cuban construction workers, and most of the Grenadian militia, wore civilian clothes.[46] The olive-green uniforms worn by regular PRA soldiers were supplied by Cuba. Grenadians were generally darker skinned than Cubans, but there were many shades of skin color represented in both nationalities. Native language was a tell-tale difference between Cubans and Grenadians, but that characteristic didn't help identify the dead. Nationality confusion, in part, accounted for the many battlefield reports of "Cuban" resistance being offered in areas away from Point Salines where their combat presence was dubious. In fact, long after the fighting stopped, American transports flew 68 dead out of Grenada for return to Cuba.[47] Only 24 bodies were accepted by Havana as their own. The others were determined by Cubans to be Grenadian and returned to their homeland. The Americans firmly believed they had killed nearly three times more Cubans than they actually did.

Cuban construction workers who weren't killed or captured as the Old Camp was overrun fled northeast toward the Cuban headquarters compound at Calliste, which the Americans called Little Havana. The focus of 1st Battalion Ranger combat action now shifted from the center of the runway toward the eastern end where the medical school campus was located. Alpha Company of the 1st Battalion gathered at an assembly point on the south side of the eastern end of the runway near Bagadi Bay. According to plan, Abizaid, the 1st Battalion's Alpha Company commander, dispatched his 2nd platoon to move south of the runway along the shoreline to the True Blue campus.[48] He directed his other two platoons to fully clear and secure the northern side of the eastern end of the runway. This hilly ground, which Rangers dubbed "Goat Hill," was occupied by a mixed force of Cubans and Grenadians who were engaging them with small arms from across the runway.[49]

Pvt. Brian C. Ivers of the 2nd platoon of Alpha Company was late to the assembly area, arriving just as units were moving out to their assigned tasks.[50] Ivers remembers watching in astonishment as a white, flat-bed, dump truck came barreling toward them from the eastern end of the still-contested runway. Sp4c. Mark Okamura Yamane, a 20-year-old, 3rd platoon machine gunner, boldly exposed himself and halted the civilian vehicle. Two men carrying AK-47s got out and dropped their weapons on Yamane's orders. A warning shot by Ivers discouraged any further resistance and the duo were taken prisoner.[51] (It was later learned that the two were PRA soldiers making a routine delivery. They claimed to be unaware that their country was at war.[52] They also warned their American captors that there were Cubans concealed in houses on the ridgeline they were preparing to climb.)

When Yamane captured the truck, he was temporarily operating with an ad hoc group of about six soldiers, including Rangers from other platoons and an Air Force controller. Sp4c. Blair Donaldson, a 1st platoon radio operator, was part of the group.[53] Donaldson and several others broke off and started moving north from the runway along a road leading toward a schoolhouse that was the 1st platoon's designated rally point. As they advanced, they started taking fire from the ridgeline to the north, pinning them down. Fearing he was caught in a kill zone, Donaldson returned to the truck. He tried to drive it to a safer position in a ditch on the north side of the runway. He only got about 75 yards when his way was blocked by a Grenadian soldier carrying an AK-47. Donaldson jumped from the cab and, with Yamane and others, took up firing positions, using the truck as cover. Yamane fired his M60 machine gun with his left hand from behind the truck's left front tire. Opposing fire from the ridgeline was intense. Both Donaldson and Yamane were hit by the same burst. One bullet took the heel off of Donaldson's right boot. Yamane was simultaneously struck in the mouth and mortally wounded. Donaldson's desperate attempts to stem the bleeding were futile. Yamane died in Donaldson's arms. Yamane, a Japanese-American from Seattle, became the first American ground soldier to die of wounds suffered during Urgent Fury combat operations, and the first of eight Rangers killed in the fighting. He was posthumously awarded a Bronze Star for valor, along with a Purple Heart.[54]

All sides were now fully engaged in the battle for control of the eastern end of airport, regardless of any restraints that may have held them back earlier. "The fighting was at least as intense as any of the fights I was in in Vietnam. And I saw two years over there," Taylor later recalled.[55] Taylor was ordered to send his men across the airfield and take the high ground on the other side as fast as he could. One enraged Ranger, Pfc. Ron

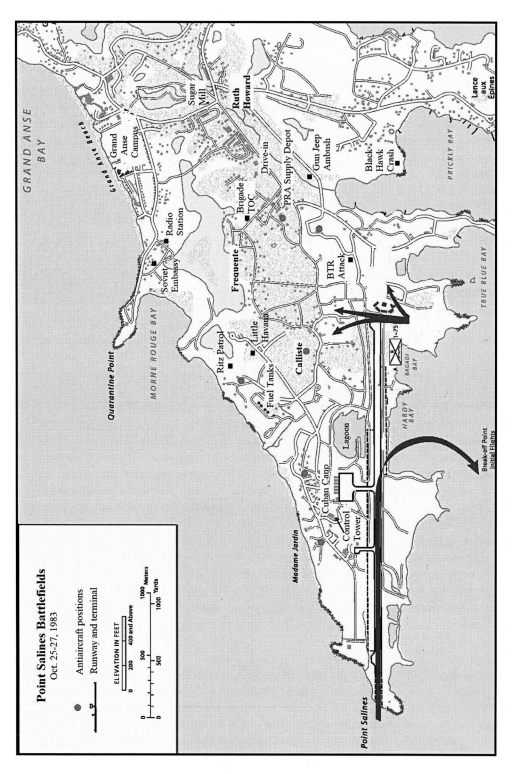

Point Salines Battlefields
Oct. 25-27, 1983

● Antiaircraft positions
⊤ Runway and terminal

ELEVATION IN FEET
0   200   400 and Above

0   500   1000 Meters
0   500   1000 Yards

GRAND ANSE
BAY

Grand Anse Beach

Quarantine Point

MORNE ROUGE BAY

Point Salines

Madame Jardin

Control Tower

Cuban Camp

Lagoon

HARDY BAY

BAGADI BAY

1-75

TRUE BLUE BAY

Break-off Point
Initial Flights

PRICKLY BAY

Lance aux Epines

Black Hawk Crash

Gun Jeep Ambush

BTR Attack

PRA Supply Depot

Ruth Howard

Sugar Mill

Grand Anse Campus

Radio Station

Soviet Embassy

Drive-in

Brigade TOC

Frequente

Ritz Patrol

Little Havana

Fuel Tanks

Calliste

This map shows the Point Salines peninsula on the southwestern tip the Grenadian mainland and key battlefields in the first two days of fighting (adapted from base map, courtesy U.S. Army Center of Military History).

Tucker, reloaded Yamane's still-hot M60 to provide covering fire for the Ranger advance. The Air Force controller with the Donaldson's group called for air support. At about 0815, an Air Force AC-130 gunship used its 40 mm cannon to destroy and set ablaze the house that was the source of the fire on the truck.[56] Other covering fire came from Ranger machine guns and mortars. The 1st and 3rd platoons of Alpha Company successfully maneuvered across the width of the runway, but not without further loss. Sp4c. Tony A. Davis, a machine gunner with the 1st platoon, was stuck in the neck as he traversed the open 350 meters, suffering a wound that left him a paraplegic.[57] Another Ranger, Sp4c. Paul N. Bell, exposed himself to fire to pull Davis off the runway, later earning a Bronze star with a V for his actions.

Once across the runway, Spanish-speaking Rangers called on concealed Cubans to surrender, but they replied with obscenities and bullets.[58] Abizaid's company improvised armored support by using a commandeered Cuban bulldozer as a tank.[59] John Wayne had famously demonstrated the use of this tactic in the Pacific in the 1944 film *Fighting Seabees*. In the later Caribbean application, Army staff sergeant Manous F. Boles, Jr., drove a captured dozer up the hill. The extended shovel shielded his following squad from small arms fire. One soldier rode shotgun by squatting on the blade.

Donaldson and others joined the assault, passing the Grenadian home that had been the source of the fire that killed Yamane. Donaldson discovered the occupants included Grenadian soldiers who were not in uniform. One man was missing part of his leg. He told Donaldson that his brother had been killed by the gunship counterfire. Nonetheless, he was grateful for the arrival of the Americans. "Thank god you are here," he said. At the top the hill, Rangers captured a 12.7 mm anti-aircraft gun. They attempted to put the four-barrel heavy machine gun into action against the displaced Cubans, but found its unfamiliar controls too complicated to safely operate. Cubans retreated into prepared defensive positions surrounding their Little Havana compound in the valley below. Boles was later awarded a Bronze Star with a V for valor for leading the advance up the hill.[60] On the hilltop, Donaldson snapped a celebratory picture of Abizaid, the victorious Alpha Company commander, beside the captured gun.

Even with the benefit of hindsight, the Army could probably have not found a better line officer to ramrod the fight to secure the eastern end of the runway.[61] Abizaid was a 1973 graduate of West Point, where he was known as "the Mad Arab" because he was of Lebanese descent. After completing his airborne training and stints as a platoon and company commander, he was awarded an Olmstead Scholarship to study abroad at the University of Jordan in Amman. On return home, he earned a master's degree in Middle Eastern studies at Harvard. As a company commander with the Ranger 1st Battalion, Abizaid was regarded by his enlisted men as a driven, but compassionate, leader who favored week-long field training exercises that closely simulated combat hardships. "We worshipped him. We felt we were the best rifle company in the world," said Ivers, a private under Abizaid, who is now a trial lawyer in Iowa.[62] Within the infantry officer ranks, Abizaid also developed a reputation as a master of improvised, quick tactics.[63] Those qualities got their first live-fire test throughout D-Day on Grenada.

Alpha Company retained their hard-won high ground until around noon when recoilless rifle fire from the Cuban compound drove them off the crest of the hill.[64] Abizaid requested an air strike, but was refused permission by Taylor because of the likely presence of civilians in the headquarters compound. Instead, Metcalf responded to the plea by making his first significant change in the Pentagon-prepared battle plan.

He directed that the Marine Cobras assigned to the 22nd MAU fly outside their designated zone to support the embattled Army and JSOC forces to the south. This decision, in turn, exposed inoperability problems between the services that were to plague the operation for the next few days. The first flight of Cobras flew south as ordered, but they were unable to make radio contact with the Army units on the ground or the Air Force Spectres overhead.[65] Low on fuel, they returned to the *Guam* in frustration. A second pair of Marine Cobra piloted by Capt. Douglas J. Diehl and Capt. Gary W. Watson took over the Metcalf-directed mission. This flight managed to pick up a common frequency, but then encountered another incompatibility problem. The Army and the Marines were using different maps. The Air Force controller couldn't give the Cobras a precise fix on the target. The controller improvised a solution by using a signal mirror to direct the Cobras.[66] The attack helicopter blasted the Cuban recoilless rifle, and a nearby building and truck, with two TOW wire-guided missiles and 20 mm cannon fire. The missiles were among nine TOWs fired by Cobras in combat for the first time during Urgent Fury.

By mid-morning, the airfield was secure enough to land the partly-emptied C-130s that had flown the Rangers to Grenada. After dropping their paratroopers, these 12 planes had headed to Barbados to refuel. Now they began landing at Point Salines, one at a time, to off-load their vehicles and remaining men. Among the new arrivals at 1000 was a five-man jeep gun crew from Alpha Company of the 1st Battalion led by Sgt. Randy E. Cline, a 28-year-old former police officer. The jeep team's mission was to secure a road junction on the northeast side of the runway, about a mile past the True Blue campus. Like all the Rangers, Cline was issued a photocopy of a British-made topographic map of the island that had no road names or longitude and latitude grid lines. The jeep missed a turn and proceeded past his assigned road junction, winding up on a dusty road leading east from the airport toward the village of Ruth Howard. Realizing their mistake, Cline's team backtracked and ran into a PRA ambush.[67] The machine-gun jeep was wrecked by a shoulder-launched rocket-propelled grenade (RPG). The ensuing firefight was detailed in a 2015 Facebook post by Joe Muccia, an Urgent Fury historian who has interviewed more than 300 Grenada veterans.[68] According to Muccia's account, three of the five Rangers were killed in the initial salvo of Grenadian fire: Cline and privates first class Russell L. Robinson and Marlin R. Maynard. The other two Rangers managed to exit the jeep on the side opposite the ambush. Sgt. Mark A. Rademacher ordered Pvt. Timothy G. Romick to go for help while he provided covering fire. Rademacher, and at least one Grenadian soldier, were killed in the ensuing exchange of fire. Romick was also hit multiple times, but managed to crawl away. He armed himself with an abandoned Soviet-made light machine gun and made his way back to friendly lines near the True Blue campus. There he yelled for help by calling out a mash-up of prearranged passwords: "Black Tape, Crusade, Teardrop, One-three!" Romick survived his wounds and was personally awarded the Purple Heart by the U.S. Army's chief of staff on the Ranger's return to a military hospital at Fort Bragg.

While Alpha Company was engaged at the east end of the runway, Bravo Company, under the command of Capt. Clyde M. Newman, was advancing on their west. By 1100, Newman had moved past the Old Camp to secure the airport's nearby fuel storage tanks.[69] From the tank farm, Bravo Company men could look down on the remaining source of Cuban resistance, the compound known interchangeably as the new camp or Little Havana. The fenced compound, about the size of football field, was located about two kilometers north of the Salines terminal in a natural bowl surrounded on three sides by hills. It consisted of the Cuban mission and new barracks buildings that were under construction about 50 meters away, across a road. The mission was the headquarters for the Cuban military advisers who had now taken charge of the construction workers. The military advisors were commanding the civilian workers who were now manning defensive positions on the hills surrounding the tactically-vulnerable compound. The compound was menaced on two sides by the Ranger 1st Battalion. Bravo Company snipers engaged any movement within the compound, killing or wounding 18 Cubans at ranges of 600 to 1,000 meters.[70]

The 1st Battalion had no immediate intention of continuing their ground advance into the defended camp, but new arrivals from the 2nd Battalion were eager to join the fight. At about 1000 two recently arrived Rangers boarded their airlanded Kawasaki motorcycles to race from the Point Salines terminal area. They followed a dirt track leading to Little Havana, unaware of the danger. Both were shot off their machines and wounded, but they fell in a no-man's land between Cuban and American positions where they could not be immediately reached. Ranger snipers from Newman's company in the 1st Battalion protected the 2nd Battalion bikers, who took cover to await rescue. At around 1400 Bravo Company took over all the Little Havana overwatch positions, replacing Alpha Company.[71] Newman decided more aggressive actions were necessary to further neutralize the compound and retrieve the wounded motorcyclists. Clayton, the Bravo Company first sergeant, a captured Cuban and a Spanish-speaking Ranger corporal were dispatched as emissaries to the compound.[72] The Rangers used a bullhorn to trumpet a direct message: "Surrender in 15 minutes or else." That edict persuaded about 175 of the encircled Cubans, including 23 wounded, to give up. The Cuban prisoners were evacuated, along with the two Ranger motorcyclists. The remaining 80–100 Cuban holdouts in Little Havana were left as a clean-up problem for the 82nd Airborne to handle when they joined the offensive hostilities on second day of the fighting. "Clayton's success practically ended the Cuban threat on Grenada, although this was not clear at the time," one Army historian later declared.[73] (Clayton was awarded a Bronze Star with a V for his actions.)[74]

The Rangers were not expecting or equipped to deal with such a large number of prisoners, but the fortunes of war provided an improvised solution. In the late morning of D-Day, the Ranger assault forces got some surprise visitors: the vanguard of the Caribbean Peacekeeping Force, a multinational force of about 300 men. The first planeload arrived by Air Force C-130 from Barbados at 1045, accompanied by Lewis, the Barbadian brigadier general who was the de facto supreme commander of the Caribbean contingent. Lewis' mission was a muddled mystery to all. Lewis had missed his scheduled link up with Metcalf the previous evening because he was preoccupied with gathering his hastily conscripted coalition force of soldiers and policemen.[75] He arrived without being briefed on the invasion plan and no clear idea of his unit's role.

Though Lewis' force nominally represented the OECS, two thirds of the force, and nearly all of the trained soldiers, came from either Jamaica or Barbados. Neither nation was an OECS member. Though the verbal vote by the OECS was portrayed as "unanimous," that consensus faltered when it came to putting words into action. Antigua and Barbuda was the only OECS-member nation to send troops, a 14-member infantry squad. Two other members, Dominica and St. Lucia, lacked standing armies and sent policemen instead. Montserrat, still a British dependency, was barred from participating by the Foreign Office in London.[76] St. Vincent, Grenada's closest neighbor, delayed sending its police contingent for four days until the outcome was assured.[77] St. Kitts-Nevis, independent

These members of the Caribbean Peacekeeping Force arrived on Grenada on November 3, after the hostilities were declared over. Their uniforms show they were a mixture of soldiers and policemen from other English-speaking Caribbean island nations (National Archives [330-CFD-DF-ST-84-09830]).

from Britain for only a month, dispatched five policemen to Barbados, but two balked at immediately going to Grenada.[78]

None of the on-scene American commanders was expecting the arrival of the Caribbean peacekeepers. They were supposed to have landed at Pearls instead of Point Salines.[79] Further, no one was quite sure how to deploy the new unit. The invasion plan worked out over the weekend at the Pentagon made no written provision for including Caribbean troops. Despite the fact that the president's National Security Decision Directive 110A had specifically called for "U.S. and allied Caribbean forces" to land at dawn on Oct. 25, the island troops were not part of the initial assault force or even the chain of command for any of the five participating American task forces. The Caribbean force's involvement in the invasion was the result of an 11th hour, verbal amendment to the execute order issued to Atlantic Command by the Pentagon on Oct. 24.[80] Lewis huddled with his American counterparts and it was agreed that the Caribbean force would be best employed as guards for the growing number of Cuban and Grenadian prisoners. The detainees were hauled off by the Caribbean peacekeepers in captured Cuban trucks. The Old Cuban Camp near the runway was turned into a temporary detention camp.

Perhaps the most puzzling aspect of the many surprising twists and turns of D-Day was the relative lack of urgency and priority attached to reaching the American medical school students at True Blue. That task was assigned to just one Ranger platoon, the 2nd platoon of Alpha Company, and did not get launched until after all the Rangers had landed and the runway had been cleared of obstacles. The True Blue facility was a sub campus, which housed first-year students who were new to the island. The compound was surrounded by a chain-link fence and consisted of five barracks-style dormitories,

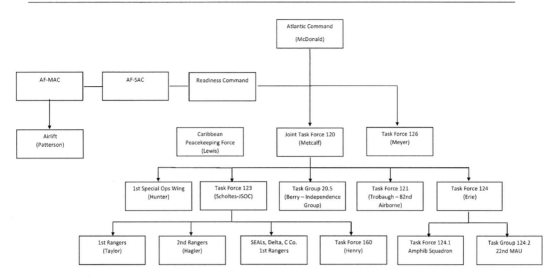

This organizational chart illustrates the complex command structure that was assembled on the fly for Urgent Fury. This chart is the author's composite version of two slightly varying charts developed by two Army historians. Even in retrospect, there is no consensus on how to graphically portray the fluid or fuzzy command authority that prevailed over some key units involved in the operation. Rangers units were "chopped" back and forth on short notice under different operational commanders before and during the fighting. On D-Day two different generals believed they were the principal forward Air Force airlift commander for the operation. No one was ever sure how the Caribbean Peacekeeping Forces figured in the formal chain of command, if at all.

a lecture hall, a cafeteria and a basketball court.[81] The first Rangers reached the campus at 0726,[82] two hours after the first Ranger set foot on the Grenadian soil. The advancing Rangers encountered only token resistance from the Grenadian soldiers who guarded the campus gates. It took another 90 minutes for the 2nd platoon to declare the campus to be secure and the 138 students safe.[83]

The students first saw the approaching soldiers outside their dorms at around 0830. "We are Americans. You are all right," one soldier shouted to them.[84] The students had been constrained in their movements for days by the dawn-to-dusk curfew, but they were not hostages in the dictionary definition of that word. They were not "held as security for the fulfillment of a condition," but all were understandably frightened by all the shooting that had been going on nearby. They applauded when an officer told them they were going home, *Time* magazine reported. Though the students were just beginning their medical studies, the Rangers enlisted them in treating casualties of the fighting. Makeshift treatment centers were set up; the school library for Americans and the lecture hall for Cubans and Grenadians. The basketball court was turned into a landing pad for helicopters to use to ferry the seriously wounded to operating rooms on the *Guam*. A school laboratory became a temporary morgue.

The students were happy to have the protection of the Rangers, but the students had disconcerting news for the soldiers. More than 200 other medical students were living at the main campus on Grand Anse Beach, about a mile and a half away along the road leading from Point Salines to the capital city. Moreover, about 200 additional students were living off-campus in various homes, mostly on the Lance Aux Epines peninsula. The Rangers had reached fewer than a third of the medical students. "Yeah, I was shocked," Taylor later recalled.[85] This egregious intelligence lapse was probably the single biggest screw-up of the entire operation. Even in retrospect, it's hard to understand how such critical information had been overlooked (or undervalued) in the planning. More fundamentally, the omission has led even military historians to conclude that the students were a secondary consideration in an intervention focused on regime-change objectives. "Congressional testimony [by Trobaugh and McDonald] suggests, by the lack of information on the number and whereabouts of the Americans, and the duration of the evacuation, that the safety of Americans was not the United States' primary concern," wrote one Air Force historian.[86]

The Defense Intelligence Agency (DIA) stumbled on the apparent multi-campus oversight at about 2100 on Oct. 21.[87] A National Security Agency employee happened to have a brother who was a medical student on the island. She had taken snapshots of the school, including the Grand Anse campus, during a recent visit. On her own initiative, she brought the pictures to the DIA for their review and analysis. The DIA maintains that an intelligence package with this information was delivered to Scholtes' Joint Special Operation Command on Oct. 22 and McDonald's Atlantic Command on Oct. 23, but that disclosure did not trigger any provision for securing the Grand Anse campus or the off-campus students. Tony Nelson, an analyst with the DIA, later speculated to a military historian that the Grand Anse location was known at the staff-officer level at both JSOC and CINCLANT on the eve of the invasion. However, by then, the "mission and the time constraints kept [the] second campus off [the] JSOC objectives list." Nelson also suggested that JSOC planners did not realize that Grand Anse was a residential campus and, instead, believed that "90%" of the students would be found at True Blue. "By this time, objectives [had] already [been] selected. Evacuation of students was [a] secondary mission. JSOC secured students anyway by eliminating enemy forces," Nelson told a post-invasion Army interviewer.[88] Accomplishing the neutralization of Grenadian resistance was more easily postulated than achieved, however. A "second campus" solution had to be improvised. Surprisingly, the phone lines were still working on the island. Rangers at True Blue called the Grand Anse campus to ask for directions. But, for now, the remaining students would have to wait. Another rescue assumed the highest military priority: Governor General Scoon and the trapped SEALs.

6

Rescuing the Rescuers

The arrival of Navy SEALs at the governor general's mansion was antithesis of the stealthy approach that the invasion planners had envisioned. SEALs in the lead Black Hawk fast-roped to the ground in daylight, under fire and onto unwelcoming terrain. They had planned to land on level ground with low undergrowth. Instead they hurtled through heavy tree branches and set foot on steeply sloping terrain that set them rolling downhill. A stone wall separated them from the mansion, about 25 yards uphill. The assault team leader, Lt. Wellington T. "Duke" Leonard, landed without either his boss, Capt. Gormly, or his satellite radio. Both had unexpectedly flown off on the other helicopter. The mission was now in the hands of Leonard and his 21 men.[1]

Scoon, his wife, and his staff fled to the mansion's cellar when the shooting started outside. Scoon heard shouts from above: "Is anyone there? Mr. Scoon? Mr. Scoon?"[2] The governor general ordered his staff to show themselves to the searchers. His wife wasn't sure that was a good idea. "Suppose they are Russians?" she asked, reflecting a fear on the island that the Soviet Union and/or Cuba might militarily intervene in the crisis before the United States. Scoon's assured his spouse that the voices he heard were American. Besides, Scoon had been expecting the arrival of U.S. troops on the island since the previous morning.[3] His driver opened the basement door and was greeted by a SEAL with a pointed gun. Leonard's men carried pouches around their neck with photographs of Scoon and his staff so they could separate friend from foe when they arrived at the residence. The SEALs cautiously confirmed the identities of Scoon and his party of 10. The displaced front gate guard balked at surrendering his AK-47, but he was persuaded by a more-senior policeman in the party. "Don't be stupid boy; give the people the gun," the older man advised.[4]

With Scoon's entourage in hand, the SEALs proceeded to clear the rooms of the mansion of any hidden threat. The Grenadians who had been firing at them on arrival had retreated. The SEALs had planned a helicopter extraction of Scoon's party within 45 minutes of their arrival. But that early exit was now in doubt given the enemy resistance they encountered. The SEALs took up defensive positions in and around the mansion and waited for a Plan B option to develop. Small arms fire directed at the house started to pick up. Several rifle-fired grenades skittered harmlessly across the tile roof. A better-aimed round exploded in one of the vacant sitting rooms. The SEALs moved the civilian party into the upstairs dining room where they were better shielded from the Grenadian military forces that surrounded them. Scoon's residence was barely guarded, but Grenadian anti-aircraft guns and mobile infantry were strategically positioned to defend all the official residences in the hilltop neighborhood, known as Mount Wheldale. Bishop's now-vacant home was located here and had a permanent guard garrison assigned to it. The house nearest to Bishop was occupied by Coard, his erstwhile friend and deputy prime minister, who was the coup mastermind.

The SEALs with Scoon watched warily from a distance as three unidentified armed men, two in uniform, approached the mansion along its U-shaped driveway.[5] The SEALs yelled a challenge; the trio raised the AK-47s they were carrying. That action brought an immediate response from two machines guns and three automatic rifles manned by the concealed SEALs. The results were unclear to the SEALs, but at least one of the three was cut in half by the bullets.[6]

While the standoff at the mansion was evolving into a bloody siege, Gormly, the nominative on-mansion SEAL commander, was trying to make his way back to the scene after being whisked away on a stricken Black Hawk. On the *Guam*, Gormly unsuccessfully sought to persuade the Army pilot of another, still-flyable, Black Hawk to ferry him back to Government House.[7] After being rebuffed, Gormly instead flew to Point Salines, where the JSOC forces set up a command post in an airport terminal building. From there, Gormly established sporadic radio contact with the embattled SEALs at Government House. They mostly communicated using a MX-360 hand-held tactical radio with limited range and battery life.[8]

At one point in the morning, after the driveway shooting, the island's police chief called Scoon by telephone to inquire about his well-being—and also about Scoon's surprise visitors. The inquisitive police chief asked how many Americans were with him, and how they were armed. Scoon coyly responded that he had never seen so many guns in his life.[9] Undeterred by this disinformation, the Grenadian military command at Fort Frederick ordered a pincer attack on the mansion. At around 1000, PRA infantry approached on foot from the northwest through a wooded area. Simultaneously, an armored personnel carrier advanced on the mansion by road from the southeast.[10] The SEALs with the governor general had no heavy weapons to counter the armored vehicle. They needed air support, but Leonard's Navy-issue radio could not communicate directly with the Air Force gunships. Instead, Leonard used his limited-range radio to contact Gormly at the JSOC command post at Point Salines. Gormly's radioman then passed the message to an Army Delta Force radioman sitting nearby. That radio operator communicated with the gunships using a Vietnam-era backup radio that the Army and Air Force had, but the SEALs didn't.[11]

Fortunately, an Air Force gunship was in the area to hear the call. Earlier, at about 0945, Couvillon's Spectre was sent north from Point Salines to support the uncompleted special operations missions in the capital city.[12] His first assignment was to attack Fort Rupert, the cancelled Delta/Task Force 160 D-Day mission. The fort was clearly marked on Couvillon's map, but he now found it to be deserted and undefended. Couvillon fired about 25 sensor-aimed 105 mm rounds into the two-building police headquarters within the fort, knocking it out of commission without any collateral damage. Couvillon was then directed to find the Richmond Hill Prison, but the forward air controller who was directing him had no coordinates for the prison. The detention facility was also not shown on the British-made tourist map that Couvillon had been issued. He searched fruitlessly for the prison for more than 15 minutes before he was ordered to break off to answer an urgent call for help from the SEALs with Scoon at Government House.

The Spectre arrived over the nearby mansion at about 1015 to find the SEALs threatened by Grenadian soldiers who were infiltrating from the north and west. Couvillon beat them back with his 20 mm and 40 mm cannons. Another Spectre piloted by Lt. Col. David K. Sims soon joined the fray. Together the two gunships squelched the pincer assault. At about 1100, Couvillon flew off to Puerto Rico to refuel while Sims circled protectively over the mansion. (Fortuitously, Sims flew in the replacement Spectre that was last to arrive over the island because Sim's first aircraft developed an engine fire.) Sims was still overhead in the mid-afternoon when two other Grenadian APCs approached the mansion from the southeast along the road from Fort Frederick. Sims' AC-130 disabled one armored vehicle and forced the other to withdraw.[13] During the battle with the APCs, Leonard used Scoon's telephone to contact Fort Bragg for help.[14] Sims later told an interviewer that the JSOC command at Point Salines thought they were controlling his fire by radio relay, but he was actually coordinating directly with the surrounded SEALs by phone via Fort Bragg—using a calling card.[15] (This is just one of several credible Urgent Fury accounts of uniformed combatants using civilian phone lines to get around military radio communication limitations.)

As the fight for the mansion continued on and off through the day, Scoon and his party lay sprawled on the hardwood floor of the mansion. During lulls in the firing, Scoon and his wife occasionally rested on a mahogany couch under oil portraits of implacable British royals and daguerreotypes of Queen Victoria.[16] Most of the SEALs remained outside the mansion maintaining a defensive perimeter around the mansion about 25 yards away, spaced 10 to 20 yards apart.[17] They were lightly armed with shoulder weapons and pistols. Their principal defense again counterattack was the AC-130 circling overheard. During the first day of the invasion, six different gunships spent an hour or more circling overhead the mansion until they broke off to refuel or for another urgent fire mission.[18]

Gormly, the SEAL commander, and his JSOC boss, Scholtes, appealed to the invasion commander for ground troops to relieve the besieged mansion. Metcalf was not happy to be asked. His pre-invasion briefing did not include any detailed information about the special operations missions. Those missions were supposed to be over before the regular forces arrived. "The rescue of the governor general had not been included in any of my earlier instructions," Metcalf later wrote in a military textbook. "But it soon became apparent, through talks with my State Department representatives, that his rescue was of paramount importance. In a political sense, the success of the entire operation hung on the rescue of the governor general."[19] Metcalf was irked by the autonomy of the special units. "In many ways, they were the problem," Metcalf said in a post-invasion interview. "They weren't the solution to anything. These special operations are independent. They go in and do things in their own way. Then mainline forces are asked to bail them out. That's what happened."[20] Metcalf was asked to attack Fort Frederick, the Grenadian military headquarters which had repulsed the attack on the prison and was now directing the counterattacks on the SEALs with Scoon. The fort was a colonial-era fortification located 750 feet atop Richmond Hill, about a mile east of the capital. Started by the French and finished by the British, it was seeing action for the first time in its two centuries. It was defended by two ZU-23 anti-aircraft guns in addition to the small arms carried by the fort's garrison of Grenadian soldiers. Other supporting ZU-23s occupied key positions elsewhere in the capital city within line-of-sight of the hilltop fort.

Because of the fort's proximity to civilian structures, Metcalf was reluctant to order bombardment by Navy ships or jets. He had been given "rules of engagement" for the operation from the Pentagon that specified that he cause "minimum damage and casualties." Metcalf interpreted that to mean "do not use one more bullet, bomb or whatever than is necessary to accomplish the mission."[21] Metcalf later complained in an oral history interview that the rules he had been issued were "very, very difficult to execute" in combat conditions where American lives are also at stake. "You take an armed force in there and you're not supposed to hurt anybody? This is absolutely against the principles in which you are trained, particularly in those days; we were trained to beat things up," he said.[22] Metcalf felt compelled to opt for the more precisely aimed firepower offered by Marine attack helicopters. But there was a tradeoff. Assaulting a fortress defended by AAA guns was a high-risk assignment for a helicopter as lightly armored as a Cobra. Two AH-1Ts, each flown by a Marine pilot and a co-pilot/gunner, were routed from Point Salines toward the capital. One Cobra was commanded by Capt. John P. "Pat" Giguere and the other by Capt. Timothy B. Howard. Arriving over St. George's after 1300, they made radio contact with an unseen Air Force aircraft, probably an EC-130E ABCCC command aircraft. The fixed-wing aircraft directed them to attack Fort Frederick, but Howard heard no mention of the anti-aircraft guns that guarded the fort.[23]

The two Cobras attacked the fort in tandem, one making a pass at the target while the other sought to distract any defenders.[24] On his first pass, Giguere fired a marking rocket that left a cloud of white smoke when it hit the green roof of the fort. His copilot/gunner, Lt. Jeffrey R. Scharver, pummeled the fort with 2.75-inch rockets launched from the Cobra's stubby wings and 20 mm rounds from the three-barrel Gatling gun cannon located under the nose. Howard's copter hurled a TOW missile at the fort. These anti-tank missiles are guided in flight from the cockpit by a wire that is spooled out the back of the missile. The wire guidance system made it an extremely accurate weapon, but it required the attacking helicopter to hold position until the missile hit. On the fifth attack run, at 1327, their luck ran out.[25] As a second TOW missile was in the air, Howard's helicopter was hit by three anti-aircraft rounds. The first went through both twin turbine engines crippling the Cobra's ability to fly. The second round exploded in the cockpit, wounding both pilots. Howard's right forearm was nearly severed. The third mangled Howard's right leg. "Take the airplane! Take the airplane!" Howard shouted at Capt. Jeb F. Seagle, his copilot. Seagle did not respond. He was knocked unconscious by the explosions; his head bobbed like a rag doll. Writhing in pain, Howard struggled to make an emergency landing in a nearby sports field without use of his right arm or leg. They were relatively low, about 1,200 feet. He couldn't use his control pedals so he set his joystick, known as a cyclic, so the copter would fly relatively level. He propped his good leg against the cyclic. Then he pulled up on the collective rotor control with his left hand to crash-land the copter. The five-ton Cobra hit so hard that the canopy-removal mechanisms activated, blowing out all the windows. The tail rotor broke off. The copter bounced, but it did not topple. It started to burn.

On landing, Seagle regained consciousness and jumped to the ground. He shouted for Howard to follow. Howard unstrapped himself from his harness and tumbled from the cockpit to the ground. He was unable to walk. His femur was sticking out of a gaping wound in his right leg. Seagle grabbed Howard by the collar and dragged him to some tall grass about 40 yards from the burning aircraft. AK-47 bullets kicked up dirt around them. The two argued over what to do next. Howard urged Seagle to leave him. Seagle refused to go. Howard threatened to shoot himself if Seagle didn't leave. The copilot relented. Seagle bound Howard's mangled arm with a radio cord he ripped off his helmet.

"I'm going for help. I'll be right back," Seagle said. Howard gave Seagle his .38-caliber pistol and the copilot ran in the direction of St. George's horseshoe-shaped commercial harbor.

Shortly after Seagle left, the burning Cobra exploded. The flames ignited unexpended 2.75-inch rockets, launching them in random directions and temporarily dissuading further enemy approach to the crash site. Howard broke out his emergency radio and called for help. Giguere's copter roared overhead, firing its cannon to beat back soldiers advancing on Howard's position. Giguere urgently called for a medevac helicopter to rescue the two downed flyers from imminent danger. (There was no room for them in the two-seat Cobra.) The call for help was heard by a Marine CH-46E transport helicopter flown by Maj. Melvin DeMars and 1st Lt. Lawrence M. King. They responded immediately, but it took them 15 minutes to arrive at the crash scene. Prudence dictated that they fly over water around the southern perimeter of the island rather than take a more direct route over land.[26]

As he lay wounded, Howard remembers thinking that, if he had to die, this wasn't such a bad place to do it. The sky was clear and blue; the temperature about 75 degrees. He looked toward the city and saw residents of St. George's on their balconies, watching him bleed to death. From time to time, he heard bullets thump into the bloodstained dirt near his body. The advancing troops got close enough for Howard to hear them taunting that they were coming to kill him. Howard raised a finger in silent, defiant retort. Each time it seemed Howard was about to be captured or killed, his attackers were beaten back by strafing runs made by the second Cobra.

DeMars and King in the rescue helicopter rendezvoused offshore with the Cobra flown by Scharver and Giguere. Giguere briefed them by radio about what to expect. He warned that the mouth of the St. George's harbor was guarded at both the north and south by anti-aircraft gun positions. The gun to the north at Fort Rupert had been silenced by air strikes earlier in the day. But the one to the south, which had not been mentioned in the pre-invasion briefing, was still shooting. This gun emplacement defended a building known as Butler House, which housed Grenadian governmental offices. It could have been fire from this gun that blindsided Howard's helicopter as he attacked Fort Frederick. Based on this information, the pilots improvised a high-risk extraction plan. Giguere's Cobra gunship would provide covering fire while DeMars' transport dashed in for the rescue. The CH-46 would have to fly into the heart of Grenada's principal harbor without advance reconnaissance. It would then land and present itself as a stationary target for as long as it took to retrieve the downed pilots. "We just took a long big breath and said: 'Well, we've got to go in there.' And that is what we did," DeMars later recounted. "I just figured we were all dead men." To minimize exposure to enemy fire, the rescue helicopter entered the mouth of the harbor from the north, flying about 10 feet above the water. A column of black smoke clearly marked the Cobra crash site to the east. As they flew in, Giguere's Cobra covered them by making a strafing run at Butler House, attacking the anti-aircraft position with rockets and cannon fire.

DeMars remembers pulling back on the cyclic so his aircraft could climb over the bow of a Greek freighter tied up at a pier. The CH-46 landed on the Tanteen, a sports field about 30 meters from the spot where Howard lay. Howard waved his uninjured hand in the air so that his rescuers could spot him in the foot-high grass. "Do you see anybody? Do you see anybody?" King, the co-pilot, urgently inquired of the helicopter crew. "Yes, I got one pilot out here," responded the helicopter's crew chief, Gunnery Sgt.

Kelly M. Neidigh, looking out the cargo door. "I am going to get him," Neidigh said. He grabbed his M-16 rifle and jumped out.

Neidigh dragged Howard back to the helicopter and then pulled him into the cargo bay with the help of Cpl. Simon D. Gore, Jr., the crew chief. Howard was bleeding from the neck, his hand was hanging on by a thread. Four inches of the bone was sticking from his leg. "Get out of the zone, it's too hot. Get out!" Giguere urged over the radio from the covering Cobra. King, the CH-46 copilot, could see enemy soldiers running from building to building all around him and he could hear the pop of small-arms fire. He thought of the white reflective tape on his helmet. "I felt like a bull's eye," King recalled. "Do you see the other pilot?" DeMars asked his crew. No one did. Giguere radioed that his Cobra would engage the anti-aircraft gun at Butler House to cover the medevac heli-copter's exit from the harbor area. King, however, saw no fire coming from the Cobra when it made its run. Giguere and Scharver had apparently run out of ammunition. They were covering the escape of the medevac helicopter with sheer bluff and bravado. Then, at 1340,[27] just as the Cobra turned to follow the CH-46 out of the harbor, the attack hel-icopter was raked by fire.

Both Giguere and Scharver were mortally wounded. Their aircraft corkscrewed out of control and plunged into the ocean just outside the harbor. The medevac helicopter did not see their protectors get hit, but they heard about it almost immediately. "Another Cobra's been shot down," an Army unit reported on an emergency radio frequency. DeMars doubled back. A disturbance in the water briefly marked the spot where the Cobra had crashed and sunk. DeMars circled briefly, but no survivors surfaced. "We better get this pilot back, I don't think he is going to make it," Neidigh radioed to DeMars. DeMars set a course to the *Guam* where Howard underwent emergency surgery that saved his life.

According to civilian eyewitnesses, Howard's copilot, Seagle was killed on the ground before the rescue helicopter arrived. Sailors on the Greek ship in the harbor later told a *Time* correspondent that they saw the pilot wave his hat, a gesture they interpreted as a signal to surrender. Unheeding, the Grenadian attackers continued firing until the flyer fell to his knees. Seagle's body was eventually taken to a civilian funeral parlor by Grena-dian soldiers, but the funeral director turned them away. The soldiers returned Seagle's body to a beach near the crash site where it as later recovered by American forces.[28] (Army lawyers later investigated reports that a Grenadian had fired a full AK-47 magazine into the body, but they concluded this did not constitute murder because Seagle was already dead.)[29] Seagle was posthumously awarded the Navy Cross, the Marine Corps' second highest award for valor, for his courage in rescuing Howard from the crashed helicopter, tending his wounds and then drawing away their pursuers.[30] Howard, DeMars, Neidigh, Scharver and Giguere were each awarded the Silver Star, the latter two posthu-mously. King, the co-pilot of the rescue helicopter, received the Distinguished Flying Cross.

The failure of the Cobra mission to subdue Fort Frederick was a bitter pill for Metcalf aboard the *Guam*. Two helicopters shot down was a high price for an attack that yielded no evident military benefit. Metcalf reconsidered using Navy jets to bomb Fort Frederick into submission. The admiral turned to Schwarzkopf, his Army liaison, to seek his opin-ion. "Bomb it," Schwarzkopf replied, pleased to be consulted. "If we let them keep up an organized resistance, we'll take a lot more casualties and eventually have to bomb it any-how."[31] Metcalf ordered a full-scale attack by A-7E Corsairs from the *Independence* on all St. George's fortified positions. The attacks at 1345[32] succeeded, but not without the civilian casualties that Metcalf feared.

Unbeknownst to the attackers, another colonial fort adjacent to Fort Frederick was being used as a civilian mental hospital. The building was shown on maps as Fort Matthew, but locals knew it as the General Mental Home or "Crazy House." There was no red cross on the roof. The exterior walls of the building were marked with a large red dot on a white background, the flag of the Grenadian revolutionary government and the military.[33] American investigators later learned that on D-Day weapons were fired from inside the hospital and from two anti-aircraft guns positioned 50 yards away. The three-story medical building was hit with a 500-pound bomb from a Navy Corsair. Twenty-one patients

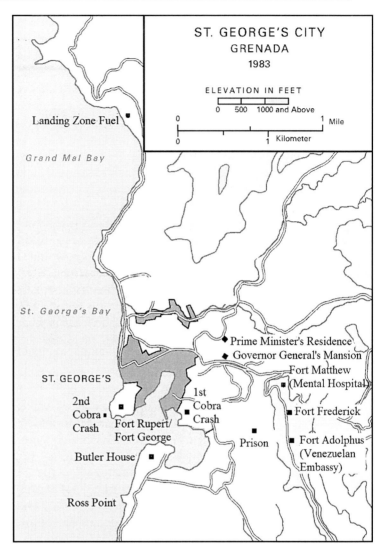

This map of the Grenadian capital and nearby shows key D-Day combat locations (adapted from base map, courtesy U.S. Army Center of Military History).

were killed.[34] Other uninjured patients were set loose to wander the streets of the capital. Aboard the *Guam*, the unintended effects of the bombing were not known until days later. The only immediately apparent result of the air strike in the flag plot of the *Guam* was a cessation of radio traffic coming from the command center in Fort Frederick.[35] "In hindsight the battle was won right there," Metcalf later recalled.[36] "From that time on, everything was local action." Metcalf personally learned that the hospital had been hit when he visited the island two days later on Oct. 27, but the mistaken attack was not publicly confirmed by Washington until Oct. 31.

The unexpectedly stout resistance at St. George's, combined with the disconcerting news of a second medical school campus, promoted another tactical conversation between Metcalf and Schwarzkopf on the *Guam* at around noon of D-Day. Metcalf asked for

Schwarzkopf's advice on how to further relieve the pressure on the SEALs with Scoon. "One of the things we learned in World War II was, if you want to give the enemy a problem, fight on two fronts," the general said to the admiral.[37] The two discussed using the uncommitted Marine company to stage an amphibious landing on the western side of the island. It was a bold idea, but a risky one.[38] The plan involved sending the invasion's only reserve force to an unsurveyed beach against an unknown enemy force. Metcalf's warrior instincts told him that Cubans and the Grenadians had likely deployed the bulk of their forces to the south of St. George's, leaving the north exposed to the "classic envelopment maneuver" that Schwarzkopf advocated.

Metcalf sent the MAU's SEAL team to reconnoiter a landing at Grand Mal Bay on the northwestern coast. Butler, the amateur yachtsman, remembered a beach just to the north of St. George's.[39] The SEALs confirmed the suitability of the unfortified leeward beach in a high-speed pass from their 36-foot Seafox.[40] H-Hour was set for 1630. The hastily drawn plan called for a landing of two Marine companies by sea and air. Golf Company of the 22nd MAU aboard the *Manitowoc* would attack the narrow beach from 13 amphibious landing tractors. Tanks and jeeps onboard the *Fort Snelling* would also be put ashore once the landing beach was secure. Later, Fox Company, already ashore near Pearls, would be ferried across the island by Marine helicopters to supplement the amphibious force. The goal was for the two tank-supported infantry companies to move on the capital to relieve the SEALs at Scoon's mansion.

The new plan hatched on the *Guam* was being developed without the participation of Smith, the Marine battalion commander. While Metcalf's command staff were conversing, Smith was onshore directing the operation of his troops on the eastern side of the island. The *Guam*, then in transit to the western shore, was at the extreme limit of radio range with Marine troops ashore. It wasn't until 1400 that the news of the change in plan was relayed to Smith by his reconnaissance platoon commander from the uppermost deck of the *Fort Snelling* using a hand-held radio.[41] Smith boarded a helicopter and headed to the *Guam*, arriving only 45 minutes before the appointed H-Hour. He pleaded for a postponement so he could coordinate the arrival of the Marines coming by helicopter with those in the landing craft. Just as the *Manitowoc* lowered its ramps to launch its amphibious vehicles, a two-hour delay was granted until 1830.

Aboard the *Guam*, Smith caught a whiff of panic in the flag plot. Intelligence officers were predicting that a counterattack by tanks and armored vehicles at Pearls Airport was imminent. Cobras were dispatched to counter the reported enemy threat. Smith was disbelieving. He knew most roads on the island wouldn't support the weight of tanks. "I got the distinct impression the intel types, having underestimated enemy strength in the south, are now being sure they give full warning of any possibility of threat in the north," Smith wrote in his journal.[42] The Cobras found nothing at Pearls. But there were other threats under active discussion on the *Guam* that Smith had no basis to doubt. "It seems the SEALs have an important person with them, no one is sure who. Reports are there are 13 SEALs, eight of whom are wounded," Smith wrote in his journal.

Communications aboard the *Guam* were chaotic. Both the Army and Marine units on the ground carried the same backpack field radios, but they were used with different voice encryption devices and so they couldn't talk securely to each other. The main means of command communication among the disparate forces on the island was a satellite radio, a Motorola URC-101. This UHF/VHF radio provided Command Net A, a secure, one-channel "party line" that all the services could use to communicate with all others.[43]

Like a CB radio, anyone with a transmission/receiver could jump on at any time for any reason. The radio on the *Guam* was not part of the standard communication gear on the ship. It had been brought aboard by two Atlantic Command liaison officers who had arrived by helicopter from Antigua with the invasion instructions.[44] The URC-101 was set up in the radar room on an upper deck of the *Guam*'s "island" superstructure. If an officer in the flag plot wanted to communicate with someone, he had to go up two levels to make the call.[45] "We only had one single channel to talk … if it was operations, if it was intel, if it was administrative, if it was logistics, if it was sheer bullshit, it all went on the same line," Schwarzkopf later recalled. "General Trobaugh and I could be talking about something very critical and all of a sudden we get just blown off the air by some guy who wants to send social security numbers." Worse, the radio contact was broken every time the ship turned.[46] Turning happened frequently because the *Guam* needed to orient itself to the prevailing wind whenever it was launching or recovering helicopters. Rudder changes caused the Motorola to lose its orientation with the relay satellite until the antenna could be manually reset by someone onboard the ship. Whenever Metcalf spoke to his Pentagon superiors, the ship needed to hold a straight course until the call was concluded. Otherwise, the *Guam* sailed on a perpetual race track pattern. Schwarzkopf observed that the radio appeared to be mysteriously linked to the ship's rudder. Every time he keyed the microphone to talk, the ship would turn and the signal would fade.

The *Guam*, however, did have hit-or-miss, secure communication with the Marine units on shore. The range of their AN/PRC-77 line-of-sight tactical radios was only about 15 miles at best and the island's mountainous terrain limited it further. Nonetheless, this radio link advantaged the Marines by reinforcing the impression on the *Guam*, and ultimately back at the Pentagon, that the Marines were doing more than their share of the fighting. "We were getting pretty detailed … on the spot reports from the Marines every time they would do something, and the only time we were getting anything from the 82nd was when we reestablished commo with each other," Schwarzkopf recalled.[47] But there was also an unanticipated benefit for all associated with the shared satellite channel. Every ship and unit equipped with a satellite radio could eavesdrop on the conversations of the top commanders. "So, all in all, despite its traditional disadvantages, for us the 'party line' worked out very well. Everyone involved in the mission decision-making knew the intended plans and the pressures on the local command," Metcalf later recalled."[48]

Smith decided to return to the east side of the island to get Fox Company at Pearls ready for the helicopter movement to Grand Mal Bay. Due to an air traffic control mix-up, he was flown to Point Salines, where the Army was, rather than Pearls. He finally made it to Pearls just 20 minutes before the pushed-back H-Hour. Putting his frustration aside, Smith collected his staff and then tried to fly out to join Golf Company on the *Manitowoc*. The moonless evening was pitch dark; the pilot was unable to navigate to the ship or make radio contact. The helicopter ran low on fuel and wound up landing instead on the *Trenton*, which was positioned on the wrong side of the islamd. From there Smith took another helicopter back to the *Guam* at 2330, his starting point six hours earlier. "I was so frustrated and so pissed off that I could hardly see," Smith later told a Marine historian.[49]

While Smith and his staff were still enduring this exasperating flight to nowhere, Golf Company and five tanks were coming ashore at Grand Mal at 1900, a half an hour

U.S. military personnel set up an AN/PRC-77 field radio in a terminal building at Point Salines during the hostilities. This line-of-sight tactical radio had limited range. Its effectiveness was further degraded by the island's mountainous terrain (National Archives [330-CFD-DF-ST-84-09896]).

late.[50] By then the sun had set and the darkness shrouded the shore. Electricity was out on the island and the moon would not rise until after midnight. Fortunately for the Marines, the landing was initially unopposed. As Metcalf had guessed, all available Grenadian troops had been deployed for counterattacks elsewhere. Capt. Robert K. Dobson, Jr., the Golf Company commander, landed with orders to secure the beach, consolidate his position and await further instruction. He had no communications with higher headquarters or the Navy ships offshore and no guide to lead him inland.[51]

Like the air landing at Point Salines, this sea landing could have easily turned into a bloodbath. The narrow, crescent-shaped beach was code-named LZ Fuel because a Shell fuel tank farm marked the exit from the beach at one end. After the Marines landed, Grenadian troops began firing illuminating mortar rounds at the beach to search out the Marine positions. The fuel tanks had exposed piping that could have produced an inferno on the beach if one of the rounds hit. A Marine historian later took pointed, if understated, note of their vulnerable position: "There were now several hundred Marines crowded onto the tiny beachhead, 750 by 100 meters, with limited exit routes and highly flammable fuel tanks close at hand."[52] Dobson ordered two of his platoons to push inland to a coastal road. One platoon took up a blocking position just to the north of the beachhead and another an equal distance to the south.[53] These movements allowed him to clear a helicopter landing area that was marked off by red lights and a pulsating strobe light.

At around the same time the Marines were landing at Grand Mal, the embattled SEALs with Scoon came yet under another armored personnel carrier attack. Butler heard radio calls on the *Guam* at around 2000 that "made it appear that they were in the last few minutes of the Alamo."[54] Naval gunfire was considered to support the SEALs, but someone made a computation error. Illumination rounds fired from the *Caron* exploded far off target. Metcalf's faith in Navy guns as a solution was shaken. At around 2215 an AC-130 piloted by Maj. Larry Strelau was directed to attack a group of 15 to 20 Grenadian soldiers who were massing to assault the governor's mansion.[55] The attack was beaten back and the gunship remained overhead until 0400, protecting the SEALs. Still, the worry on the *Guam* was that the Marines sent to rescue them might arrive too late. At the mansion, Lady Scoon broke down and began to cry. Then around midnight, the phone rang. The Most Rev. Sydney Charles, the Roman Catholic bishop on the island, called Scoon to offer his prayers and support.[56] The couple's courage was restored.

Smith finally arrived at Grand Mal Bay sometime around 0100–0200. His transport helicopter landed at LZ Fuel, but the only available open spot on the crowded beach was at the water's edge. The copter landed with its back wheels in the water. Smith and his staff had to wade ashore. "That was a first for all of us—a heliborne ship-to-shore movement where you still had to wade through the surf," Smith later observed.[57]

Smith's arrival came at the beginning of a new calendar day that occasioned a grim reckoning on the *Guam* of the results of the first 24 hours of combat on Grenada. "What was supposed to be a highly unconventional situation that was going to be cleaned up in one day, turned into a very conventional ground operation," Schwarzkopf later recalled.[58] The bold *coup de main* plan had been a failure in its execution. The uncoordinated initial blows did not fully subdue either the Cubans or the Grenadians. None of the three first-day special operations objectives had been accomplished by Atlantic Command's later estimation.[59] The radio station at Beausejour had been briefly taken, but not held. The hoped-for "lay down your arms" broadcast by Scoon was not made. The governor general had been reached by the SEALs, but his safety was more in doubt than before they arrived, even after the loss of two Marine Cobras and three pilots. The attack on the prison had been repulsed with one pilot killed, and dozens of Delta commandoes wounded. The surviving Task Force 160 Black Hawks were effectively out of action. One Black Hawk was totally destroyed, another wrecked on the deck of the *Guam* and five more significantly damaged by Grenadian gunfire. Only a third of the American medical students had been reached by American forces. The *Guam*'s limited medical facilities were overwhelmed by the near simultaneous arrival of 36 first-morning casualties.[60]

On the plus side, both airports were now in American hands and a second front had been opened just north of the capital city. The military situation brightened further before dawn on Oct. 26, the second day of fighting. During the night, Golf Company and the command element at Grand Mal was joined by Fox Company arriving by helicopter from Pearls via Point Salines. There was only room on the beach for one helicopter to land at a time so it took about two hours for the entire company to land. From Grand Mal the two companies pushed south to the capital through the jet-black night on a narrow road that was barely wide enough for two cars. Smith proceeded cautiously, based on mistaken intelligence that he was opposed by two battalions of Grenadian and/or Cuban troops.[61] In the event, the Grenadian troops in the area were ineffectual and the Cuban force was entirely fictional. Smith's two companies encountered scant resistance as they pressed on toward the capital and the beleaguered SEALs. Smith later learned that the advancing Marines actually passed through a hidden force of Grenadian soldiers who were so frightened by the Marines' tanks that they let them travel through their lines essentially unopposed. The Marine column consisted of 5 tanks and 13 amtracs, but the noise that these machines made carried through the night. The 18 tracked vehicles sounded like an armored battalion to the ears of their enemy.

The column arrived at the Queen's Park Racetrack on the northern fringe of the capital city at around 0430.[62] The absence of resistance and the arriving daylight emboldened Smith to advance quickly to the Governor General's mansion. Golf Company moved as near as they could in their heavy vehicles before dismounting. They then followed a steep, stepped path up Mount Wheldale. At the summit, Dobson's men made contact with members of the SEAL team who led them to the mansion. Dobson took two squads of Marines with him to the Government House while other Marines were sent to Bishop's nearby home, which had been used as a staging area for the assault on Scoon's mansion. The Grenadian attackers had fled during the night, leaving behind three trucks full of arms and equipment.

The vanguard of the Golf Company arrived at Scoon's residence on Wednesday, Oct. 26, at dawn. The compound was cleared and secured by 0710 without incident. The new arrivals linked up with the 22-man SEAL team and a Scoon party totaling 11 civilians. The Marines were surprised to learn that none of the SEALs were wounded seriously enough to require immediate medical evacuation. However, one stoic SEAL suffered a deep gash in his elbow on landing that was later found to have been caused by a 23 mm cannon shell fragment.[63] Scoon and his wife packed a small bag with personal items. Lady Scoon broke apart a bracelet to pass out charms to her SEAL protectors as souvenirs.[64] The SEALs also carried out a Grenadian flag they found flying from a flagpole. The rescuers and the rescued traveled in a group on foot back to Queen's Park. They arrived at around 0900 to find an American military helicopter waiting. The governor general and wife were flown to the *Guam* for a quick shower, a change of clothes and a hearty breakfast. The couple had late morning tea with Metcalf on the *Guam* and stayed until the afternoon. At that point, Scoon informed his hosts that he felt his proper place was back on the island with his countrymen.[65]

The couple traveled by helicopter to Point Salines where they made their way to the Great House, a colonial-era residence being used as an impromptu headquarters by the Caribbean forces. Lewis, the Barbados Defence Force general commanding the multinational force, presented Scoon with a batch of four draft letters back-dated to Oct. 24.[66] The identically worded letters were individually addressed to Reagan and the heads of Barbados, Jamaica and Dominica requesting their intervention.[67] Scoon made one unspecified "alteration" and then signed the letters. (Rossin, the safari-suited State Department officer, was also present at this scene, but it's unclear from his oral history account if he arrived before or after the letter to Reagan was signed.[68]) Scoon wrote in his memoir that he was then asked by "an American functionary" (apparently not Rossin) to authorize a prepared press release. He refused. "Perhaps he [the functionary] thought that in the current circumstances, he and others like him could get me to do whatever they required of me," Scoon sniffed in his memoir. "Quite mistakenly the gentleman did not realize that Caribbean public figures were less gullible and more alert and self-confident than hitherto [assumed]."[69] Scoon and his staff next took up temporary residence in the borrowed home of a friend.

Rossin offered Scoon a list of names of Grenadians the CIA thought would be suitable for Scoon to appoint to an interim government. He also urged Scoon to make a public broadcast that the United States could use to dampen the mounting international indignation over the American violation of Grenadian sovereignty. Scoon put the offered list aside without comment, careful not to display any message of endorsement. He also rebuffed an immediate broadcast to his nation. Instead, Scoon sought political advice from Dr. Vaughan Lewis, the director general of the OECS—and Buckingham Palace.[70] Scoon was determined to chart his own political course, guided by the queen, the Grenadian constitution, the British Commonwealth tradition, the Eastern Caribbean community, and his personal knowledge of the island's political players.

"The Governor General must be impartial and he is expected to be above politics," Scoon declared in his autobiography. "For the next few months I would have to explain all this to foreign media people who never understood the Commonwealth concept, and they usually started by posing the question: 'How long have you been in politics?' They seem amazed when I replied that I was never in politics."[71] In fact, Scoon showed himself to be a master politician through the entire crisis. He deftly dealt with nearly all the major players in the crisis, except for the Cubans who shunned him.[72] By signing the letter of intervention and assuming the reins of government in Grenada, Scoon effectively culminated a military counter-coup. With his signature, he asserted that a "vacuum of authority" existed on Grenada that allowed him to take executive action on behalf of his nation. He brushed aside the ruling authority of both the Bishop regime and the short-lived military council. He also undid the suspension of the Grenada constitution that he had once accepted. He unilaterally reasserted the Westminster-style form of government that existed back in 1979, at least on paper, when Gairy was deposed.

While Scoon was conducting a regime change with the power of his pen at Point Salines, U.S. Marines to the north were completing the subjugation of the military council by force. After freeing Scoon and seeing him safely off to the *Guam* by helicopter, Golf Company was ordered to move south toward Fort Frederick, the Grenadian military command center that had caused so many casualties in the early hours of D-Day. Although it wasn't immediately apparent to the Marines on the ground, Grenadian resistance crumbled quickly once daylight arrived and American tanks rolled through the streets of the capital. During the night, Grenada's military leaders furtively changed into civilian clothes and slipped away from the fort to hide within the general population. "If I had known then what I know now, I would have landed five tanks off Point Salines, and that would have done it," Metcalf later said. "They had nothing set up to deal with that, and people are afraid of tanks."[73]

At around noon, Golf Company set off on the winding road leading from Mount Wheldale to Fort Frederick.[74] Along the way the Marines encountered two abandoned armored cars which gave mute testimony to the PRA's unannounced surrender. The first vehicle was neutered by a platoon leader who tossed a hand grenade inside. The second vehicle was about 100 yards farther on. The engines were still running and the hatch was open. This time the platoon leader just turned the ignition off and shouted: "All clear!" When the colonial-era fort eventually came into view, Dobson, the company commander, watched as eight or 10 men dropped themselves off the fort's back walls.[75] The fleeing enemy emboldened him to advance his men to the fort without calling for suppressing fire. "Let's go in," he shouted and his men double-timed it to the fort's wooden door.

Golf Company entered the bastion unopposed at around 1700 on Oct. 26. Inside they found a deserted underground command post and cantonment. The Marines were later told by a captured PRA staff officer that least 16 Cuban advisers were present at Fort Frederick up until the morning of Oct. 26.[76] Cuban military advisors were attached to all the Grenadian military commands, but they had been directed by Havana to withdraw to their compounds after Bishop's assassination and relations chilled with the Coard faction. Cuban presence at the Grenadian battle headquarters on D-Day would have been in direct violation of Castro's orders. Cuban involvement in a coordinated defense of the island with Grenadian forces could not be confirmed a year later in an all-sources intelligence assessment led by the CIA.[77]

Although there were no Cubans present when Marines arrived, the Americans discovered abundant evidence of Soviet Bloc influence on the island. The Marines captured a large store of weapons and ammunition in the fort and nearby, including three trucks full of anti-aircraft ammunition, two trucks with three brand-new, Soviet-made 82 mm mortars and ammunition and many assault rifles and machine guns.[78] One Marine corporal also found a leather briefcase with a passport belonging to Austin, the PRA's commanding general. The briefcase also contained official papers including recently signed arms agreement involving Grenada, the Soviet Union and Cuba. These documents were proof of Bishop's secret military relationship with the Soviet-Bloc. The briefcase was immediately flown out to the *Guam*, along with captured military maps.

In the flag plot, the maps were of more immediate interest than the arms agreement. One map showed all the Grenadian military positions on the island. Schwarzkopf used that information to plan out the remainder of the ground campaign. He resolved that hostilities could not be declared over until every military location on the map had been reached and neutralized.[79] As a career military officer, Schwarzkopf considered himself neither a hawk or a dove, but an owl.[80] He was wise enough to do everything possible to avoid war, but once committed, ferocious enough to do everything necessary to achieve victory. The one-day unconventional *coup de main* that had been planned was now being fought as a conventional war that took seven more days to officially conclude.

7

Rescuing the Students

After the successful rescue of Scoon and the SEALs, the American commanders turned their undivided attention to reaching the remaining American citizens on the island as soon as possible. Washington was disconcerted to learn that the Rangers had reached fewer than a third of the medical students on the first day. Metcalf was under pressure from the Pentagon to get to the medical students at the Grand Anse campus on the western shore halfway between Point Salines and St. George's. A land advance by the 82nd Airborne was problematic because the overland terrain was difficult and intelligence reports incorrectly indicated a large enemy force was blocking the way north from Point Salines.

Schwarzkopf on the *Guam* radioed Trobaugh on shore. "When are you going to get to Grand Anse?" he asked. "Based on the resistance we are getting, we probably won't be there for another day or two," Trobaugh replied.[1] Schwarzkopf didn't find that to be a satisfactory answer and he began to search for a quicker solution. At this point, the *Guam* had moved to a point directly west of Grand Anse beach, a crescent of white sand with calm surf regarded as one of the best in the Caribbean. Schwarzkopf looked from the bridge of the *Guam* to the beach, where the students were, and then down to the flight deck, where a dozen Marine helicopters were at the ready. A light bulb lit and he radioed Trobaugh. "Look, if I can get you helicopters, how about an air mobile assault over on the beach and we'll pull them out that way?"

Trobaugh agreed, provided he could use the Rangers under his temporary command. Raid-type missions were their combat specialty. Schwarzkopf brought Metcalf to the bridge and proposed using the *Guam*'s Marine helicopters to fly Rangers from Point Salines to reach the students. "Great!" Metcalf declared. "Make it happen."[2] Schwarzkopf summoned the Marine colonel in charge of the entire battalion landing team to the bridge. His autobiography does not name the officer, but the rank and job description cited matches Faulkner, the 22nd MAU commander.[3] Schwarzkopf explained his brainstorm. The Marine colonel listened and replied: "I'm not going to do that…. We don't fly Army soldiers in Marine helicopters." He wanted his Marines to do the job, and 24 hours to prepare. Schwarzkopf was incredulous. He restated his wishes, this time as a direct order backed by Metcalf and the threat of a court martial if the subordinate officer disobeyed. (Another account avers that the argument also involved cursing and shoving.)[4] In any case, the leatherneck colonel eventually, grudgingly acquiesced to the Army's use of his Marine transports.

The tactical plan for the landing at Grand Anse was crafted by two lieutenant colonels who found themselves on opposing poles of this inter-service standoff. Amos, commander of the Marine helicopter squadron, sat on a concrete block at Point Salines with Hagler, commanding officer of the 2nd Ranger Battalion, to hash out a battle plan.[5] Amos was no stranger to hastily planned helicopter rescues, he had participated in the chaotic evacuations of Saigon and Phnom Penh at the end of the Vietnam War. Trobaugh, the 82nd Airborne commander, happened by and attempted to interject himself in their huddle, but Amos successfully shooed him away until he and Hagler finished their one-on-one conversation.[6]

Thirty minutes later they had roughed out a three-phase rescue plan. First, they would fly a Ranger assault force in Marine CH-46 transports to establish a protective perimeter around the campus, located just two miles away from Point Salines by air. The only suitable landing zone they could identify was the mile-long arc of Grand Anse Beach. Once the campus was secure, the *Guam*'s heavy-lift CH-53D Marine helicopters would retrieve the students. Finally, the CH-46s would return to extract the Rangers. Amos and Hagler would fly together in an UH-1 (Huey) command helicopter to oversee the operation and direct fire support from Army mortars, Navy ships and jets, Air Force gunships and Marine Cobra attack helicopters. The whole mission would be over within half an hour. But, however short the operation, it was daunting assignment for the Marine transport helicopter pilots because no reconnaissance had been done on the landing zone and enemy resistance was expected. Failure was not an option. "Don't think the aborted Iranian rescue attempt wasn't on everyone's mind," Brewer, Amos' executive officer, later confided to a Marine historian. "It could have turned into a shit sandwich."

On the plus side, the Rangers on Point Salines had managed to establish telephone contact with the students at Grand Anse. Hagler was able to develop the plan to rescue them with the help of James F. Griffee, a resident assistant at the True Blue campus.[7] Griffee, an Army Vietnam veteran, had been instrumental in setting up two student-staffed triage facilities at True Blue for the immediate treatment of wounded Cubans, Grenadians and Americans.[8] He now worked with Hagler's battalion staff to communicate with the Grand Anse students and gather intelligence on enemy positions near the campus.[9] He drew maps, reviewed aerial photographs and answered questions about the campus layout.[10] Other valuable counsel was provided separately on the *Guam* by two State Department officers who knew the island and its politics: Rossin, the safari-suited emissary to Scoon, and E. Ashly Wills, another veteran of the U.S. embassy in Barbados. (Rossin, Wills and Griffee were all later presented awards by the Pentagon for their civilian service to the military effort.) The *Guam* was also receiving short wave radio updates from Mark Barettella of Ridgefield, New Jersey, a medical student who had a ham radio transceiver in his Grand Anse dorm room, and from Don Atkinson, an American expatriate who had a home near the airport.[11]

The Grand Anse students were instructed by phone to gather at noon on Oct. 26 in the ground floor of a two-story residence building near the beach.[12] They crammed into five rooms facing the beach where they spent the night and prepared for rescue. They hung white sheets on the exterior to mark their location and piled mattresses up on the windows. They made white armbands to identify themselves as non-combatants. When the shooting started, they were to lie on the floor with their hands over their heads until the Rangers arrived. The Rangers expected the landings to be opposed by 15 to 20 Grenadian soldiers who had been observed near the school. However, the students had told the *Guam* that the defensive positions were oriented to repel an attack by land coming

The long-haired civilian shown riding with Army Rangers on this gun jeep is James Griffee, then a student at the St. George's Medical School. Griffee, an Army veteran of Vietnam, offered Rangers valuable intelligence information on the school's second campus at Grand Anse. Griffee was later awarded the Army's Distinguished Civilian Service decoration for his assistance in the Grand Anse rescue (National Archives [330-CFD-DN-SN-84-12021]).

from the south of the north-facing beach. The approach to the campus from the sea to the west was an open door. The principal heavy weapons threat was a Grenadian 12.7 mm anti-aircraft gun, the Soviet Bloc equivalent of a four-barrel, 50-caliber machine gun,[13] positioned 500 meters northeast of the campus. The waiting students kept up their spirits by singing patriotic songs: "God Bless America" and "It's a Grand Old Flag."

The original plan called for Rangers to arrive at the campus at 1530. Fifteen minutes before the deadline, Hagler's intelligence officer asked that the attack be delayed so that an additional 50 students living just off the campus could join their classmates on campus. The number to be evacuated now swelled to 233. The landing was rescheduled. A 10-minute, pre-assault bombardment of suspected enemy positions by Army mortars and howitzers, Navy A-7 jets and an Air Force AC-130 gunship began at 1605. Couvillon's Spectre was given the mission of attacking the Carifta Cottages, government-owned rental residences clustered in a rectangular plat immediately to the south of the medical school campus. The buildings were considered a threat because they were being leased to Cuban engineers and supervisors who were working on the runway.[14] Navy A-7s from the *Independence* were given the job of attacking a hardened structure to the northeast of the campus. The building was shown on maps as the Police Training College, but staff at the medical school knew it as a roofless former hotel.

Couvillon savaged the wood-frame cottages nearest the campus with his 20 mm gun. Meanwhile, a Navy A-7 made bombing and strafing runs on the police training building. Couvillon's AC-130 gunship finished it off and set it ablaze. The Grenadian-manned 12.7 mm anti-aircraft gun near the campus got off a few shots at the gunship, but was quickly silenced by return fire from the Spectre. Some of these airstrikes came within about 100 meters of the dormitory where the now-terrified students were huddled.[15] At the last minute, a Navy lieutenant questioned whether the naval gunfire plan would land five-inch shells too close to the student-occupied building. His doubts prompted Metcalf to countermand the order to fire that he had just given.[16] "We almost blew away the students with naval guns," Butler, the *Guam*'s chief of staff, later told a Marine historian. But he was nonetheless bedazzled by Metcalf's ability to improvise a joint operation on short notice by "grabbing all concerned by the short hairs."

At 1630 nine CH-46s in flights of three rolled in on the pristine white sand beach. One of the students watched the approach in awe, comparing to the famous "Ride of the Valkyries" helicopter assault scene in Francis Ford Coppola's 1979 Vietnam War film *Apocalypse Now*. The beach at Grand Anse was narrow and lined by palm trees. The pilots scrambled for suitable landing spots, landing farther up or down the beach than intended.[17] Some dropped their passengers into waist-deep water. The spinning rotors of one CH-46 drew in the fronds of a shoreline palm tree. The pilot shut the engine down and the air crew and the Rangers abandoned the stricken aircraft on the beach. The other eight CH-46s took off undamaged.

Companies Alpha and Bravo of the 2nd Battalion quickly established a defensive 180-degree cordon around the campus. Charlie Company dashed to the campus gym where the students were told to assemble.[18] "U.S. soldiers! Friend or foe?" shouted the Rangers. "Friend!" the students replied. The Rangers led the students outside in groups to the beach to await the arrival of their rescue helicopters. While the CH-53s were in the air, the crew chief of the disabled CH-46, Lance Cpl. Martin J. Dellert, ran back to his aircraft to take a second look at the damage. After a quick inspection, he ran back to report to the pilot. "I think we can fly it," he said. The pilot and two crew members returned to the copter. It shook violently on takeoff, but it managed to stagger back to safety at Point Salines.[19]

The CH-53s landed on the beach one at a time and loaded aboard about 50 students in each of five successive flights. Because of the last-minute additions, one aircraft carried 60-plus passengers on one flight, well over its maximum load.[20] A total of 233 civilians were flown from Grand Anse to Point Salines. Among the evacuees was a British couple who had the misfortune to choose a nearby beach bungalow for their honeymoon.

Once the civilians were all safely out, the Rangers threw a yellow smoke grenade to signal the CH-46s to come back to pick them up. The plan was to extract them gradually in three flights, about 50 Rangers on each flight. Pilots reported heavier resistance leaving than when they arrived. Brewer, a Vietnam vet, saw six or seven mortar rounds exploding nearby as he was extracting a load of Rangers. On the second landing, another CH-46 came in accidental contact with a palm tree. The tree trunk fell into the rotor blades, making the helicopter unflyable. The crew jumped aboard one of the other CH-46s. But, in the final extraction scramble, and with two CH-46s out of action, 11 Charlie Company Rangers were left behind. The attack plan had anticipated this eventuality and provided for the anyone left behind to "evade and escape." They were briefed to wait until dark and then move southwest along the coast to link up with 82nd Airborne troops advancing north from Point Salines. But the Rangers were fearful of friendly fire if they approached the 82nd lines unannounced in the approaching darkness. Instead, the lieutenant leading the stranded 2nd platoon improvised a better solution. Rummaging through the wrecked CH-46 at the water's edge the Rangers found rubber life rafts. Using their weapons as oars, they rowed out to sea toward Navy ships just offshore.[21] They were eventually spotted by a helicopter and picked up by the destroyer *Caron*. Even officers of the 82nd believed the Rangers were prudent to avoid nighttime encounters with their lines. "I think they made a very wise choice," Col. Stephen Silvasy, Jr., the 2nd Brigade commander, told an audience of military students at a briefing a month later. "If you are faced with going to a bunch of trigger-happy airborne troops or going out to the Navy who was floating around in boats out there, you probably made the right choice."[22]

The Rangers were not the only ones left behind. At the last moment, Dr. Robert Jordan, then an assistant professor of anatomy at the school, decided he didn't want to be evacuated along with his students.[23] As an Air Force veteran and a student of military history, he was drawn to witness the combat that was occurring around him. Two chance companions also weighed in his decision. One was the very pregnant German Shepard named Brandy that had been entrusted to his care by a student. The other was a histology instructor at the school who wore a leg brace that inhibited her from making the mad dash to the helicopter.

The trio elected to shelter in place and await the arrival of 82nd Airborne troops in trucks, which they thought to be imminent. Rather than joining the students in the designated evacuation dorm, they chose to ride out the preparatory fire in the school's anatomy lab. Jordan thought the safest place would be the refrigerated locker where the cadavers were stored. He and his companion slid into the shelves next to the cadavers and waited out the barrage and the evacuation. When the campus grew silent, Jordan emerged for a look. The students were all gone, but he still saw Grenadian soldiers nearby. He decided to defend his hideout by moving cadavers from the locker to conspicuous locations near the door and a window to scare off Grenadian visitors. The ruse worked. The trio emerged at nightfall to a deserted campus. They then moved down the beach to the Spice Island Hotel where Jordan and his companions spent a sleepless night in the hotel's fruit locker. They were kept awake by a running duel between an AC-130 and a truck-mounted Grenadian anti-aircraft gun. In the morning they emerged to see 82nd Airborne troops cresting a ridge heading their way.

The successful action at Grand Anse came at the cost of one CH-46 wrecked, another damaged and five Rangers wounded by shrapnel or small arms.[24] None of the students were injured, but they were very frightened. The pre-extraction barrage, the race under fire to the helicopters and the hurried liftoff from a narrow beach certainly put students in the most danger they would face during the entire intervention. "We just got absolutely lucky," Brewer later declared. The Marines, however, concluded that there was more than good fortune involved in the successful rescue. Brewer was awarded Distinguished Flying Cross with a Combat V for the courage and skill he showed in leading the 16-helicopter flight that evacuated the students from Grand Anse.[25]

The Rangers and the students returned to Point Salines separately. They linked up again when the Rangers returned to defensive positions near a guarded compound that held the evacuated the students. When the civilians saw the soldiers, they started cheering their rescuers. Paul Andreasen, a Ranger sergeant, raised his fist in acknowledgment and shouted: "WE DO EMBASSIES TOO!"[26] On board the *Guam*, Butler marveled that securing the safety of the students at Grand Anse had been a totally improvised operation that had no prior planning by the Pentagon. "This business of rescuing the students out of this place was almost a side show and not a central piece of what was going on that day.... It just happened," he later told a Marine historian.

By coincidence, the first top-level, on-the-record official press briefing on Grenada convened at the Pentagon just as Marine helicopters arrived at Grand Anse. Up until this point, with reporters barred from the island by the U.S. military, the international press was largely relying on ham radio operators and Radio Havana for reports on conditions on the island.[27] As the press conference was underway, Vessey, the Joint Chiefs' chairman, interrupted the questioning to report that the Grand Anse campus had been evacuated without casualties. Defense Secretary Weinberger interjected: "that means that all of the students are now out and safe and that is a very great relief, that's again one of the things that I think was extremely skillfully done."[28] In fact, Rangers on the ground in Grenada had learned the day before that there was yet a third group of more than 200 other medical students living off-campus mostly on the Lance aux Epines peninsula. They would not be reached by American forces for another 24 hours. Yet another group of 21 off-campus students and staff were living on the Westerhall peninsula and were overlooked completely and never left the island.[29]

After the Washington press conference concluded at around 1800, an AC-130 gunship piloted by Capt. David Tarpley was ordered to return to the evacuated Grand Anse campus. Tarpley was instructed to destroy the abandoned CH-46 on the beach to prevent its weapons and equipment from falling into enemy hands after dark.[30] Most of the visible damage to the much-photographed wreckage was caused by 20 and 40 mm fire from the

St. George's University Medical School students displayed their happiness and patriotism after being evacuated by Rangers and Marines from the Grand Anse campus on the second afternoon of the invasion (National Archives [330-CFD-DF-SN-84-10902]).

Spectre gunship, not by hostile fire or the palm tree. The photo became an oddly appropriate iconic image of the fighting on Grenada. During Urgent Fury, appearances were often deceiving; grievous wounds to men and machines were sometimes the result of accidents or friendly fire.

Meanwhile, back in the United States, another iconic photograph was soon snapped by news photographers in South Carolina. The first C-141 with 71 students and staff from the True Blue campus landed at Charleston Air Force Base at 1719 on Oct. 26.[31] They were escorted home by a special team of State Department officers dispatched from Washington.[32] Before deplaning, the civilian passengers were screened by the Air Force to select those who would present the most positive impression of their rescue. "The greatest challenge in the [airlift] operation was management of the media," an Air Force after-action report declared. "The first press conference was critical. The commander boarded the first aircraft [and] evaluated student responses to his greeting and selected four to be interviewed by media representatives ... this procedure became standard for the remainder of the evacuation flights as long as press representatives were present in large numbers."[33] One of the first students off the first plane was Jeff Geller, 24, of Woodridge, New York, who dropped to his knees, spread his arms and kissed the runway. This image

This chewed-up Marine CH-46 Sea Knight became an iconic image of the invasion, but was much misinterpreted. The military-supplied caption for this photograph incorrectly states this helicopter was shot down by anti-aircraft fire on October 25. In fact, it was damaged in a contested landing the next day to rescue American medical students at the Grand Anse Beach campus. The helicopter was disabled and abandoned when a rotor blade came in contact with a palm tree. The damage to the nose was caused later when an Air Force AC-130 was ordered to fire on the wreck to prevent classified components from falling into enemy hands (National Archives [330-CFD-DD-ST-86-03409]).

Jeff Geller, 24, a St. George's University Medical School student from Woodridge, New York, famously kissed the tarmac at Charleston Air Force Base in South Carolina on his arrival back to the United States on October 26. Geller was among 67 Americans who were on the first flight of U.S. and UK citizens to be evacuated from the island on U.S. military aircraft (National Archives [330-CFD-DF-SN-84-10873]).

appeared on TV network broadcasts and on newspaper front pages around the county. "I have been a dove all my life," Geller told reporters. "I just can't believe how well those [Army] Rangers came down and saved us.... I don't want anyone to say anything bad about the American military."[34] The Grand Anse rescue proved to be both a military and a political triumph.

Later, as night was falling in the Lesser Antilles, Schwarzkopf revisited the resistance he had encountered earlier in the day over the use of Marine helicopters to fly Army Rangers. "I'm more than happy to run your ground campaign, but I've got to have some authority," Schwarzkopf told his boss. "I can fix that," Metcalf responded. He called in his entire senior staff and announced that Schwarzkopf was now his deputy commander, his second in command.[35] Metcalf reinforced the message by leaving the command center to get some sleep for the first time in a day and a half.[36]

8

The Enemy Is Us

The 82nd Airborne was supposed to arrive on Grenada as an occupation force when the fighting was essentially over. The invasion plan called for two battalions of the 325th Infantry, about 1,200 combat troops, to mop up whatever resistance remained and then keep the peace until a new civil government could be formed on Grenada. Trobaugh, the 82nd commanding general, was expecting his principal mission to be more administrative than tactical. "We didn't think there was … very much of a possibility of us getting involved in the fight," he later told a military historian.[1]

The airport under construction at Point Salines was the only practical entry point for such a large force because of the limited length of the runway at Pearls. The Pearls runway was too short to safely land the C-141 four-engine jet aircraft which had been assigned to transport the 82nd.[2] The expectation was that the unfinished airport would be successfully secured by the Rangers before the 82nd arrived to air-land their men and materials on the runway. But the satellite radio reports that Trobaugh heard beginning at 0500 on Oct. 25 persuaded him to make alternative landing plans. After consulting with his three-star Army boss, Mackmull, Trobaugh decided the wisest choice would be to prepare for the entire force to land by parachute if necessary. This was a prudent precaution, but much easier said than done because it required a major last-minute reshuffling. An air drop meant further restricting the number of men and/or vehicles assigned to each aircraft. Still the preference was to air land if at all possible, because of the hazards associated with an air drop of so many paratroopers on a narrow landing zone that had water areas on three sides. "I was convinced that, had we dropped with 1,200 or 1,300 jumpers, that I would have had 100 of them put out of commission just like that," Silvasy, an 82nd Brigade commander, later remarked in a post-invasion briefing.[3] The first transport plane was scheduled to be "wheels up" from Pope Air Force Base at 0900 on Oct. 25, four hours after H-Hour. In the event, just like the other forces before them, there were delays getting the men and aircraft assembled, loaded and airborne. The first of an initial wave of 13 C-141s departed at 1007,[4] more than an hour late. The delay was of limited concern because the entire operation at that point was also running behind schedule.

The C-141B transports were "stretched" versions that could carry twice as many paratroopers as the smaller C-130s which had carried the Rangers into battle. The jet transports were also faster than the turboprop C-130s, but not much more comfortable for the passengers. Each C-141 crammed in a maximum load of 120 paratroopers and their gear. Trobaugh insisted on flying in the first plane along with his 31-man command staff. Four times in flight the men on the first plane took their parachutes on and then off according to the latest radio reports from Point Salines. Trobaugh had to finally decide whether to land or jump no later than two and a half hours before their scheduled arrival over Point Salines. Twenty minutes before the decision deadline, word was relayed to him that the airport was secure to land.[5] That news allowed the paratroopers to de-rig from their parachutes, but the report conveyed an overly optimistic impression of conditions on the ground. When Trobaugh's plane arrived at Point Salines at 1405, the passengers didn't have to jump, but they did tumble to the tarmac. When Trobaugh's C-141 touched down, the passengers were told to exit the tailgate door before the aircraft came to a full stop. Patrick O'Kelley, an 82nd Airborne sniper, watched as his commanding general ran off the back of the plane, lost his balance and bounced painfully along the runway. Seconds later O'Kelley attempted the same feat, with similar results.[6] Bruising was just the beginning of Trobaugh's discomfort. He was surprised to hear sounds of gunfire at the eastern end of the airport. O'Kelley heard fire even closer. Bullets passed over his head at supersonic speed making a noise that sound to him like someone clapping their hands next to his ear.

Trobaugh stopped the first Ranger he saw and asked: "Where's your CP?" The Ranger directed him to his battalion's command post which was just located just 20 meters away on the edge of the runway. Trobaugh got a quick briefing from a Ranger battalion commander (apparently Taylor) and ordered his men to take cover until more 82nd troops landed. Trobaugh's arrival made him the ranking Army officer on the Grenadian territory, including Schwarzkopf, but that didn't make him in charge. His presence, though expected, further muddled an already complex command structure and introduced a new level of confusion that took hours to sort out. Trobaugh's first order of business was to meet at 1530 with Scholtes, the JSOC general, to get an up-to-date briefing on a battle he had been following by radio while in the air. The original invasion plan envisioned that the special operation missions would be completed by the time the 82nd arrived on the island. Scholtes would then turn over combat operations to Trobaugh. All the initial JSOC assault forces, including the Rangers, would immediately return to the United States before the press was allowed in. Instead, Trobaugh learned from Scholtes that the attack on the prison had been a bloody failure and that the SEALs tasked with taking the radio station and the governor general's mansion were still embattled. Task Force 160's brand-new Black Hawks had been badly shot up and two were wrecked. The airport was secure only as far as the immediately surrounding hills. Only about a third of the medical students were under Ranger control.

Scholtes resisted turning over the airfield to Trobaugh. He wanted to stay on the island until all his SEALs were safe. Trobaugh was unmoved by the plea. "If you special f**kers get out of the way, we'll win this war," he declared, but he eventually relented.[7] The two Army two-star generals agreed to temporary set up separate headquarters at the half-finished airport terminal complex. Scholtes wanted extra time on the island to settle his unfinished missions. Trobaugh's troubles were just beginning. The chaotic condition of the airfield was a major complication for all the services, but especially the 82nd Airborne. The Americans learned on arrival that the airfield was not fully up to the task they envisioned for it. Only about two-thirds of the runway's length was finish-paved with five layers of asphalt. The western one third nearest the ocean was only paved with gravel and oil.[8] Worse, the airstrip was narrow and cramped. Fixed-wing planes could only turn around at the eastern end and there was only enough apron space at the mid-point near the terminal to allow one plane to unload at a time. The terminal apron was littered with construction materials, equipment and debris typical of an active construction site.

"One of the most important decisions made during the deployment was the decision by the 2nd Brigade commander to remove a truck from his assault echelon and replace it with a 6.000-pound-capacity, rough-terrain fork lift," one Army after-action report observed.[9] For days, this vehicle was the only piece of equipment capable of off-loading and moving heavy palletized loads from the transport aircraft. But the forklift was only a partial solution to the 82nd's logistical problems. Because of the airport's limitations, the C-141 transports would be unable to land in rapid succession as planned. The 19 planes would have to land at least 20 minutes apart, not counting the times the runway needed to be shut down because of hostile fire or other safety concerns. When darkness came, and temporary lighting proved inadequate, the runway was shut down by the Air Force.[10] The remaining C-141s were diverted to Barbados where they transferred their passengers to smaller C-130s. It ended up taking until 0245 the next morning to land all the troops and materials in the two battalions that Trobaugh expected to be at his disposal on the first day.[11]

At about the same time Trobaugh was getting bad news from Scholtes, he was further discomforted when the eastern airport perimeter came under counterattack. According to a top-level Grenadian party official, the armored counterattack was specifically urged on the PRA headquarters by the Cuban ambassador. He belatedly sought Grenadian help in defending the Cuban positions around the airport.[12] This sourcing establishes this counterattack as the only documented coordinated military action by the Grenadians and Cubans, who otherwise fought separately on Castro's insistence. The airport attack was mounted by Grenada's elite Motorized Company, which was composed almost entirely of professional, ideologically committed, full-time soldiers. The 24-man sortie was led by Warrant Officer Stephen F. McEwan, who died in the courageous, but tactically flawed, assault.[13] The plan was for three Grenadian-manned armored personnel carriers to make a sudden appearance on the runway, firing their turret-mounted heavy machine guns. The hope was that the APCs would disable one more American aircraft and shut the airport down.

In the event, surprise was lost before the attackers even sighted the airport. Unbeknown to the Grenadians, a Ranger patrol had been dispatched east of the airport to look for any survivors of the earlier jeep ambush. The 10-man recon patrol was led by 1st Lt. Sydney Farrar, 2nd platoon leader in Abizaid's Alpha Company. One enlisted member of the patrol, Pvt. Jose E. G. Gordon, offered a detailed eyewitness account of the ensuing meeting engagement in 2004 posts to an online bulletin board serving the special operations community.[14] According to those posts, at about 1430 on D-Day, Farrar's patrol was about two and a half kilometers northeast of the airport. They had just sighted the wrecked jeep about a kilometer away. They were about to move closer when they heard the noise of the approaching BTR-60s. Farrar radioed a flash warning to Abizaid, his company commander. "I have three Bravo Tango Romeo Sixties moving toward me," Farrar declared. He then immediately deployed his patrol to engage the vehicles. Farrar and two of his men prepared to fire their LAW anti-tank weapons, each aimed at a separate BTR-60. The gunners hit two of the vehicles, but did not disable them. The three vehicles raced past them toward the eastern end of the airport, where two Rangers companies were then located. As the vehicles approached the larger force, a wild firefight developed.[15] The Rangers from the Alpha companies of both battalions responded with a fusillade of fire from rifles, mortars, machine guns and shoulder-fired LAWs. One or more LAWs struck the lead vehicle, causing it to unexpectedly reverse and crash into the second. The immobilized vehicles were then further attacked by two Rangers with 90 mm recoilless rifles. When these shells hit the armored plates, the crews abandoned their stricken vehicles, leaving two dead. More fell as the Rangers fired on the retreating Grenadians. The third vehicle, trailing behind, attempted to escape, but was engaged by a Spectre gunship. (The late-arriving AC-130 piloted by Sims always seemed to be in the vicinity when a BTR-60 appeared on D-Day.) An artillery round from the gunship's 105 mm main gun hit near the third vehicle, blasting it over on its side.

The counterattack failed, in part, because the armored vehicles were not supported by either dismounted infantry or indirect fire, as they should have been according to textbook military tactics. Nonetheless, the timing and objective was astute. "All they had to do to stop the whole thing was to knock down one plane. If one C-141 had gone down, they would have shut down everything. I'm convinced of that…. I guess they tried that in the BTR-60 [attack], but they should have tried harder," Silvasy, the 2nd Brigade commander, later observed.[16]

The end of the counterattack, however, was not the end of fighting that afternoon around True Blue. After the BTRs were dispatched, Farrar, the 2nd platoon leader, got the order to continue on with his gun jeep recon mission.[17] Farrar gathered three men and moved on to the wrecked jeep, leaving six others behind in overwatch on a hill. The

The Grenadian armored counterattack at True Blue at mid-afternoon on D-Day was a daring, but foolhardy, gamble. It left one vehicle blasted off its wheels by aerial gunfire (National Archives [330-CFD-DD-ST-86-03407]).

Two other armored vehicles were disabled by ground counterfire in the failed assault (National Archives [330-CFD-DF-ST-84-09829]).

four point men moved parallel to a road leading west from the runway toward a north-south intersection. Along the way, they discovered a wheeled ZU-23 anti-aircraft gun sitting in the road. The towed weapon evidently had been hurriedly dropped off there by the third BTR-60 around the time of the initial LAW attack. An armed black man in a camouflage uniform then appeared near the unmanned AAA gun. He fired three shots from his AK-47 up the road to where Farrar stood exposed to the unnoticed threat. Farrar went down in a heap with a bullet in his left arm and two in the chest. Those shots triggered an extended gun battle between the remaining Rangers and a concealed force of enemy soldiers, believed to be the survivors of the failed BTR attack. The firefight raged inconclusively for about 90 minutes until Navy jets appeared overhead indicating that close air support was now available. One member of the patrol, Sp4c. Kelly D. Venden, decided to take personal action to help Farrar. Venden signaled for covering fire as he exposed himself and dragged Farrar off the middle of the road to the roadside tree line. Gordon kept the Grenadian soldiers at bay with automatic rifle fire as Spc5c. Johnny Bowen, a medic, administered first aid to the stricken patrol leader. At that point the Navy jets were cleared to cover the further evacuation of Farrar. Red smoke was used to mark Ranger positions as A-6 Intruders made bombing and gun runs on the enemy positions. The patrol members moved Farrar up a hill to a secured house where other members of their platoon were waiting with a jeep. The wounded lieutenant was taken to the True Blue campus where a battalion aid station had been set up in the cafeteria. Venden and Bowen were later awarded Bronze Stars with valor for their shared roles in saving Farrar.[18] The platoon leader was also honored with an Army Commendation Medal with a V for his valor, in addition to a Purple Heart.

The unexpected BTR attack succeeded to the extent that it made Trobaugh concerned about the security around the airport and the possibility of further counterattacks. Trobaugh contacted the *Guam* to discuss the situation with Schwarzkopf, who was junior to him in date of rank. The two men were long-time friends and shared the same current boss. They each commanded subordinate Army divisions under the XVIII Airborne Corps and reported to Mackmull, the corps commander. Trobaugh thought the situation on the ground required more manpower than the two 82nd battalions that were then planned to arrive. Equal contests were not part of Trobaugh's Vietnam-bloodied combat creed. "I just don't like the idea of going in light where it might be a fair fight.... I want to overwhelm the guys, that's all there is to it," Trobaugh later explained to a military historian.[19] Schwarzkopf, though also a Vietnam combat veteran, disagreed with the need for more troops. Trobaugh rejected his advice and sent a fateful message back to Fort Bragg: keep sending battalions until I tell you to stop.[20] That turned out to be yet another heavy-handed Urgent Fury command decision that, in hindsight, had more negative consequences than positive. Eventually, six battalions were dispatched, instead of just two.

What Trobaugh didn't know at the time was the armored attack was the last gasp of organized Grenadian resistance to the invaders. More importantly, the decision to unleash a continuous flow of fresh troops to the island overwhelmed the half-finished, debris-littered airstrip. The call for additional troops disrupted the logistical flow of supplies and equipment for troops already on the ground. The lightly equipped Rangers were already scrounging for food, fresh water and transport vehicles. The tropical heat and cloudless sunshine were becoming the new enemy of the assault troops, who were carrying rucksacks weighing 100 pounds or more. Flies, mites and gnats added to the foot soldiers' misery.

In addition to summoning more 82nd troops from the U.S., Trobaugh appealed to Metcalf to temporarily put the Rangers under his command. He needed the Rangers to maintain their positions at Salines until enough of his men arrived to take on both the airport defense and the unfinished offensive missions. Metcalf agreed and issued the order at 1900 putting the two Ranger battalions under Trobaugh's control. Scholtes protested the Ranger transfer, but he was overruled. In any event, it took until the next morning for both of the Ranger battalion commanders to learn that Trobaugh was their new boss and that their return to the United States would be delayed.[21]

The 82nd did not join the offensive battle until just before dawn on Oct. 26. Trobaugh ordered the 2nd Battalion of the 325th Infantry to assault the holdouts at the Cuban compound north of Calliste known as Little Havana. The plan called for Bravo Company, then holding a position near the airport tank farm, to attack from the west at 0630. Alpha Company would provide supporting fire for the assault from its position on the Calliste hills to the southeast. Charlie Company was also nearby, in reserve, ready to join the attack if necessary.

Capt. Michael F. Ritz, the Bravo Company commander, decided to conduct a "leader's recon" in advance of the assault. He asked all three of his platoon leaders and one sergeant to join him on the night patrol to get a better mental picture of the three hills that separated them from the Cubans.[22] The first stop was an observation post on the first hill where they discussed the scheme of maneuver they would follow in the dawn attack. From there, Ritz decided to push past friendly lines to get a look from the top of the last of three hills on a ridge line. On the way there, Ritz checked the time and ordered two of the platoon leaders to turn back to be sure they would be with their men for attack. The remaining three men, Ritz, Sgt. Terry L. Guinn and 2nd Lt. Stephen M. Seager, a newly arrived platoon leader, pressed on to the top of the third hill where they stumbled into a Cuban outpost. A firefight ensued that instantly killed Ritz, who fell on the Cuban-held side of the hill. Guinn, the NCO, was shot through the chest, but fell to the friendly side. The rounds went over the head of Seager, the platoon leader, who returned fire and hit several Cubans. He then retreated down the hill seeking help. The trio did not have a radio.

Bravo Company's first sergeant had assumed effective command of the company until Ritz returned. Hearing the firefight, he ordered Sgt. Rodolfo Capetillo to move Seager's 3rd platoon in the direction of the shooting.[23] The platoon soon came upon a deserted Cuban position with two recoilless rifles. One squad, under the leadership of Staff Sgt. Gary L. Epps, was left behind to guard the guns while the rest of the platoon continued on. Capetillo then met up with Seager and the platoon moved to the top of the hill to reengage the Cubans. A fierce firefight ensued that quickly depleted the paratroopers' available ammunition. The paratroopers were not issued hand grenades before they left Fort Bragg for flight safety reasons. They only acquired one each after arrival. They continued the fight with captured AK-47s and three boxes of Soviet-made hand grenades. The platoon held off the Cubans long enough to retrieve the wounded sergeant (Guinn) and return down the hill to resupply. The platoon then went back up the hill a second time to fully evict the Cubans and secure the position prior to start of the assault. Capetillo was then ordered to withdraw to allow for bombardment of the Little Havana compound by Navy A-7s and Army artillery.

With Ritz missing, Bravo Company was now under the direct control of Lt. Col Jack L. Hamilton, the 2nd Battalion commander. Hamilton appointed a platoon leader the acting company commander to prepare for the ground attack.[24] As Bravo Company approached the compound, they came under automatic weapons fire from Cubans and took several wounded. Alpha Company, positioned in "overwatch" support, responded with M60 machine guns mounted on tripods. Hamilton also called for strafing runs by A-7 Navy jets. Explosions blasted the cinderblock buildings of the compound in a savage display of coordinated firepower. The jets killed Cubans on each pass, forcing the defenders to move from building to building, eventually retreating to the headquarters building where a large Cuban flag flew. Castro had sent the trapped men a radio message urging them to continue the fight to the last man, but their cause was hopeless.[25] As the A-7s came in on their fourth bombing run on the compound, white sheets were displayed in the windows of the headquarters to signal capitulation. A cease fire was called and eventually the Cubans emerged with their hands up. Bravo Company swept into the compound. Emotions ran high, as both sides had suffered casualties. "We could have very easily had a My Lai in that incident," Silvasy later remarked.[26] The attack killed a total of 16 Cubans, including Diaz, the late-arriving Cuban diplomat. More than 80 Cubans surrendered, of whom 29 were wounded, nine seriously. Three Cubans carrying code books and other secret material managed to slip away before the final surrender. They found sanctuary in the Soviet Embassy near Grand Anse. The escapees included Col. Tortoló, who had been dispatched from Havana to organize the Cuban last stand. Little Havana was declared secure by 0835.[27]

One additional Bravo Company fatality occurred after the shooting stopped at the compound. Epps, the leader of the left-behind squad, was killed when he attempted to neuter one of the captured recoilless rifles he had been assigned to guard. An explosion occurred that wounded four of his nine squad members.[28] That brought the total cost of

This captured Soviet-made, recoilless rifle was the type of the weapon that was involved in the death of a 82nd Airborne squad leader on the second day of the invasion. The sergeant attempted to neuter a captured Cuban-deployed gun, triggering a blast that also injured at least four of his squad members (National Archives [330-CFD-DF-ST-84-09906]).

subduing the Calliste compound to two Americans killed and 10 wounded, all from Bravo Company.

From Calliste, Hamilton's 2nd Battalion pushed west toward the nearby village of Frequente, which was the principal source of the anti-aircraft fire on the lead Ranger drops on D-Day. The advance was led by Charlie Company under the command of Capt. Mark D. Rocke, who was brand new to the brigade and still feeling his way among strangers. Rocke's unit actually belonged to a different battalion (2nd Battalion, 505th Infantry) in the 82nd Airborne. It had been selected as a last-minute replacement for Hamilton's Charlie Company, which had not yet been combat certified. That Silvasy-ordered switch was not popular with the men left behind. It placed an extra burden on their fill-ins, despite the honor implied by having been chosen. "I was a bastardized element and a bastard company," Rocke later remarked.[29]

At Frequente, Rocke's unit came upon the Grenadian Army's logistics compound. This barbed-wire-enclosed facility consisted of six warehouse-type buildings, two ammunition dumps and a covered vehicle park.[30] The lone sentry on duty surrendered himself and the huge store of weapons, ammunition and heavy vehicles he was guarding. At this point, 1400, the afternoon tropical heat was more of a threat to Rocke's company than the enemy. His men were wilting in 85-degree heat and 90-plus humidity while wearing flak jackets and lugging heavy rucksacks. He halted his man and had them drop their packs. They found water in a rain barrel behind a nearby house. Temporarily refreshed, the men then made a quick clearing check of the abandoned supply depot. A later inventory found enough weaponry at Frequente and other smaller caches to equip six infantry battalions: 6,322 rifles, 65 82 mm mortars, 13 anti-aircraft batteries, 15 recoilless rifles, 111 machine guns, 68 rocket-propelled grenade launchers and five million rounds of ammunition.[31] The capture of this trove was a double loss for the PRA. The loss of Frequente deprived Grenadians of their principal arms depot and handed Americans a propaganda prop to demonstrate the belligerent intentions of the island's secretive Communist leaders.

Roche's men did not tarry at the depot. They took up a defensive line on a ridge just north of the compound where Rocke was joined by Hamilton, the battalion commander. As the two officers talked, they saw an ambush unfold near a drive-in theater about a kilometer away.[32] A reconnaissance platoon of six jeeps from the 82nd had been ordered to retrieve the bodies of the four Rangers who had been killed in their gun jeep on the first day.[33] The retrieval detail was itself ambushed on the return trip. The recon platoon returned fire from their jeep-mounted machine guns, as did the machine gunners and mortarmen of Rocke's Charlie Company. The ambushers were beaten back at the cost of four claimed killed and a BRDM-2 scout car destroyed. There were no American casualties in the firefight, but Rocke did end up losing five men as serious heat casualties before the day's action was done. The ambushers were Cuban, according to one otherwise authoritative Army historian.[34] However, there are multiple circumstantial reasons to question this identification. This ambush came after the surrender of holdout Cubans at Little Havana, when Tortoló, the Cuban commander, was on the run. The Soviet-made armored car was a component of the Grenadian motorized company and the ambush site was located outside the Cuban defensive zone. Whatever the nationality, this firefight unit in the afternoon of Oct. 26 represented the last organized unit action by either Grenadian or Cuban forces on the Point Salines peninsula.

On the third day of the operation, Thursday, Oct. 27, friendly fire and accidents now emerged as more of a threat than enemy action. A key objective of the day was linkup of Army and Marine forces on the island at a point south of the capital city. Toward that goal, Smith's Marines were ordered to start their day by capturing Richmond Hill Prison, the target that had cost U.S. forces one KIA (Lucas) and at least 28 unreportable WIAs (18 Delta Force and 10 Nightstalkers) on D-Day. As was the case at Fort Frederick, the guards at Richmond Hill lost their resolve by daybreak on Wednesday and had abandoned their posts. Several hundred prisoners, a mixed group of criminal lawbreakers and about 100 political detainees,[35] began breaking out of their cells as soon as their jailers left. As prisoners got out, they helped others who were still confined. The political detainees included those imprisoned during the four-year Bishop reign and also the six-day reign of the military council. Notable among the newer detainees was Alister Hughes, a Grenadian journalist who was scooped up in a purge that followed the assassination of Bishop.

Three international journalists who made their way to the island soon after the invasion managed to reach the prison in advance of the Marines. They found 10 prisoners still in their cells, including Hughes, who was a "stringer" (a regular freelance contributor) for both the *Miami Herald* and *Time*, among other news organizations. The arriving journalists convinced the prisoners that it was safe to leave. The trio also made contact with Smith, the Marine battalion commander, to report that the prison was undefended. Smith radioed the news to Dobson, the Golf Company commander. Golf Company moved immediately to secure the unguarded prison. One prisoner was found shot to death in his cell, apparently the victim of a too-early escape attempt when the guards were still present.

The company's next objective was to attack Fort Adolphus another colonial-era fort located further south on the same ridgeline. As Golf Company approached the stone fortress, they could clearly see that it was occupied. Figures were moving about and a flag was flying over the building that Dobson did not recognize. It was a horizontal design with three colored bands and stars. Dobson guessed it was Cuban and reported his observations to his boss.[36] Smith had been given the go-ahead from Metcalf to level the building with gunfire from ships and planes, if he needed air support. A voice in the back of Smith's mind held him back. The policy of restraint that the Marines had been employing since landing was working well for them. Smith saw no reason to change tactics. He advised Dobson to scout out the position and withdraw if he came under fire. Bombardment would be a fallback option.

Dobson's men advanced and discovered to their surprise that the fort was actually an embassy compound. The unidentified pennant flying over the fort was the flag of Venezuela. Smith belatedly recalled reading an intelligence report mentioning that Venezuela had one of the three embassies on the island. At the fort, Smith was greeted by the Venezuelan ambassador who told him that two of the Grenadian coup's leaders, Austin and Coard, had spent the previous night at the embassy. Smith got the impression that the fugitive leaders were not particularly welcome and had left just prior to the arrival of the Marines. They had headed into St. George's instead of seeking sanctuary in the nearby Cuban ambassador residence at Morne Jaloux. Smith was puzzled by that decision and concluded the duo weren't expecting to be welcomed there either—though he didn't understand why.[37]

In retrospect, Smith's impression was certainly correct. Less than a month after the invasion, Castro publicly denounced the Coard-led faction that had deposed Bishop as "a group of extremists drunk on political theory" who "unleashed the events that opened the door to imperialist aggression."[38] While Golf Company advanced along the Richmond Hill ridge line, Fox Company moved into St. George's to take control of government and military offices. The door to the capital was wide open. Resistance had evaporated. Welcoming Grenadians were pointing them toward hidden arm caches and identifying PRA officers and Coard loyalists. "My basic guidance is that anyone important enough or infamous enough for the people to finger is worth going after," Smith wrote in his journal. "By now, my discussions with the local population have convinced me that a good percentage of the PRA should be considered criminals. I am told horror stories of PRA firing into crowds and summarily executing civilians before and especially after the coup."

In order to accommodate the Marine advance, Metcalf twice shifted south the east-west boundary separating the Army area of operation from the Marines. After the second shift on the evening of Oct. 27, the line was stretched to encompass the entire capital city and the southern shore of St. George's harbor.[39] Washington was under pressure from the Canadian government to assure the safety of their citizens on the island. The surprise invasion had preempted Ottawa's independent plan to get their citizens out on a chartered civilian jet. Smith was ordered to press on to the Ross Point Inn where as many as 400 foreign nationals, mostly Canadians, were believed to be sheltered. The Pentagon wanted a headcount before Reagan made a televised address to the nation at 2000. Fox Company Marines arrived at the 12-room hotel at about 1930, just after dark, to find just 17 guests. Other English-speaking foreigners soon trickled in from nearby. Marines eventually collected 40 to 50 civilians at the hotel, mostly Canadians.[40] Few accepted the American offer of an evacuation.[41]

The accommodations were more comfortable for the hotel guests than for the Marines, who set up a defensive perimeter outside. The next morning, Friday, Oct. 28, they had a disconcerting encounter with 82nd Airborne troops who were advancing north from Point Salines. The Marines had been expecting a link-up at the hotel, but their presence came as a surprise to the Army paratroopers. Word of the boundary line shift had not reached the commander of the lead company of Hamilton's 2nd Battalion. The company commander told the Marines that he considered the hotel to be in a "free fire" zone and said the Marines "were lucky that he hadn't reconned the area by fire."[42]

The strict security rules governing the operation prevented the pre-invasion distribution of standard land maps for the operation, although such maps were in the possession of the Defense Mapping Agency. Instead, the various units found their own maps and photocopied them. Subsequent studies found at least five different maps were used, each map of a different scale or with a different grid system.[43] The maps served basic navigation purposes, but all lacked the precision and standardization necessary for safely directing supporting fire from planes, ships or artillery.[44] "The confusion caused by these multiple grids was considerable," was the characteristically deadpan comment offered by McDonald in his Atlantic Command after-action report.[45]

The main Army action of the third day, Thursday, Oct. 27, was a mission that was of murky, off-island origin. At noon, Metcalf received orders from the Atlantic Command

Map differences among the combat units on Grenada were the source of great confusion during the hostilities and considerable friendly-fire danger. Subsequent studies found that at least five different maps were used by Urgent Fury combat units (National Archives [330-CFD-DF-ST-84-09825]).

to immediately assault a restricted Grenadian military complex near the village of Calivigny on the thinly populated Egmont peninsula east of Point Salines. The Cuban-built camp was the main base and training facility for the Grenadian Army. It consisted of barracks buildings, a water tower, an obstacle course and a firing range. Intelligence officials in Washington believed the compound also served as a clandestine Cuban training camp for exporting communism through the Caribbean. The Reagan administration had previously highlighted this military facility in its public warnings about Soviet and Cuban expansion in the Caribbean Basin.

Metcalf and Schwarzkopf were aware of Calivigny's political importance, but surprised that a tactical military decision was being dictated from the Pentagon on such a tight deadline. Every other order they had received up to that point came from McDonald's CINCLANT command in Norfolk. Their Pentagon bosses had been pretty much hands-off. Schwarzkopf was enraged. "That's the stupidest goddam order I've ever heard," he told Metcalf.[46] It didn't sound to the on-scene commanders like an order that a "mud soldier" like Vessey would approve. Metcalf directed his staff to confirm the directive. The reply from Norfolk came back: "JCS has ordered you to take Calivigny barracks before dark."[47] At noon, Metcalf dutifully passed the order on to the 82nd commander to execute.

Trobaugh's own 82nd troops were advancing by foot on Calivigny, but they were unlikely to cover the remaining distance before dark. Because of the extremely tight deadline, Trobaugh again turned to the Rangers to carry out the attack. The Rangers had turned over their defensive positions at Point Salines and were currently unengaged, awaiting airlift back to the United States. The Rangers had more helicopter assault experience than his own paratroopers. They were also familiar with the target because it had been an uncompleted part of the 2nd Battalion's D-Day mission. The logic of all those arguments convinced Metcalf to put the Rangers back under Trobaugh's direct command instead of flying them home. Trobaugh sought to smooth over any rough edges by assigning tactical command of the assault to Col. James T. Scott, an 82nd Brigade commander, who was also a former Ranger battalion commander. Scott further eased the leadership transition by delegating tactical control back to Hagler, the Ranger 2nd Battalion commander, once the attack was underway.[48]

A plan was hastily drafted to assault the camp with Hagler's reinforced Ranger battalion transported on Army Black Hawks. The force of about 180 Rangers were told that the camp contained about a battalion of Grenadian troops, 300 or more Cubans, 60 Soviet advisers and was defended by up to six ZU-23 anti-aircraft guns.[49] If true, that made it a highly hazardous daylight assault. The bloodshed in the failed Delta assault on Richmond Hill prison was fresh in everyone's memory. Only two of the nine Task Force 160's Black Hawks that flew into battle on the first day were still fit to fly. Instead, the airlift was assigned to newly arrived Army Black Hawks belonging to the 82nd Airborne's Combat Aviation Battalion. These pilots averaged only 600 hours of flight time, compared to an average of more than 2,000 hours for the now bloodied and withdrawn Task Force 160 pilots.[50] Lt. Col. Robert N. Seigle, the helicopter battalion commander, tried to stiffen his pilots for a mission they feared would be suicidal. "Guys, we don't know what's out there. Just remember that your primary job is to fly the aircraft until it won't fly anymore. Concentrate on that," he advised.[51]

The plan of attack called for the assault to be preceded by an intense 15-minute Army-Navy barrage at 1600. The bombardment began with three 82nd Airborne batteries at Point Salines firing 500 shells at Calivigny. But, due to aiming miscalculations, all but one of the rounds from seventeen 105 mm howitzers fell harmlessly into the sea.[52] Only one round was fired by the USS *Moosbrugger* before the 1615 firing deadline.[53] The destroyer's guns did not respond because naval doctrine prohibited fire by surface ships when Navy jets were aloft in close proximity to the target. A furious Trobaugh radioed the *Guam* demanding to know the name of the Navy officer who refused to give the order to fire. Butler on the *Guam* interjected himself between the general and the gunnery lieutenant. He radioed an argument-ending reply: the name of the offending officer was spelled "CJTF," the acronym for Metcalf as Chief of the Joint Task Force.[54]

The attack was delayed 15 minutes to allow for an aerial bombardment by Navy A-7 Corsairs and an Air Force AC-130 Spectre. The Navy bombs knocked down most of the buildings and set two 1,000-gallon oil drums ablaze. The Spectre gunship piloted by Twiford also hurled two 105 mm rounds into each of the 15–20 corrugated-roof buildings, but they appeared to be currently uninhabited. The gunship got no return fire, but it did set off a small secondary explosion in one of the buildings, suggesting an ammunition or fuel store.[55]

The way was now cleared for the Rangers to arrive in four flights of four Black Hawks each at 1645. Each helicopter carried 15 soldiers. The aircraft approached the target by flying low at 100-plus knots over Westerhall Bay and then climbing 125 feet over a steep coastal slope to a plateau. The pilots were misled by the aerial photos and maps of the camp they had been supplied. They came up on their designated landing zone sooner and faster than expected. The zone was also partially obscured by thick black smoke coming from the burning oil drums. The pilots flared their helicopters nose-up to quickly reduce speed.

Disaster struck almost immediately. The first two aircraft landed successfully, but the third suffered explosive damage to its tail boom while it was still about 15 feet in the air. Chief Warrant Officer 2 Wayne P. Sinibaldi, suddenly lost all hydrologic control of his aircraft.[56] The fire could have come from ammunition stores that were cooked off by the airstrikes, misaimed machine gun fire from the Black Hawk door gunners or small arms from a squad of Grenadian soldiers who were spotted on a distant ridgeline.[57] Whatever the source, the Black Hawk landed violently and started bouncing to the right toward the second Black Hawk. The rotors of the two helicopters meshed, tearing their blades apart. Meanwhile, a fourth Black Hawk, still airborne, veered off to avoid the wreckage of the other two and landed hard in a ditch. Rangers from three helicopters were now on the ground, but some were seriously wounded. Sgt. William C. Sears, Jr., was hit in the right shin above the boot as he exited his helicopter. Unable to get up, he yelled for help. Sp4c. Kevin J. Lannon, a medic, heard his call and responded.[58] Lannon had just bandaged Sears' wound when the fourth helicopter attempted to take off. The pilot was unaware that his hard landing had caused critical damage. The main rotor blades had flexed down and sliced through the drive shaft of the tail rotor.[59] The Black Hawk design gave no cockpit warning while on the ground that the rear rotor was inoperative. The helicopter struggled on liftoff. Sears heard the turbine engines screaming and looked up to see the shadow of the crippled craft careening toward them. Sears pushed the medic away and attempted to crawl away. He yelled for Lannon to run. Neither escaped the second crash.

Rotor blade shards from the three wrecked helicopters sliced through the 2nd Battalion Rangers like scythes. Three were killed: Lannon, Sgt. Stephen Eric Slater and Sp4c. Philip Sebastian Grenier. Three more Rangers were badly wounded in the chain-reaction crash. Sears was crushed and left permanently paralyzed by the falling helicopter. Three pilots were also injured, one with a broken back.[60] The landing zone was now a mass casualty scene.

The surviving Rangers sprinted away from the carnage on their mission to clear the burning buildings in the compound. Sgt. Stephen Trujillo, a 23-year-old Ranger medic from the only unscathed helicopter, was ordered back to the crash scene to do what he could for the casualties. Trujillo recalled the bloody scene in a 2017 e-book memoir.[61] Trujillo's initial search for trapped survivors was cut short by a secondary explosion that blew him away from the wreckage, searing his skin and shirt. Then he heard shouts and found 1st Lt. William E. Eskridge, a Ranger platoon leader, buried in mud at the base of a smoking Black Hawk. Trujillo pulled Eskridge free and into a nearby shell hole where he immediately began administering first aid. Eskridge had a wound in his left leg and his right was severed above the knee. Trujillo applied a tourniquet, started two IVs and gave the paralyzed officer a shot of morphine. A second medic, Sgt. Gerry Eric Holt, arrived and went off to search for other casualties. More help soon arrived in the form of medics and doctors in the following waves. Sears was discovered and pulled from the wreckage near death. Trujillo and the other medics saved his life by keeping him breathing when his lungs collapsed. Trujillo was officially credited with saving at least one life at Calivigny and was awarded a Silver Star for conspicuous gallantry.[62] Holt was awarded a Bronze Star with a Combat V for his role. A third medic, Lannon, was posthumously awarded the same medal for giving life-saving care to Sears and several others in the course of the first two days of fighting. Lannon's death was especially poignant because he had been away at Fort Bragg for advanced medical training when his battalion was recalled for Urgent Fury. Lannon went AWOL from his temporary assignment to hitchhike back to Savannah, GA just in time to deploy to Grenada with his parent unit, Company A of the 2nd Battalion. Slater, a 22-year-old Ranger who was killed at the same time as Lannon, was a team leader with that same company.

Some of the wounded 2nd Battalion Rangers were brought to the *Guam* by helicopter. Schwarzkopf went to see them in sick bay and found blood splattered everywhere from horrible slashing wounds. A lieutenant who had lost a leg tried to get out of bed to stand at attention. Schwarzkopf pushed him back. The young officer inquired if the mission had been accomplished. Schwarzkopf assured him that the Rangers had done well.[63] "Rangers lead the way—hooah!" responded the lieutenant, reciting the battle cry that Rangers bellow from their ranks before and after missions. (Schwarzkopf's memoir does not name this junior officer, but his description matches Eskridge.)[64] Schwarzkopf was deeply moved—and enraged. "[T]here had been no military reason we had to take the Calivigny barracks that day. I wondered which son of a bitch had ordered the attack," he wrote in his autobiography. The rest of the battalion landed successfully. They swept through the camp only to find it totally deserted of either Cubans or Grenadians: no bodies, no wounded, no prisoners. The exact source of the fire than set off the chain reaction collision was never conclusively determined. The compound was declared under control by 2100.

No record was ever found at the Pentagon of the Joint Chiefs ordering the attack on Calivigny.[65] Schwarzkopf later speculated that the purported JCS order originated in McDonald's headquarters in Norfolk because of impatience in both Norfolk and Washington to secure the compound.[66] As word of the calamity at Calivigny spread through the ranks, so did the skepticism about hostile fire as a cause of the crash. Schwarzkopf was among the doubters. "What happened is when they got to Calivigny Barracks, in their haste, they went into a lousy landing zone," he later told a military historian.

"There still is a question in my mind whether there was any ground fire at all, and certainly if there was any ground fire at all, it was probably minimal ground fire. It was, in fact, the crashing aircraft that end[ed] up killing and wounding so many people, more than it was the actual enemy, because. when they actually got there, it was a dry hole."[67]

At around the same time that the Rangers were savaged at the Calivigny complex, another tragedy was in the making near Frequente involving the 82nd Airborne. At about 1600 on Oct. 27 a Combat Support Company attached to the 2nd Brigade came under small arms fire near a road junction in an area east of Frequente known as Ruth Howard. The fire came from two or three directions and may have been from both enemy snipers and friendly counterfire.[68] Units from two different brigades were operating in close proximity in this area. Sniper fire was also reported around this time, and perhaps from the same hostile source, by two other units: Bravo Company, 1st Battalion, 505th Infantry of the 3rd Brigade[69] and Bravo Company of the 307th Engineers, another support unit attached to the 2nd Brigade.[70]

The sniper fire was witnessed by a jeep at the Ruth Howard crossroads carrying a joint Navy/Marines fire support team that was supposed to be operating with the 3nd Battalion, 325th Infantry, of the 2nd Brigade.[71] This Air and Naval Gunfire Liaison Company (ANGLICO) unit was newly arrived and, like most units operating on the island, its communication was spotty. In addition to signal limitations, this unit was also operating without its usual higher-echelon supervision at brigade headquarters because of coordination complications at Fort Bragg prior to the short-notice deployment.[72] The Marine-led team spotted a house near a drive-in theater to the west that they thought was the source of the hostile fire.

Bravo Company of the 307th Engineer Battalion had also identified sniper fire coming from the same area. Lt. Scott A. Snook, the engineer company executive officer, was dispatched by his company commander to seek help in silencing the threat. Snook trudged up a steep hill to the 2nd Brigade command post which had recently been established on a ridge line adjacent to his unit. There he found the tactical operations center for the 2nd Brigade commander, Silvasy, and his 44-man command staff. Silvasy's three radio operators had set up a communication center inside a crudely built, tin-roof structure on the hilltop that had been used by the Grenadians as a barracks. The three radiomen collectively controlled naval, artillery and air support for both Ranger and 82nd Airborne units. It was a particularly busy place at this time because the Ranger assault on the Calivigny compound was then in progress.[73] Snook met with the Capt. August J. Fucci, the brigade's fire support officer, outside the shack to discuss using Army artillery fire to subdue the pesky sniper. Meanwhile, unbeknown to them, the ANGLICO jeep made direct radio contact with a flight of four Navy A-7 Corsairs, which were then flying in support of the Calivigny raid.

The ANGLICO unit identified the source of the harassing sniper fire as a white house with a red roof on a ridge north of the drive-in movie theater.[74] Normally an attack on a target like this would need the approval of the battalion commander, in this case Lt. Col. John W. Raines. But the Marine officer was not in radio contact with either Raines or Silvasy and decided to act on his own initiative to suppress the hostile file. On his direction, the A-7 flight leader flew in low over the drive-in on several practice runs. The pilot radioed he had located the target and was cleared hot at 1645. On the ensuing live-fire run, the Corsair mistakenly strafed Silvasy's nearby command post. The jet's 20 mm cannon rounds blew the roof off the brigade's radio shack and sent shrapnel and splinters everywhere. Both Fucci and Snook were thrown from their feet and wounded. Snook landed down the hill, ending up next to another fire support officer he did not know. That officer had blood oozing from holes in his boot, a sharp pain in his back and a radio at his side. Snook heard him desperately plead for the Navy jets to cease fire. "I watched helplessly as the one person who was supposed to be able to talk to the Navy screamed into his microphone," Snook later wrote. "No reply. He couldn't raise the carrier group. He couldn't raise the fighter pilots."[75]

Meanwhile, the Marine ANGLICO officer also called for a cease fire with more success. He immediately realized that the Corsair had hit the wrong structure, but he did not yet know that casualties had resulted. The leader of the A-7s refused to further engage and returned to his carrier.[76] Still, the Marine officer persisted and directed another flight of Navy jets, A-6 Intruders, to continue the attack on the original red-roof target. Snook watched as different jets dove to the attack. Snook tried to shelter his head next to a nearby rock, expecting another strafing attack. Instead, an A-6 dropped two MK-20 cluster bombs at the end of its dive. One bomb exploded several hundred yards away; the other was a dud. Finally, the air attack was called off.

The strafing attack left at least 17 wounded at the command post. A tropical downpour added to the misery and delayed the arrival of Army helicopters to evacuate 12 of the wounded. Two radio operators, Sgt. Harry E. Shaw and Sgt. Sean P. Luketina, suffered severe injuries that resulted in the loss of both legs in the attack.[77] (Luketina died eight months later of further medical complications, bringing the final American combat death total to 19.) Two Air Force liaison officers, Capt. Jimmy H. Alexander and Capt. Robert M. Awtrey, were also among the command post wounded, the only casualties the Air Force suffered in Urgent Fury, according to that service's post-invasion final tally.[78] (Another unnamed Air Force liaison serving with the Rangers was also a combat casualty, according to a Tactical Air Command history of Urgent Fury.[79] It's unclear why this additional wounded airman was not included among the reportable Air Force wounded.)

Lt. Col. George A. Crocker, the commander of the 1st Battalion of the 505th Infantry, witnessed the devastating Frequente friendly fire attack from his position 1,000 yards away. After the cease fire, he went in search of who was controlling the Navy jets. He walked down a road where he encountered a distraught Marine fire controller. "Do you know that air strike just hit the 2nd Brigade?" he asked. "Yes," murmured the Marine who hung his head in remorse.[80] A subsequent investigation laid the blame for the mistaken attack on the Marine officer for supplying the A-7 with the wrong coordinates and exonerated the Navy pilot.[81] Despite the carnage that the friendly fire wrought on his brigade command post, Silvasy was forgiving of the mistaken attack, chalking it up to fortunes of war. "The guy made an assessment, he seized the initiative, he did what every one of us want a young officer to do. He thought we were in big time trouble and he called in the air," Silvasy said in a post-invasion briefing at Ft. Leavenworth. "So, you know, I understand. I can't condone any of it, but I can understand it."[82]

Ironically, the last major Army mission to be accomplished on Grenada was the same as the first: the rescue of yet another group of Americans. Even after the rescue of students at the True Blue and the Grand Anse campus, there still were additional Americans, including medical school students, living in private homes on peninsulas in the southwest quadrant of the island. The 82nd Airborne troops were slowly working their way toward them from Point Salines. The paratroopers used portable public-address systems to broadcast their presence in residential areas and advise any American listeners to "lay low" until rescued. On the third day, an additional 200 American, Canadian and British civilians and were reached in this fashion by Cocker's battalion.[83] Cocker was moved when he saw medical students running toward his paratroopers "crying, laughing, praying ... hugging and kissing" though he was secretly annoyed they called his men "Marines."[84] Meanwhile to the north, Marine units moving south from St. George's collected 35 more Americans in their area of operations. So, by the end of the third day, a total of 595 American civilians had been collected by various American units. The final extraction of the scattered Americans on the 82nd Airborne's Black Hawk helicopters didn't begin until 1128 on Friday, Oct. 28, 78 hours after the invasion began.[85] Later on Friday, the first planeload of Rangers also returned home to American soil. The 1st Battalion was greeted at Hunter Army Airfield by the Army chief of staff, Gen. John A. Wickham, their loved ones and an Army band. Mop-up operations were now entirely in the hands of the Marines and the 82nd Airborne.

For a variety of reasons, the pace of the advance by the 82nd was the subject of mounting concern at the Pentagon as a one-day operation stretched on to a week. The 82nd Airborne's deliberative pace was partly by plan and partly the result of circumstances beyond their control. With intention, Trobaugh directed that the advance include thorough searches for hidden combatants and arms caches. Drawing on his Vietnam experience, he wanted to forestall any opportunity for an insurgency to take root when the Americans departed. He thought he was facing a determined force of Cuban soldiers, perhaps supported by Russian and Eastern European military advisers. He also thought a controlled advance would reduce the risk of friendly fire incidents as his paratroopers moved closer to the Marine forces in the north.[86]

This inclination for caution was amplified by the supply snarl at the airport which delayed arrival of his transport vehicles and needed supplies, especially water. Paratroopers had to advance over difficult terrain on foot in tropical heat. Even the most physically fit needed frequent stops for rest and rehydration. Their rucksacks were too heavy and their medium-weight, 50/50 cotton-nylon battle dress uniforms (BDUs) were too hot for the tropics. (Rangers wore Vietnam-era, hot-weather fatigues.)[87] On Oct. 26, the first day of combat for the 82nd Airborne, five heat-related casualties were suffered in the assault on Little Havana, five more securing Frequente and 30 advancing over steep terrain toward Grand Anse. Based on these alarming reports, Hamilton, the 2nd Battalion commander, ordered all his men to shed the 20-pound flack vest they wore over their uniforms. Eventually, the entire brigade was given permission to shed their vests.[88]

Water was a problem that manifested itself in different ways at both the squad and the command level. For the individual soldier, the problem was the fragility of the standard-issue, two-quart canteen that every soldier carried, in addition to two one-quart canteens. The two-quart model was prone to rupture, which instantly cut a paratrooper's supply in half.[89] At the division level, the problem was supply and distribution. Army engineers scrounged for local supplies to supplement the 5,000 gallons a day that were arriving from off the island in five-gallon jerrycan containers. A storage tank was found near the airport with water that tested pure. Then the problem was how to get the liquid from the airport to soldiers in the field without the vehicle-drawn "water buffalo" tanks that the division normally used. Captured vehicles were pressed into service as delivery vehicles.[90]

The capture of the Grenadian Army logistics complex at Frequente on Oct. 26 was a fortuitous boon to the over-heated, over-burdened paratroopers. The complex included a truck park with 19 vehicles, most of them loaded with ammunition. The arms cache

Water was a precious commodity on tropical Grenada for overburdened ground combat troops, like this thirsty Marine. Potable water was flown in by military aircraft until safe supply sources were identified on the island (National Archives [330-CFD-DN-SN-85-02083]).

proved a propaganda bonanza for American policy-makers seeking evidence that Grenada was to be a staging area for exporting communist revolutions throughout Latin America. But, from the paratroopers' perspective, the vehicles were far more valuable as a solution to their mobility and supply problems. Army maintenance specialists immediately set about hot-wiring the fleet. Regardless of the vehicle's originally designed purpose, all captured vehicles were converted to military transport use. Dump trucks carried rucksacks, food and water. Sedans transported mortar tubes in their trunks. Even garbage trucks were deputized for hot-wired military convoys, until their absence threatened public sanitation. Most repurposed vehicles had USA hastily painted on their chassis. One well-read commander compared the sight of his battalion's supply train coming down the road to the over-laden "California or bust" caravans that fled the Dustbowl during the Depression, as described by John Steinbeck in *The Grapes of Wrath*.

By the next day, the vehicle park at Frequente was totally stripped of vehicles aside from one armored personnel carrier and a dump truck with a dead battery. That morning Silvasy, the brigade commander, invited a staff officer to join him for a personal tour of the captured motor pool. When they arrived, Silvasy was surprised to see most of the vehicles gone. He was also annoyed to see an 82nd paratrooper working on the brand-new BTR-60. He had issued orders for troops to keep their hands off this combat vehicle for fear that they would be mistaken for the enemy. Silvasy accosted the soldier saying: "Look friend, I told one of your buddies yesterday to stay the hell off that vehicle. You're going get yourself killed ... what in the world are you trying to do?"[91] The grease-soiled, backyard mechanic explained to the colonel that he wasn't trying to drive the vehicle; he

The 82nd Airborne arrived without its customary transport vehicles. Captured vehicles, like this Soviet-made dump truck, were pressed into military service (National Archives [330-CFD-DF-SN-84-10785]).

was cannibalizing it for parts to fix a disabled truck. Silvasy was dubious. "I'm going to sit right down here and eat some C-rations and I am going to watch you," he retorted. Under the brigade's commander skeptical gaze, the soldier extracted a giant-size battery from the personnel carrier and single-handedly dragged it over to the fender of the truck. Then he connected the battery to the ignition and started the engine. He waved at Silvasy as he drove off with his prize.

After the third day, the principal focus of military operations was a roundup of PRA and NJM leaders, uncovering arms caches and extending the military control to the entire island. The American forces were assisted in all of these efforts by Grenadians who provided them with actionable intelligence information. Coard, the leader of the coup, and his wife, Phyllis, were captured by 22nd MAU Marines, who were tipped to their location by Grenadians. The Coards and four friends were found hiding in a private home on the eastern outskirts of the capital on Saturday morning, Oct. 29. The fugitives were induced to surrender when an antitank weapon was pointed at the house. Coard was the last to emerge and kept saying, "I'm not responsible, I'm not responsible" according to the gunnery sergeant who demanded the surrender.[92] The next afternoon, Austin, the head of the military council, and two PRA lieutenant colonels were captured by 82nd paratroopers in a private home in the expatriate enclave at Westerhall Point.[93] The Austin group and the Coards were flown separately to the *Guam* where they were held in cells and the men were interrogated by Americans.[94] After eight days, the prisoners were taken to Richmond Hill Prison to face civil criminal charges for the murder of Bishop and 10 of his supporters at Fort Rupert on Oct. 19.

9

The Enemy Is the Media

The first invasion of Grenada on Oct. 25 by American and Caribbean military forces was closely followed by a second, mounted by the Anglo-American press corps. The first action was opposed by Grenadian troops and the Cubans in residence. The second incursion was opposed, at least initially, by the American military.

The Pentagon-approved invasion plan made no prevision for taking the news media along with the invading troops, or for tolerating their presence on Grenadian soil while significant fighting was going on. To an extraordinary extent, reporters were barred from observing American troops engaged in overt combat against another sovereign nation on foreign soil. That exclusion was not received well by the American news media. "While Grenada was a skirmish in terms of warfare, it may also have been the information-warfare 'mother of battles,'" Metcalf wrote in a 1991 article for a naval journal.[1] (The maternal reference played off Iraq president Saddam Hussein's defiant prediction that the 1991 conflict over Kuwait oil fields would be "the Mother of all Battles.") Metcalf's epic battle with the media over Grenada in 1983 was not the result of any written directive from Washington. Metcalf opined that the "no press" policy was initially decided more by implication than by assertion. "In my opinion, it probably 'just happened'… a logical extension of the tight security that covered the early planning," Metcalf wrote.

The available historical record indicates that the role of the press first came up indirectly in two national security planning discussions on Thursday, Oct. 20, before Metcalf had any role in the operation.[2] The worry at that time was that the preparations for intervention would leak prematurely and result in a parrying response from Cuba and/or Moscow. The particular fear was that Cuba would move to introduce troops, or that the Grenadian coup leaders would move the American students to hidden locations. The Oct. 20 meetings resulted in the "prepare for action" National Security Decision Directive 110, signed by Reagan on Oct. 21. That presidential order directed the Defense Secretary and the Joint Chiefs to take "all possible measures … to preserve the secrecy of these activities and reduce the possibility of pre-emptive action by the Soviets/Cubans." Although the order did not explicitly not say so, Reagan also wanted to avoid any domestic objection being raised through the American press. "Frankly there was another reason I wanted secrecy. It was what I call the 'post–Vietnam syndrome,' the resistance of so many in Congress to the use of military force abroad for any reason," Reagan later wrote in his memoirs. "I suspected that, if we told the leaders of Congress about the operation, even under terms of strictest confidentiality, there would be some who would leak it to the press.... We didn't ask anybody, we just did it."[3] In the event, the possibility of an invasion did leak in an ambiguous way on Friday night, Oct. 21, but the information embargo remained in force.

Vessey later remembered the subject of media coverage coming up again in the course of a series of one-on-one conversations he had with McDonald in the frenetic last 48 hours before the invasion. "We had agreed that we were not going to take any press along; that there wasn't time enough to get things ready to take press along on the operations. We gave it just sort of transitory consideration saying: we've got a problem," he recalled.[4] In subsequent conversations, Vessey said the two four-star officers agreed that press would be allowed access to the battlefield after the special forces had departed the island, likely "at the tail end of the first day ... or at least on the second day." The mere existence of the Joint Special Operations Command was then considered a secret at the Pentagon. Vessey didn't want the special operators and their equipment and tactics exposed to press scrutiny. He was also wary of the new anti-terrorism forces being perceived as "a tool for quickly invading third world countries."[5]

For his part, Metcalf recalled the subject first coming up in passing at about 2030 on Sunday, Oct. 23, in Norfolk, just six hours after he was informed that he would lead the invasion. A lieutenant commander on the Atlantic Command's staff came up to him and said: "There will be no press. Do you have a problem with that?" Of the many problems on Metcalf's mind at that point, not having to deal with the press sounded like an easy solution to him. "My answer came more from the attention to urgent operational matters than a thought-out position on the issue of the press," Metcalf later wrote.[6] "Was that a formulation of a media policy by acquiescence, or did I have an option?" As a practical matter, the only public affairs officer on his Second Fleet staff at that moment was an ensign straight out of college who was subbing in a position usually filled by a mid-career officer. The ensign got left behind when Metcalf selected his "fly away" staff of 17.

Though Pentagon officials were being tight lipped, that did not translate to reporters being unaware that something was brewing in the Eastern Caribbean. Beginning on Friday evening, Oct. 21, when the news of the ship diversion broke in Washington, the international press was aware that some sort of American military intervention in Grenada could be in wind. However, it wasn't clear to reporters working the story what form that intervention might take. The dominant impression through the ensuing weekend was that, if an intervention occurred, it would be a humanitarian evacuation of American citizens. That assumption was challenged on Monday, Oct. 24, when Bill Plante, the White House correspondent for CBS, was told by a source that the United States was about to "invade" Grenada. Plante asked Larry Speakes, Reagan's top press spokesman, about the possibility of an invasion occurring the next morning. Plante left the impression that the tip had come from someone connected either directly or indirectly with the CIA.[7] Speakes promised to get back to him with a response. At this point, according to Speakes, he was not fully trusted to keep a secret by more senior White House staff. He was as much in the dark about the impending action as the press corps. In any case, Speakes was far more focused on responding to questions associated with the 241 American lives lost in Beirut over the weekend than on what could be happening on Grenada. "I had suspected we might send troops into Grenada at some point to rescue the American medical students, but I had no inkling that was imminent, nor did I have any idea that we might launch a full-scale invasion of the island," Speakes later wrote in his White House memoir.[8]

Les Janka, Speakes' deputy for foreign affairs, got similar calls from CBS news staffers early Monday afternoon, as did Robert Sims, the press officer for the National Security Council. The multiple inquiries led Sims to check with Poindexter, the deputy NSC director, who knew the invasion was planned for the following day. "Preposterous. Knock it down hard," was the guidance from Poindexter that came back to Speakes and Janka. Speakes passed Poindexter's one-word answer verbatim to Plante. The strong denial, sourced to such an informed official, effectively put the kibosh on the story. "[W]ith that much of a knockdown there wasn't much choice," Plante later recounted. "Given the normal rules of the game you have to assume they are not lying."[9] Speakes later concluded that Poindexter was under orders from Baker, the White House chief of staff, not to reveal what was going on. When asked about this suspicion later, Baker demurred. "I never, ever ordered anyone to lie to the press. I might have told [Poindexter] not to tell the press office about it [the invasion]. That's different." (They both may have been influenced by the fact that Reagan's final National Security Decision Directive 110A reaffirmed the need to maintain strict security controls, and specifically authorized "appropriate cover and deceptive measures to mislead the present Grenadian regime and the Cubans concerning our true intentions.")

Poindexter's knockdown punch didn't KO the invasion story entirely. The Oct. 31 issue of *Newsweek*, which was sent to press on Oct. 23, before the shooting started, carried a prescient look to the future in the Windwards. The three-page report on Grenada included a detailed account of the Bishop assassination and the international outcry it precipitated. Noting that the bloodshed had led Reagan to dispatch a naval task force toward the island, lead writer Mark Whitaker concluded his first paragraph with the rhetorical question: "was the president intent on a simple exercise in gunboat diplomacy—or was he, in fact, considering a U.S. military invasion of Grenada?" By Monday evening, Oct. 24, Speakes was belatedly aware that something big was stirring in the White House. He learned that Reagan was having an unscheduled, after-hours meeting with congressional leaders to which he had not been invited. He went home in disgust for being excluded. He called the White House chief of staff from home later that evening and learned for the first time from his boss that "something" was afoot. Baker told him to report to the White House at 5:45 a.m. on Tuesday, but did not further explain.[10]

Closer to the action, other reporters were also suspecting that an invasion was imminent, based on hints they were getting from Caribbean government officials. Meetings of the two regional organizations, OECS and the Caribbean Community (CARICOM), over the weekend had occasioned on-the-record confirmation from Caribbean leaders that military intervention was being discussed, as well as economic sanctions against Grenada. Moreover, the Grenadians themselves were expecting an armed intervention of their territory—and shouting alarms from the rooftops. On Sunday night, Radio Free Grenada broadcast government warnings that an invasion was imminent.

Reading the abundant tea leaves on Monday morning, 24 hours before the invasion began, an ad hoc group of seven international journalists set out from Bridgetown to the expected scene of action in St. George's. The seven included reporters for the *Miami Herald*, the *Washington Post*, *Newsday* on Long Island, New York, and *Time*. The others were two British journalists and a photographer for Sygma, a French photo news service, who was working on contract for *Time*. One of the British reporters, Hugh O'Shaughnessy, later wrote an account of their odyssey in a book about the invasion.[11] The seven began their shared journey on Oct. 24 with a 55-minute charter flight from Barbados to Union

Island on St. Vincent, Grenada's nearest island neighbor. There they found a boatman who was willing to take them 10 miles south to Carriacou, the second largest of Grenada's three principal islands. Carriacou, a largely undeveloped island of about 6,000, was removed from the repressive political sway of the main island. The foreign journalists breezed through routine customs checks and were officially admitted to Grenadian soil. They stayed in a Carriacou hotel overnight and awoke at dawn to hear a Radio Free Grenada broadcast that the invasion had begun. They hurried to the harbor and found a Grenadian fisherman who was willing to take them the final 34 nautical miles to St. George's. His 20-foot boat, the *Odin C.*, was fittingly named for the Norse god of war.

A tense, spray-soaked, five-hour journey ensued through choppy waters. En route, the journalists heard commercial-frequency radio reports that U.S. Marines were in control of the quay at St. George's. Fearful that they would miss the fighting entirely, they urged the boat captain to increase speed. Later the *Time* correspondent on the boat learned that some of the broadcasts they heard originated from the U.S.–controlled "Radio 1560."[12] The military-run station broadcast prerecorded "news" reports and music produced by a Navy audiovisual unit. Radio 1560 initially broadcast on the Voice of America (VOA) frequency before switching to the Radio Free Grenada frequency when the station was knocked off the air by the American invaders. The replacement signal came from a mobile 10-kilowatt mobile transmitter on a Navy ship offshore and also from an airborne transmitter carried by a Pennsylvania National Guard EC-130.[13]

Radio 1560's scripted D-Day morning propaganda reflected Pentagon expectations, not reality. The seven journalists were shocked to find the air battle over St. George's to still be in full fury when they arrived at the capital's harbor quay at 12:30 p.m. Their landing coincided with the ill-fated Cobra helicopter attacks on Fort Frederick, and the ensuing A-7 bombing of the mental hospital and AC-130 strafing of anti-aircraft sites in the capital.[14] The seven took refuge in a fire station across the quay. During a lull in the air-to-ground gunfights, the journalists were approached by a Grenadian policeman who said he was an immigration officer. He checked their passports and bags and told them that the PRA had ordered that they stay put while the battle over the capital raged.[15]

The seven were held at the firehouse for six hours under what one of them later described as "mostly friendly detention." A truck filled with eight Grenadian soldiers stopped to check on them and discouraged them from straying too far. The journalists appealed to the soldiers to help them file their reports to their publications. "The Grenadian soldiers appeared to be as anxious for us to put out the news as we were," Don Bohning, the *Miami Herald* reporter later wrote.[16] The PRA soldiers tried to help, but they couldn't locate the keys to the nearby telex office where a backup generator was providing power. When darkness fell, a mixed group of journalists and soldiers broke into the closed office, but couldn't find a working telex or voice line. The soldiers then took the civilian visitors to the St. James Hotel near Fort Rupert, where they told the owner that the journalists should be considered "guest of the revolution." (It's ironic that, at this point, the leaders of a Marxist-military coup which had expelled international reporters were more accommodating to uncensored, first-hand reports by Anglo-American journalists than anyone in charge in the Pentagon or the White House.)

The journalists slept fitfully as distant explosions interrupted their sleep. The next morning, Oct. 26, the visitors woke to reports from locals that Marines had entered the capital overnight and had established a position at Queen's Park Racecourse at the northern edge of town. Members of the group made their way there in the pursuit of news from the American military and the means to transmit that information back to their editors. The journalist delegation arrived at Queen's Park at around the same time as Scoon and his party arrived there on Oct. 26 for evacuation by U.S. helicopters back to the *Guam*. The reporters also met Marines who were as thirsty for accurate information as they were. After checking identification of the *Washington Post* reporter, a junior officer said to him: "We just got here last night. Can you please tell us what the f … is going on?" The reporter shared a brief update and then the platoon leader asked: "Is the Grenadian Army on their side or ours?"[17] The questions were entirely understandable given the warm reception the Marines were receiving from Grenadian civilians. The journalist also got a cordial welcome from Smith, the Marine infantry commander who was then the ranking American officer on the ground at St. George's. They asked to use military communication equipment to contact their editors. Smith told them that the *Guam* had such facilities and, by their account, offered the journalists a ride on a Marine helicopter to Metcalf's offshore command ship. Four of the journalists who were working for daily newspapers accepted: Edward Cody of the *Washington Post*, Don Bohning of the *Miami Herald*, Morris Thompson of *Newsday* and Greg Chamberlain of *The Guardian* of London. The three others, working under less urgent deadlines, opted to remain on the island and continue reporting and photographing.

Metcalf and his command staff where startled by the arrival of the four print journalists on the *Guam* while they were in the midst of a still-active battle. The reporters had hopped aboard a Marine helicopter that Metcalf had dispatched to retrieve members of the Scoon party—not American reporters. The pilots let the civilians aboard thinking they were with Scoon.[18] When this unexpected development was reported back to Washington, the Pentagon affirmed a continued "no press" policy and admonished Metcalf for letting reporters aboard.[19] Metcalf promised the reporters he would pass word back to their editors that they were safe, but the four were told that there was too much priority message traffic for them to use the *Guam*'s radios to file their stories.[20] Meantime, the journalists became Metcalf's guests on the *Guam*, but with no way to leave without the military's help.

About two hours after Metcalf had reported the arrival of American reporters on his flagship, the Pentagon changed its tune about press coverage. Now feeling the mounting outrage of the excluded press corps, Metcalf's superiors asked him how soon the press would be allowed into the war zone. When the admiral heard that as many as 400 reporters wanted to come, he put the issue aside, at least for the moment. His personal feelings about the press after his Vietnam experiences didn't incline him to do journalists any favors. "I had little confidence in the press to report events accurately or to make balanced interpretations of what had occurred," he later wrote.[21] Metcalf decided on his own that reporters would not be not allowed onto the battlefield until the situation was stabilized sufficiently for the media to be shielded from hostile fire—and could be escorted by public affairs officers. "How many casualties are worth the presence of one press guy?" Metcalf later rhetorically asked in an interview.[22] "I say zero. By the second day, we had actually secured most of the island, but then there wasn't any water or electricity, or any place to put this gaggle of 400."

Reporters on Barbados, undeterred by such logistical considerations, continued to try to report the news by any means they could. At 1100 on D-Day, the *Guam* received a radio report of a civilian speedboat heading toward Grenadian shores. The approach was in defiance of an announced military cordon around the island that was intended to keep

Grenadian officials from escaping or Cubans from entering. A Navy fighter was dispatched to make low passes over the boat to get it to stop, without success. "Who could be doing this?" Schwarzkopf heard Metcalf ask.[23] "Is someone trying to pick up Hudson Austin?" Metcalf authorized the Navy jet to fire warning shots. Still the boat did not turn. A second burst was fired and the boat finally turned. It wasn't until later that that Metcalf learned the boat contained reporters trying to reach the island.

In the afternoon of Oct. 26, two of the journalists aboard the *Guam* attempted to hop on a Marine helicopter headed to Point Salines in preparation for the Grand Anse airlift. Schwarzkopf spotted them and sprinted across the flight deck to order them out. "You're interfering with a military operation," he barked. All the reporters were barred from the flight deck and spent the rest of the day, and night, on the ship. Metcalf later acknowledged to two of the journalists that, acting on orders from Washington, they were deliberately held on the ship for 18 hours to prevent them from filing their firsthand reports.[24] But, in Washington, Metcalf's superiors were telling a different story about the source of press restrictions. At a press conference on Oct. 26 conducted by both Weinberger and Vessey, the defense secretary said that the decision to exclude the press came from the commanders outside the Pentagon.

> Q: "Why weren't any reporters allowed along this time and when will reporters get into combat?"
>
> A: (Weinberger) "The reason is, of course, the Commander's decision, and I certainly don't ever, wouldn't ever dream of overriding Commander's decisions ... their conclusion was that they were not able to guarantee any kind of safety of anyone."

As questioning persisted of Weinberger on this topic, Vessey joined the colloquy. "I think one of the most important reasons that we didn't [allow reporters] was the need for surprise in this operation," Vessey interjected in answer to a question addressed to Weinberger. "We were going in there very quickly and we needed to have surprise in order to have it be successful."

The four detained journalists remained incommunicado onboard the *Guam* until Thursday morning. Metcalf invited them to join a planned Marine assault on Richmond Hill Prison which Metcalf still believed to be a Grenadian stronghold. But when the four flew from the *Guam* to the island they learned that the prison had already been liberated by the three journalists who had remained behind on the island: O'Shaughnessy of the *London Observer*, Bernard Diederich of *Time*, and Claude Urraca, a Sygma photographer. The trio had been eye-witnesses (from a distance) to the uncontested Marine seizure of Fort Frederick and the Ranger rescue at Grand Anse on Wednesday afternoon.[25] Later on Oct. 26, they went looking for Hughes, the Grenadian journalist and *Time* stringer who had been imprisoned by the coup leaders. At 1700 they made their way to Richmond Hill Prison where they found about 100 prisoners still in their cells.[26] They released Hughes and nine other political prisoners. They pragmatically advised the common criminals to remain in their cells for their own safety. Marines might mistake their gray prison garb for green Grenadian military uniforms. At around 1930 the journalists reported to a Marine command post that the prison was unguarded, but Smith's handwritten journal states that he did not learn this news from the journalists until just after dawn on Thursday. Smith then dispatched a platoon to the hilltop prison and it was reported secure by 0800 on Thursday, Oct. 27.

The seven enterprising journalists who had arrived by boat on D-Day were reunited on shore in Grenada on Oct. 27, but still had no way to file their stories. They hitched a ride on a military helicopter to Point Salines. From there, an Air Force C-130 flew them back to Barbados on Thursday evening.[27] On Barbados, the seven joined about 300 journalists who had assembled at a press center near Grantley Adams Airport. They were all clamoring for information from the military officials there who were running the logistical support for the forces on Grenada. The new arrivals had the only uncensored, firsthand accounts of the first days of the fighting, and even they missed the critical events of the first morning. Cody's account of his D-Day journey to the island and subsequent detention on the *Guam* started on the front page of the Oct. 28 *Washington Post* and filled nearly an entire page inside. Diederich's two-page account of his two days on the island was published in the Nov. 7 issue of *Time*, accompanied by Urraca's photographs. One of published photographs showed the body of an American helicopter pilot (Seagle) dead on a beach at St. George's. This raw image was a departure from customary news practice and provoked protests from veterans who felt it dishonored the dead.

The blackout on first-hand reporting on the fighting was principally enforced by the establishment of an 80-kilometer military zone around the island by Metcalf.[28] The U.S. military warned that any aircraft within this zone would be regarded as enemy. On the first day, a plane chartered by a CBS news crew tried to land at Pearls Airport, but they were denied permission to land five times by the Marines who were manning the control tower.[29] The next day, another CBS charter flight was chased away by a Navy jet when it filmed naval activity around the island. Another group of journalists managed to land at Pearls Airport by boat, but they were ordered back to Barbados.[30] As the operation progressed into multiple days, the *Guam* launched two 65-foot patrol boats to conduct interdiction patrols around the main island. A destroyer with the *Independence* group also started plying the northern coast between the main island and Carriacou.

Ostensibly, the cordon was intended to keep leaders of the military regime from getting out by boat, but the Navy net also snared boats carrying reporters in. The destroyer intercepted a boat carrying ABC correspondent Josh Mankiewicz and cut across its bow. The warship came close enough for Mankiewicz to inspect the gun on the foredeck and he decide that discretion was the better part of valor.[31] Another ABC television crew hired a 35-foot fishing boat in Barbados to ferry them to Grenada, a 30-hour sea journey. As the boat neared Carriacou, Grenada's northernmost island, a Navy fighter appeared overhead and wagged its wings. The boat continued on and the jet made a low lateral pass. Still the boat continued on. The jet finally dropped a buoy just 30 feet ahead of the fishing boat's bow.[32] The newsmen got the message and turned around. Onboard the *Guam*, Butler, the chief staff officer of the amphibious squadron (and a former reporter), viewed these interdiction efforts with increasing skepticism. By this point, he thought that all the "bad guys" had either had made good their escape or had gone into hiding. He concluded the main purpose of the patrols was to keep the press out. "The first two or three boats [stopped]were carrying newspapermen," he recalled. "That increased interest a lot."[33] Sailors on the USS *Moosbrugger* dubbed the area off the main island's northwest coast the "CBS Patrol Zone."[34]

Eventually a few journalists managed to elude the Navy net around the embattled island. The successful odyssey of three *Newsweek* staffers was particularly epic, and ultimately blessed by good luck.[35] On Tuesday afternoon, Oct. 25, the news magazine chartered a small passenger jet to fly a team of staffers and freelancer photographers directly to the front lines in the Caribbean. They flew from Teterboro Airport in New Jersey to Miami and then on to Grenada. The military-trained civilian pilots radioed for permission to land at the Point Salines airstrip, but they were turned away by military air controllers. The jet diverted to Barbados and arrived around midnight. The next morning, the jet continued on to three different islands around Grenada, leaving passengers at each stop to separately attempt to gain entry by boat. Wally McNamee, a Washington bureau staff photographer who was also a former Marine, got off at a stop in St. Vincent. He was accompanied by a Linda R. Prout, a *Newsweek* reporter, and Jean-Louis Atlan, a Sygma agency photographer working on contract with the weekly news magazine.

The trio went to a marina and offered $10,000 to a local couple with a Boston Whaler if they would take them to landfall on the west side Grenada. On approach to the island from the north, the open boat ran into a picket line of Navy ships—and bit of good fortune. One of the Navy ships started to make smoke and head to the east. The low-profile Whaler made for the smoke cloud and slipped past the military vessels to reach the western coast of Grenada on the afternoon of Oct. 27. The travelers came ashore just north of the now-vacant Grand Anse campus, a day after the helicopter rescue. They then made their way to a nearby road where they encountered leading elements of the 82nd Airborne advancing north from Point Salines toward the capital. The paratroopers took the newsmen to their battalion commander, Lt. Col. Jack L. Hamilton. By then the first off-island reporters were making escorted visits to Point Salines. Hamilton made a battlefield decision to allow the *Newsweek* journalists to do their reporting and photographing and to follow his advancing troops. The trio split up. Prout, the reporter, initially staked out a nearby Grenadian coffee shop that also served as an impromptu command post for the 2nd Battalion of the 325th Infantry.[36] There she was able to report on the paratroopers mopping up the last pockets of resistance. She also got news from Grenadians who were stopping in for food and drink and to pass intelligence information to the American soldiers. Three Cubans with diplomatic passports showed up at one point to ask for—and get—permission to travel by road to the nearby Soviet Embassy, which had become a sanctuary for all displaced Soviet Bloc diplomats. The *Newsweek* photographers, operating separately, encountered some off-campus students left behind after the Grand Anse rescue who were belatedly on their way to Point Salines for evacuation. McNamee enlisted one student as a courier to get his film back to New York City. As darkness approached, the two photographers "liberated" a room in a closed beachfront hotel where they dined on C-rations and Cognac before spending the night. The next day, Friday, Oct. 28, the two freely roamed St. George's and the vicinity until Saturday when McNamee made his way to Point Salines. He hitched a ride on a military plane to Barbados where he caught a civilian flight back to New York in time for the rest of his film to make the magazine's next issue, dated Nov. 7, but available earlier.

Meanwhile, on Barbados, a hoard of frustrated reporters yearned for the freedom of movement that the *Newsweek* journalists had claimed for themselves. In response to intense pressure from the press corps, and an order from Weinberger, McDonald drafted a plan to allow media access to the battlefield on Thursday, Oct. 27, the third day of the operation.[37] The Pentagon set up a Joint Information Bureau on Barbados and organized the first reporting pool to be flow to the island. The military offered to fly 15 television, magazine and wire service reporters to the island to collect a report that would be shared with their colleagues back on Barbados. The pool was confined to the Point Salines area for a three-hour visit under military supervision. They were allowed to interview American students and inspect captured arms warehouses. Metcalf also gave them a briefing.[38] The first pool included three television network correspondents and one pool camera crew to record a shared film and sound report. The hope was that pool would be back in Barbados by 1700 in time for the correspondents to make their reports on the nightly network newscasts. Their reports would be a lead-in to an address to the nation on Grenada and Lebanon that President Reagan had scheduled for 2000. But, in the event, the pool plane was delayed on the congested runway at Point Salines and did not land in Barbados until 2045, more than 15 minutes after Reagan had finished speaking. The only film from Grenada available to the networks before the speech was just-released footage shot by the military and cleared by the Pentagon. The footage showed medical school students smiling and flashing "V" for victory signs. All three networks used the hand-out film, but CBS superimposed "cleared by Defense Department censors" over the images. Dan Rather, the CBS anchor, emphasized that viewers were seeing film that was "shot by the Army and censored by the Army."[39] But his attempt at journalistic transparency only served to enrage many viewers. After the broadcast, the CBS switchboard lit up with calls from viewers saying that network report was unpatriotic. (Both the footage supplied by the military and the press pool missed the big news event of Thursday: the helicopter crashes in the Calivigny assault and the friendly-fire bombing of the brigade command post. These mishaps were not disclosed by the military until the following Monday.)[40]

On Friday, Oct. 28, the press pool was expanded to 27. On Saturday, 47 were flown in.[41] Metcalf was on hand at both Point Salines and Bridgetown on Saturday to spar with journalists with a characteristic mix of good fellowship and bluster.[42] On Grenada, Metcalf met the pool plane dressed in an olive jump suit and wearing a baseball-style cap. The embroidered brim had a "lightning bolts and storm clouds" design, signifying senior command, and "COMSECONFLT" (Commander Second Fleet) stitched in an arc across the crown. He shook hands with new arrivals and asked their names. One journalist described the admiral as having "the vibrancy of a TV game show host and a hard edge of George Patton."

Later, facing a larger group of frustrated reporters on Barbados, Metcalf defiantly took full responsibility for the restrictive media policy. "The buck stops with me," he declared. "If you want to argue with somebody about it, you've got to argue with me, not the DOD [Department of Defense], not anybody else but me." One of Metcalf's interlocutors had been aboard a boat that had been turned away by a Navy jet. "Admiral, what would have happened if we hadn't turned around?" the reporter asked. "We would have blown your ass right out of the water," he growled.[43]

By Sunday, the military began running three C-130 media flights a day from Barbados. The number of visiting journalists swelled to more than 100 a day for the next five days before interest began to trail off. Metcalf's personal assessment was that, despite their complaints about their belated arrival, the press had done a "more than adequate" job of ferreting out what went on in their absence. He noted that the press learned about the bombing of the mental hospital before he did. The hospital bombing could have become a My Lai–like incident, but Metcalf was grateful that reporters on the scene uncovered the full circumstances of the bombing.[44]

With victory now in hand, the military was anxious now to quickly spread the laurels widely. Combat Infantryman Badges were issued to the 1st Battalion Rangers on Oct. 28 as soon as they returned to their home base in Savannah. A flood of other medals followed, eventually leading to public embarrassment over the number that were authorized by the Pentagon. The Army was especially generous, pushing the eligibility criterion to the edge of credibility. One out of every two of the 7,000 Army soldiers who set foot on

Grenada (3,534) got Combat Infantryman Badges, an award only supposed to be issued to infantrymen or special forces who personally come under hostile fire during ground combat with the enemy.[45] Only about 1,000 of those 7,000 soldiers were present on the island during the first two days when nearly all the unit-level combat occurred. The rest of the soldiers arrived on or after Oct. 27, but the eligibility period for the badge was officially extended until Nov. 21, 1983. Similarly, the Army issued 812 Bronze Stars for Urgent Fury participation, though only 59 were issued with the "V" device for valor.[46] (A Bronze Star can be issued either for merit or heroism but, in either case, only in connection with "military operations against an armed enemy.") Other uniformed services were more parsimonious in their awards, leading one military commentator to call out the "rampant medal inflation" by the Army in an op-ed column for *Washington Post*. "Perhaps elated by the first significant, clear cut, American military success in over three decades, [the Army] cared to make little distinction between the deserving and the underserving. Simply showing up for the invasion was worth at least one medal," he wrote.[47]

10

The Enemy Is Cuba

The United States invaded the territory of Grenada, but Cuba was regarded as America's ultimate adversary on the island. The invasion planners in the Reagan administration believed that the Coard-led coup could not have happened without the tacit approval of Cuba and/or Moscow. The subsequent assassination of Bishop and his supporters was seen as a sudden destabilizing move left that could lead to Cuba dispatching troops to Grenada to shore up the newly installed military regime. This was a Cuban muscle-flexing pattern that played out in the 1970s in Angola, Mozambique and Ethiopia.[1] Based on this ideological interpretation of recent events, the Grenadian military was seen to be already under effective Cuban control with the arrival of Col. Tortoló and Diaz. Statements to the contrary coming from Cuba were disbelieved. The nuance of Cuba's role in, and view of, the crisis was either misinterpreted or disregarded. Relatedly, the Pentagon gave too little credence to the possibility that Grenadians themselves might put up an effective fight against the Americans.

The possibility that Cuba would try to dispatch military reinforcements to Grenada was a prime reason offered by the Pentagon leadership for the tight secrecy that was imposed on the American intervention planning. Cuba's military was no match for the U.S., but a superpower among the many microstates of the Caribbean Basin. In 1983, Cuba had more than 200,000 combatants in uniform, two hundred jet fighters and two submarines.[2] The first overt acts aimed at keeping Cubans at bay came on late on Oct. 22, three days before D-Day. Four E-3A AWACs aircraft based at Tinker Air Force Base in Oklahoma were deployed to the Caribbean to begin looking around the clock for any unusual aircraft movements by the Cubans.[3] At the same time, a detachment of eight F-15 Eagles based at Eglin Air Force Base in Florida was also sent to the Naval Station Roosevelt Roads, Puerto Rico. From this forward position, the fighters could interdict any planes sent from Cuba to Grenada once hostilities commenced. At least one F-15 was continuously on 15-minute alert through Nov. 2. Twice F-15s were scrambled to close on Cuban planes, but both the aircraft were identified as civilian airliners before contact was made.[4] The Strategic Air Command also deployed an array of reconnaissance aircraft to collect intelligence on Cuban intentions and Grenada's preparations. Air Force SR-71s, U-2Rs and the RC-135s flew a total 42 missions over, or on the periphery of, the two islands.[5] In addition to the SAC planes, the Tactical Air Command sent RF-4Cs from Bergstrom Air Force Base in Texas on a total of 50 photographic, infrared and electronic reconnaissance missions.[6]

There was also a psychological warfare objective at work in the decision to sortie so many different aircraft to the Caribbean from so many U.S. bases. The JCS was intent on making Urgent Fury a "narrow" operation aimed at ousting the Revolutionary Military Council and extracting Americans on the island, without Cuban interference. "We went to considerable extent ... to make sure that Cubans got the message that 'You have no opportunity to intervene in this thing,'" Vessey later told a military historian. "We put a carrier task force out there; we very blatantly put naval forces out there; put air surveillance and all these sorts of signs to make it clear to the Cubans."[7]

As H-Hour approached, diplomatic signals were also sent by Washington to Havana in the hope that Cubans would not resist the arrival of American troops. This approach proceeded along two channels: one through the American Interest Section of the Swiss Embassy in Havana and the other through General Manuel Antonio Noriega, the military dictator of Panama. Noriega was a Central America power broker who had intelligence dealings with both the United States and Cuba.[8] He later said in an oral history interview that a phone call came to him "at the moment of invasion" from CIA director William J. Casey, who told him that Vice President Bush was listening on the same line. Casey asked the Panamanian despot to pass an urgent message to Castro advising him that the United States wanted to avoid an armed confrontation with the Cubans on Grenada. Noriega dutifully conveyed the American message to Havana in a separate phone call, but he was told by Castro that the call came too late: Americans were already firing on his people.[9]

The White House had hoped to alert Cubans to the invasion early enough to avert combat with them. During the night of Oct. 24 and into the early morning of Oct. 25, Washington also attempted to directly notify Castro that his people were not a target.[10] However, that diplomatic approach was frustrated by the absence of working telephone or telegraph lines between Washington and its Interest Section in Havana. The 17 lines were suddenly cut off at 7 p.m. on Oct. 23 and could not, or would not, be immediately repaired when the American diplomats complained about the outage to their counterparts in the Cuban Foreign Ministry. Ultimately, Washington reached the head of the mission on his home phone and the message was relayed to the Cuban Foreign Ministry in Havana at 0830 (Cuban time) on Oct. 25, hours after the first American troops arrived on the island.[11] The U.S. message assured Cuba that all efforts would be made to ensure the safety of its citizens "while order is being restored." It urged Cuba to instruct its citizens on Grenada to "avoid any steps which might exacerbate the delicate situation in Grenada" and cautioned the Cuban government to "refrain from sending any new military unit or personnel to Grenada." But, by the time this plea arrived, unrestrained combat had already broken out between Cuba construction workers and Rangers at Point Salines, which would continue sporadically until the surrender of Little Havana the following day.

According to Cuba, later on D-Day, the United States sent a follow-up, truce-seeking message declaring: "The Cuban personnel station in Grenada are not a target for action by U.S. troops." The message stated that the United States was ready to cooperate with Cuba on the "evacuation" of its personnel and pledged not to portray their departure as a surrender. It concluded by stating that the United States "regrets the armed clashes between men from both countries, and considers they have occurred due to confusion and accidents brought about by our men's proximity to the area of operations of the multinational troops."[12] (One American international law legal expert later characterized this statement as a near admission that the United States initiated the hostilities with Cuba.)[13]

But, the conciliatory tone of this message was not reflected in the public statements being made at the same time in Washington. Reagan's and Shultz's press conference on D-Day both conveyed the suspicion that the Soviets or the Cubans were behind the Grenadian coup, but stopped short of outright accusation. Shultz gave this equivocal response to a question on the Soviet/Cuban responsibility for Bishop's overthrow: "We don't have any direct information on that point. However, the O.E.C.S. states feel that such is the case."

The first detailed, on-the-record account of the battle for Grenada did not come from the Pentagon until 1630 Wednesday, Oct. 26, 37 hours after the invasion began. The fog of war hung heavily over the banks of the Potomac that afternoon. Preconceptions and preferred outcomes colored the statements made by the invasion's top two military leaders. Weinberger and Vessey overstated the role of the Cubans in the initial fighting, under-reported the number of Americans killed in action at that point and prematurely declared that all the medical school students had been rescued. There was no mention at all by either man of the resistance offered on the island by the People's Revolutionary Army of Grenada. (It took four more days for Metcalf to indicate for the first time in a press briefing that some of the resistance to U.S. forces came from the PRA.)[14] In his opening remarks, before taking questions, Weinberger said, "We've captured about 600 Cubans, many of them combatants, almost all of whom were with rifles who were shooting at us, and a large number of weapons including a number of Soviet AK-47s." His omission of any reference to Grenadian resistance conveyed the impression that all opposition came from the Cubans. That misimpression was amplified by the phrasing of the questions posed by reporters. The press queries parroted inaccurate information that had been previously supplied to them in Washington on a not-for-attribution basis. The first question-and-answer exchange set the tenor of the rest of misleading briefing.

> Q: General Vessey, we understand that when you landed, when the Rangers landed on Tuesday morning, they encountered not just armed construction workers, in fact a combat battalion that had dug in very well-prepared positions and fierce resistance. Did you anticipate meeting organized Cuban military units and what did you do to offset that apparent surprise?
>
> A: (Vessey) No, we didn't anticipate meeting Cuban fighting units. We knew there were Cuban construction workers in there who might have been reservists and might have been armed, but the first planes coming into the area received anti-aircraft fire, which is a contrast to the statements coming out of Havana, which says that they have only construction workers in Grenada.

In response to a question about U.S. casualties, Weinberger stated that the tally was "killed 6, missing 8, wounded 33." The killed and missing numbers were reasonably accurate if lumped together. The bodies of the three dead Cobra pilots had not yet been recovered, and the bodies of the four drowned SEALs were never recovered. However, the number of known Americans wounded at that point was easily double the number acknowledged. (The Pentagon reported to the White House at 8:59 p.m. on Oct. 25 that the D-Day toll as of then, nearly a full day before the press conference, was "14 KIA and 40 WIA," records show. The records also show that the Pentagon asked that that tally be kept within the Oval Office circle. Weinberger intended to personally call Reagan with the news.)[15]

The theme of Cuban-led resistance was repeated and amplified two days later on Friday, Oct. 28 when McDonald replaced Vessey and Weinberger at the Pentagon podium. The press conference came 24 hours after the attack on the nearly deserted Calivigny compound attack that was defended by a PRA squad at most. In his opening remarks, McDonald declared that major military objectives had now been secured even though "resistance was much greater than expected due to extensive Cuban military involvement on the island…. Heavy fighting occurred on the evening of 27 October at the Calivigny military barracks area."

"The overwhelming evidence from our ground troops is that Cubans, not Grenadians, were in the forefront of the fighting," he declared. The four-star admiral made passing, vague mention of Grenadian resistance, lumping them in with the Cubans. He said he had only "sketchy" information about "opposing force" casualties. He could only confirm a total of 18–23 "opposing force" wounded. He said 17 "Grenadian personnel" were being detained at the airports along with 638 Cubans, further buttressing the impression that Cuba was the main military opponent. (This characterization of the combat infected many subsequent battlefield reports for years to come. "Cuban" was offhandedly used as a synonym for any enemy soldier.)

McDonald noted that, prior to the invasion, a Cuban transport ship with arms (the *Vietnam Heroico*) had arrived in St. George's on Oct. 6 and Col. Tortoló had arrived on the island by air on Oct. 24. "When it appeared that U.S. intervention was likely, Cubans took control of the island. All evidence indicates the entire Point Salines facility was Cuban controlled and sealed off from Grenadians…. Impersonating as construction workers, Cuban soldiers' resistance was well organized with fire being well-aimed and directed. Assessment indicates they were well-trained professional soldiers. Documents indicated that at least 1,100 were on the island." (The 1,100 figure came from claims made by two captured Cubans that were accepted at face value by their military interrogators and then passed on to McDonald in an Oct. 27 message from Metcalf.[16])

The 4-digit number was nearly double the estimate that had been initially offered by the Pentagon for the Cuban presence on the island. "We're estimating there is probably about 300 maybe 350 Cubans unaccounted for at the present time," McDonald also asserted. But, in fact, the 638 Cubans that McDonald reported to be in American detention at the airports (not counting Cuban nationals at the Cuban and Soviet embassies) was in line with the 697 Cubans (counting diplomats) who were eventually returned to Havana. Also on Friday, McDonald inaccurately asserted that Cuba was planning to send 341 additional officers and 4,000 reservists to the island in the near future.[17] Within days, however, a then-secret, all-agency intelligence assessment debunked this claim as "a misinterpretation of a captured document that referred to efforts to expand the Grenadian army and military to a force of 6,800."[18]

The same day McDonald gave his grossly misleading press briefing, he was directed by the Joint Chiefs to submit a plan to track down and eliminate the hundreds of Cubans then believed to have fled into the mountainous interior to wage a guerrilla war.[19] Within eight hours McDonald submitted a plan to secure of the entire mainland and also to assault the northern island of Carriacou. But the battlefield looked much different on Oct. 28 from the bridge of the *Guam* than it did from the five-sided headquarters on the Potomac. Butler, the chief of staff on the *Guam*, was surprised, even bemused, by the Pentagon's perception that Grenada was still full of Cubans. Butler knew that Americans had more than 600 Cubans in custody and doubted there were many more to capture. "I was willing to believe the statements coming out of Cuba that 'This is all we got.' I was beginning to think most [had been] rounded up," he later recalled. Butler's perception proved accurate. Much of the weekend was spent on wild goose chases in pursuit of phantom Cubans. Confirmed encounters with resistant Cubans on the island were few and even then, ambiguous. By Saturday, the Pentagon was no longer contesting Havana's claim that there were 784 Cubans on the island at the time of the invasion.[20] The Cuban government said that figure included 636 construction workers and 43 members of their armed forces. Half of the 43 were officers and the rest support personnel. The remaining 105 Cubans were civilians of various occupations, including 16 diplomats and their dependents.[21]

One of the final combat clashes of the entire operation happened in the late afternoon of Oct. 28 in a chance meeting between Cubans and Marines from Echo Company, the unit that had conducted the helicopter assault on Pearls Airport on D-Day. Capt. Henry J. Donigan III, the Echo company commander, was with his unit at Pearls at around 1400 when he received orders to investigate a report of a large arms cache believed to be stored in caves in the nearby agricultural settlement of Mirabeau.[22] Donigan found the caves to be empty, but decided to further scout the area on foot, leaving the company jeeps with a security detail. Shortly after, Donigan's dismounted Marines encountered three men standing next to a Range Rover on a ridge line. The lead Marine ordered them to freeze but, after a brief, inaudible conversation among themselves, the men took off running. The Marines opened fire on the trio. One was fatally wounded, another suffered multiple, but treatable, wounds. The third got away. Donigan loaded the wounded man and the dead man in the Range Rover to return to Pearls with along with his jeeps. During the return trip, the caravan came under fire from six or eight uniformed assailants. One Marine fired a LAW at the attackers and silenced their fire. Donigan exited the area without casualties to his company. Donigan was later told by a superior officer that the two men shot on the ridge were Cuban, but their presence was not explained to him. Based on reports he heard from friendly Grenadians, Donigan believed the uniformed troops to have been local members of the PRA. The Cubans were probably civilian advisers rather than military personnel based on the date, location and circumstances of this encounter.[23]

On Sunday, Oct. 30, Joint Chiefs chairman Vessey and McDonald arrived on the island from the United States for a first-hand perspective. Vessey's purpose was a battle-field inspection, not a photo op or a victory tour. The chairman was met at Point Salines by three top-ranking service commanders: Metcalf from the Navy, Trobaugh from the Army and Faulkner from the Marines. Vessey took a quick look at the Cuban detention camp at Point Salines and the weapons cache discovered at Frequente. Vessey and his party also got a motor tour of St. George's courtesy of the 22nd Marines who had the only jeeps on the island with passenger seats. Smith, the Marine infantry commander, rode with Vessey and used his proximity to the chairman's ear to air complaints about the Army's use of force.

"I told General Vessey, as I understood it…. I thought I had the [same] mission that [the] 82nd had, [but] it was different. I thought my mission was to liberate Grenada and [the 82nd] thought their mission was to attack Grenada," Smith later recounted to a Marine historian.[24] Smith said his message to Vessey was essentially "General, you know the 82nd is down there blowing the hell out of civilians?" Smith was alarmed by repeated reports he was hearing from otherwise friendly Grenadians about excessive use of supporting fire by the advancing American troops. Smith knew the complaints were about the 82nd Airborne and not his Marines because the Grenadians specified their grievances were with the soldiers with the "funny helmets." The Marines and Rangers were wearing standard-issue "steel pots" helmets, but the paratroopers were equipped with new Kevlar-layered combat helmets. These helmets, though more effective as protection, had a profile that resembled the protective headgear that German soldiers wore during World War II. Smith had twice flown out to the *Guam* to protest to Metcalf about excessive bombardment of civilian areas by the Army, but to no avail. That emboldened him to make his case to the man at the pinnacle of the Pentagon pyramid.[25] "You know, I think he [Vessey] was a little offended. I think he thought I was out of line a little bit, but I think he also believed me. They had different rules of engagement after his visit, but … they couldn't turn around the attitude," Smith later recalled. "I told my guys more than once that I was a hell of a lot more concerned of the 82nd Airborne than I was the People's Revolutionary Army."

General John W. Vessey, Jr., chairman, Joint Chiefs of Staff, and Maj. Gen. Edward L. Trobaugh, commander of the 82nd Airborne Division, toured the True Blue Campus of St. George's University Medical School during an inspection visit by Vessey on Sunday, October 30, 1983. Vice Adm. Joseph P. Metcalf III, the invasion commander, is visible in the center background. Vessey urged the commanders to move more quickly to subdue the entire mainland (National Archives [330-CFD-DA-ST-85-02245]).

Whatever his private takeaway from Smith's pleadings, Vessey admonished the ground commanders to get moving to fully secure the mainland and then assault Grenada's lesser island, Carriacou. Vessey wanted the 22nd MAU Marines to sail on to Lebanon and the 82nd Airborne to return to Fort Bragg as soon as possible. The Marines were urgently needed in the Middle East and Congress was already asking when combat troops would be fully withdrawn from Grenada. In one of his conversations with Vessey, the chairman reportedly spurred Trobaugh to move more aggressively by declaring: "We have two companies of Marines running all over the island and thousands of Army troops doing nothing. What the hell is going on?" (Asked years later about the accuracy of this quote, Vessey said he "didn't recall those words," but acknowledged he thought the 82nd was moving too slow.)[26]

For the 82nd Airborne, the directive to fully secure the main island translated to mounting an immediate assault on a mountain lake area called Grand Etang, thought to be the home of a Cuban-run unconventional warfare center. At 0700 on Monday, Oct. 31, Hamilton ordered three of his 2nd Battalion companies to assault the training camp. Two arrived by helicopter and one by road. When all three converged at the camp, they found it to be deserted except for one armored personnel carrier. Local citizens told them that the camp had been abandoned for two months.[27]

For the Marines, Vessey's "get going" urgings translated to an aggressive moves up the west coast to reach the northern communities of Gouyave and Victoria, which remained outside American military control. Smith ordered Golf Company to move up the coastal road from St. George's. A column of armored amphibious vehicles left the capital at 1530 on Sunday under the command of Dobson. Smith also loaded two tanks on a Navy landing craft, known as a "Mike Boat." This square-bowed, 73-foot vessel sailed

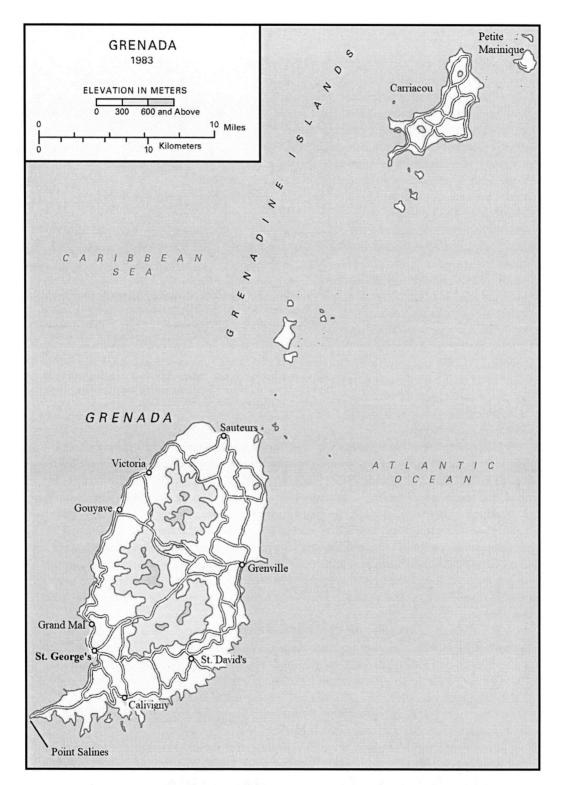

This map shows the three major islands which make up the multi-island nation of Grenada. Carriacou, the second largest island, was the last territory to be secured by American troops in a simultaneous air and amphibious assault on November 1, 1983 (adapted from base map, courtesy U.S. Army Center of Military History).

parallel to the shore, along with two other landing craft and a destroyer, to provide fire support if the advancing column needed it.[28] Amos' Cobra gunships were launched to fly aerial escort. The Marine vehicles ran into a road block near Gouyave, but Dobson managed to fill in the tank ditch with a hotwired bulldozer. By nightfall the column had moved past Gouyave to Victoria, the northernmost settlement on the leeward coast.[29]

Meanwhile to the east, even before Vessey landed on the island, Echo Company of the 22nd MAU had begun a parallel move up the windward coastline to Sauteurs, the largest town on the northern tip of the island. Donigan, the company commander, led a motorized patrol that left Pearls at 0330 on a six-mile trek along winding roads to the coastal town.[30] Donigan had obtained detailed intelligence on PRA positions in the area from a captured Grenadian regional officer. When the residents of Sauteurs rose from their beds at dawn, they found their streets occupied by armed Marines. The shock of their arrival made the residents wary at first, but the military operation soon morphed into an unheralded, and inspiring saga of person-to-person diplomacy.

The Marines knew the civilians might be short of food so they brought extra rations with them. Donigan made contact with two local Red Cross workers and two local priests, one Anglican and the other Catholic. He enlisted their aid in equitably distributing the supplies among the populace. By mid-morning more than 300 residents had received free food. The residents reciprocated by offering information about former Grenadian army and militia members who were in their midst. One woman said that she was the girlfriend of the PRA district commander. Donigan told her to bring him in for questioning—and she did.

Since it was a Sunday, the two priests proposed holding an ecumenical service that would be attended by both civilians and the Marines. The service was held at 1330 in the Anglican church. Prayers were offered for both the Grenadian and American casualties of the fighting. (Marines were aware by then that three of the MAU's Cobra pilots had been killed in the early fighting at St. George's.) Donigan recalled a large part of the service was devoted to hailing the Marines as liberators. The spirit of the day extended into evening when the principal focus of the Marines was arranging an emergency medevac flight. A local 43-year-old woman hemorrhaged after giving birth to a baby boy with the aid of a midwife. Navy corpsman HM2 Glenn Scott did what he could for the woman, but he lacked the supplies and training to appropriately care for her.[31] Not unusually, the radio link between the Marines on shore and the *Guam* was broken. It took hours to summon a rescue. Finally, a CH-46 arrived to evacuate the woman to the *Guam*'s sick bay. Both mother and newborn recovered.

By the end of the weekend, Marines were loosely holding two-thirds of the Grenadian coastline stretching clockwise from St. George's on the west to Requin Bay on the east. The remaining one-third was Army turf. Echo Company returned to the *Guam* by helicopter on Monday afternoon, Oct. 31. Before they left, Donigan wanted to give thanks to the Grenadians who had supplied them with intelligence information. He organized an impromptu commendation ceremony. He collected his company in formation and marched them from town to a nearby soccer field, singing as they marched. At the open field, with his men in company formation, he called forward four civilians and a Grenadian police corporal who had been particularly helpful. He presented each with a military arm patch and shook their hands as a crowd of several hundred Grenadians looked on.

As a new week began, the 82nd Airborne's commanding general pondered his orders to take the outlying island of Carriacou. Again, Trobaugh opted to assign the assault task to troops other than his own. After the Calivigny assault mishaps, Trobaugh's aviators did not want to mount another helicopter attack without artillery support. Trobaugh distrusted naval gunfire and Carriacou, about 20 miles away, was beyond range of his land-based howitzers. Based on these factors, Trobaugh assigned the assault to the 22nd MAU.[32]

The final Marine action of Urgent Fury came at 0530 on Tuesday, Nov. 1, with a coordinated helicopter and amphibious landing on the second largest of the three-island Grenadian chain. American electronic eavesdropping had picked up radio broadcasts in Spanish from the island suggesting the possible presence of Cuban troops.[33] But, the assault was unopposed. The islanders greeted the Marines as liberators. Smith arrived at the dirt airstrip at Lauriston Point to find Marine air crews giving aircraft tours to Grenadian civilians. "The first question they [Grenadians] asked me was, 'When are you going to raise the U.S. flag? We want to be part of the United States,'" Smith later recalled. "And they meant it. A lot of people on Carriacou had spent time in the United States, like 20 percent of the population."[34] The 19-man PRA platoon assigned to defend the island scattered as soon as the Marines arrived and changed into civilian clothes. Marines rounded up their leaders and ordered them to muster their men for a formal surrender. The entire PRA platoon duly reported that afternoon. Smith dismissed them and ordered them to return again at 0800 the next day.[35]

That night the island took on the atmosphere of a liberty port. Smith gave his men permission to drink a few beers with the locals; there was even talk of a wet T-shirt competition. The threat posed by Cubans on Carriacou proved vaporous. However, the omnipresent menace of friendly fire never abated. The 82nd Airborne came to Carriacou to relieve the Marines at 0700 Wednesday, Nov. 2. A company from the 505th Infantry arrived by Army Black Hawk helicopters prepared for a hostile reception. The paratroopers scrambled off the helicopters with loaded weapons and ran to assume firing position. Marines watched the arrival with incredulity. Puzzlement quickly turned to alarm that a firefight might break out.[36] Smith was infuriated by the display of force and moved to deescalate the dangerous situation. The local PRA detachment mustered as promised at 0800. Smith turned his prisoners over the 82nd and then he and his Marines flew off the island and back to the *Guam*. "There is a large crowd of civilians around the 22nd waving goodbye. It is a fitting end to what has been a fabulous personal and professional experience," Smith wrote in his concluding journal entry. Hostilities were officially declared concluded at 1500 on Wednesday, Nov. 2, eight days after the invasion began. Also on that date, the Marine force set sail for their delayed peacekeeping duties in Lebanon. Metcalf decamped from his command post on the *Guam* to return to Norfolk, leaving the Army in charge.

The principal problem now facing the American military command was the repatriation of the Cubans who were in their custody. The original "done in a day" invasion plan had never anticipated the need to care for more than 650 Spanish-speaking prisoners for a week. As Rangers advanced, they also displaced and detained Grenadians living in private homes near the airport. Telling combatants from civilians on sight was difficult because the Cuban civilians fought in work clothes and not all Grenadian combatants wore uniforms. The first-sort criterion was anyone carrying a gun was considered a combatant. Grenadians and Cubans combatants were herded together until they could be separated after interrogation and physical examination. Most Cubans were lighter skinned and did not speak English. Detainees were initially held by the Rangers near the terminal, which was also being used as an American command post. When the first elements of the Caribbean Peacekeeping Force arrived at Salines, the prisoners were turned over to them. The Caribbean soldiers then used captured Cuban trucks to move them away from the terminal to a new location to the west, a grassy area next to the runway. Cuban prisoners started to pile up on the afternoon of D-Day. Maj. William D. Archer, the 82nd Airborne's civil affairs staff officer, became involved in the problem and decided to find a better location that an uncovered spot that was subject to both the tropical sun and live fire.[37] The next morning the Cubans, along with Grenadian military prisoners, were moved to the captured workers' camp on a hill behind the terminal buildings. The Caribbean forces continued to act as guards, but the 82nd Airborne assumed responsibility for providing food, water and other essential supplies to the detainees.

By the end of the second day, Oct. 26, the number of Cuban prisoners was swelled by the fall the Little Havana to the 82nd Airborne. Many detainees spent all day and night outdoors because the barracks could not accommodate them all. None of their Caribbean overseers had any training in guarding prisoners and some policemen from the smaller islands lacked zeal for their assignment. Some Cubans managed to slip away with weapons on the first night from the unfenced camp.[38] On Oct. 26, the first specialized Military Intelligence team arrived by C-141 to begin interrogation of the prisoners. When Capt. John F. O'Shaughnessy arrived with his Alpha Company, 519th Military Intelligence Battalion, he found more than 650 Cuban and Grenadian prisoners milling about in the old camp. They were under armed guard, but "there was no barrier wire, no perimeter, no segmentation or identification, or even a total count of the prisoner population," he later wrote.[39]

There were also thorny legal questions to consider. Principal among them was how the captives would be classified and treated under the terms of the Geneva Convention of 1949 governing the treatment of POWs. The central problem was that there had been no declaration of war by the United States against either Grenada or Cuba, or vice versa. Army lawyers determined that Urgent Fury fell under of Article 2 of the 1949 convention which states that, in addition to declared war, it also applies to "any other armed conflict" that involves two or more parties to the convention.[40] This interpretation was further extended to mean that all Cubans and Grenadians taken into custody, whether civilian or military, would be treated, at least initially as prisoners of war. This was a significant determination because it afforded more rights and privileges to the detainees than persons classified as being "retained" or "interned" under the convention. Later, all the detainees were screened and either affirmed as POWs or classified as retained personnel or civilian internees. The 82nd Airborne considered 141 of the captured Cubans in their custody to have been combatants and another 159 were "sympathizers" who had a dual function as construction workers and combatants.[41] The remaining 366 Cuban prisoners were simply classified as "workers." This accounting implies that only slightly more than half the 666 Cubans then in custody were considered to have participated in, or otherwise actively supported, combat action. (The number of Cuban prisoners reported by the U.S. military was fewer than the total number of Cubans on the island reported by Havana: 784. This is mostly because some Cubans took refuge in their embassy or the Soviet embassy and were never taken captive. Still other Cubans were killed in the fighting.)

By Oct. 27, the care and feeding of the refugees and prisoners became Metcalf's biggest logistical problem.[42] The 118th Military Police Company arrived from Ft. Bragg on a C-141 and was assigned to take charge of security for a total of about 1,500 Cuban prisoners and Grenadian refugees who were then gathered in and around the Old Cuban camp behind the terminal. "It was an instant nightmare," recalled Capt. Russell J. Cancilla, the commanding officer of the 102-member company. "It looked like Woodstock '69. There were people all over that hill, most of them in open areas."[43] The MPs initially set about enclosing the detainees in concertina wire and organizing them into work groups. Food supplies were running low. Americans learned from the Cubans that food was stored at the recently captured supply depot at Frequente. A convoy of jeeps was organized to liberated the food to feed the prisoners. On Oct. 28, enough military police had arrived on the island for the American troops to replace the Caribbean forces as guards. The Caribbean troops were then assigned to police duties in St. George's that were more suitable to their training and experience. This transfer allowed for a by-name list of detainees to be created for the first time and reclassification of prisoners according to their Geneva convention-defined status.[44] Forty-four of the Cuban prisoners were female, but all of the American military guards were male, at least initially. Four female MPs from Fort Bragg arrived on the island on Oct. 29, but were sent home the next day by Trobaugh.[45] Trobaugh's order was based on his misinterpretation of the then-existing Army policy that barred woman from positions likely to experience "direct combat" with the enemy during hostilities. After protests to Mackmull, the corps commander at Fort Bragg, female MPs returned to Grenada on Nov. 2 when hostilities were officially declared to be over. They were subsequently joined on Grenada by about 100 other women soldiers who were also serving as MPs or in other combat support roles.

Conditions at the detention camp during the first 10 days of the operation were unsatisfactory, regardless of who was guarding them. When Vessey stopped at the camp on his Sunday morning visit to the island he was displeased to see Cuban prisoners penned up in barbed wire enclosures on a macadam parking lot in the tropical sun. He ordered McDonald and Trobaugh to get them under some shade immediately.[46] Vessey's edict, combined with the winding down of hostilities, and the belated arrival of tents and building materials, allowed construction of a new detention camp to begin on Nov. 1. The construction was done by Cuban construction workers supervised by Spanish-speaking American sergeants. It was completed on Nov. 3.

The many difficulties that the 82nd Airborne experienced in performing their peace-keeping role on Grenada were the unintended consequence of Vessey's decision at the outset of the operation to exclude corps-level involvement. "The 82nd Airborne ended up being tasked to do things that a division headquarters just flat does not have the capability to handle," Schwarzkopf later declared. The inadequately supported divisional duties Schwarzkopf enumerated included running a POW compound, taking care of civilian refugees, securing the Russian and Cuban embassies and evacuating American and foreign-national civilians.[47] The 82nd Airborne got scant help on these underestimated issues from the invasion planners in Norfolk. "Ad hocism prevailed," wrote one active duty Army commentator. He opined that McDonald and Metcalf had organized a command and control structure "better designed to keep the various services at odds than to ensure cooperation."[48]

Once hostilities ended on Nov. 2, the repatriation of Soviet Bloc citizens, both living and dead, began. The task became the shared responsibility of the military and the newly established U.S. embassy on Grenada headed by Charles A. Gillespie. The newly named ambassador arrived on the island on the night of Oct. 26 and set up a temporary embassy in the Ross Point Inn just south of St. George's.[49] The next morning, Thursday, Oct. 27, he set out to establish contact with the nearby Soviet and Cuban embassies, which, by

Captured Cubans were moved from the airfield to the nearby Old Cuban Camp for detainment. The barracks were too small to house all the prisoners indoors. Vessey was displeased to see prisoners still held outside, exposed all day to the tropical sun, when he arrived for an inspection visit on Sunday, October 30. Blue shirts and straw hats were customary work wear for the civilian construction workers (National Archives [330-CFD-DF-ST-84-09893]).

then, had both been swept past by the ground advance of American troops. Initially, the Soviet bloc diplomats were allowed nominal freedom of movement on the island, though they often were stopped and temporarily detained by suspicious American soldiers. On the evening of Oct. 31, orders were issued to 82nd Airborne to cordon off both embassies and not to let anyone in or out without Gillespie's permission.[50] The next day Scoon exercised his admittedly questionable constitutional powers to break relations with the Soviet Union and other Communist Bloc nations, with the exception of Cuba. Scoon felt his nation's ties to Cuba were too extensive to sever entirely so he, instead, declared the Cuban ambassador *persona non grata*.[51] This action set the stage for talks to begin for the eviction of all government-sponsored visitors from Cuba and Soviet Bloc states, including diplomats.

Gillespie found the Soviet ambassador to be accepting of the eviction, at least at the professional level. Gennadiy I. Sazhenev was a veteran diplomat who spent two decades in the Caribbean serving variously in Cuba, Colombia, Peru and Argentina. He was posted to Grenada in July 1982 to be the first Soviet ambassador in residence on the island.[52] The ambassador wore a diplomatic dress uniform when he presented his credentials to the governor general, but Scoon was more amused than threatened by the sartorial display of medals.[53] After the invasion, an opinion column in the right-leaning *Washington Times* identified Sazhenev as a four-star Soviet general in the military intelligence branch of the Kremlin. This identification was denied by the Soviet Embassy in a letter to the editor. Intelligence experts consulted by the *New York Times* were divided on his intelligence affiliations.[54]

For his part, Gillespie found Sazhenev to be a scholarly, refined man who spoke good English. Gillespie checked with the CIA and found no known intelligence connection with either the ambassador or his second-in-command, Boris Nikolayev, the senior commercial officer.[55] As a nominally uninvolved party in the hostilities, Sazhenev asked Gillespie if he could use American communications to pass a diplomatic message back to his superiors in Moscow seeking instructions. He offered to write his report in English to save both sides the time and trouble of translating the message before it was sent.[56] With the communication problem amicably settled, Gillespie was surprised to discover that his counterparts' next pressing concern was arranging a distress sale of their personal automobiles. The ambassador and his deputy had both purchased expensive cars: a Mercedes 300 S sedan from the 1950s and a late-model Japanese luxury sport sedan. They told Gillespie they urgently needed to convert the cars to hard currency: British pounds or American dollars. "That was really something to see," Gillespie later marveled. "That was a major, major point."[57] With American acquiescence, the cars were purchased by the Grenadian merchant who had originally sold them to the Soviets. The car dealer profited again, much to the annoyance of the Soviet diplomats. They ended up getting 10 cents on the dollar.[58] The way was now clear to discuss repatriation.

The Soviet embassy was located in a former bungalow hotel on a hillside just to the southeast of the Grand Anse campus. Forty-nine Soviets civilians lived inside the walled and fenced compound. In the fighting, 15 North Koreans, six East Germans and three Bulgarian took refuge here. Fifty-three Cubans also fled here and they now constituted the new majority of the occupants. The Cuban contingent included several dozen armed construction workers led by Col. Tortoló, the Cuban military commander. As a result of the Cuban influx after hostilities began, the compound functioned as a Cuban military citadel, as well as a Soviet diplomatic enclave.

The embassy had an anti-aircraft gun mounted on its roof that Trobaugh's staff suspected had shot down a Marine Cobra on the first day,[59] though that suspicion was not later affirmed by the Pentagon. On the second afternoon of the invasion, there were battlefield reports that combatants believed to be Cuban fired a mortar from the compound on Rangers who were executing the Grand Anse extraction.[60] American eyewitnesses said these attacks triggered retaliatory strikes by Marine Cobras that blew a roof off an embassy building.[61] Moscow subsequently received word that a member of its embassy staff had been wounded by fire from an American aircraft during the course of the fighting Oct 26.[62] This prompted a formal diplomatic protest by the Kremlin to the resident U.S. embassy. The chiding note was also read on a Moscow evening television news broadcast. A TASS commentator added his tongue-lashing of Reagan as "a bandit, liar and murderer."[63] The U.S. State Department denied that the embassy had been deliberately targeted, but one unnamed official conceded to a *New York Times* reporter that it might have been hit by bomb fragments.[64]

The vicinity of the embassy at Morne Rouge continued to be a hot spot for shooting into Oct. 27. Sp4c Brent Taylor of Bravo Company of the 325th Infantry had become separated from his squad that morning as his unit moved through the area. At about 0800, as Taylor was passing through an open field within about 50 yards of the Soviet compound, he came under fire from three nearby uniformed soldiers. The first bullets knocked off his helmet and glasses. Subsequent fire hit him in the leg and then the arm. Taylor took cover behind a dirt mound and then engaged in sporadic fire with his unknown assailants for several hours. Eventually, an American jeep passed by and heard Taylor call for help. The wounded paratrooper was rescued, but his attackers had disappeared.[65] The nationality of the attacking trio was never established, but the circumstantial evidence points to Cubans operating from the embassy.

The armed Cuban presence inside the compound worried Sazhenev as much as the Americans. Sazhenev told Gillespie privately that he would not leave the embassy because he "was concerned about what would happen if he left the compound and relinquished authority to someone else." In post-invasion testimony before Congress, Defense Secretary Weinberger affirmed that the Soviet embassy complement did not include armed military personnel and that there was "no evidence to suggest any Soviets participated in hostilities."[66] At this same hearing, Weinberger also publicly knocked down a published report suggesting that a Soviet-backed assassination team had been involved in the killing of Bishop.[67]

Before the Cubans were sent home, the White House briefly considered rubbing Castro's nose in his defeat. Some zealots in the administration suggested that the returned group should include the Cuban criminals who had been released from jail by Castro to join more than 125,000 refugees who fled their homeland during the Mariel Boatlift in 1980. Secretary of the Navy John F. Lehman liked the idea, and, according to him, so did Weinberger.[68] The National Security Council asked the State Department on Oct. 27 for an options paper on the topic, but diplomatic and military opposition scuttled the idea.

Even after more than three decades, collecting an accurate assessment of the human toll of the invasion on all the parties is elusive. The official U.S. military count, as of 1988, was 19 killed and 125 "reportable" wounded.[69] But, if unacknowledged SEAL, Task Force 160 and Delta force casualties are included, the true number of wounded increases by at least 32 to 157. The military's owns records strongly suggest the true number of American combat casualties could be doubled if all the combat-related injuries that required medical treatment are included. The Army's official count of "reportable" wounded soldiers is 108, but twice as many soldiers (219) were issued Purple Heart medals for Grenada service.[70]

Of the 19 acknowledged Americans killed as a result of Urgent Fury combat, nine died as the result of combat-related accidents. This includes the four SEALs who drowned; the three Rangers who were killed in the Calivigny helicopter crashes; Luketina, who was maimed in the friendly fire bombing of the brigade command post; and Epps, who was killed trying to neuter a captured recoilless rifle. Just five combat units accounted for all the acknowledged American killed. Eight were Rangers, three were 82nd Airborne paratroopers, three were 22nd MAU Marine pilots, four were SEALs and one was a Task Force 160 pilot. As for the 125 reportable wounded in action (WIA), the vast majority (105) were from the Army's front-line, combat-ready units: Rangers (69) and 82nd Airborne (36).[71] Of the remaining 20 WIAs, 15 were Marines, two were Air Force controllers and three were Army soldiers of other unit affiliation.

As for the 784 Cubans, 25 were killed and 59 were wounded, according to the JCS—a casualty rate of more than 10 percent.[72] Only two of the Cubans killed, and just eight of the wounded, were professional soldiers, according to Cuba. The uninjured returned to Havana on passenger jets as released prisoners or expelled diplomats and their dependents.[73] Havana television announced on Oct. 27 the last six Cubans to die on the island were holding the Cuban flag in their arms. The returned Cuban prisoners were initially welcomed as heroes by Castro when they returned home. But that public display was just for show. According to a 1984 "all sources" CIA intelligence assessment, Castro personally ordered a board of inquiry to examine the conduct of the Cuban defenders. The board found "a broad pattern of cowardice" by the Cubans. "All those who were not wounded have been demoted, reprimanded or otherwise punished," the CIA report said.[74] Further, the CIA found no convincing evidence that Cubans had coordinated the Grenadian defenses or defended any ground other than their own positions at Point Salines. "Most of the Cuban resistance came from the 40-odd military advisers and an unknown number of construction workers who were trained reservists in the Cuban military. It appears, however, that the majority of the construction workers had insufficient arms and ammunition and offered little resistance," the report concluded.[75]

The final casualty count indicates that Grenadians bore the brunt of the fight—and the casualties. According to a 1997 Joint Chiefs historical study, 45 Grenadian combatants were killed in the fighting and "at least" 24 civilians were accidentally killed.[76] (The Department of Defense later told Congress that 21 of the 24 confirmed civilian deaths occurred in the mental hospital bombing.[77]) No corresponding official count of the killed in action was ever made by the Grenadian government, but an accounting was eventually compiled from various published reports by a resident journalist, Ann Elizabeth Wilder. Her online list identifies 18 PRA regular soldiers or militia by name as having been confirmed or claimed to have been killed during the invasion.[78] According to the JCS study, 358 "Grenadian forces" were wounded in the fighting, a figure that apparently lumped together soldiers, militia and civilians. (About 60 Grenadian civilians were injured seriously enough during the fighting to be flown off the island for treatment in American military hospitals.[79]) These numbers of Grenadian wounded are not easily reconciled with the American rules of engagement and the abundant anecdotal evidence that Grenadian civilians generally welcomed the invaders as liberators.

Military critics of the operation have also found significance in comparing the total "reportable" number American military killed and wounded (144) to the comparable Grenadian/Cuban figures (511).[80] "The most striking aspect of the Grenadian casualties is that [the] U.S. suffered about one-fourth of the casualties suffered by the Grenadians and the Cubans combined. This is surprising as usually an attacker in a conventional war suffers twice as many casualties as the defender," wrote Maj. Vijay Tiwathia, an Indian army officer, in a 1987 critique of the Grenadian operation.[81] He suggested the roughly 1:4 U.S.–enemy casualty ratio was a reflection of American overreliance on firepower, especially aircraft, to achieve military objectives and domestic sensitivity to combat casualties. (In addition, this ratio was further skewed by the systematic under-reporting of American special forces casualties.)

In dollar terms, figures cited compiled by the Defense Department, put the cost of the first three days of the operation at $134.4 million, including $22 million for helicopter replacements, but not the salaries of the troops. *Time* magazine observed that total was equivalent to $1 million for every square mile of territory or $224,000 for every American evacuated.[82]

11

The Route to Intervention

For most of America, and most of the world, the intervention into Grenada was viewed as the geopolitical equivalent of a late-season tropical hurricane. It was seen as a sudden storm, spawned by an overheated climate, that just happened to make a random landfall in the Windwards. In fact, an American intervention in Grenada had long been idly contemplated by some in Washington and anxiously feared in St. George's.

The roots of the intervention go back four years to the very beginning of Communist-inspired rule on the island—even before Reagan became president. Bishop seized power in Grenada in a nearly bloodless revolution on March 13, 1979, when President Jimmy Carter was in the White House. Eric Gairy, a flamboyant labor leader regarded as the founder of Grenadian independence, was the elected prime minister at the time. His populist rule had become increasing autocratic, corrupt, brutal and eccentric. Gairy believed that God spoke directly to him. He also believed in flying saucers and unabashedly claimed to have communicated with aliens.[1] His excesses spawned opposition parties. In March 1973, a merger of two fledgling anti–Gairy groups brought together young idealistic men who would, a decade later, become the leaders of their nation and principal players in the intervention drama.

One opposition party was called JEWEL, Joint Endeavor for Welfare, Education and Liberation, and another called MAP, Movement for Assemblies of People. They joined to form a new organization they called the New Jewel Movement (NJM) party in a mashup of the two organization names. Bishop had been a co-founder of MAP with Kendrick Radix, then his law partner, who would later become his justice minister. JEWEL likewise had two founders: Unison Whiteman, later Bishop's foreign minister, and Selwyn Strachan, a sugar worker who later became Coard's right-hand man. With the merger of MAP with JEWEL, Bishop and Whiteman shared the leadership of the new NJM party as coordinating secretaries. Initially, their organization espoused a nationalist, socialistic ideology and focused on ousting Gairy from power by political means. Coard was living in Trinidad and teaching economics at the University of the West Indies when the NJM was formed. He joined the party in 1974 as its third coordinating secretary. He returned to Grenada permanently in 1976 with his wife, Phyllis, who was also active in the NJM.

In the general elections of 1976, the NJM formed a coalition with three other opposition parties. Collectively, they came close to defeating Gairy by garnering 48.6 percent of the votes and six of the 15 seats in the legislature. Within the anti–Gairy coalition, the NJM party emerged as the dominant force winning three of the six seats. Bishop, then

160

32, took one of the seats and became the opposition leader. Coard, newly relocated from Jamaica, took another seat. Coard now emerged as the party's resident ideological guru and the organizational complement to Bishop's charismatic style. Bishop was the populist and Coard was the pedant. (One Grenada scholar later wrote a psychological analysis of the two personalities that was titled "the Hero and the Apparatchik.") The two schoolboy chums were now party partners. Their espoused policies were the result of a Creole mix of ideological influences: West Indian nationalism, the Cuban Revolution, Marxist-Leninist economic theory, Tanzanian socialism and the American Black Power movement.

After winning the legislative seat, Bishop stirred the pot by traveling through the Caribbean denouncing the Gairy regime. Sometimes he took off his shirt to show the scars he suffered when he was beaten by Gairy's "police aides" for his political agitation in 1973.[2] Gairy's enforcers were pejoratively known as the Mongoose Gang, named for a weasel-like omnivore, native to the Caribbean jungles. Mongoose forage in packs and are regarded as indiscriminate killers. Bishop's hatred for the Gairy regime was fanned white-hot on Jan. 21, 1974, when Gairy's enforcers killed his father, Rupert, in the course of disbursing a demonstration in the capital city.

By 1979, Gairy resolved to take an even-tougher line against his ascendant leftist opposition. He correctly suspected that the NJM was plotting to overthrow his repressive government with bullets, if ballots failed. Those suspicions were independently confirmed by Washington in February when federal and local agents arrested a Grenadian national in Maryland on gun-running charges.[3] Forty M-1 carbine rifles and several hundred rounds of ammunition were found concealed in six 55-gallon drums labeled as "grease" destined for shipment to the island. The seizure triggered a federal grand jury investigation that found that the guns had been fraudulently purchased from American gun shops in a smuggling scheme linked to the New JEWEL Movement.[4] Two Treasury agents were authorized to travel to Grenada in March to collect records and witnesses for an upcoming trial.[5] Meanwhile, on Grenada, Gairy ordered sweeps for hidden arms caches. Tensions came to a boil on March 12 when Gairy left the island on a previously planned official visit to New York. Gairy had secured a meeting with UN secretary general Kurt Waldheim to urge creation of an agency to study cosmic phenomena, including UFOs. He also planned to address the UN General Assembly about his conversations with God and aliens. As Gairy passed through Barbados in transit to New York, he met the arriving federal investigators.[6] The prime minister suspected that Bishop would attempt a coup in his absence. Gairy gave orders for his police to arrest NJM leaders while he was away. One leader was picked up, but the rest got tipped off and went underground to plan their counter-move.[7] Top leaders gathered clandestinely at a safe house and voted 3–2 to execute an armed coup, despite not having enough guns to go around.[8] Tellingly, Coard was one of the yes votes. Bishop voted no, but only for readiness reasons.

The putsch was tactically led by Austin, a 40-year-old former corporal in Gairy's army and a former prison guard. Austin had fallen under Bishop's charismatic sway during one of his prison stays. Austin commanded an armed group of 46 much-younger NJM members from the clandestine military wing of the party. Twelve of them had secretly completed a four-week training course in Cuba two years earlier.[9] However, aside from this prior training, Cuba played no material role in the coup, according to Joseph Ewart Layne, one of the 12 Cuban-trained "apostles."[10] The plotters has asked repeatedly for Cuban assistance in overthrowing Gairy, but Havana held them at arm's length, probably because the Cubans doubted their organizational ability to bring off a revolution, according to Layne.

The coup's primary objective was the Point Salines barracks that housed Gairy's 200-man army. The soldiers were known on the island as the "Green Beasts" for the color of their uniforms and their comportment. The insurrection was launched at 0415 on March 13, 1979, with 16 M-1 rifles, nine shotguns and revolvers and Molotov cocktails.[11] Gairy's soldiers were surprised in their beds. They fled in panic and their barracks was burned to the ground. Within 12 hours the uprising secured control of the entire island and its democratically elected, but not particularly popular, government. Gairy was stranded in exile in the United States as a revolutionary government led by the NJM was proclaimed on Grenada. Two of Gairy's men were killed in brief fighting and one NJM supporter died in a gun accident.[12] Subsequent commentators assigned the coup an oxymoronic adjective: "near-bloodless."

The NJM party came to power without benefit of an election, but nonetheless enjoyed wide public support. Gairy's mismanagement had run the country amuck. At the time of the coup, about half of the island's workforce was unemployed. The treasury was in shambles and basic infrastructure was crumbling. Broad popular support for the coup allowed the leaders to later claim that they had actually taken power in a revolution. "[I]f there had been no response by the people, there would not have been a revolution," Bishop later asserted. "We all would have been dead from the start."[13]

Still, the armed overthrow of an elected, independent government was without modern precedent in the 18 English-speaking Caribbean countries. The initial regional reaction was shock and wariness. Bishop sought to allay apprehensions about his new regime in a radio broadcast to the nation on the morning of the coup. Bishop's "A Bright New Dawn" speech promised "all democratic freedoms" would be restored. Within three days, a new, 14-member People's Revolutionary Government (PRG) was formed. Nine were NJM revolutionaries but the group also included two representatives of the conservative Grenada National Party and three moderates from the business/professional sector.[14] The participation of non-revolutionaries signaled Bishop's intention to preserve the private sector as a component of the island's mixed economy.

These comforting assurances led to conditional endorsements of the coup from established, unaffiliated institutions on Grenada including the Torchlight newspaper and the Chamber of Commerce.[15] That led to a conditional support for recognition by the Caribbean Community (CARICOM), a regional trade organization then representing 13 neighbor states.[16] CARICOM's recognition was secured when the new foreign minister publicly affirmed his party's commitment to constitutionality. Recognition was also supported by Canada and the United Kingdom, the two Western powers most closely connected to the island. Following the lead of their Atlantic allies, the U.S. State Department announced its recognition of the new regime on March 22, 1979, in order "to continue the friendly and cooperative relations our two countries have enjoyed since Grenada's independence in 1974."[17]

But the spring bloom on U.S.–Grenada relations lasted only 12 days. On March 25 Bishop made a major speech promulgating 10 new "People's Laws." People's Law #1 used two sentences to sweep away five years of Westminster-style government parliamentary rule and inoculate the coup from all legal challenges.[18] It declared: "The Constitution of Grenada is hereby suspended and has been suspended as of 12:01 a.m. on March 13, 1979. All acts and/or deeds by or under the authority of the People's Revolutionary Government are hereby deemed and declared to have been legally done." This blow to democracy was something of a pulled punch, however, because it was accompanied by a simultaneous pledge "to return to constitutional rule at an early opportunity." People's Law #3 established the island's new government as an odd hybrid: a revolutionary monarchy with the queen of England as the nominal head-of-state and an unelected, Marxist-influenced, revolutionary party calling the shots.

The person obligated to personify this schizophrenic national identity was the governor general, a post then held by Scoon, a respected Grenadian-born educator and public administrator. Scoon had been picked for the ceremonial post by Gairy, but he was asked to stay on in a reduced capacity by the new regime. The governor general's already-limited executive powers were reduced to "such functions as the People's Revolutionary Government may from time to time advise."[19] The post was retained by the revolutionaries to smooth the way to international recognition for the new regime and also to encourage desired close relations with the United Kingdom and Canada.[20] Scoon acquiesced to the new arrangement, but he did not totally surrender himself to puppet status. Scoon recognized he was now engaged in a "no-holds-barred, political power game" in which the "new, cock-a-loop regime held virtually all the cards."[21]

Another early player in this floating political poker game was Frank V. Ortiz, a career diplomat, who was then the U.S. ambassador to the Eastern Caribbean, based in Barbados. The State Department instructed Ortiz to visit Grenada twice in the immediate aftermath of the coup to check out how the new regime intended to play its hand. On the second visit on April 9–10, Ortiz carried with him a 10-point list of instructions he had received from his superiors at Foggy Bottom.[22] On the subject of aid, Ortiz outlined four U.S.–funded loans available to the new regime through the Caribbean Development Bank totaling $1.34 million.[23] For immediate assistance, Ortiz could only offer small project grants totaling no more than $5,000 each from a fund the ambassador personally controlled. Ortiz pledged that the United States would not countenance any attempt by Gairy to launch a counter-coup from American soil. But he cautioned Bishop against seeking military assistance from Cuba. "We would view with displeasure any tendency on the part of Grenada to develop closer ties with Cuba," he warned in a note he handed to Bishop.[24] To make sure there was no misunderstanding, Ortiz also deliberately left behind a "non-paper"— a complete copy of the talking point instructions he had received from Washington.[25]

The American ambassador thought they parted amicably, but Bishop and Coard were offended by both the substance of the demarche and the manner of delivery. On April 13, three days after the meeting with Ortiz, and a month after taking power, Bishop responded with a 22-minute radio broadcast that later came to be known as his "backyard" speech. Bishop gave his version of the meeting with Ortiz, focusing on the $5,000 immediate aid fund. He contrasted that "paltry sum" from the "wealthiest county in the world" with the no-strings-attached offers of goods and technical assistance his new regime had received from then left-leaning governments in Guyana and Jamaica. In summary, he declared: "No country has the right to tell us what to do, or how to run our country, or who to be friendly with. We certainly would not attempt to tell any other country what to do. We are not in anybody's backyard, and we are definitely not for sale."[26] The next day, Grenada and Cuba established diplomatic relations.[27]

Though Bishop publicly blamed Ortiz for giving diplomatic offense, Bishop had secretly decided to look to Cuba for political guidance and military aid even before he met with the American ambassador. On April 9, a Guyanese cargo ship with a shipment of rice arrived after dark in St. George's. It also carried several wooden crates of arms, which originated in Cuba.[28] The day before Bishop's backyard speech, a Cuban cargo ship arrived in St. George's harbor with cement—and 10 to 12 cases of additional arms. In both cases, the arms were offloaded and trucked to Grenadian army sites.

In Washington, these clandestine weapons shipments alarmed Zbigniew Brzezinski, President Carter's national security advisor. On May 8, Brzezinski wrote a memo to then CIA director Stansfield Turner suggesting that the spy agency embark on a covert program to expose the growing Cuban presence in the international press.[29] Turner responded with his own amplifications for neutering Castro's influence on the island.[30] This CIA response led Carter on July 3 to sign a "finding" that sanctioned covert efforts to overthrow the island's new government. Two weeks later, the finding was briefed to the Senate Intelligence Committee, which gave it a hostile reception. The next day the committee sent a letter to President Carter saying they would not support covert action against Grenada. That was enough cold water to halt the nascent destabilization effort in its tracks.[31] But Grenada's leaders were not privy to these then-secret Washington judgments. For years after, the Grenada revolutionaries invariably saw the CIA's hand behind political discord, suspect fires, and attempted assassinations. The Bridgetown embassy initially sought to show these accusations to be false, but soon came to the conclusion that the new regime was not interested in constructive dialog. "The PRG [People's Revolutionary Government] in its pursuit of a chimeric CIA destabilization plan and of propaganda advantage, has accused the United States of a series of actions which are either fabricated from whole cloth, or hanging on to a morsel of fact, are self-serving interpretations of events," the embassy reported to Washington.[32]

Meanwhile, Grenada's ideological flirtation with Cuba blossomed into a multifaceted, mentor-tutor relationship. Cuba eventually dispatched more than 50 doctors, teachers and technical specialists to the island to aid in the social, economic and political development of the island on the Cuban model. Forty-three military advisors were also sent to shape a major expansion of the Grenadian army. But the largest Cuban investment in Grenada in terms of both money and personnel came in the construction of a new airport. The first word of this joint effort came in December 1979 when the Bishop regime announced that it would begin construction of an international airport at Point Salines with Cuba as its principal construction partner. It was a surprising announcement because, up to that point, the NJM party had opposed the idea of a new airport as an overly ambitious use of limited resources. Once in power, Bishop and Coard quickly came to appreciate the merits of the project for both economic and political reasons.

Grenada's only commercial airport was then located at Pearls on the island's east coast. The airstrip was built by the British for Allied military use in World War II. By the mid–1950s Pearls was obsolete and making a poor impression. The 5,151-foot runway was 23 serpentine miles from the capital of St. George's, a 45-minute, bone-jarring ride. The airport's principal commercial carrier was Leeward Islands Air Transport (LIAT) which flew prop planes from nearby islands. LIAT's on-time record was spotty; its acronym was derisively translated as standing for "Leaving Island, Any Time." A succession of outside consultants recommended that Grenada replace Pearls with a new airport at Point Salines on the southwestern tip of the island. A longer runway would be capable of handling long-haul commercial passenger jets originating from points in the United States and Europe. Extending the landing field at Pearls was deemed to be impractical because it was hemmed in by high hills on three sides. Point Salines was much closer to the capital, where 30 percent of the population lived, and the island's mile-long showcase beach at Grand Anse. The shoe-shaped Point Salines peninsula was mostly undeveloped, but, nonetheless, presented some formidable construction challenges. The instep of the shoe was carved out by Hardy Bay. This inlet was at the center point of the proposed 9,600-foot runway and would need to be bridged by a causeway. In addition, hills would need to be leveled, marshes filled and aprons and taxiways laid. Finally, a tower, a terminal, support buildings and fuel storage tanks would need to be erected.

The construction would take many years and cost many millions. Still, Grenada was able to make a good case for the airport as a public works construction project. The project would put jobless island laborers to work and then welcome international tourists attracted by the island's pristine beaches and tropical breezes. The price tag for the project was initially estimated to be $70 million (U.S.), but eventually ballooned to an estimated $80 million. Grenada put out its hand and many countries responded. Cuba footed about half the total cost, mostly in the form of manpower, equipment and materials. Algeria, Venezuela, Syria and Iraq also provided grants. Loans were provided by Iraq, Libya, private Finnish banks and a British construction company. Two multinational organizations in Europe and the Middle East provided limited financial assistance for airport equipment.[33] But not all the promised foreign help actually arrived. By fiscal 1983, the Grenadians themselves were supporting about 30 percent of that year's planned capital expenditures for the airport.[34] The Soviet Union was asked to help, but was notably absent from the list of direct foreign contributors to the project.

Cuban engineers and laborers built the runway with the help of Grenadian laborers. The Cuban workers were civilians, employees of the National Union of Enterprises—Caribbean (UNECA), a state-owned construction firm.[35] Specialized work was contracted out to American and European companies. METEX, a Finnish firm, was hired to install exterior lighting for the runway, roads and parking areas.[36] An American firm, Layne Dredging Company of Miami, built the runway causeway and filled in the tidal salt ponds for which the promontory was named. Another American company, Norwich Engineering of Fort Lauderdale, designed the fuel storage complex. A British firm, Plessey Airport, Ltd., was hired to install the airport navigation and communication systems. The runway was originally planned to be just 7,800 feet long, too short to handle the latest generation of wide-bodied commercial jets, including a fully loaded Boeing 747. About a year after construction started, in October 1980, Grenadian officials persuaded Cuba of the need to lengthen the runway to more than 9,000 feet to accommodate the civilian international standard.[37]

The project was expensive, but comparable to facilities that Grenada's island neighbors had already built to attract tourists from Europe and the United States. A dozen other Caribbean islands had airports with runways of 9,000-foot-plus length. Most of the other islands, however, had a much better-established tourist trade than Grenada. Once built, the new Point Salines airport would face the next challenge of attracting new commercial airline service to the island, not to mention new hotels, restaurants and other traveler amenities.

The building of the new airport was intertwined with the growth of St. George's Medical School which was just three years old when Bishop seized power. Like the airport project, Bishop was initially wary of an enterprise that had been conceived under the Gairy regime but, like the airport, its obvious economic advantages overcame its ideological impurity. The medical school was a for-profit enterprise founded by Charles R. Modica, an American entrepreneur. Modica was a foreign medical school dropout who then turned to law for a career. He saw that there was money to be made catering to Baby Boomers whose college grades were not quite good enough to rate a classroom seat in an American medical school. Modica initially cashed in on their frustrated aspirations by publishing a directory to foreign medical schools and working as an admission officer for a medical school in the Dominican Republic.[38] Based on this market knowledge, he convinced 12 investors, many of them doctors who were parents of rejected students, to put up a total of $10 million to create an American-run, offshore school. Modica focused on the Anglophone Caribbean where there were more than a dozen island nations looking for outside investment to pull themselves out of endemic poverty. After unsuccessfully exploring Jamaica and Puerto Rico, Modica got an especially encouraging response from Grenada.

In 1976, the 29-year-old Long Island lawyer negotiated a draft agreement directly and quietly with then Prime Minister Gairy and his staff.[39] Grenada granted Modica's investment group a "sole and exclusive" charter to create a medical school on the island, as well as the sole rights to use the island's general hospital for teaching purposes. The government also offered a 10-year lease on a building and six acres of land at True Blue for $21,500 per year. Tax breaks were offered that would benefit the school's faculty, staff and students.[40] In return, the investors agreed to a number of financial inducements: $75,000 for expansion of the hospital laboratory, an annual payment of $100,000 for hospital supplies and equipment, $75,000 a year to the government for "general purposes" and free tuition for five Grenadian medical school students a year.

Typical of Gairy's autocratic style, an establishment act was rushed through the Parliament his party controlled. The House of Representatives debated and approved the measure in a single day, two weeks before it became law on Aug. 4, 1976.[41] The packaged deal cleared the way for Modica to hire a faculty and draft a curriculum on an equally hurry-up schedule. The first classes started in January 1977 with six part-time professors and 152 students. Tuition was about a third of what most American medical schools were charging. By the spring of 1979, the school had expanded to a full-time faculty of 23 and an island-resident student body of about 600.[42] Students came from 18 countries, but 80 percent of the students and staff were Americans. Many were New York residents. Modica presided as chancellor from an office building in Bay Shore, New York, on Long Island.

The vice chancellor and resident chief executive of the school was Geoffrey H. Bourne, Ph.D., Sc.D., an Australian by birth who had a distinguished medical career in England. He was an anatomist and nutritionist who at one time served as both the chairman of the anatomy department at the University of London and director of Yerkes Primate Center at Emory University in Atlanta. When Gairy was ousted on March 13, 1979, the school suspended classes for one day and everyone held their breath waiting to see how the new regime would regard the school. Bourne had a personal relationship with Bishop so he got in touch with him on the first day of the coup and was privately assured that the school would remain.[43] After Havana also endorsed the school's continuation, Bishop made a personal visit to the campus where he publicly extended his welcome.

So began a separate peace that prevailed on Point Salines through the on-and-off belligerence that characterized U.S. and Grenadian-Cuban relations in the ensuing four years. Bishop shook his fist at Washington in fiery speeches that blamed the CIA for fomenting discord and subverting his rule. The Carter administration shunned the island firebrands as a matter of policy, against the recommendation of Sally Shelton-Colby who replaced Ortiz as the regional ambassador until 1981. "I simply lost that battle," Shelton-

Colby later recalled. "So, we basically disengaged, and we developed a policy of trying to build up all the neighboring countries."[44]

Nonetheless, on Grenadian soil, the citizens of the three diplomatically antagonistic nations got along amicably on a day-to-day basis. The American medical school students followed Cuban doctors on their rounds in the general hospital. The students also played softball with the Cuban construction workers who lived and worked nearby. In 1978, the school's professors and student embarked on a mass immunization campaign financed by North American charities that succeeded in immunizing 80 percent of the population against seven infectious diseases.[45] The apex of harmonious town-gown relations was reached in the spring of 1982 when Bishop addressed the graduating class at the school with resident Soviet, Cuban and Libyan diplomats as invited guests. "Our government … is very happy to have the school with us in Grenada. We are very, very conscious of the benefits which the school has brought to our people and our country over the years," Bishop declared. The prime minister concluded his address by the shouting "Long Live St. George's Medical School!" and received a standing ovation.[46] But, under the surface, there was also tension in the local tri-lateral relationship. The Bishop regime suspected the school of harboring CIA spies and had their international phone and telex conversations recorded.[47] The school administration hedged its bets on the future in Grenada by maintaining a facility on nearby St. Vincent, putting feelers out to other Caribbean nations and keeping the U.S. embassy up to date whenever school officials were passing through Bridgetown.

As relations with Washington cooled to ice under the Bishop regime, relations with Moscow warmed. The Bishop regime in St. George's sought to formalize its ideological kinship with the Soviet Union in September 1979 by establishing diplomatic relations with Moscow for the first time. In early, Grenada stood alone with Cuba among Western countries in opposing a UN resolution calling for the withdrawal of Soviet troops after the invasion of Afghanistan. That vote was such an extreme position for a self-professed "non-aligned" nation that the Carter Administration lost all hope for reaching any accommodation with the Bishop regime.[48] Other concerns took precedence, notably the Iranian hostage crisis and the 1980 presidential campaign, which Carter lost to Reagan.

Grenada became an Ahab-like "obsession" of the new Republican administration when Reagan took office in January 1981.[49] The new administration was determined to stem, and ideally reverse, Soviet-supported Communist expansion throughout the world—and especially in the Caribbean, which had been regarded as an American lake since the days of President Monroe. For Reagan, Cuba was a *bête noire*—and Grenada was its surrogate.

On the military front, sabers were rattled in annual military exercises in the Caribbean through the early 1980s. In August 1981, the U.S. military conducted a three-month exercise code-named Ocean Venture '81 that sprawled across the Atlantic, the Baltic and the Caribbean. It involved 250 warships, 1,000 aircraft and more than 120,000 troops from 14 nations. One Caribbean component of the exercise was a mock invasion of a fictional country code-named "Amber and the Amberdines" that bore an unmistakable similarity to Grenada and the Grenadine Islands. Marines staged an amphibious landing on the island of Vieques off Puerto Rico that also involved a hostage rescue scenario and an airdrop of 350 Rangers.[50] The Grenadians were understandably spooked by the operation. Bishop issued a statement calling it "a practice run for a direct invasion of Grenada by U.S. troops."[51] Despite his protests, similar exercises were repeated in 1982 and 1983.

As relations with the United States became even chillier with the change in administration, relations with the Soviets further warmed. In July 1982, the Soviet Union assigned a resident ambassador to Grenada for the first time, replacing a previous ambassador who had been resident 1,121 miles away in Jamaica.[52] An embassy compound was established in a former bungalow hotel near Grand Anse Beach and the Radio Free Grenada broadcast studio. Moscow financed an upgraded relay transmitter for the radio station capable of covering all the Caribbean. The Soviet news agency TASS opened an office on the island and replaced the BBC as the source of radio station's off-island news.[53] By contrast, the new Reagan administration did not seek Grenada's accreditation for Milan Bish, the new Barbados-based regional U.S. ambassador, when Congress confirmed his appointment in November 1981. But this diplomatic posturing was belied by reality in both countries. Whatever their government-to-government relations, Grenadians were far more socially connected to the United States than either Cuba or the Soviet Union. More Grenadian expatriates lived in the United States than in their homeland. The number of Americans present on Grenada as tourists or temporary residents during the Bishop era always exceeded the number of Cubans. The American-run medical school was one of Grenada's largest employers and a major contributor to the government's annual budget and island's economy.

Reagan visited the Eastern Caribbean for the first time as president on a working vacation in April 1982. His first stop was a late-night working dinner in Jamaica with his friend and ideological ally, Edward P.G. Seaga, the prime minister. Seaga was a Boston-born, Harvard-educated, music entrepreneur before he turned to politics. He was the first foreign leader to pay a state visit to the White House after Reagan's inauguration in January 1981.[54] After a press conference at which each heaped praise on the other, Reagan flew on to Barbados for a luncheon meeting with the leaders of five more English-speaking Caribbean islands: Barbados, St. Vincent and the Grenadines, Antigua and Barbuda, Dominica and St. Kitts and Nevis. The Reagan visit was a rare opportunity for a leader of a microstate to have extended face time with the leader of the Free World, even if it was a group session. In fact, just to be clear about who said what to whom across the table, a microphone was hidden in the flowered centerpiece to record the 105-minute luncheon discussion.[55] Grenada was not invited to attend, but its Marxist-inspired leaders were the subject of luncheon conversation. Reagan voiced a Cold War message in his public remarks, declaring "the overturn of parliamentary democracy in Grenada ... bears the Soviet and Cuban trademark."[56] Significantly, all six of the Caribbean leaders he met on this vacation trip urged Reagan 18 months later to lead a military intervention in Grenada.

Reagan turned up the heat on Grenada with rhetorical attacks in early 1983 when the airport project was nearing completion. The one-week war in October was preceded by a six-month war of words beginning in the spring. In 1983, the Cold War had turned as chilly as it had ever been since the Cuban Missile Crisis. The tenor of times was exemplified by Reagan's address to the National Association of Evangelists in Orlando, Florida, on March 8, 1983. Reagan declared the Soviet Union to be an "evil empire" that is Godless and indifferent to morality that springs from religion.[57] Two days later, in a March 10 speech to a manufacturing trade group in Washington, Reagan pushed back against critics who suggested that Grenada was too inconsequential a county to be worth worrying about, considering its principal distinction was its production of spicy nuts. "People who make these arguments haven't taken a good look at a map lately or followed the extraordinary build-up of Soviet and Cuban military power in the region or read the Soviets' discussion about why the region is important to them and how they intend to use it,"

Reagan retorted. "It isn't nutmeg that is at stake in the Caribbean and Central America. It is the United States' national security," he said.[58]

The Republican president amplified on the theme of Grenada as Soviet surrogate in an address to the nation from the Oval Office on March 23, 1983. The topic of the speech was the Soviet threat and American plans to counter it. It became known as the "Star Wars" speech because Reagan proposed that the United States embark on a new weapons program to destroy Soviet ballistic missiles from space.[59] In an overshadowed portion of the same speech, the president used reconnaissance photographs to document Soviet military capabilities in Central America and the Caribbean Basin. He showed separate photos of a radio eavesdropping facility and airfield in Cuba that were used by the Soviets. A third photo showed an airfield in Nicaragua with eight Soviet-made helicopters on the ground. The final photo showed Point Salines. Of the latter, the president said: "On the small island of Grenada, at the southern end of the Caribbean chain, the Cubans, with Soviet financing and backing, are in the process of building an airfield with a 10,000-foot runway. Grenada doesn't even have an air force. Who is it intended for? The Caribbean is a very important passageway for our international commerce and military lines of communication. More than half of all American oil imports now pass through the Caribbean. The rapid buildup of Grenada's military potential is unrelated to any conceivable threat to this island country of under 110,000 people and totally at odds with the pattern of other eastern Caribbean States, most of which are unarmed."

The same night that Reagan made his televised speech from the Oval Office, Maurice Bishop addressed his nation in a broadcast on Radio Free Grenada. Alarmed by the drumbeats coming from the Reagan administration, Bishop cut short a visit to India, believing a U.S.–planned invasion was imminent. Bishop told his listeners that his intelligence staff had uncovered a CIA plot to launch an attack on Grenada by "counter-revolutionaries and mercenaries 'any day now.'"[60] To forestall that anticipated move, he called his countrymen to attention. But, instead of ordering his army to its posts, Bishop announced stepped up recruitment for the militia and a massive military maneuver—in another month. The spring invasion Bishop feared never materialized. Nonetheless, Bishop's remarks indicate that, even at the height of his regime's invasion paranoia, he was anticipating a Bay of Pigs–like attack by U.S.–supported surrogates, not a surprise attack by elite, uniformed American forces.

Reagan rhetorically returned to the U.S.–Grenada tensions a month later in an address to Congress on problems in Central America. On April 27 he appealed to federal lawmakers to support foreign aid programs that would "hold the line against externally supported aggression" in the Caribbean Basin.[61] One example he offered was that Libyan cargo planes might use the new airport on Grenada as a refueling stop for military aid they were ferrying to the Marxist Sandinista government in Nicaragua. Despite the impression repeatedly conveyed by the president, the airport at Point Salines was designed as a civilian facility, not a military base. A *Washington Post* reporter visited the construction site a month after the "Star Wars" speech and found American cruise ship visitors taking photographs of the same construction area that the president showed in satellite photos. American medical school students were also using the unguarded runway to race motorbikes.[62] After the invasion, Plessey, the British engineering firm hired to do electronics work at the airport, took the unusual step of issuing a statement debunking the military potential of the unfinished airport at Point Salines. Plessey declared that the airport design lacked 11 key characteristics of a military airbase, including radar, hardened aircraft shelters and underground fuel and weapons storage.[63] However, runways are agnostic as to the planes that land on them. It's certainly true that Soviet or Cuban military planes could potentially have used the Point Salines runway. American Air Force C-130s and C-141s demonstrated that on Oct. 25, even before it was completed.

A then-secret CIA intelligence report, dated April 21, 1983, offered a nuanced, strategic assessment of what was happening at Point Salines. "The ongoing airfield construction project will improve the island's capability to support Soviet forces and can be used to sustain Cuban interventionism in the hemisphere and Africa," the report declared in its first-page summary.[64] However, the full 11-page assessment went on to take a skeptical view of the airfield's military potential. The most likely military use, according to the report, was as a way station for Cubana Airline civilian transports ferrying Cuban troops to Angola and other trouble spots in Africa. The Soviets also could use the runway for "periodic deployments" of submarine patrol aircraft, but the report stated that such reconnaissance flights from Grenada "would only marginally improve the USSR's surveillance capabilities in the Atlantic" beyond those then being staged out of Cuba or Angola.[65] The report noted the nearby Galleons' Passage between Trinidad and Tobago was a primary route for oil tankers in the Caribbean, but the CIA added "we do not believe that interdiction of the sea lines of communication in the Caribbean would be a major mission of the Soviet Navy or is it a major stimulus for Soviet interest in the region."[66]

This restrained view was later affirmed by the Yuri Pavlov, a career Soviet diplomat who was the Ambassador to Costa Rica in 1983 and went on to become head of the Latin American division of the Soviet Foreign Office. Disillusioned by Russian-style communism, Pavlov immigrated to the United States from the Soviet Union at the end of 1990 just prior to its collapse. "No one in his right mind was thinking in Moscow ... along the lines of any possibility of turning Grenada into yet another Cuba. It was too small, too susceptible to economic and political pressures and could not be defended militarily," Pavlov later told CNN in an interview broadcast in 1998 as part of a 24-part series on the history of the Cold War.[67]

The Grenadian relationship with the Soviets in mid–1983 is probably best summarized in a confidential report by W. Richard Jacobs, Grenada's ambassador to Moscow. His memorandum to Bishop, Coard and two others offers a revealing glimpse of Grenada's place in the Communist world as viewed from Moscow.[68] Jacobs wrote that the Kremlin considered Grenada to be a proto-communist state, which was in the early stages of transformation from a socialist to a Soviet-style regime. This assessment rated them treatment as a "fraternal" state; essentially a second cousin who was part of the Soviet family through Cuba, but not a close relation. "[T]hey regard Grenada as a small distant country and they are only prepared to make commitments to the extent of their capacity to fulfill, and if necessary, defend their commitments," the resident Grenadian ambassador wrote. "The Soviets have been burnt quite often in the past by giving support to Governments which have either squandered that support, or turned around and become agents of imperialism, or lost power.... They are therefore very careful, and for us sometimes maddeningly slow, in making up their minds about who to support." In order to advance their standing in the eyes of the Soviets, Jacobs said they would have to be seen in Moscow as "the sponsor of revolutionary activity" in the English-speaking countries of the Caribbean Basin. However, Jacobs suggested that this proselytizing be accomplished by political means, such as hosting regional party meetings, modeling the benefits of a USSR alliance and acting as a diplomatic conduit to Moscow.

The escalation in the war of words between the United States and Grenada in Reagan's first years as president also gave rise to a mutual reconsideration that could have reset the relationship. On Dec. 5, 1982, Vice President Bush spoke at an annual conference on the Caribbean in Miami and declared Grenada to be a dependency of Cuba and the Soviet Union.[69] The Grenadian government took umbrage at that characterization and proposed to send a "high level emissary" to the United States to argue its case to the contrary to the vice president. A long pause followed without a reply. Meanwhile, Grenada's ambassador to the Organization of American States worked behind the scenes with sympathetic members of the Congressional Black Caucus to facilitate a trip by Bishop to the United States. Two members of the caucus agreed to sponsor a visit. Both the NJM's Political Bureau and the Reagan Administration were separately persuaded to go along, but for much different purposes. The Grenadian Politburo saw the trip as a public relations tour that would project a "statesman" image of Bishop and promote tourism, primarily by black Americans.[70] The Reagan Administration saw the trip as an opportunity to plumb rumors that Bishop was reconsidering his embrace of Cuba. Shultz's objective was to "size him up and see how committed he was to the present course."[71] Top-level White House policy discussions in May and June resulted in Reagan approving an offer of better relations in return for a reduction in anti–American rhetoric, improved human rights and a more non-aligned foreign policy.[72] Bishop sought to meet with Reagan personally, but that was rebuffed.

An 11-day, multi-city spring visit was arranged. The itinerary eventually included a 30-minute meeting on June 7 at the State Department in Washington between Bishop and two Reagan administration surrogates: William P. Clark, then the president's national security advisor, and Kenneth Dam, assistant secretary of state.[73] On June 4, Grenada sought to soften the frozen diplomatic ground by announcing the formation of a commission charged with producing a new constitution for Grenada within two years. Both sides rehearsed for the June 7 sit-down and came prepared with a script and scribes. According to unsigned notes taken by the Grenadian side, Bishop opened the session by expressing thanks for the meeting and proposing a joint commission that would help resolve their differences.[74] Clark responded that he had no problem with dialogue, but he was more interested in conduct. He said he was particularly concerned about Soviet influence in the region and expected to see a moderation of criticism of the United States in the future. Bishop responded that toning down of attacks must be mutual, but he was encouraged that Americans appeared willing to conduct talks on the normalization of relations. At that point, Clark departed the meeting. He left it to Dam to reiterate and amplify on American concerns about Soviet/Cuban influence on the region, according to the Grenadian account later captured by the Americans.

Dam later reported to Reagan that the "amicable" conversation had included Bishop's assurances that Grenada "would not be a security threat to the U.S. or any other government in the hemisphere." Dam wrote that the meeting had achieved its desired dual purpose: laying out the administration's concerns about the Bishop regime while also quelling domestic criticism that the United States was "stonewalling" him.[75] "Bishop now knows what we expect of him," Dam wrote. "We will judge his sincerity by the actions he takes in the coming weeks."

Whether Bishop ever seriously intended to alter his political course as a result of the meeting is still a matter of unresolved conjecture. As far as the Reagan administration was concerned, any subsequent course correction on Bishop's part was slight. "It is quite clear that he [Bishop] understood the message that was given to him," Fred C. Iklé, the under secretary of defense for policy, later told Congress.[76] "It is not quite so clear, but it is possible, that he tried to indicate a somewhat less hostile position toward the United States by a slightly less hostile tone in his radio broadcast. It is also not clear whether if, indeed, he wanted to move toward a less hostile stance toward us and eventually work with us; whether that had something to do with his downfall."

The principal effect of the Bishop-Clark meeting turned out to be its unintended consequences for Bishop. The Soviets were irked that they hadn't been informed in advance about the meeting with Clark and they let the Grenadian ambassador in Moscow know of their displeasure.[77] Some historians suggest that Bishop may also have accelerated his troubles with his own Central Committee by departing from his prepared script for the meeting.[78] The CIA agreed that the trip had a deleterious domestic effect on Bishop, for a different reason. "Bishop's trip to the United States appears to have had a catalytic effect on Coard…. Coard seemed to fear that the trip and Bishop's performance would undercut Coard's own standing in the party," an all-sources, post-invasion analysis later declared.[79]

By the late summer of 1983 the Grenadian revolution was faltering and near collapse. Roads were rutted, electricity unreliable, the militia in disarray, party and worker morale at low ebb and overworked leaders were exhausted or sick. On Sept. 14, a pivotal meeting of the party's Central Committee was convened that ended up stretching over three days.[80] Bishop found himself the target of a caustic attack on his personal leadership. The verbal assault was spearheaded by Lt. Col. Liam James and Layne, two Grenadian army officers who were Coard loyalists. Also joining in was Coard's wife, Phyllis, who served on the Central Committee in her capacity as head of the National Women's Organization. The source of the attack made it clear that the sentiments they expressed were shared by Coard, though he was not in attendance. The prescription offered for the island's current ills was "firm Leninism." This castor oil remedy called for applications of organization, discipline and ideological "clarity"—qualities lacking in Bishop. The humiliating critique led up to a surprise proposal that Bishop formally share leadership with Coard, his erstwhile friend and current rival. Bishop wanted time to consider the idea, but the proposition was put to an immediate vote. It was approved 9–1, with Bishop and two others abstaining.[81] The lone recorded no vote was cast by George Louison, then the agriculture minister, who now emerged as one of Bishop's principal defenders. Louison, 33, was the son of poor farmers, who became a teacher and social activist. He was also an established leader of the NJM party and who had held a number of senior government positions before assuming his agrarian ministry. Louison personified the populist wing of the party, which was in increasing conflict with the ideological orthodoxy of the Coards and the military faction of the party.

Since Coard was not present for the leadership discussion, he needed to be officially consulted on the joint plan. Bishop also appealed for more time to consider the implications of sharing the reins of government. Formalization of the joint leadership plan was put off until a meeting of the full party membership set for Sept. 25.[82] That meeting began with about 50 of the 300 party members attending, and neither of the two protagonists present. Both had to be summoned to the session as it was in progress, with Bishop the last to arrive. Seeing his cause was lost, Bishop accepted joint leadership. He embraced Coard and the party members sang "The International." Everyone may have been singing a song of unity, but Coard's political victory was near total. As deputy prime minister,

Coard was now in control of the party's organization, ideology and strategy. In addition, he was chairman of the Politburo, the small power group than ran both the party and the government. Bishop nominally retained the chairmanship of the Central Committee and the title of prime minister. Essentially his job was reduced to being the public face of the government to the masses and the international community. Bishop remained commander in chief of the PRA, but most of the officer corps was loyal to Coard. Shortly after the climatic meeting, Bishop and two loyalist ministers, Whiteman and Louison, left on a previously planned diplomatic mission to Eastern Europe. But, on consideration, Bishop resolved in the ensuing days to revisit the joint leadership idea when he returned from his 12-day trip.

Bishop returned on Oct. 8 to discover that his domestic opposition had been further emboldened in his absence. Bishop's itinerary included a final, unscheduled stop in Havana to see Castro, his friend and mentor. From Cuba, Bishop sent a message alerting the Central Committee of his scheduled time of return to Grenada—and also his desire to revisit the joint leadership issue. He got a non-verbal response to the latter, when his plane landed at Pearls Airport. No reception party was waiting to welcome him, as was customary. Instead, Bishop was met by a single official, Strachan, the minister of national mobilization who was closely identified with Coard.[83] Strachan was dressed in a T-shirt, jeans and slippers, a sartorial display of disrespect. After a cold exchange, Bishop returned to his home in St. George's to rest before reengaging in the leadership struggle with Coard.

The simmering tensions between the two men came to a boil on Wednesday, Oct. 12, at a morning Political Bureau meeting held at Fort Rupert. The eight-member committee, which included both Coard and Bishop, represented the inner-circle of the party. It met weekly, chaired by Coard, to made the day-to-day decisions for both the party and the nation. While Bishop was away, the bureau's sessions were temporarily merged with the larger 15-member Central Committee.[84] The practical effect of this change was to further shift party power toward Coard and away from Bishop. Controlling these two committees put Coard in de facto control of the government, the military and the party.

Bishop and Coard both maneuvered for advantage before the showdown meeting. Bishop wanted the Political Bureau agenda to include a review of the joint leadership proposal.[85] He had practical questions to raise about how such an arrangement would work. But the Coard faction interpreted this request as a direct challenge to the joint leadership idea, which they considered a closed matter. Bishop was equally apprehensive about the ultimate intentions of the Coard faction. He told his two bodyguards that he believed that Phyllis and Bernard Coard were planning to kill him. He asked them to spread the word to a list of his most trusted supporters.[86]

The Coard faction also sought to bind their supporters closer in advance of the meeting. While Bishop was abroad, and Coard was in charge at home, the PRA was given long-promised pay raises.[87] The night before the showdown meeting, members of Bishop's security detail were awakened and brought to a secret meeting. The bodyguards were warned that Bishop was developing dictatorial tendencies and reminded that they owed their first loyalty to the Central Committee and not the prime minister.[88] Before day's end, these men would be confining Bishop, instead of protecting him, but that turnabout was not yet preordained.[89] At 7 a.m. another secret session was held with Army soldiers who were also members of the party. These were mostly officers who were already Coard loyalists. They were briefed on efforts to reconsider the Central Committee's decision on joint leadership and urged to support the expulsion of "opportunists" who opposed the will of the party. The army officers approved a strongly worded resolution calling for the party to expel "all elements who do not submit." They also demanded an immediate end to "cultism" and "egoism"—a thinly veiled reference to Bishop and his followers.[90]

Bishop, meanwhile, started his day by stopping at the Cuban embassy on his way to the Political Bureau meeting. He told Julian Torres Rizo, the Cuban ambassador, about the deep divisions that were threatening to tear apart his party and his revolution. The substance of their conversation was summarized in a Cuban government statement later issued in Havana, after Bishop's assassination, but before the intervention.[91] The Cubans maintained that they found Bishop's report of party trouble on Grenada both "surprising" and "disagreeable." Bishop had spent 36 hours in Cuba on his way back from Eastern Europe, but "he made not the slightest mention in his conversations with Comrade Fidel and other Cuban leaders" of his domestic political problems. Bishop disclosed to the Cuban ambassador that, on his return home, he found his problems to be far more serious than he imagined while he was away. Bishop said he feared that he might be assassinated by his adversaries.[92] Still, he conveyed the impression that he could manage the situation on his own. Bishop wanted Cuban leaders to know what was happening, but he did not ask for their help in any way.

The deck was thus stacked against Bishop when he arrived for the start of the 9 a.m. meeting in a secure meeting room at Fort Rupert, the military headquarters. Instead of a *de novo* discussion of the complexities of a shared power arrangement, the agenda was set by Coard. The session focused mostly on the recent conduct of Louison, the agriculture minister. Louison was accused of persuading Bishop to balk at shared leadership during their Eastern Europe trip.[93] Louison denied sowing discord. He counter-attacked, blaming the laziness of some of his Central Committee members for the party's current woes.[94] A motion was offered to expel Louison from the Central Committee and he left the meeting.[95] According to Coard, Bishop was also defiant and announced he now opposed joint leadership. A lunch break was taken. The morning meeting molted into an emergency afternoon session of the Central Committee to resolve the leadership stalemate.

When the meeting resumed at 3 p.m., Coard was not present. During the break, Coard learned that rumors were spreading that he and his wife were plotting to kill Bishop. Fearing that these rumors would put his family in danger, he opted to take refuge in a "safe house" until the rumors were dispelled.[96] The assassination rumors became the focus of the Central Committee meeting that lasted seven hours. An investigation by PRA counter-intelligence officers traced the source of the rumors to Bishop's bodyguards. One of the guards, Errol George, admitted that he and the other guard, Cletus St. Paul, were acting on instructions from Bishop. When this was reported to the committee, St. Paul and Bishop were summoned. They denied responsibility for the rumors, but they were not believed. St. Paul was arrested.[97] Emotions ran high. John Ventour, a Coard supporter on the Politburo, chaired the raucous meeting. One point he pulled a gun to maintain order.[98] As the meeting was coming to an end, word came that some militia members outside the capital had seized weapons from an armory with the intent of coming to Bishop's rescue. Orders were given to put the regular army on alert and to remove arms from the armories in two troublesome militia districts.[99] The motion to expel Louison from the Political Bureau and the Central Committee was affirmed. His brother, Maj. Einstein Louison, the Army chief of staff, and the top-ranking officer loyal to Bishop, was suspended and put under house arrest.[100] Bishop was confined in his home and pressured to make a calming statement on Radio Free Grenada.[101]

Bishop taped a brief announcement that was broadcast after midnight when the government-run station normally went off the air. Bishop declared the rumors about the Coards to be untrue and denied any dissention existed with the party leadership. But the ultimate message conveyed was far from reassuring. Astute listeners noticed that Bishop was introduced on the after-hours broadcast as the leader of the New JEWEL Movement party, not as Prime Minister, as was customary.[102] Pandora's Box was opened. Up to this point the power struggle had been closely contained within the party leadership committees. Now it was in the public arena, where Bishop held far more sway.

At around 11 a.m. on Thursday, Oct. 13, the Central Committee met again at Coard's home to decide on their next course of action in an internal crisis that had now spilled out to involve to the entire nation. Coard and his followers feared that Cuba would intervene militarily to oust them and reinstate Bishop's authority.[103] After three hours of discussion, the committee resolved to head off this eventuality by tightening their grip on Bishop. The loose form of the house arrest that had been imposed on Bishop was formalized to include removing any communication equipment he might use to contact the Cubans.[104] Coard thought the enforced confinement would prevent Bishop from spreading any more rumors about him. He also hoped that Bishop would reconsider and bend to the will of the Central Committee.

Later that day, Bishop was brought before the full party membership in a session that was more of an inquisition than a hearing. This meeting was held in a huge room at Butler House, the former hotel that now served as the offices for the prime minister and the meeting place of the cabinet. About 250 people were present and 31 spoke.[105] Coard attended, but let others speak for him.[106] Bishop was brought to the meeting shortly after it began, but only the top party leaders knew he was under house arrest. Bishop was greeted by a standing ovation from the rank and file. Ventour again chaired the meeting and brought the membership up to date on events of the previous day. Bishop delivered a 45-minute speech in which he acknowledged failing to accept the joint leadership directive, but he denied spreading any rumors about the Coards. However, Bishop's denial was immediately thrown into doubt by the surprise appearance of George, the bodyguard, who proceeded to detail his role in the rumor dissemination scheme. This public unmasking prompted some members to weep for their shamed leader and others to become enraged with him. There were calls for Bishop to be put on trial. Others called on Bishop to rebut the bodyguard's testimony, but he declined to speak further.[107] The pro–Coard audience applauded a suggestion from the floor that Louison be expelled for the party for his suspected role in undermining joint leadership. There was also general support for a motion to expel Bishop from the party, but, in the end, no formal expulsion action was taken against either man.[108] Bishop ended the day under detention at this home.

The next morning, Friday, Oct. 14, two top party leaders visited Bishop to inform him that the Central Committee had expelled him from the party he co-founded.[109] Radix, the Justice Minister, a longtime Bishop friend and political ally, was so outraged by the Central Committee action that he resigned his government post and began agitating for Bishop's immediate release.[110] The shocking news spread quickly through the population and into the diplomatic community. The Cuban ambassador was alarmed and met with the Central Committee to find out what was going on.[111] Ordinary Grenadians were also roiled. By late morning, small public demonstrations had formed in both

St. George's and Grenville that swelled to several hundred by the mid-afternoon. Coard was well aware that the escalating leadership crisis would not play well with average Grenadians—not to mention their already wary island neighbors. He reached out to Whiteman, the foreign minister, by phone that morning and offered to open negotiations. An agreement was reached for Whiteman and Louison to meet at Coard's home at 3 p.m. on Saturday, Oct. 15.[112] Coard's belief that the crisis had reached a tipping point proved correct within hours.

Also on Oct. 14, Strachan, the mobilization minister and Coard confidant, appeared at the office of the government-run *Free West Indian* newspaper in St. George's. He announced that Bishop was under arrest and Coard was the new prime minister. The news did not go over well. By the afternoon, an angry crowd of Bishop supporters had gathered outside the newspaper offices to demand Bishop's reinstatement. The scene was shared off-island by Hughes, the Grenadian journalist who worked as a stringer for the regional Caribbean News Agency (CANA) and other English-language news organizations.[113] Bishop loyalists in his cabinet added to the pressure by resigning in protest of the treatment of their popular leader. Whiteman announced his resignation as Foreign Minister as he was passing through Barbados on the way home from New York. On Grenada, Jackie Creft, the mother of a son by Bishop and pregnant with another child by him, announced her resignation as the minister of education. Louison, who had already been purged from the leadership of the party because of his loyalty to Bishop, also resigned his agriculture minister post.[114]

Coard sought to counter this flood of resignations by also resigning. At 4 p.m., Radio Free Grenada reported that Coard had just phoned the station to say that he giving up his minister posts immediately to put to rest rumors that he had seized power.[115] Five minutes after reporting the news about Coard's resignation from the government, the station broadcast a muscle-flexing statement from the People's Revolutionary Army. The Army warned that unnamed "counter-revolutionary" elements were causing unrest and that full measures would be taken to restore order.[116]

On Barbados, these rapid developments took the regional American embassy by surprise. Milan Bish, the U.S. ambassador to Barbados and the Eastern Caribbean, first learned of the recent events from the British embassy on Barbados. The British reported to him that Coard had been "all but successful" in seizing control from Bishop with the intent of declaring Grenada to be a Marxist state.[117] Bish cabled the White House, the secretary of state and others with news he had collected from the British and Radio Free Grenada, but he added nothing of his own.

Bish, a 54-year-old Nebraska businessman and Republican Party activist, was a political appointee, not a career diplomat. He got a patronage appointment to the ambassador post as a reward for having served as a regional campaign director for Reagan in his 1980 presidential bid. Bish had insider access in Washington, but he was unschooled in the profession of diplomacy or the ways of the West Indies. He was a Nebraska real estate developer who had never been to Barbados until he assumed the ambassador post there on Nov. 26, 1981.[118] Though Grenada nominally was part of his nine-nation jurisdiction, Bish had not yet set foot there. By 1981 the United States had balked at exchanging ambassadors with the Bishop regime.

Consular-level visits to the island had been drastically reduced under Bish's administration.[119] His embassy relied heavily on Caribbean radio stations and a regional wire service for the latest news from Grenada. Bish's cables indicate his insights into the working of Grenada's politics and players came largely from friendly nations, notably the Barbadians and the British. The U.K. Foreign Office had a well-informed counselor officer (John Kelly) resident on the island, not to mention two centuries of shared history with the island. The American diplomatic deficit was compounded by the fact that the CIA also lacked active human assets on the island, despite the strategic priority that the Reagan administration had assigned to it after taking office.

In this vacuum, Barbados Prime Minister Tom Adams took on an early leadership role. He personally rallied a multinational response to the disquieting news coming from his closest island neighbor. Adams, then 52, was in his second term as prime minister and at the apex of his political power. He was an Oxford-educator lawyer of wide-ranging intellectual interests and a passion for politics. He was only the second man to serve as prime minister after Barbados gained its independence in 1966, but learned the job from his father, Sir Grantley Herbert Adams. The elder Adams led the island's government for a dozen years at the end of the colonial era. Grantley and his wife were unable to agree on a single first name for their only son, so they gave him four. As an adult they were commonly reduced to four initials, J.M.G.M., but the son preferred his nickname: Tom. The younger Adams was a personable man with a sarcastic wit, a mathematic mind and a special skill for both oratory and organization.[120]

Adams sensed immediately that further disorder on Grenada was inevitable. His instinct was to reach out to help those he saw most in harm's way. In the afternoon, he made phone contract with Whiteman, Grenada's foreign minister, while he was in transit through Barbados back to Grenada. Adams offered Whiteman asylum, but Whiteman declined and continued on home.[121] (Adams' premonition proved correct. Both Bishop and Whiteman would be executed within a week.)

At 7 p.m. Friday evening, Oct. 21, Torres, the Cuban ambassador, and Gastón Diaz González, his deputy, paid a visit to Coard's home at his invitation.[122] Coard wanted to know Castro's reaction to Bishop's ignominious fall from party favor. "The Cuban position and possible actions were central to our … concerns," Coard later recalled.[123] Coard was mindful of Castro's surprise decision in late 1975 to send 25,000 Cuban troops to Angola to support a leftist movement in a multisided Cold War power struggle precipitated by that country achieving independence from Portugal. Coard remembers asking the Cuban ambassador directly: "Is Cuba likely to intervene militarily in our Party dispute, as it did in Angola?"[124] According to Coard, both Cuban diplomats ducked a direct answer to his question. Coard was now convinced that Bishop had secretly secured "decisive" support from the Cubans in the leadership crisis and was prepared to "call in the Cubans," if necessary, to win the contest of wills.

In Washington, however, the Grenada crisis was not a sufficiently urgent matter to interrupt weekend plans. The principal national security concern inside the Beltway was who would replace William P. Clark as national security advisor. On Thursday afternoon, the White House announced the surprising news that Clark was resigning his current post to accept Reagan's nomination to be secretary of the interior.[125] James A. Watt, the previous secretary had resigned under pressure leaving a cabinet seat unexpectedly vacant. Clark, long at odds with Shultz and others in the White House inner circle, saw an opportunity to change horses.

At first, Reagan was primed to appoint Baker, the White House chief of staff, to the national security post. Michael K. Deaver, Baker's deputy, would move up to fill his boss' job. The double move had been conceived by Baker as his way out of a "brutal" staff job and, more significantly, as a means of quelling internal conflicts within the administration over national security policy.[126]

Reagan initially agreed to Baker's plan, but temporized when Meese, Clark, Casey and Weinberger joined forces in a last-minute lobbying offensive against the linked appointments.[127] Reagan left for Camp David to mull the appointment options. He took calls over the weekend from political moderates, who favored Baker, and conservatives, including Casey, who favored Jeane J. Kirkpatrick, then the U.S. ambassador to the United Nations. In the end, Reagan settled on McFarlane, Clark's deputy, as a compromise choice to succeed his departing boss.

In contrast to Washington's preoccupation with personnel matters, the events unfolding on Grenada were perceived by the right-leaning leaders of the English-speaking Caribbean as a clear and present threat to their sovereignty. They all had radical leftists on their islands whom they feared might be inspired to follow the quick path to power paved by the Grenadian coup leaders.

Barbados prime minster Adams had also recently come to believe, rightly or wrongly, that Bishop was becoming disenchanted with the communist path for his people.[128] So, when Adams learned of the internecine campaign to depose Bishop, his first thought was how to save Bishop from his dogmatic party insurgents. "I concluded that, whatever our differences in the past, Mr. Bishop deserved the support of the Caribbean governments in the circumstances," he later declared in a speech to his countrymen.[129] That view was also evidently shared by some in Washington, at least initially.

According to Adams' public account, on Oct. 15 "a United States official" approached a senior official in the Barbados Defence Force about mounting a joint effort to rescue Bishop from house arrest. Adams did not mention the name of the official in his address and refused to identify the person by name or rank in a follow-up interview with a *Washington Post* reporter. But, in 1988, Bish, then an ex-ambassador, confirmed in an interview with an American academic that the offer of an airplane to conduct the rescue had been made by him to the Barbadian permanent secretary of defense and security.[130] In a subsequent interview in 1994, Bish told a British historian that he believed the Bishop rescue plan had originated with the CIA.[131] It's noteworthy that the first U.S.–floated multinational rescue plan for Grenada was a rescue of the island's ostensibly Marxist prime minister, not the Anglophile governor general or U.S. medical students. The plan to rescue Scoon and the students would come later, after Bishop's assassination rendered his rescue moot. (After the invasion, Deputy Secretary of State Dam told Congress that there had not been any "authorized" discussion between U.S. government officials and any Caribbean country regarding a military action on Grenada prior to the OECS request on Oct. 21.)[132]

Why would any America official propose a rescue of a Marxist-inspired leader whom they had worked to isolate for so many years under two administrations? The *Washington Post* reported that speculation in the Caribbean at the time was that some officials (including Coard) feared that Bishop's house arrest would drive him to seek an armed intervention by Cuba on his behalf to regain power. This could potentially render Grenada a de facto Cuban protectorate, rather than a mere protégé.[133] Whatever the American motive or authority at the time, the possibility of a joint rescue of Bishop was taken seriously enough by Adams for the Barbados Defence Force to draft a plan that bore superficial similarity to the invasion plan that later emerged from Washington and Norfolk. Key targets were identified, including Bishop's house, the governor general's residence and the airports. The principal architect of the Barbadian plan was Maj. Adkin, the staff officer of operations and training, who would later write the first definitive popular history account of Operation Urgent Fury.[134]

Meanwhile, on Grenada, Radix, the just-resigned justice minister, organized a week-end rally in the market square at St. George's. Radix was a boyhood friend and former law partner of Bishop. Like Bishop, he was a skilled orator and champion of the poor. Several hundred turned out to hear him denounce Coard as power obsessed.[135] Radix urged the crowd to seek out Coard if they wanted to free Bishop. But, by then Coard had withdrawn from public sight to pull the stings of power behind the scenes. Soon after the rally, Radix was arrested at his home and put behind bars at Richmond Hill Prison as a counter-revolutionary.[136] The Coard faction also attempted to exert control over media coverage by expelling about a dozen members of the international press who had come to the island to report on the turmoil.[137] With foreign reporters ousted and Bishop and Radix in custody, Coard now focused his attention on negotiating a lasting solution to the crisis. Conversations between representatives of the two sides went on for two and a half hours on Saturday and continued for the next two days.[138] The negotiators were Coard and Strachan, a Politburo member, for the Coard-controlled party and Whiteman and Louison, both just-resigned ministers, for the Bishop faction.[139] Bishop's negotiators pressed for his reinstatement. Coard reluctantly agreed to put the question to the Central Committee, but he continued to maintain a low public profile.

Just after noon on Sunday, Oct. 16, a gruff, unpracticed voice was heard on Radio Free Grenada as an official spokesman for the party and the government: Austin, the former prison guard who was the titular head of Grenada's army, police and its security services. Austin's message carried special significance because all Grenadians knew his name as a daring leader of the 1979 coup that installed Bishop. Reading from a prepared text, Austin blamed Bishop for provoking and perpetuating an internal power struggle within the New JEWEL Movement that had paralyzed the party and weakened the country. He accused Bishop of insisting on "sole and exclusive" rule, a one-man governing style that "our party cannot, and will not, permit."[140] Austin asserted that the Central Committee was now in full control of the nation and called on Grenadians "to maintain unity in order to ensure that imperialism does not take advantage of this moment of difficulty." He concluded by assuring his listeners that Bishop (though deposed and humiliated) was still beloved by party members and "is at home and is quite safe."

On the same Sunday evening, Castro let his views be known to the new Grenadian leaders with a dramatic flourish. At around 8 p.m. Coard and a few of his close advisers were conferring at his home when a convoy of cars unexpectedly pulled up at this front door. Torres, the Cuban ambassador, emerged, accompanied by about a dozen armed personnel. Coard's security detail immediately formed a protective cordon. Only Torres was permitted to enter Coard's home. The ambassador strode to the center of the room and read a letter from Castro to the Central Committee. The letter was a reply to the questions that Coard and Strachan had posed to Torres two days earlier about Cuba's suspected role in Bishop's change of heart on joint leadership.[141] (A copy of the letter later fell into the hands of the American military and was made public along with other seized NJM documents.) "We are indignant at the very thought that some of you would have considered us capable of meddling in any way in the internal questions of your party," Castro scolded.[142] He decried as "a miserable piece of slander" the notion that Bishop had stopped off to see him to seek his support in the power struggle. "Bishop did not mention a single word to me, nor did he make the slightest allusion to the matter," Castro declared. He cautioned that the divisions that have since emerged "will result in considerable damage to the image of the Grenadian Revolution."

Coard was stung by the censorious tone of the letter, which was reinforced by the form of the signature. According to Coard, Castro usually signed his communications to Grenadian leaders over his title as president of the Cuban government or as first secretary of the Cuban Communist party. This letter was signed under a third title: commander-in-chief. "We all read Fidel's letter as a warning," Coard later wrote.[143] Coard's fear at this point was oddly congruent to Washington's. Leaders in both St. George's and D.C. believed the crisis might prompt Cuba to intervene militarily to restore Bishop to power.

While the Central Committee struggled to find a way out of its leadership dilemma, Bishop's supporters acted to tilt the scales in favor of their beloved "Maurice," which they commonly pronounced as "Morris." On Tuesday, Oct. 18, schools went on strike. In Grenville, the eastern port town, several thousand persons marched to Pearls Airport. The young protesters shouted anti–Coard slogans and carried banners that read, "We don't want communism" and "We want democracy."[144] Meanwhile, in the capital city, Coard's negotiations with Bishop's supporters stalemated and then broke off with angry words.

Bishop's negotiators decided to take their case directly to the people. Whiteman gave telephone interviews to radio journalists from several nearby Caribbean islands.[145] Whiteman disclosed to the world that a total of seven of 11 cabinet minister posts were now vacant as a result of the party turmoil.[146] These vacancies effectively meant that Grenada no longer had a functioning government, as Coard had also resigned his Finance Minister post for his own political reasons.[147] Some ministers were in custody, as well as out of office. Louison was arrested by security forces, allegedly for inciting violence. He joined two other Bishop supporters who were also being detained at Richmond Hill Prison for similar reasons: Radix and Einstein Louison, the army chief of staff and George's brother. Creft, the minister of education, who was also Bishop's mistress, was under voluntary detention. She elected to join Bishop in house arrest at his home as a condition to visiting him on Oct. 17.[148] These detainments left Whiteman as the top-ranking spokesman for Bishop who was still free to act. He made preparations for a massive public pro–Bishop demonstration at Market Square the next morning.

Meanwhile, the Central Committee decided to convene a late-night, emergency general membership meeting at Butler House to bring the party rank-and-file up to date on the crisis and to secure their endorsement of a final compromise offer.[149] The 10 p.m. meeting was chaired by Ventour, a trade union leader, without Coard present. The membership agreed to a proposal to reinstate Bishop as prime minister and the nominal leader of the party—provided he accepted a big downside. Bishop would no longer be a member of the Central Committee and would only attend Political Bureau meetings in an advisory capacity. The post of commander-in-chief would be abolished. Military affairs would be handled by the Central Committee instead of the prime minister. Finally, he would have to accept full responsibility for the crisis by broadcasting an appeal for calm and meeting with Coard to hash out their remaining differences.[150]

A four-member delegation delivered the six-point proposal to Bishop at his home around midnight.[151] Bishop asked for time to consult with his supporters, including the Cuban ambassador. At a minimum, Bishop wanted to retain his seat on the Central Committee and the Political Bureau. He agreed in principal to make a broadcast, but he appealed for time to draft the text. At this point, Washington was also looking for calming gestures. A note was sent to the Grenadian foreign ministry through diplomatic channels seeking assurances about the safety of U.S. citizens on the island.[152] Ironically both Grenadian and the American policy makers were now both actively seeking the same elusive objective: statements that would reduce the threat of violence the crisis was posing to their respective citizens. The Bishop radio address was never made and the RMC diplomatic response failed to allay American concerns. The furies unleashed by the crisis could not be contained.

The next day, Oct. 19, became known as "Bloody Wednesday." On Grenada, the morning began with Louison, the freshly-expelled and detained agriculture minister, being brought under guard to a 7 a.m. meeting with Bishop at his house on Mount Wheldale. The two men discussed the Central Committee's compromise offer for nearly two hours. The conversation was private, but it was closely observed by the Coard faction. Coard watched Louison leave Bishop's home from a vantage point in his house, just 150 yards away. The Coard faction feared that Bishop would use that meeting as an opportunity to call for more active Cuban intervention. Cornwall, the just-recalled ambassador to Cuba, was dispatched to the Cuban compound in the morning to warn restive pro–Bishop Cuban construction workers against joining in the protests planned for later that day.[153] As Louison was departing, members of the delegation that was sent to Bishop's home the previous night were arriving at Coard's home. They told Coard that they were optimistic that a settlement could be wrapped up at a session with Bishop set for 10 a.m. Coard was anxious for an answer from his estranged friend that would peaceably abate the crisis.[154] Instead, he got his answer directly from the Grenadian people in the form of defiant shouts.

St. George's school children now became the standard-bearers for pro–Bishop sentiment in the capital city. The student council at the all-girls Anglican High School sent out emissaries to recruit protesters from the government-run Grenada Boys' Secondary School, Coard's alma mater, and Presentation Brothers' College, the parochial secondary where Bishop had once been a star student. Students poured out into the streets. While the students were gathering, Whiteman and Vincent Noel separately led other pro–Bishop demonstrators through the city streets to the Market Square where loudspeakers had been set up for the planned rally. Still more protesters arrived by bus and private vehicle from the countryside. By 9 a.m. an estimated crowd of 15,000 people had assembled at the city square to hear speeches from Whiteman and others. The gathering represented 15 percent or more of the island's entire population.

At around 10 a.m., Whiteman proposed that the crowd march directly to the prime minister's residence on Mount Wheldale to free Bishop.[155] About a third of the assembly set off up the hill to the nearby house. Some stopped at the start of the road leading to the compound, but others proceeded on to a sentry box at the entrance to Bishop's driveway. "We want we leader. B for Bishop, C for Coard and C for Communism," the crowd chanted.[156] Their shouts where heard by the Central Committee which had gathered on the veranda of Coard's home. Marchers had to pass Coard's house to get to Bishop's. Two top Army officers left the Coard residence to confront and quiet the crowd.[157] They were booed until they retreated. Two armored cars were dispatched from Fort Frederick to take up defensive positions at Bishop's home. The protesters were not intimidated by the armored vehicles and started breaking down the fence to the compound at around 10:30

a.m. The soldiers fired four bursts into the air. Hundreds fled in panic, but others slipped behind the armored vehicles and made their way to where Bishop and Creft were being held. They found the two ministers tied to beds in separate rooms.

Once freed, Bishop and Creft revived sufficiently to be taken by the arm by their rescuers to the main road. Private vehicles were waiting to take them to the center of town where a large group of supporters was still gathered hoping to hear from Bishop. Instead, Bishop directed that he be taken to Fort Rupert, the headquarters for the People's Revolutionary Army. Bishop wanted to use the communication facilities at the fort to make phone calls and a broadcast to the nation by radio or a public-address system.[158] He may also have wanted to avail himself of some medical treatment from the nearby general hospital. Some of the demonstrators followed their leader to the fort. Others, perhaps sensing trouble, returned to Market Square where they started.

The crowd with Bishop streamed into the car park at the fort. A tense standoff between civilians and soldiers ensured. Maj. Christopher Stroude, the senior officer at the 60-soldier headquarters, parleyed with Fitzroy Bain, a Bishop supporter and a trade union leader on the Central Committee. Bain informed Stroude that Bishop had rejected joint leadership and reasserted his control of the party.[159] Stroude sought the advice of about a dozen party members who happened to be at the fort that morning for a meeting, and then made his decision. He ordered his soldiers to disarm, rather than resist the mob. Bishop set up an impromptu headquarters in the operations room on the first floor joined by dozens of his supporters. Bishop told Stroude he intended to arrest Coard, Layne and Cornwall. Bishop's supporters freed Maj. Einstein Louison, the former chief of staff who was being held prisoner at the fort because of his Bishop loyalties. Bishop appointed him the new head of the PRA, replacing Austin.[160] He also directed that the fort's armories be opened to arm militia members in the crowd against a counter-attack. Other protestors with military training took weapons directly from the soldiers in the garrison. The fort's officers were held under guard by armed civilians in one section of the ops room. The party members present were also held separately at gunpoint on an upper courtyard.[161]

Bishop dispatched an emissary to the Cuban embassy to appeal for the airport construction workers to intervene on his behalf. But the Cuban ambassador was not free to act without Fidel's approval. An urgent wire was sent by the embassy to Havana, but Bishop was assassinated before there was time for a response.[162] In any event, the answer would have been no, Castro later asserted. Castro was wary of placing his workers in the middle of a civil war where Cuban personnel would be engaging in combat against Grenadian soldiers loyal to the Coard faction. "Even if things had turned out in Bishop's favor and the U.S. intervention hadn't occurred, Bishop would have had to rule the country without his party, without the army, without the police and security units, and without the revolutionary cadres," Castro later told two American interviewers.[163]

Meanwhile back at Mount Wheldale, the Central Committee sought safety from the angry crowds by moving from Coard's home to Fort Frederick, a sprawling, colonial-era fortress on a ridge two miles east of the city center. Coard rode in the back seat of a government ministry van to avoid being recognized.[164] Witnesses later testified in court that they saw him arrive carrying a briefcase in one hand and a pistol in the other. At Fort Frederick, Coard and key Central Committee members regrouped in a communications room in an underground tunnel. Coard, an obese man weighing 285 pounds, called for a bed so that he could lie down to relieve his aching back.[165] The committee made phone contact with Fort Rupert. Bishop refused to take the call. Whiteman, the resigned foreign minister, came onto the line to declare, "No negotiations; no compromise" and then he hung up.[166]

At that point, three more armored personnel carriers (APCs) and their crews had just arrived at Fort Frederick after being summoned by Layne from the PRA base at Calivigny. After conferring with the Central Committee members, Layne ordered the armored unit to retake Fort Rupert.[167] The 25-year-old Army lieutenant colonel believed that decisive military action was needed to head off a civil war. He ordered his soldiers to ride on the top of their vehicles until the lead vehicle arrived on the one-lane road leading to the fort. At that point, the soldiers would dismount, fire their weapons in the air and, ideally, use the "shock effect" to retake the fort without bloodshed.

When the vehicles reached Fort Rupert at around 1 p.m., the crowd initially assumed the soldiers had come to join them. The martial demeanor of the soldiers quickly disabused the civilians of that hope. The lead APC stopped about 30 meters away from the two-story headquarters which was located just inside the north wall of the fort. Hundreds of Bishop's supporters had gathered in the parking lot that separated the APCs from the headquarters. They were expecting Bishop to speak to them from a balcony on the second floor.

What happened next would become the basis of murder charges brought against Coard and 17 others who were subsequently accused of causing the death of Bishop and seven of his supporters. Eyewitness offered varying accounts of the bloodshed, spawning controversies that have persisted to this day. However, key sworn testimony was offered over successive days in the spring of 1986 at a drawn-out trial that led to the conviction of 14 of the accused. Cecil "Tony" Buxo, a Grenadian optician, was a star witness for the prosecution because of his vantage on events and his military knowledge. Earlier in life, Buxo was trained at the Royal Military Academy Sandhurst near London and then went on to rise to the rank of captain in the Trinidad and Tobago Defense Force.[168] On Bloody Wednesday, Buxo was visiting a friend at a home in St. George's that had a line of sight to both Mount Wheldale and Fort Rupert. He was able to observe the day's drama at both locations through an 80-power telescope. Buxo testified on May 9, 1986, that he watched as the armored column from Fort Frederick made its way through narrow, winding city streets to the fort at the harbor entrance.[169] Upon arrival at Fort Rupert, he saw soldiers in the two lead vehicles dismount and take up a V-shaped formation that would funnel anyone leaving the area to a single point. Then the lead APC fired off a long burst from its turret machine gun. A loud explosion followed and a vehicle parked in the courtyard in front of the operations room erupted into flame. The initial machine gun burst was immediately followed by firing from multiple directions.

In the maelstrom of bullets two enlisted soldiers were killed and one officer was mortally wounded: Conrad Mayers, the officer candidate who was leading the APC detachment. The surviving soldiers unleashed a fusillade on the fort's defenders. They fired heavy machine guns from their armored vehicles and small arms, including AK-47s, hand grenades and rocket-propelled grenades (RPGs). They then advanced on the crowd, sending them fleeing to the battlements of the hilltop fort. Faced with a choice of facing a machine gun or a jumping over the edge, some chose to leap onto rocks 20 or more feet below. An RPG round penetrated the operations room, killing two young women and injuring others. Noel, a trade union official who had dedicated his life to the revolution in 1979, was mortally wounded. The attackers called on the surviving occupants to come out with their hands up. Bishop shouted his surrender and called on his supporters to lay down their arms. The fort's captive cadre now rearmed themselves and joined forces with the armored unit sent to their relief.

Three PRA officers took charge: Lt. Callistus Bernard (then better known as Iman Abdullah), Capt. Lester Redhead and Maj. Stroude, the senior officer at the fort that morning,[170] Bishop and seven of his most loyal supporters were gathered up and told to keep their hands on their heads. They were marched up to an upper square which was level with the second story of the headquarters. The prisoners then were ordered to stand facing a four-foot high wall with their hands still on their heads. Enlisted soldiers guarded them as two officers, Bernard and Redhead, sought direction from the Fort Frederick about what to do next. The 10 Central Committee members present at the hilltop fort met and agreed that Bishop and his clique should be executed, according to a contested signed statement later made by Colville McBarnette, one of the 10.[171]

Bernard and Redhead returned to the square where the eight prisoners were anxiously waiting to learn their fate. Bernard took up a parallel position about 20 meters away on the other side of the square, facing their backs. He carried a machine gun. Another armed soldier took up a position to Bernard's right and two more were to his left. Key testimony at this point was offered by Fabian Vernon Gabriel, a warrant officer who was one of the three subordinate soldiers. Gabriel was among the 17 later accused in the murders. Gabriel was granted a conditional pardon in return for testifying for the prosecution on May 12 and 13, 1986.[172] Gabriel testified that he heard Bernard order: "Comrades, turn around." The prisoners turned to face their executers. Taking a piece of paper from his pocket, Bernard declared: "This is an order from the Central Committee that you shall be executed by fire." He instructed them to turn back to face the wall. "Comrade, I am seven months pregnant," Creft pleaded, to no avail. "Prepare to fire, one, two, three," Bernard ordered.

Bullets from four automatic weapons cut through the condemned like a scythe, shredding flesh and exposing vital organs. Seven died immediately. Fitzroy Bain, a trade union leader on the Central Committee, clung to life. Gabriel executed him with one shot to the head, according to statements by both Gabriel and Bernard. Besides Bishop, three of the eight assassinated were his cabinet ministers: Norris Bain, the minister of housing (no direct relation to Fitzroy); Whiteman, once the foreign minister; and Creft, the pregnant, resigned education minister. The three others killed, two insurance workers and a garage manager, were Grenadians who were committed to Bishop, but held no party or government leadership positions.

The total death toll at Fort Rupert has never been conclusively established. However, a two-year investigation in 2003 by senior students at Presentation Brothers College, Bishop's alma mater, put the total number of confirmed deaths at Fort Rupert at 19.[173] Beyond the eight who were assassinated by the firing squad, this total includes three PRA soldiers killed in the initial fighting with Bishop's supporters. Noel and five other civilians were also killed in the initial shooting. Two more civilians died in falls over the wall. Another 100 civilians suffered injuries either by falls or gunshots, the study found.

When the shooting stopped for a final time at around 2 p.m., a white flare arced over Fort Rupert. Radix saw the flare from his jail cell at Richmond Hill Prison and was told by soldiers that it was a predetermined signal that the executions had been carried out.[174] At Fort Frederick, the immediate task at hand was to form an interim group to take control of the government. The body created was a 16-member Revolutionary Military Council (RMC) officially composed entirely of Army officers who were also party members and Coard loyalists. Austin, a hero of the 1979 coup, was chosen to be figurehead leader of the council, as the Coards remained out of the public eye. Austin's name signaled to the population there were serious problems with Bishop's leadership that even his most loyal followers could not excuse. The group was not the clean-slate list that is normally associated with a violent military coup. Austin and four RMC members were also prominent members of the Central Committee.

At 45, Austin was a generation older than the rest of the military council members, who were mostly in their mid–20s.[175] All the members were officers in the PRA, but their military training was limited. Their collective combat experience came exclusively from participation by some in the one-day coup that brought Bishop to power in 1979. Austin had proved his mettle as a combat commander in the earlier coup, but was unprepared by intellect, education or temperament to be an effective leader of a nation, even on an interim basis. He was the son of a shoemaker who had received six months of military training in Trinidad when he was 20. That experience led to a job as a prison guard in the 1960s, before full independence. He met Bishop through the prison and became a convert to his rebellious cause. He trained in construction engineering by correspondence courses with the Jamaica Institute of Science and Technology, but he had no polish. "You have only to talk to Austin to know that he was barely more than literate," said one journalist in neighboring Trinidad.[176] Though he wore the rank of a general as head of the Grenadian army and security services, he spent most of his time working in his civilian role as the minister of communications and construction. He looked like a brute and acted the part. In 1981, Phyllis Coard shamed him before the Central Committee by accusing him of beating his wife, pulling a gun on her and maintaining a public liaison with another woman.[177]

The British embassy on Barbados considered Austin "a man of erratic judgment, fickle loyalties and no particular intellect."[178] The British diplomats saw the real leaders of the council to be three Coard loyalists who held military rank immediately under Austin: James, Layne and Cornwall. All three were members of a Marxist study group led by Coard called "the Organization for Revolutionary Education and Liberation" (OREL). Their standing in the Army hierarchy was due to their political zealotry and organizational skill, rather than the training or experience that would be normally associated with their advanced military ranks. Louison, the Bishop loyalist minister, concurred with the British view that Austin, the general, was actually subordinate to the politically oriented officers under his command, especially James, who commanded the police and the intelligence apparatus, and Layne, the Army's representative on the Politburo. "Their militarism was a militarism bent on political power," Louison later told an interviewer.[179]

Austin addressed his nation at 10 p.m. on Radio Free Grenada by reading a two-page statement that recounted a funhouse-mirror version of the momentous events of the past 24 hours.[180] The statement painted Bishop as the villain in the drama for spurning further leadership negotiations with the Central Committee and then using a crowd of supporters to seize Fort Rupert. Austin claimed that Bishop intended next to "wipe out the entire leadership of the party and the army." When the PRA sent a company of soldiers to retake the fort, they were fired on by Bishop's supporters, killing two soldiers and wounding several others, he asserted. "The Revolutionary Armed Forces were forced to storm the fort, and in the process the following persons were killed: Maurice Bishop, Unison Whiteman, Vincent Noel, Jacqueline Croft, Norris Bain and Fitzroy Bain among others," he declared, without further explanation. In order to preserve the revolution, a military council had been appointed to run the government "until normalcy is restored." Until then the army will govern with "absolute strictness" by banning demonstrations, closing schools and businesses and confining residents to their homes at least for the next four days. Anyone violating the curfew "will be shot on sight." The restrictions on movement were an onerous burden in a subsistence society where fewer than 40 percent had running water and fewer than 25 percent had in-home toilets.[181]

At 11 p.m. Bernard, now an appointed member of the RMC, returned to Fort Rupert to dispose of the bodies of the eight who had been executed by the firing squad on his orders.[182] Soldiers under Bernard's command wrapped the bodies in blankets and drove them by truck to Camp Fedon, the Grenadian name for the training facility near Calivigny on the Egmont peninsula. Once there, the soldiers dumped the bodies into an open grave, spread gasoline over the copses and set them on fire. The pyre burned until the next day when Bernard returned to cover it. Just before midnight, Hughes, the 64-year-old publisher of the independent *Grenada Newsletter*, heard a knock on his door. Grenadian security officers arrested him and took him to Richmond Hill Prison where he was thrown into a tiny annex called the goat pen. He joined 11 other political prisoners being held in the 12-by-10-foot cell.[183]

On Barbados, Ambassador Bish concluded a frenetic day by sending a top-priority, CRITIC (critical intelligence) cable to Washington, a message form reserved only for the most urgent situations.[184] The message said in part: "There appears to be imminent danger to U.S. citizens resident on Grenada due to the current deteriorating situation, which includes reports of rioting, personnel casualties [possibly deaths].... Embassy Bridgetown recommends that the United States should now be prepared to conduct an emergency evacuation of U.S. citizens residing in Grenada."[185]

In Washington, the Joint Chiefs issued a "warning order" to Atlantic Command just before midnight.[186] The dispatch gave McDonald until dawn to prepare an estimate of what it would take to evacuate U.S. and other designated foreign nationals from the island. McDonald was expecting the message. He took only two hours to respond with his plan for an operation code named: Urgent Fury. The assigned name, as per Pentagon practice, was both random and calculated. The random part was the Defense Department's assignment of two-letter alphabetical sequences to individual commands as a starting place to describe operations they were planning. In this case, Atlantic Command started with the randomly assigned grouping of UM-UR. From that prompt, military wordsmiths settled on Urgent and then Urgent Fury as a *nom de guerre* for the time-pressed, *coup de main* they were planning.[187]

12

Securing the Victory

The inevitable military victory on Grenada was essentially achieved within 48 hours, but the public relations war it provoked continued on for many weeks. The repercussions of the invasion played out in Congress, the United Nations and foreign capitals. The PR battle in Washington began at the White House at 5:45 a.m. when Reagan's chief of staff handed the president's principal spokesman an inch-thick packet of information and told him to announce the invasion to the press at 7 a.m.[1] At 6:07 a.m., ABC news reported from Barbados that Marines were landing on Grenada. NBC and CBS followed within an hour.[2] News managers at all three television networks, as well as newspaper editors around the country, were unprepared for war in the Lesser Antilles. Aides were dispatched to find a Caribbean map that showed Grenada as more than a fly speck. The government-run media in Moscow was equally unprepared. A Soviet television broadcast reporting the invasion showed a map of the Granada region of Spain instead of the similarly named Caribbean island.

Editors everywhere were expecting that the Beirut bombing aftermath was going to be the dominant news story of the week. With 241 U.S. servicemen dead, mostly from hometowns on the East Coast, virtually every major city east of the Mississippi had a local casualty on the front page of the daily newspaper. Just as in the Pentagon, newsrooms now had to simultaneous deal with both international stories, unavoidably intermingling the two narratives in the public mind. Presented with a near total news vacuum on Operation Urgent Fury, news executives welcomed the advisory that Reagan would shortly be addressing the nation from the White House.

At 7:30 a.m. a first-time official visitor arrived at the White House: Eugenia Charles, the Dominica prime minister and a Caribbean champion for the intervention. Her powerful presence proved to be fortuitous for the Reagan administration. Charles played a critical role in shaping how the invasion was perceived by the American public and the world. She was invited to Washington by the Reagan administration. She hitched a ride on an unmarked jet with Ambassador McNeil, Reagan's special envoy, who was returning home from pre-invasion consultations with the OECS in Barbados.[3] McNeil's Gulfstream landed in D.C. after midnight on Oct. 25 and Charles spent the night in a hotel. In the morning, McNeil escorted her to the White House where she was met by Constance C. Menges, a National Security Council staffer who had been an early and outspoken advocate for the intervention.[4] Menges led her to the Oval Office where Reagan was waiting, along with seven of his top advisers. Reagan greeted her warmly and a steward served juice and coffee. The president gave her a preview of the announcement he was about to make. "I'd like you to come on television with me when I go to explain to the nation," Reagan said. Charles readily agreed. After their 20-minute meeting, Menges took Charles aside for a coaching session on what to expect in her first encounter with the White House press corps. Menges was joined in the White House dining room by Dam, Shultz's long-time friend and his top deputy at the State Department. Menges played the role of a hostile interrogator. For 10 minutes he asked Charles the hardest questions he could think of. The threesome then rehearsed the phrasing of substantive answers. In the course of their rehearsal, Menges was handed the latest version of the president's statement on the invasion. He noticed that the phrase "to restore democracy" had been deleted from the earlier draft by the State Department. Menges appealed to Dam and "democracy" was immediate restored in Washington—and, later, also in St. George's.

While Charles was getting prepped, Reagan met privately with his advisers. He began the tense session with a wisecrack about his get-away weekend: "You fellas ought to try golfing in Augusta sometime,'" he quipped.[5] First, he got an early invasion update from Shultz and Weinberger. That was immediately followed by a briefing for 25 Congressional leaders in the Cabinet room.[6] At 9:07 a.m. President Reagan, a former actor, and his new leading lady were ready to appear together in a live television performance from the White House Briefing Room. Almost immediately the administration ran into trouble getting the President's prepared remarks to correctly line up with the facts.[7] Reagan said in the first sentence that the United States was intervening after receiving an urgent formal request from "five member nations" of the OECS. But then, in the second sentence, he named six Caribbean nations as participating in the multinational force along with the United States. In the third sentence, he clarified that two of the six he just named (Jamaica and Barbados) were not actually members OECS, but they had been approached by them. (That subtraction left four, not five, OECS members actually participating in the intervention.) In the fourth sentence, Reagan ambiguously declared that "all of them" had joined "unanimously" in asking the United States to participate. This implied that the formal request from the seven-member OECS had been unanimously affirmed when it wasn't. Montserrat, as a British territory, was prohibited from participating by the Foreign Office. St. Kitts-Nevis, newly independent from Britain, also did not sign[8] and neither did Grenada, which was also an OECS member. In the fifth sentence, Reagan further asserted: "Early this morning, forces from six Caribbean democracies and the United States began a landing or landings on the island of Grenada in the eastern Caribbean." That phrasing evoked memories of the simultaneous, multinational Allied landings on Normandy beaches at dawn on June 6, 1944. But, on Grenada, it would be nearly 11 a.m. before the first uniformed Caribbean coalition member set foot on the Ranger-secured runway at Point Salines—and none ever had any role in combat.[9]

Reagan offered three reasons for intervening: protecting innocent lives, particularly Americans on the island; forestalling further chaos; and restoring law and order and democratic institutions. He made no mention of thwarting subversive expansionism by Cuba or the Soviet Union. Reagan also made no mention at all of Scoon or his supposed oral request for intervention on behalf of his country.[10] The address was not the administration's definitive justification for the invasion. A nuanced explanation evolved as occasions arose in various forms and forums. The justification process took no less than 12 statements from seven different spokesmen over the ensuing four months.[11]

After his brief statement, Reagan introduced Charles, who launched into her own rehearsed, but unscripted, comments.[12] Charles said Grenada's neighbors were "horrified" by recent events on the island and took them as an affront to the entire region because "we belong to each other; we are kith and kin." At one point a reporter asked the president a question that Charles thought was outside his personal knowledge. She hijacked the answer. Shultz started laughing; he was impressed by her spunk.[13] The question was a loaded one, asking whether Reagan thought Russia and Cuba were behind the Grenada takeover. "Yes, we do have this information," Charles declared, though, in fact, the CIA found no evidence that either country had any role in the Fort Rupert killings.[14] Her answer, however, conveyed a suspicion that some of Reagan's top advisors shared, but relieved the president of responsibility for the accusation. Reagan was charmed. "You can come and do this for me every month," the president said to her later.[15] He then asked Charles to join him in a meeting with his Cabinet. Shultz gave her his chair next to Reagan. She explained the OECS call for intervention and got a standing ovation from the assembled. Her appearance also played well with the national and international audience. Her presence affirmed the invasion as a multinational action and, more subtly, dispelled any impression that the intervention was a white superpower's unilateral response to a black micronation's provocations.

The morning's official announcements were followed in the early afternoon by a raucous, hour-long press briefing, which Speakes conducted. Reporters threw Speakes' denial of the previous day back at him, along with questions like "Are you going to

Reagan conferred at the White House with Dominica prime minister Eugenia Charles on the morning he announced the invasion to the world with her at his side. Charles had flown to Washington to urge Reagan to intervene to restore order and democracy on Grenada. Secretary of State George P. Shultz, left, was delighted with her presence, and Reagan was also charmed by her (courtesy Ronald Reagan Library).

resign?" Speakes was furious at Poindexter for having deceived him, but he liked his job too much to quit. He was further enraged when the *Washington Post* reported the next evening that he was planning to quit. Speakes traced the source of that story back to Janka, the deputy who had also been deceived by Poindexter, and was considering resigning himself. Speakes called Janka into his office the following morning and fired him for leaking something about him that was untrue.[16] Speakes offered to soften the blow by keeping Janka on the payroll as long as possible. The two worked out a joint statement presenting his departure as a resignation under pressure.[17]

Once he departed the White House, Janka was outspoken in his criticism of the administration's "no press" policy. He believed that the media could have gone ashore on Grenada after the initial assaults with "no compromise" to the mission or security.[18] "The twin decisions of excluding its own press officers from the pre-invasion planning and denying/delaying media access to the island were not only a serious breach of constitutional responsibility toward informing the public, they were also acts of political stupidity for the most practical of reasons: our military forces performed superbly and the overall operations was a domestic political success. But the positive results were under-observed and ultimately tarnished by the controversy over media access," he wrote in a post-invasion assessment for a military journal.

Janka was not the only White House casualty of Urgent Fury. David Gergen, the White House communication director, was also disheartened by the news blackout surrounding the invasion. He was an advocate for engagement with the press corps on the belief that, over time, it would result in a more favorable portrayal of the Reagan presidency. He saw the Grenada experience as a strategic victory for those within the administration who wanted a tougher line with the press. Gergen resigned in January 1984, citing personal reasons. He later conceded that Grenada was "a major break for me.... You fight a certain number of these battles, and after a while I found that I was losing some."[19]

Reporter anger over the press restrictions and deceptions was evident in the Tuesday afternoon press briefing at the White House, but that pique took a while to manifest itself in the coverage of the invasion. None of the three major television networks made mention of the exclusion of the press in its coverage of the first day of the invasion. However, the *New York Times* did run a story on the "Communique War" that reported that the information in stories from Washington was entirely based on American government sources.[20] That restrained tone changed by the second day when it became evident that the exclusion was continuing and would not immediately be lifted. The Oct. 27 *New York Times* put the issue on the front page under a headline that read: "U.S. Bars Coverage of Grenada Action; News Groups Protest." The "censorship" accusation became louder and more widespread in the days ahead. Formal and public protests were lodged by top news department representatives at all three networks, as well as by the American Newspaper Publishers Association.

The administration reaped an unexpected public relations boost in the late afternoon of the second day of the invasion when the first planeload of 69 American medical school students landed at Charleston Air Force Base in South Carolina. The stateside arrival of the first medical students had been anticipated with apprehension at the White House by Reagan's embattled press staff. As soon as the president's chief press spokesman saw a student kiss the ground, he knew his public relations problem was over. "That's it! We won," Speakes shouted as his fellow staffers cheered and pounded the table.[21] Speakes personally had doubts that the invasion was necessary, but those reservation were rendered moot by the reaction of the American public to the Charleston arrival. Other welcome support for Reagan's decision also came from Modica, the chancellor and founder of the medical school. On the first day, Modica decried the invasion to the press as unwarranted. The next day, he received a half hour briefing from a State Department official who changed his mind.[22] "It's not a very clear-cut issue. It never was," Modica said. "The people that I had been dealing with [in Grenada] were not necessarily fully in charge of the government, and therefore the assurances they were giving about the security of Americans could not be fully guaranteed." More unexpected public relations help was provided by the Grenadian revolutionaries themselves in what was left behind on the battlefield.

The stores of weapons seized at Frequente and other depot sites were evidence of the Bishop's regime's disproportionate military capabilities. More than 11,000 captured weapons were inventoried and then shipped back to Washington where examples were put on public display at Andrews Air Force Base. Captured documents proved that the displayed weapons have been supplied to the Bishop regime under the terms of separate, secret military agreements with the Soviets, Cubans or the North Koreans. The weapons had arrived in a series of clandestine deliveries between April 1979 and August 1982. They were mostly light machine guns, rifles, shotguns and sidearms meant to be carried by individual infantry soldiers. Some Soviet-made, crew-served Soviet weapons were also captured, including two undamaged armored vehicles, 12 ZU-23 anti-aircraft guns, 10 medium mortars and eight recoilless rifles. Captured documents showed more heavy weapons had been promised by the Soviet Union, but not yet shipped: 30 field guns, 30 anti-tank guns, and 50 more armored vehicles. The addition of crewed weapons would have augmented an expansion of the Grenadian military to four regular and 14 reserve battalions force by 1985.[23] Such a force of 7,200 to 10,000 soldiers would put roughly 10 percent of the population in uniform, proportionately one of the largest military forces of any country in the world.[24]

The captured arsenal was touted by Reagan to support his assertion that "we got there just in time" to prevent Grenada from becoming "a major military bastion to export terror and undermine democracy."[25] But, at the same time the president was playing up the offensive capability of the captured weapons, secret intelligence estimates were playing down the threat they posed to Grenada's neighbors. An all-agencies assessment prepared by CIA, dated Oct. 30, 1983, was kept secret for 25 years until it was declassified and approved for public release in 2008. The report declared: "[I]t is reasonable to believe that the captured arms stocks inventoried to date were intended to insure internal security and to defend Grenada against attack—particularly in view of apparent plans to expand the size of the Grenadian armed forces."[26] The report acknowledged the possibility that some of the arms could have been used as a stockpile for revolutionaries elsewhere in the Caribbean or as a prepositioned contingency store for Cuban forces. But the intelligence agencies found no clear documentary evidence at the time to support these speculations, and, instead, cited reasons to doubt them. "The use of identifiable Soviet arms to support guerilla movements would be uncharacteristic," the CIA report stated. "Moreover, we doubt that the weapons found in Grenada were stockpiled for use in an invasion of neighboring island states because Cuba and Grenada would be deterred by anticipated U.S. responses."

This 10-page assessment roiled the executive offices at CIA headquarters when it reached Casey's desk on Oct. 31, 1983. Its qualified findings ran counter to the President's public pronouncements, as well as Casey's personal beliefs.[27] At one critical point in the Oct. 20 White House discussions, Casey had shown his cards on the Grenada matter. "Hey, fuck it, let's dump these bastards," Casey declared.[28] Casey now viewed the all-agency, post-invasion assessment to be "unimaginative." He shared his disapproval with the coordinator of the report, John R. Horton, then the CIA's national intelligence officer for Latin America.[29] A year later, Horton resigned in protest when Casey ordered a rewrite of another of his inter-agency reports, an evaluation of Mexico's internal troubles, in order to better support the administration's Central American strategy.[30] "There is pressure from Casey on subjects that are politically sensitive to jigger estimates to conform with policy," Horton asserted in a rare on-the-record airing of a high-level internal CIA dispute.

Nonetheless, a majority of the American people were readily persuaded that Reagan had done the right thing. Two independent polls of Americans were conducted separately on Oct. 26 and 27, one a partnership of the *New York Times* and CBS News and the other, a Gallup Poll for *Newsweek*. They both found that over 50 percent of America adults approved of the decision to send troops into Grenada, compared to a disapproval percentage in the mid–30s. By one way of thinking, the invasion of Grenada had been approved in advance by the American people, at least in concept, when Reagan derailed Carter's bid for a second term. "In 1980 the American people consciously chose a president who saw the world as battle between good and evil and was willing to use force to protect what he perceived as good. Last week, Ronald Reagan kept those campaign promises," *Newsweek* wrote in the concluding paragraph of its 14-page special report on the invasion.[31] Reagan played up the favorable domestic reaction to the rescue of the Americans from the island. He invited the returned students to a celebration event on the South Lawn on Nov. 7. Almost 500 St. George's students turned out to cheer their approval of the president's action. Reagan used the occasion to brush off criticism of the invasion. "It is very easy for some smug know-it-alls in a plush, protected quarter to say that you were in no danger," he declared to student applause. "I wonder how many of them would have changed places with you."

The invasion also played well in the Eastern Caribbean islands, especially on Grenada. A snap poll conducted by CBS on Nov. 4, 10 days after the invasion, found that 91 percent of the 304 people polled by Grenadian interviewers said they were "glad the United States troops came."[32] That favorable impression persisted through the military occupation of the island. At the end of 1983, a public opinion survey firm from Trinidad interviewed 711 Grenadians to plumb their view of recent events. Eighty-six percent of those polled said they regarded the intervention by the multinational force as a "good thing," though that sentiment was stronger among those over 40 than it was among those under 40.[33] October 25 is now celebrated annually on Grenada as National Thanksgiving Day, a public holiday of gratitude, remembrance and reconciliation. Public opinion also ran strongly in support of the intervention in the English-speaking Caribbean nations that participated in the peacekeeping coalition. On Jamaica, Prime Minister Seaga seized on a surge in his popularity to call snap elections, which the opposition boycotted. The result was the election of a one-party Parliament that made governing easier for Seaga, but had the unintended effect of eroding the quality of Jamaica's democracy.[34]

On the South American continent, the most significant immediate reaction came from Suriname, a former Dutch colony that was under leftist military rule. Lt. Col. Dési Bourterse, the country's leader, made a television address to his nation on the night of the invasion to announce the end of his flirtation with Cuba. "The leadership of the Suriname revolution is convinced that a repetition of developments in Grenada should be prevented here," he declared.[35] In a political move that was also motivated by other factors, Bourterse gave the Cuban ambassador six days to leave the country and ousted 25 other Cuban diplomats and 60 advisers.

The invasion also had an effect on Cuban-connected revolutionaries in Central America. In Nicaragua, the leftist Sandinista government took the intervention as a signal that they were next on America's hit list. A minister of interior privately suggested immediate talks with the United States. "The Sandinistas made a great to-do to make sure the United States knew they had no intention of permitting Soviet bases on Nicaraguan soil," McNeil, the American envoy to the OECS coalition, later wrote in his memoirs.[36] In retrospect, McNeil saw the Grenada aftermath as "a magnificent opportunity for a durable peace in Central America."[37] He kicked himself in print for not pressing harder for an immediate American peace offensive. At the end of 1983, to further relax tensions, the Sandinista regime moved to halve the number of Cuban civilians in their schools, loosen internal censorship controls and encourage the departure of El Salvadorian rebel leaders from their capital. Reagan administration officials dismissed the limited measures as propaganda ploys.[38]

In the United States, the surprising strong domestic support for the Grenada operation emboldened plans already under discussion for a CIA-led, paramilitary offensive against the Sandinistas. Duane R. "Dewey" Clarridge, a James Bond–like CIA spymaster, personified the invigorated Central America policy. Clarridge pasted two bumper stickers onto his personal jeep: one read "We kicked ass in Grenada" and the other said "Nicaragua next!"[39] In 1983, Clarridge served as the financier and field marshal of the Contra's guerrilla war with the Sandinistas. In the fall of 1983, with the support of Reagan, the CIA and the Contras launched a joint campaign to force the Sandinista regime to the bargaining table by the spring. The Contras made hit-and-run ground attacks inside Nicaragua seeking to ignite a civil war. Meanwhile, the CIA separately organized and supported seaborne attacks on the Nicaragua's ports and infrastructure.

As part of the CIA-led offshore offensive, Clarridge hatched a plan to sow mines in Nicaragua's shipping harbors. The Ivy League–educated spy was inspired by reading about the Russo-Japanese War of 1904, during which both sides used floating mines to severely damage or sink opposing battleships. In the Central American application of these weapons, the goal was not to sink warships, but to scare off civilian shipping, especially oil tankers. A de facto naval blockade would strangle Nicaragua's trade-dependent economy and enhance the perceived prowess of the Contra insurgents. To limit the threat to civilian ships and sailors, the CIA custom-manufactured "firecracker" mines designed to cause more noise than damage. The devices were made out of sewer pipe packed with 300 pounds of C-4 explosives. The bottom-sitting mines were armed with fuses that could be variously activated by the water pressure, acoustics or the magnetic properties of a passing ship.[40] The CIA supervised the mining operation from a chartered "mother ship" outside Nicaraguan territorial waters. Speedboats manned by Latino mercenaries, hired and trained by the CIA, dropped the mines in ports on Nicaragua's Pacific and Caribbean coasts. Air cover was provided by weaponized civilian helicopters flown by CIA contract pilots off the mother ship. Reagan approved the plan in December 1983 and the mines were sown in January and February 1984.[41] The mining campaign was announced as the action of the Contras, but the hand of the CIA in the sophisticated operation was transparent.

As in Grenada, nothing worked quite as planned.[42] The announcement of the mining did not deter commercial shippers, who shrugged off the threat as another hazard of the seas in a volatile area. The first mines to explode sank two small Nicaraguan boats and damaged a Dutch dredging ship. In early March, Manuel Ortega, the Sandinista leader, accused the CIA of being behind a "military blockade" of his nation and his government sent a letter of protest to the State Department. On March 20, a Soviet oil tanker was struck by a mine that badly damaged the ship and injured five civilian crewmen.[43] That prompted the Soviet foreign minister to formally protest to the United States, calling the mining "an act of a banditry and piracy," the same nouns that Moscow used to describe the Grenada intervention six months earlier. The Soviet protest also implied that the United States had supplied the mines to the Nicaraguan rebels, arousing the attention of Congress. The mining figured in a Senate floor debate in early April on a then-pending bill to supply $21 million more in aid to support Nicaraguan rebels. In the course of debate, Sen. Barry Goldwater, R–Arizona, the chairman of the Senate Select Committee on Intelligence, denied that the president had any role in the mining. He was infuriated when he learned the next day that the CIA was directly involved in the mining, with Reagan's approval. He sent off an indignant letter of complaint to Casey, the CIA director, which was later leaked and published in the *New York Times*. Goldwater, a conservative normally supportive of Reagan, wrote that the mining was an "an act of war" that "I don't see how we are going to explain."[44] The public furor resulted in an apology to Goldwater by Casey and, eventually, a two-year suspension of Congress-approved military support for the Contras.[45]

Clarridge's relations with Congress soured to the point that he was transferred to head the CIA's European Division. At the end of his Central American tenure, in May 1984, as U.S. funding was temporarily running out, Clarridge had a meeting with Contra leaders in Honduras at which he introduced Lt. Col. Oliver North as his alter ego on the National Security Council staff. The Marine officer had played outsize role in Urgent Fury planning that exceeded his mid-career, field-grade military rank. In an ad hoc role as an expeditor and facilitator, North had connected the intelligence community with the military and vice versa. He also gave everyone who asked the lay of the land at 1600 Pennsylvania Avenue. According to McFarlane, his boss, "the actual writing of the plans was military, and the briefing of allies was the State Department. But the reporting what was going on and making sure, from the White House perspective, that what needed to be done was being done was North's job."[46] All this was heady responsibility for an officer who did not pin his lieutenant colonel silver oak leaves on his epaulets until November 1983, after the Grenada operation was essentially over.[47]

The aid cutoff, the public scolding of the CIA and the transfer of Clarridge shifted Contra support from the CIA to the NSC, with North assuming primary operational responsibility.[48] Beginning in May 1984 the NSC staff began to look to private parties and foreign nations for funds and weapons for the Contras. That, in turn, gave rise to the Iran-Contra Affair that brought public disgrace to many in Reagan's core Central America policy team.

Criminal charges were filed against five government officials who had earlier played key roles in the Grenada intervention: McFarlane, North, Poindexter, Clarridge and Weinberger. McFarlane subsequently pleaded guilty to four counts of withholding information from Congress. North was convicted of obstruction counts after a two-month trial, but his convictions were either overturned or vacated on appeal. Poindexter was also convicted in a separate trial of five felonies, but an appeals court reversed the convictions. Clarridge and Weinberger were still awaiting trial on charges against them on Christmas Eve, 1992 when they and four others were pardoned by George H. W. Bush at the end of his one-term presidency.[49] McFarlane was one of the four also pardoned by Bush.

On Grenada, it took a while, but democracy was eventually restored. On Nov. 15, 1983, Scoon invoked his executive authority to appoint a nine-member Advisory Council to serve as an interim administration until elections could be held. Elections were held in December 1984 for the first time since Gairy was elected prime minister in 1976. Gairy, the eccentric autocrat deposed by Bishop, returned home from exile after the invasion. He revived his old Grenada United Labor Party (GULP), but he failed to regain his sway over the island. Herbert Blaize, a lawyer who had twice served as Grenada's chief minister prior to full independence, won overwhelmingly. Blaize's center-right coalition, the New National Party, sweep away all but one of the 16 seats of Parliament.

Outside the borders of the island nations that had participated in the intervention, the sentiment on the invasion was overwhelmingly negative, even among America's closest NATO allies. The British were incensed and humiliated. Foreign Secretary Geoffrey Howe told Parliament that the American action was "a matter of regret." An opposition leader derided Thatcher as Reagan's "obedient poodle." Reagan tried to personally make amends with a phone call to Downing Street on Oct. 28. "If I were there Margaret, I'd throw my hat in the door before I came in," Reagan began.[50] He then proceeded to do most of the talking in a 10-minute phone call, during which he reiterated his reasons for intervening and apologized for causing her embarrassment. Thatcher was cool to his approach and cut the conversation short. Thatcher's chilliness was indicative of the reaction in other major European capitals. A spokesman for the West German ruling coalition declared that their government would have advised against the intervention "had we been consulted." France also said it was also not consulted and archly described the intervention as "a surprising action in relation to international law."

The United Nations membership was unequivocally hostile to the intervention. On afternoon of the invasion, Nicaragua and Guyana called for an emergency session of the Security Council to consider a resolution "condemning the intervention as a flagrant violation of international law and Grenada's sovereignty."[51] On Oct. 28, 11 nations voted in favor of the resolution, including three putative allies: France, Pakistan and the Netherlands. Three others, including Britain, abstained. The United States vetoed the resolution by casting the lone negative vote.[52] The shunning exercise was repeated on Nov. 2 when the full General Assembly considered a similar resolution and approved it by a 108 to nine margin with 27 abstentions. U.S. diplomats, however, did successfully manage to stem the negative tide when the matter was taken up by two other multinational organizations. The Organization of American States met in emergency session but, with sentiment divided, avoided a vote. The Commonwealth discussed the intervention at its heads-of-state conference in New Delhi in November 1983 and found itself similarly divided. Unable to reach a consensus, the then 49-nation group instead issued a consensus communiqué calling for reconstruction of the island.[53]

Reagan professed to be unconcerned about the negative international reaction to an operation he came to characterize as a "rescue mission" rather than a collective security action. In a question-and-answer session with reporters on Nov. 3, after the end of the hostilities, a reporter asked why so many nations had opposed the intervention in the

United Nations. "One hundred nations in the United Nations have not agreed with us on just about everything that's come up before them where we're involved, and it didn't upset my breakfast at all," he quipped. Doubling down on the flippancy, the White House press office offered up the president's menu that morning: one poached egg, toast and coffee.

Still, the administration squirmed to come up with a rationale for Urgent Fury that would be consistent with both the facts and the standards of international law. In the aftermath of the invasion, at least six noteworthy discrepancies in fact or argument in the administration's legal case arose.[54] Those discrepancies prompted the international law section of the American Bar Association on Dec. 3, 1983, to commission a report on the intervention. A committee of four international law experts, including three law professors, set out to independently, and quickly, assess the administration's legal defense of its action. By early 1984 they had finished a draft report that they shared with the State Department for comment before publishing their final findings in a legal professional journal.[55] The report concluded that the invention was "incompatible" with the restraints on the use of force contained in the charters of the United Nations and the Organization of American States, and under the terms of the Rio Treaty of 1947. That finding prompted a predictably dissenting letter signed by Davis R. Robinson, the State Department's legal advisor, dated Feb. 10, 1984.[56] Because of the circumstance and authorship, the Robinson letter is considered by legal scholars to be the administration's final "best case" justification for the intervention. Robinson wrote that the intervention was essentially a three-legged stool that stood on a triad of "well-established principles of international law," none of which "standing alone" was sufficient to support the action.[57] As for the facts, Robinson emphasized the "unusual circumstances" that had prompted the action. Robinson specifically asserted that the American intervention into Grenada was in no factual way analogous to the "illegal" Soviet occupations of Czechoslovakia and Afghanistan.

The Congressional Research Service eventually concluded that the invasion of Grenada was neither a war nor a rescue mission. In a 1990 study prepared at the request of the House Armed Services Committee, the congressional research arm studied 60 "low-intensity conflicts" of the 20th century that had involved the American military. The study then subdivided the 60 case studies into subcategories based on their key characteristics. The researchers labeled Urgent Fury a "punitive expedition" more akin to the U.S. Army operations against Pancho Villa in 1916–17 during the Mexican Revolution than a "rescue mission" like the Marines dispatched to free American merchant sailors on the USS *Mayaguez* from their Cambodian captors in 1975.[58] (None of the American operations classified by historians as rescue missions also involved invasion, overthrow of a government and occupation of foreign soil.)[59]

However difficult the diplomatic blowback was for the United States; the aftermath of the invasion was worse for Cuba. The Castro regime felt the lash of America's "punitive campaign." In the space of a few weeks, an expensive four-year investment in the cultivation of communism on Grenada had literally and figurative been blown away by the United States. The repatriation of the Cuban dead and the survivors of the fighting was arranged in testy negotiations with the Americans, brokered by Spain, Colombia and the International Red Cross. The return home was a sad spectacle and a humiliating defeat for Castro. The first to arrive were 57 (of 60) wounded who were flown to Havana on Nov. 2 on a chartered Swiss jet accompanied by a 10-member Cuban medical staff.

According to the Havana, only 8 of the combat wounded were regular soldiers. Castro and Cuban Politburo greeted each of the 57 as they emerged from the plane.[60]

Castro put off any public remarks until the rest of the Cubans, including the dead and the evicted diplomats, arrived in other flights over the following days. A national day of mourning ceremony was held in Havana's Plaza de la Revolution on Nov. 14. Caskets with the bodies of the 24 Cubans who died on Grenada were put on display for an event witnessed by millions of Cubans either in person or on live television. Castro launched into a 90-minute speech in which he recounted how Havana's relationship with St. George's had come to such a sudden and inglorious end.[61] Somewhat surprisingly, he blamed the Coard faction for recklessly provoking the United States response. "In our view, Coard's group effectively destroyed the revolution and opened the door to imperialist aggression," he declared in the stem-winding oration. At various points he derisively referred to the Coard faction as "the Pol Pot group," "hyenas," and "extremists drunk on political theory." He mourned his friend, Bishop, as a "noble, modest and unselfish" leader whose only fault was "excessive tolerance and trust." Predictably, he also accused the Reagan administration of using the Fort Rupert assassinations as a pretext to intervene and then telling "nineteen lies" to justify its actions. He then enumerated them in succession as the crowd cheered "Lie!" to each American assertion. "The United States did not achieve any victory at all—not political or military or moral. If anything, it was a pyrrhic military victory and a profound moral defeat," Castro declared.

The speech made no acknowledgment of Cuban fault in its handling of the Grenada crisis, but Castro later publicly reproached his resident diplomats for failing to detect the developing leadership struggle.[62] Castro also blamed his military advisers for failing to adequately defend the national honor. Tortoló and others were court-martialed and punished.[63] Raul Castro, Fidel's brother and the Cuban defense minister, was videotaped ripping the shoulder boards off Tortoló's shoulders before he was demoted to private and shipped off to Angola. The tape was later shown to party members as an object lesson. Torres, the ambassador, was also reportedly demoted within the Foreign Ministry.

At the Pentagon, one of Vessey's principal take-aways from Urgent Fury was the need to foster a less contentious military-media relationship. "The huge mistake at the national level was failing to find a way to take some press along. We missed a great opportunity to have the American people get reports about how well the Rangers and Marines operated. We compounded the error by permitting Admiral Metcalf to keep the media out longer than intended," Vessey later declared in a letter to the general in charge of the history office for the Joint Chiefs.[64] On reflection, Metcalf also agreed that the story of Urgent Fury was not adequately reported to the public. Writing seven years later, he acknowledged that the press restrictions had interjected a negative narrative line in the Grenada story that distracted from its ultimate success as a contingency military operation. "In the actual reporting of Grenada to the U.S. public the media expended more column inches and time talking about their prerogatives than in reporting the story.... The story that was not told by the media was the one of an operation put together in hours by forces that never operated together and yet were successfully controlled by a command structure that was invented on the spot." he wrote.[65]

A month after the invasion, on Nov. 29, Vessey announced the formation of a commission to recommend "workable solutions" to military-media relations in future military operations.[66] Invitations went out to broadcast and print associations seeking members to serve on the panel, but no names of working journalists were offered in response.

Journalists felt it was inappropriate to serve on a government-appointed panel, reflecting the widely shared view in their profession that their job was to report on government policy, not make policy. A second attempt was made to assemble a panel by soliciting the participation of retired journalists and journalism educators. A panel was eventually formed that included journalism professionals. Vessey named Winant Sidle, a retired major general who was a former chief of information for the Army, to chair the group.[67] The commission became known as the "Sidle panel" and held five days of hearings in February 1984. It heard presentations from 25 representatives from 19 news organizations as well as testimony from the heads of public affairs for the Army, Navy and the Air Force. The following August, the panel's final report was released at a Pentagon press conference.[68] The group unanimously agreed that American news organizations "should cover U.S. military operations to the maximum degree possible consistent with mission security and the safety of U.S. forces." To achieve this end, the group offered eight recommended changes in Pentagon policy or procedure. The key recommendation was the creation of a press pool as an integral part of the planning for any future military operation. In return for voluntary compliance with security guidelines, the pool members would receive advance notification of a military operation, transportation to the battlefield and help transmitting their stories back to their news rooms. The chosen reporters would also follow an established "pool" convention, commonly employed when many news organizations were vying for limited access to a major news event. Reporters chosen to be the "pool" reporters agreed to share their reporting with other news organizations which had previously agreed to be bound by the pool's guidelines. The Sidle panel report was favorably received by the news media establishment and public affairs professionals at the Pentagon. After further consultation by the Pentagon with media representatives, a follow-on agreement was reached on a pool that would ideally consist of up to 12 journalists: four network television reporters, two wire service reporters, one newspaper reporter to be chosen by a publishers' association, a news magazine reporter, a radio reporter, one still-picture photographer and a two-person television camera and sound crew.

A "Sidle pool" was deployed for the first time in April 1985 in a test that was part of a planned military exercise in Honduras. A 10-member pool was formed that was to be escorted by three military public affairs officers. It did not go especially well for either institution.[69] The military was irked that news of the pool's activation leaked within six hours of the members being alerted, and also annoyed by media jockeying for competitive advantage or special accommodation. The pool members complained that the military had not adequately provided for them to file their stories in a timely fashion. After a formal debriefing session, both sides chalked the test up to a learning experience and resolved to try again. Three more test runs were conducted over the next two years with similar mixed results. The first limited operational use of the pool concept came in July 1987 when the Iraq-Iran war spread to involve attacks on foreign-flagged ships in the Persian Gulf.

The press pool nearly fell apart on its second combat deployment on Dec. 19, 1989, as part of Operation Just Cause, a secret attack on Panama that had many similarities to the invasion of Grenada six years earlier. A 16-member press pool from Washington was alerted in advance by the Pentagon and flown to Panama, but the logistical support was deeply flawed.[70] Complaints were serious enough for the Pentagon to commission yet another special review. Fred S. Hoffman, a former newsman working for the Pentagon, was asked to make a report that would document the problems and make recommendations for the future. The shaky pool concept, with some patching, continued to be employed in the 1991 Gulf War with unsatisfying results. In the 2003 Iraq War, pool reporting was largely supplanted by the "embedded" reporter system which became the new standard for later full-scale combat in Iraq and Afghanistan. In short, correcting the public relations failings of Urgent Fury was not an easy fix and took many flawed attempts and decades to sort out.

Congress was late to be advised of the Grenada intervention, but it lingered much longer on the subject than the Reagan administration would have liked. Initially the two principal questions from Congress were: was the intervention lawful and how soon will the troops be home? Reagan engaged on both of those questions on D-Day by formally notifying the leaders of the House and the Senate of the deployment of American troops to Grenada, using a carefully-worded letter[71] The political and legal artistry of the Oct. 25 letter came in its oblique reference to the War Powers Resolution. Passed a decade earlier, overriding a presidential veto, this federal law was intended to provide a procedure for legislative and executive branches to share war-making powers as the Constitution intended. But Congress and the presidents of both parties had sparred ever since enactment over the constitutionality of Section 5 of the 1973 legislation.[72] That section of Public Law 93-148 sets a maximum 90-day limit on the participation of U.S. armed forces in "hostilities" without Congressional assent. Accordingly, Reagan's letter said the Grenada deployment was "consistent with" the War Powers Resolution, essentially saying he was complying with the spirit of the law, but not necessarily the letter. The "consistent with" phrase was borrowed by Reagan's lawyers from previous administrations to avoid conceding the constitutionality dispute over Section 5.[73] The Reagan missive also merely reported the "deployment" of American troops to Grenada and avoided any mention of "hostilities" having resulted once they arrived. This effectively kept the 90-day clock (60 days, with one 30-day extension) from starting.

In the Democratic-controlled House there was strong sentiment for a quick response that would emphasize the need for an early withdrawal. On Oct. 27, the House Foreign Affairs Committee approved a bill 32–2 demanding that troops be withdrawn within 90 days unless the deployment was extended by Congress. Republicans and Democrats were ideologically divided on the wisdom of introducing American forces, but they found common ground in asserting the role of Congress in committing American troops to combat on foreign soil.[74] The next day, the full Senate adopted the same language 64–20 as a rider to a debt bill. The measure stalled at that point, but the Reagan administration got the message. Congress wanted the troops home by Christmas, 60 days after the invention. The administration acted accordingly. The last of the combat troops were withdrawn on Dec. 12, 1983, though a 400-man force of military policemen, support specialists and trainers stayed on into 1984.[75]

First-hand Congressional investigation of the Grenada incursion was delayed until the shooting was over. Both the House and the Senate Armed Services Committees scheduled fact-finding missions to Grenada in early November. On the Senate side, John G. Tower (R–Texas), the committee chairman, traveled to Grenada on Nov. 4 accompanied just by three staffers. As a Reagan loyalist, his principal purpose was to collect evidence justifying the President's decision, but he also wanted to learn about any operational problems that the military encountered.[76] Tower and his staffers returned from the two-day trip to prepare a report largely devoted to supporting the invasion. While in Grenada,

Tower's entourage heard about problems of coordination and command among the services and deficiencies in maps and radios, but they chose not to delve into those anecdotal complaints. Instead, Tower tucked what he heard away for later pursuit. In his public remarks on releasing his report on Nov. 9, Tower went so far as to declare Urgent Fury "almost a textbook example of how a joint operation should work."

But, in the House, where Democrats were in the majority, members were not so easily persuaded that the intervention was a just war. On Oct. 28, the day after the Cubans surrendered at Little Havana, Speaker O'Neill broke his silence on Grenada and condemned the action on the House floor as "gunboat diplomacy" that violated international law.[77] But, as the nation rallied behind Reagan's action, O'Neill eventually opted to leave the House's judgment on Urgent Fury up to a bipartisan fact-finding committee. He appointed a 14-member delegation, which made a trip to the island in early November. The committee was led by Majority Whip Tom Foley (D–Washington) and Rep. Dick Cheney (R–Wyoming), who was destined to later become vice president and secretary of defense. Chris Matthews, then an aide to O'Neill and later a cable television news show host, went along as a staff member on the trip. He soon discovered the unannounced political purpose of the trip was to support the president, not to assemble a bill of particulars in opposition to the intervention. "Whatever the Speaker [O'Neill] thought at the time, the fix was in," Matthews wrote.[78] "When it came to Grenada, nobody wanted to fight a fight that was already won. After hearing from the Foley-Cheney committee, the Speaker went along with its finding that Reagan's intervention was justified."

The House Foreign Affairs Committee took the lead in assessing the international ramifications of the Grenada action. Two subcommittees held public hearings over the course of three days in a two-week period beginning Nov. 2. The purpose of the hearings was to learn the administration's justification for its actions and solicit comment from other expert witnesses, including two former ambassadors to the Eastern Caribbean. Though the hearings got limited press attention at the time, the testimony provided detailed information about the invasion that had not been previously available. The principal spokesmen for the administration were Dam, the deputy secretary of the state, and Maj. Gen. George Crist, a Marine general who had accompanied McNeil on his eleventh-hour, gut-check mission to Barbados. During the fighting, Crist had served as the liaison between the Caribbean forces and the American military. He was sent to Capitol Hill to discuss the weapons and equipment captured on the island from Cubans and Grenadians. Dam presented a detailed prepared statement that laid out the chronology of events leading up to the intervention and amplified on the three legal grounds for military action. "Sometimes action is necessary to keep a bad situation from getting worse. This was such a time," he declared.[79] Dam emphasized the circumstances that provoked the intervention were unique. "We have not made, and do not seek to make, any broad new precedent for international action; we think the justification for our actions is narrow, and well within accepted concepts in international law," he testified.[80]

The most extreme Congressional reaction came on Nov. 10 when seven House members, led by Rep. Ted Weis (D–New York), offered a resolution of impeachment against Reagan. That measure went nowhere.[81] Ted Weiss and 10 other Congressmen then sued Reagan in federal court seeking the immediate withdrawal of American troops and the court's declaration that the invasion was illegal and unconstitutional. That plea was dismissed short of trial by a federal district judge who rejected the case as unwarranted judicial interference in the legislative process.[82]

In early 1984, the House Armed Services Committee turned its attention to a Pentagon-focused assessment of Urgent Fury. A day-long "lessons learned" hearing was held on Jan. 24, but most of the testimony was conducted behind closed doors. Shultz and Weinberger did not attend and, instead, sent second-tier officers and officials who had been most directly involved in the operation. McDonald, the invasion's stateside commander, set the tenor of the prepared public testimony by unequivocally declaring Urgent Fury to have been a total victory. "In summary, history should reflect that the operation was a complete success," he said. "All phases of the assigned mission were accomplished. U.S. citizens were protected and evacuated. The opposing forces were neutralized. The situation stabilized with no additional Cuban intervention, and a lawful, democratic government is being restored. U.S. students are returning to resume their studies at the medical school."

That broad-brush summation triggered no immediate on-the-record comments or questions for McDonald from the assembled congressmen. Instead, a classified executive session was immediately convened to pursue what one member called the main purpose of the hearing: "what we learned, good and bad." Whatever the committee heard on that topic that day behind closed doors has remained secret ever since.[83] Journalistic interest in pursuit of the untold aspects of the Grenada saga was on the wane. The Washington press corps was more focused on what Reagan would say the next day in his State of the Union message. The *Washington Post* ran a story on the public portions of the House hearing on page 20 and the *New York Times* didn't run a story at all.

The flickering flame of public controversy over Grenada revived momentarily in spring of 1984 with the public release of the so-called Lind report. The assessment was named for its author, William S. Lind, a national security aide to Sen. Gary W. Hart (D–Colorado) on defense matters. Hart was then actively campaigning for the Democrat nomination for president. Hart was also a member of the Military Reform Caucus, a bipartisan congressional alliance pushing for better battlefield results from the money spent on national defense. Lind's critique of Grenada was in the form of a five-page memo to the reform caucus.[84] Rep. James A. Courter (R–New Jersey), then caucus chairman, was so impressed with Lind's analysis that he released it to the press. He added his personal call for an investigation of the Grenada operation by the House Armed Services Committee, of which he was a member.[85] In summary, Lind criticized the Pentagon's planning for the operation, the battlefield performance of some of the units, and raised an eyebrow over the American helicopter losses suffered in the fighting. The latter was, arguably, his most telling point. He noted that of the roughly 100 helicopters used on Grenada, nine were eventually reported as destroyed. "A loss rate of 9% in three days against an opponent with no anti-aircraft missiles, only guns [which can be highly effective] is not easy to pass over. What does it suggest our helicopter losses would be, for example, in a war in Europe?" Lind wrote.

The called-for congressional investigation never materialized, but, two months later, the Joint Chiefs issued a five-page, item-by-item response to Lind's report.[86] The service chiefs found virtually no merit to the criticisms of the operation and praised the performance of the American forces. As for the key issue of helicopter losses, the JCS response confirmed that nine of 107 helicopters used in the invasion were destroyed or badly damaged. But the Pentagon suggested these losses were the regrettable result of restrictive rules of engagement that sought to reduce civilian casualties. "[We] therefore did not support helicopter operations with the supportive air and artillery fire to the extent we could have," the Pentagon report asserted. The Lind report and the JSC response both played out in military publications and the back pages of the *Washington Post*. However, the charge and rebuttal served to keep the Grenada debate on the public agenda. *Army Magazine* furthered the counterattack in its June issue with a supportive summary of the Pentagon rebuttal written by L. James Binder, the editor in chief. Binder chided the Reform Caucus for "giving its name to the nebulous nitpicking that Mr. Lind has assembled into a scurrilous and unfounded attack."[87]

But, behind the scenes, the military bureaucracy was quietly conducting a bottom-up review of its own performance. Most conventional units which took part in Urgent Fury wrote after-action reports, which were passed up the chain of command. Army chief of staff Wickham wasn't satisfied with just the standard post-hostilities scrub-up. A special study team, the Grenada Work Group, was assembled at Fort Leavenworth, Kansas, to conduct an in-depth Urgent Fury review. That ad hoc effort, in turn, led to the permanent creation of the Center for Army Lessons Learned (CALL) at the site of Army's Command and General Staff College. "I think it is fair to say Grenada was our catalyst," Ken Harrison, CALL's founding director, told a newspaper interviewer in 1986.

In addition, historians working for the Army, Air Force and the Marines were dispatched to conduct formal oral history interviews with key participants, sometime within days of the fighting. These three Pentagon branches used these classified interviews and reports to prepare revealing, but critically restrained, historical monographs on their service's or command's performance. These monographs were all also initially classified, but some have since been made public.[88] The Navy alone was not much disposed to a historical examination of its performance. McDonald's Atlantic Command produced a tersely written after-action report of the entire operation, later partially declassified. The report summarized "lessons learned" in broad subjects areas such as "communications" and "tactics" in an unclassified sentence or two, but much of the amplifying detail was redacted.[89] Still, Schwarzkopf, the invasion's deputy commander, found the military's general impulse to document the mistakes of Urgent Fury, instead of papering them over, to be "the best evidence" that the uniformed services had changed for the better since Vietnam. "[T]he brief war had a lot of shortcomings—an abysmal lack of accurate intelligence, major deficiencies in communications, flareups of interservice rivalry, interference by higher headquarters in battlefield decisions, our alienation of the press, and more," he wrote in his autobiography.[90] "Yet I was heartened that these deficiencies had come to light in our *own* after-action reports."

Meanwhile, at the Pentagon, the civilian secretary of defense was doing his own year-after analysis of the lessons of October 1983 and coming to much broader, strategic assessment. On Nov. 28, 1984, Weinberger delivered his lawyerly assessment in a speech at the National Press Club that had been reviewed in advance by both the president and the National Security Council.[91] His vetted remarks were interpreted as a signal of the administration's policy for the president's second term, which would begin in January. Weinberger set a high bar for America's future use of U.S. combat troops abroad. He posited six tests to be applied:

- The objective should be of vital interest to the United States or its allies.
- The commitment should be wholehearted, with the intention of winning.
- The political and military objective should be clearly defined and accomplishable.
- The force used should be continuously reassessed to assure victory is achieved.

- There must be "reasonable assurance" that the commitment of forces will have the support of Congress and the American people.
- Combat should be a "last resort" measure.

Though he did not expressly say so, the implication was clear that Vietnam did not fully meet this punch-list. He did, however, specifically assert that Grenada passed the bar, because "our vital interests were at stake" and America had committed the "strength necessary to win the fight." Looking to the future, Weinberger said that adherence to these benchmarks would avoid the danger of a "gradualist" approach to interventions. "The President will not allow our military forces to creep—or be drawn gradually—into a combat role in Central America or any other place in the world," Weinberger declared in an unequivocal sentence that put the story on the front page of *New York Times* the next day. It wasn't until two days later that the *Washington Post* editorial page, playing catch-up on the *Times*, reprised Weinberger's speech and dubbed his six tests to be the "Weinberger Doctrine." Shultz, ever Weinberger's foil, thought the defense secretary's standards were too black and white for the gray world of diplomacy and did not hesitate to express his immediate dissent. "The need to avoid no-win situations cannot mean that we turn automatically away from hard-to-win situations that call for prudent involvement," he declared.[92] But Weinberger clearly was speaking for Reagan on this subject. Reagan itemized Weinberger's principles in his memoirs, embraced them as his administration's policy and recommended them to future presidents.[93] Still, however often Weinberger and Reagan publicly declared Urgent Fury to have been an operation justly launched and laudably waged, they could not fully beat back critics who gnawed on its flaws. The perceived mismanagement of the military by the Pentagon hierarchy became a major political issue in the first two years of Reagan's second term.

Before that bureaucratic war was fully joined, the military had to suffer through an embarrassing public relations kerfuffle involving the two Navy admirals who led the invasion. The controversy had its roots in an off-handed decision that Metcalf made after the fighting stopped, just before he left Grenada to return to Norfolk. Metcalf directed a member of his command staff to requisition from the captured stores eight AK-47s, which he intended to give away as gifts to unspecified dignitaries. The assigned officer took it upon himself to also collect additional AK-47s as trophies for Metcalf's staff, attaching their names to individual weapons. In total, 24 AK-47s and empty magazines were packed into five wooden crates and put aboard Metcalf's plane for his flight home.[94] These withdrawals from the captured Grenadian arsenal emboldened others from other services to seize their own battle souvenirs without the benefit of paperwork. Still more war trophies were picked up on the battlefield by American troops. Hundreds of soldiers and Marines collected enemy weapons, especially AK-47s, which they intended to bring home. This trophy gathering was tolerated after World War I and II and Korea. The military tightened up its rules after the Gun Control Act of 1968 prohibited the import of automatic weapons like the AK-47s into the United States.[95] Marines embarking on their ships from Grenada for Beirut were reminded of this law and many surrendered their banned trophies under an amnesty program.

Metcalf should have been aware of this rule as well, but the AK-47s flew back with him in his plane. U.S. Customs, reportedly acting on an anonymous tip, discovered the weapons on the plane when it landed at the Naval Air Station Norfolk on Nov. 3.[96] The weapons were seized as contraband. The case was referred to the Naval Investigative

Service, but it did not immediately come to public attention.[97] It was then required that Navy investigators seek the approval of the commanding officer before beginning a probe. McDonald summoned Metcalf. Metcalf told the investigators he took full responsibility and then declared: "What is there to investigate?"[98] The investigation ended after three days. Metcalf was supposedly given a nonpunitive "letter of caution" for his actions, but a later investigation could find no official record of this in Navy legal files.[99] The matter eventually reached the desk of the secretary of the navy in early 1984. Lehman concluded that there was nothing more to be done. Other servicemen who had had voluntarily given up captured weapons under the amnesty program had not been punished. In fact, some of the surrendered weapons (but not AK-47s) were disabled and returned as acceptable "war trophies."[100]

That might have been the end of the issue, if it hadn't been for what happened to other military weapons that were smuggled back from battle zones at the same time by lower ranking members of other services. Some of these contraband weapons were offered for sale in the Fort Bragg area. That triggered a new investigation in North Carolina that resulted in the court martial of nine 82nd Airborne soldiers. Five soldiers were sentenced to one year or more in prison and four other enlisted men were reduced to private and given bad-conduct discharges. In addition, four Marines were accused of stealing, and trying to sell, contraband weapons acquired during duty in Beirut or Grenada including American-made, shoulder-fired rockets and grenades.[101] Three had been court-martialed when a reporter for Hearst newspapers learned of the Metcalf incident and wrote a story contrasting the punishment meted out in the related cases. That story got wide distribution through the Associated Press. The Navy secretary was ordered to make "a complete report" on the importation of war trophies by seaborne servicemen after Grenada.[102] Simultaneously, the Navy released a statement drawing a distinction between the Navy admiral and the enlisted Marines because Metcalf had requisitioned his weapons as trophies, not for illegal sale. The Navy statement indicated that Metcalf mistakenly believed that automatic weapons could be kept as souvenirs "as long as they were disabled." The embarrassing news reports also triggered further inquiries by Congress, the Defense Department's inspector general and the Pentagon's general counsel. Those inquiries uncovered the role played by Cmdr. Woodrow John Roble, an assistant air operations officer under Metcalf, in expanding the number of weapons requisitioned to two dozen. The investigations were finally resolved with Metcalf cleared of further wrongdoing, but the episode is believed to have cost him a fourth star and led to his premature retirement.[103] McDonald was scolded for "poor judgment" by the inspector general and Roble was issued an administrative "letter of caution" by the Navy.[104] The Army also granted clemency to three of the court-martialed soldiers.[105]

The final, epic battle of Grenada was fought in Washington, not the Caribbean. It was a bruising, but bloodless, civil war that divided the national defense community into opposing camps of reformers and traditionalists. The live-fire combat on Grenada amounted to scattered firefights that were over in a week. The years-long policy clash was fought later, stateside, over what lessons Urgent Fury should teach the American military. Was Grenada just a quirky, one-off, mostly successful, otherwise excusable, contingency operation? Or was Urgent Fury a case study that provided fresh evidence of an organizational malaise that had hobbled the American military for the past century?

This bureaucratic conflict had already been declared, skirmishes fought and battle lines formed when Urgent Fury occurred. The first salvo was fired in early 1982, 20 months before the Grenada operation, by Gen. David C. Jones, then the chairman of the Joint Chiefs. Jones was a cerebral, energetic administrator who speed read, wrote with both hands and worked standing up.[106] He was intimately familiar with the workings of the Joint Chiefs based on eight years of top-echelon Pentagon service. He served as the Air Force's chief of staff, appointed by Nixon, and then another four as chairman of the Joint Chiefs under Carter and Reagan. Jones was near the end of his second four-year term as chairman. The Reagan administration was actively looking for his replacement. Jones resolved to make organization reform his personal mission in his final months in uniform—even though he knew from previous conversations that Weinberger did not favor major reform.[107]

Jones launched his campaign in closed-door testimony on Feb. 3, 1982, before the House Armed Services Committee, a session billed as a preliminary budget review session with Jones and Weinberger.[108] Jones surprised the committee members, and to some degree his boss, by using the occasion to declare that the military had major organizational problems that needed repair. "It is not sufficient to just have just resources, dollars and weapons systems: we must also have an organization which allows us to develop the proper strategy, necessary planning and the full warfighting capability," he said. Jones observed that the organization structure at the pinnacle of the Pentagon was "basically a committee" system that required unanimity for action and perpetuated inter-service rivalry. He proposed instead a new structure that would promote joint-thinking by strengthening the role of the chairman, strengthening the role of war-fighting commanders in the field and upgrading the advice offered by the joint staff. Jones' rehearsed statement lasted only 8 minutes and barely made an impact on his unprepared audience. Still, the fuse was lit. Jones amplified on his reform message in a mid–February breakfast meeting with major TV and newspaper organizations. A seminal article by him was published in the February issue of *Directors & Boards*, a business journal, and the March issue of *Armed Forces Journal*. The two nearly identical articles were both titled "Why the Joint Chiefs of Staff Must Change."[109] Jones compared the Joint Chiefs to the directors of a private corporation. The Joint Chiefs consisted of a chairman (him) and four "insider" directors, each representing one of the corporation's line divisions. "Committees can serve a useful purpose in providing a wide range of advice to a chief executive ... but they are notoriously poor agents for running anything—let alone everything," he wrote.

Jones asserted that the then-existing organizational scheme was hobbled by two fundamental flaws. One key failing, was, contrary to public perception, the chairman of the joint chiefs did not by statute have any command authority over the uniformed service branches or their chiefs. Instead, the chairman's role was to serve as moderator of the committee he headed. The Joint Chiefs as a body had the statutory role of offering military advice to the president, the secretary of defense and the National Security Council. The concept was that uniformed service chiefs would collaborate to offer advice to top civilian national security leaders whose decisions would flow back to the military as orders—guaranteeing that the military would be subordinate to civilian authority. Further, the chiefs customarily arrived at their advice by unanimous agreement. This one-voice policy tended to reduce recommendations to the lowest common denominator. The offered advice represented everyone collectively, but often only up to a point of critical disagreement. The other perceived flaw was the conflict-of-interest inherit in the job of being the head of the Army, Marines, Navy or Air Force. Every service expected their top officer to be loyal to their military branch and to promote their interest. But this down-the-ranks view necessarily burdened the service chiefs with parochial concerns when acting on higher-minded joint issues. This was frequently referred to as the "dual hat" or the "statesman-spokesman" dilemma.

The solution Jones proposed was to strengthen the role of the chairman by freeing him to act unilaterally on joint matters and to appoint a deputy who could fully represent him when he was absent. The system then in place called for the ranking service chief present at the Pentagon to fill in whenever the chairman was away, often triggering a Pentagon game of "musical chairs" among the peripatetic chiefs. During one trip Jones took to Korea, eleven different officers served as acting chairman.[110] Jones believed that the service chiefs should remain focused on their respective service responsibilities. He proposed they draw their advice on joint matters from an invigorated joint staff, which would be better prepared, better motivated, less parochial and longer tenured than in the current system.

Jones initial salvo was immediately followed by an even bolder organizational broadside by Gen. Edward C. "Shy" Meyer, the Army chief of staff, who was also nearing the end of his final term as the Army's top officer. In an article for the April issue of *Armed Forces Journal*, Meyer endorsed Jones' analysis of the JCS's structural problems, but argued that Jones solutions did not go far enough.[111] Meyer proposed creation of a full-time panel of four-star officers called the National Military Advisory Council. This body would discuss and debate joint issues and act as "the developers of the prime military input to the President and the Secretary of Defense."[112] Their freedom to act unconstrained by service loyalties would be guaranteed by a requirement that the four-stars "never return to their respective services" before retirement.

These two salvos from within the tight circle of the Joint Chiefs had the calculated effect of encouraging reform forces in Congress to propose legislation to correct the identified flaws of the JCS system. Both Jones and Meyer were among 43 witnesses called to testify before the House Investigations Subcommittee, which held 20 hearings on Pentagon reform over three months.[113] A bill was drafted by the subcommittee chairman, Richard C. White (D–Texas), aimed at fixing the flaws cited by Jones and Meyer. The draft got a quick markup and whisked through the full House Armed Services committee in a week. Four days later, on Aug. 16, 1982, H.R. 6954 passed the Democratic-controlled lower chamber on a voice vote. But, at that point, the legislative reform push stalled.

The Senate Armed Services Committee was then chaired by Tower, a Texas Republican who did not favor legislative reform. Weinberger also did not believe that major reform was necessary and, with the retirement of Jones and Meyer, neither did the reconstituted JCS. Eventually, Tower agreed to a hold a single courtesy hearing on the House bill before it died at the end of the session. Over the next two years Pentagon reform effort drifted into legislative stalemate. No bipartisan, bicameral consensus emerged on what Pentagon problems needed fixing or the appropriate legislative remedy. Solutions offered to various perceived organizational problems ranged from elimination of all the service chiefs (following the Canadian military model) to abolishing the Joint Chiefs on the other. Weinberger and Vessey sought to ease the pressures for legislative reform by making administrative changes that were narrowly aimed at encouraging joint thinking at the top of the Pentagon pyramid. In October 1984 a rider was attached to a Defense Authorization Bill mandating six procedural changes at the Pentagon that incrementally increased the power of the chairman or lessened the ties between the services and the joint staff.[114]

The reform logjam further shifted at the end of 1984 with a turnover in leadership in Congress and in the Pentagon. In the Senate, Tower retired and Goldwater (R–Arizona), the GOP's 1964 presidential nominee, assumed the chairmanship of the armed services committee. Goldwater was a retired major general in the Air Force Reserve, but also something of a policy maverick who was personally and politically inclined toward bipartisanship.[115] He found easy alliance with Sam Nunn (D–Georgia), the ranking Democrat on the committee. Nunn was a conservative-leaning moderate who was a strong reform advocate. On the House side, Pentagon reform had the support of Les Aspin (D–Wisconsin) who had taken control of the Armed Services Committee in a coup. Another reform advocate, Bill Nichols (D–Alabama), had assumed the chairmanship of the House Investigations Subcommittee when White retired. Both Aspin and Nichols were conservative-leaning Democrats with military credentials. Aspin was a former economics professor and Pentagon analyst. Nichols was a World War II combat veteran who lost a leg when a German land mine shattered his foot.

At the Pentagon, Vessey declared his intention to retire on Oct. 1, 1985, clearing the way for the Reagan administration to begin a replacement search. On July 10 Reagan announced he would appoint Adm. William J. "Bill" Crowe to be the next chairman. Crowe was unconventional thinker who was scornful of the parochialism that was rampant in the tradition-bound Navy. He had a Ph.D. in politics from Princeton and was more open to organizational reform than Vessey. But, initially at least, he supported the view of Weinberger and the other service chiefs that no major legislative change was necessary.

With the pro-reform moons coming into alignment over Capitol Hill and the Pentagon, the stage was set in 1985 for an invigorated push in Congress to pass a significant reform bill that President Reagan would feel compelled to sign. The debate started to come into focus with the publication of think-tank reports on the arcane, but suddenly hot, topic of Pentagon organizational reform. A pair of reports prepared by experts at the Center for Strategic and International Studies (CSIS), then housed at Georgetown University, framed the debate early in the new year. One was a book, titled *The Pentagon and the Art of War*, by Edward W. Luttwak, a senior fellow at CSIS. Luttwak's central premise was that the failings of the modern military all have their roots in the "rudderless" bureaucracy at the Pentagon. Grenada served as one of several case studies where he traced battlefield snafus back to their origins on the banks of the Potomac. Luttwak laid the principal blame for Urgent Fury's failings on the Joint Chiefs and the "unified" commands immediately below the service chiefs. The Joint Chiefs system was dysfunctional, he argued because was no single person was effectively the commander of all uniformed American combat forces. The president was nominally the commander-in-chief of the military, but he wore that hat only sometimes, in addition to his considerable executive branch and ceremonial responsibilities. The chairman of the Joint Chiefs did not serve as the president's surrogate because, by statute, the unified commands reported to the secretary of defense, not to the chairman. (Weinberger finessed this organization anomaly during Urgent Fury by delegating his command authority to Vessey.)

The other CSIS-sourced study was a group effort that spread its arms wide both in terms of the breath of its examination and the diverse group of defense experts who signed on to the book-length final report.[116] The report was funded by the Ford and Rockefeller Foundations and overseen by a steering committee that included Jones and Meyer, now both retired, as well as Aspin and Nunn. The CSIS reform package stretched far beyond how the Joint Chiefs functioned to include the organization of the secretary of defense's office, the Pentagon's combat forces, how the defense budget was prepared and reviewed and how weapons are acquired. In sum, the *New York Times* described the report as advocating "the most drastic changes in military management since the Eisenhower Administration."[117] The closer on this sales package was the signed, conceptual endorsement of the report by six of the seven former secretaries of defense. Their joint statement affirmed that there were "serious deficiencies" in how the military was organized and managed. They declared the recommended changes to have "compelling merit" that deserved bipartisan support. The report had particular currency because its release came at time when the defense buildup that began when Reagan took office was topping a record $1 trillion. That attention-getting benchmark was leading to increasing pointed questions about how well the money was being spent. A steady stream of news stories documenting Pentagon waste were making embarrassing headlines: a $600 toilet seat for a Navy submarine-hunting plane, a $404 socket wrench for a F-14 fighter, a $7,400 coffee pot for an Air Force C-5A cargo plane, $5,098 for a wine and stereo cabinet for a "captain's gig" assigned to a Navy aircraft carrier, and $900 for a china and crystal service for the residence of a Navy admiral in Philadelphia.

The CSIS report eschewed such sensationalism. It was written in the dusty prose of a business school textbook. It sought to influence Washington policy-makers more than the general public. One reviewer called it "stolid." Its broad-brush focus on the Pentagon's procedures and structures avoided extended examinations of particular cases. The flaws of Urgent Fury, for example, rated just two passing mentions in the 247-page book form of the report. The incompatibility of the tactical radios used by the various services on Grenada was cited as an example of why the Pentagon needed to place greater emphasis on selecting weapons and equipment that would be of maximum use in the integrated battlefields of the future. The "ad hoc planning" and "curious command structure" of the Urgent Fury illustrated why unified commands like Atlantic Command needed to be better staffed, trained and organized for future missions.[118]

The mounting reform pressure prompted the Reagan administration to search for a way to get ahead of the political wave before it crashed on the Pentagon. In June, over the objection of Weinberger, Reagan announced the formation of his own commission to study Pentagon procurement.[119] The study group came to be known as the Packard Commission, after its chairman David R. Packard, the co-founder of Hewlett-Packard and a former deputy secretary of defense under Richard Nixon. The 14-member committee was asked to present its initial findings to Reagan by March 31, 1986.

Meanwhile, the CSIS report served as a table setter for the bipartisan debate on military reform that played out in the fall of 1985 before the Senate Armed Services Committee (SASC). Goldwater and Nunn planned a two-pronged strategy to focus the attention of both the national media and the Congressional leadership on the hearings. On the media front, the plan was to open the Senate's consideration of military reform with alternating floor speeches by Goldwater and Nunn over the course of six straight sessions. This would be quickly followed by the public release of a massive 625-page staff report on military reform, which the committee staff had compiled in two years of study. Nunn encouraged the committee staff to include extreme recommendations in the final draft that would serve both as attention-getters and bargaining chips in future negotiations with the anti-reform forces. "We need staff recommendations that scare them so badly that when we do what we really intend to do, they will take out their handkerchiefs and wipe their brows," Nunn told James R. Locher III, the director of the study.[120]

The speech offensive was launched by Goldwater who told his colleagues and the listeners in the Senate gallery on Oct. 1, 1985, that they will be shocked by "the serious deficiencies in the organization and procedures" in the national defense that would be publicly documented in the days ahead. The second day was devoted to a shared Goldwater-Nunn recitation of organizational problems that were exposed in military operations from the Spanish American War to the present day. Grenada played a prominent role in this cavalcade of past snafus. Nunn believed that Urgent Fury was an ideal case study because, unlike the ultimate defeat in Vietnam or the abortive Iranian hostage rescue, it "avoided the sensitivities that surround a failure."[121] In his floor speech, Nunn declared: "Grenada has been touted as a victory.... But it is sobering to look at how many failures of coordination and communication there were. One cannot help but wonder what would have happened if the opposition on the island had been better armed, organized, or larger."[122] The second component of the Congressional strategy was to organize a weekend "retreat" for a bipartisan core group of nine Senators who had been receiving periodic briefings on the draft report. This skull session also included 15 experts. whom Goldwater described as "the most prestigious and knowledgeable group of experts in this area that had ever been assembled." At the end of the two-day session, Nunn and Goldwater counted six of the nine Senators as solid backers of sweeping reform, including Ted Kennedy (D–Massachusetts).[123]

With that assurance of support, Nunn and Goldwater were now emboldened to offer courtesy, pre-release briefings to other key Washington players in the reform debate. The Pentagon briefing was attended by Weinberger, Deputy Defense Secretary William Howard Taft IV, Maj. Gen. Colin L. Powell, Weinberger's top military assistant, and Crowe, the new JCS chairman. (Crowe had just replaced Vessey who retired on Sept. 30.) Locher gave a 20-slide presentation as the leader of the staff study. Goldwater and Nunn accompanied him as paladins for the fight the presentation was expected to provoke.

The session was also complicated by bad blood lingering from Goldwater's opposition to Taft's nomination to the second-ranking position at the Defense Department. Taft was a Harvard-trained lawyer who was also the great grandson of a president and nephew of a senator. Despite that impressive pedigree, Goldwater felt he lacked the managerial training and experience to be, in effect, the chief operating officer of the largest corporation in the world.[124] Taft objected to both the tone and substance of Locher's presentation. "This briefing makes it seem like the Defense Department couldn't even defend the Pentagon's River Entrance," Locher recalled Taft remarking. Goldwater rose to Locher's defense. "Your operational performance has been so piss poor, you guys would have trouble defending the River Entrance from an attack by a troop of Boy Scouts," Goldwater retorted. By Locher's account, the top two defense secretaries and the two senators sparred for the next 15 minutes to no resolution. Locher remembers that Powell was the only one of the Pentagon partisans who shook his hand when they left the meeting. Two years earlier, Powell had observed Urgent Fury as a self-described "fly on the wall" in Weinberger's office. The organizational shortcomings he saw and heard made him a closeted believer in the need for major change at the Pentagon. "The operation demonstrated how far cooperation among the services still had to go," he later wrote in his autobiography.[125] "The invasion succeeded, but it was a sloppy success."

The stage was now set for the orchestrated public release of the Senate committee's staff report on Wednesday, Oct. 16, 1985. Forty-three print and broadcast reporters attended a pre-release briefing by Locher on the condition that their stories not be aired or published until after the hearing, a common arrangement for the orderly release of complex information.[126] Two thousand copies of the 645-page document were distributed within 24 hours to meet the demand.[127] Both ABC and CBS included reports on the study in their network evening news broadcasts on the day of the release. The *Washington Post* ran the report on the front page the next morning, but the *New York Times* put the story inside.

Like the CSIS study that preceded it, the Senate staff study was wide-ranging. It called for significant changes in the Office of the Secretary of Defense, the Joint Chiefs, the Pentagon headquarters of the four military branches, the nine war-fighting unified commands and within the career military officer professional development system. The report made 12 key recommendations in these five arenas.[128]

1. The Joint Chiefs was targeted for the most radical change. The report called for the existing committee-of-equals system to be scrapped entirely and replaced by a Military Advisory Council composed of four-star representatives of each uniformed service. Membership would be limited to generals or admirals in their last tour of duty who, presumably, would feel freer to offer advice that deviated from the parochial interests of their respective services. That advice would include, not just their majority recommendation, but "all legitimate alternatives." The council would be presided over by the chairman, who also would be specifically empowered to offer his own personal military advice to civilian decision makers, regardless of what the council advised. The chairman would also be able to choose the officers the services assigned to joint duty and ensure that they were properly prepared and rewarded for their joint service. Finally, the chairman would be allowed to select a four-star officer from a different service who would be fully empowered to act as his replacement in his absence.

2. The service chiefs of the four uniformed branches would be relieved of their presidential advisory responsibilities and refocused on their duties to their respective services. The service chiefs would also be removed from having any operational command authority over the war-fighting commands, including the ones headed by an officer of their own service. These top regional or specialized-function commanders would instead get their orders from chain of command that came directly from the president through the secretary of defense.

3. The staffs of the Pentagon headquarters of the four service branches would be shrunk by consolidating them with the staff of their respective service secretaries.

4. Within the office of the secretary of defense, the report called for the creation of three mission-oriented, under-secretary positions to better align the organization of that office with three major strategic goals: nuclear deterrence, NATO defense and regional defense. Also, the report called for the creation of a new assistant secretary position for strategic planning.

5. Within the uniformed officer ranks, a new career specialty for joint service would be created for mid-career officers to promote this work as a path to flag rank rather than a dead end.

In making the case for change, the report authors looked to the military history of the past century for illustration. Appendix A of the report reprised the organizational problems that had plagued six military operations since the Spanish-American War. Urgent Fury was the most recent of the six case studies and was covered in the most detail.[129] Evidently heeding Nunn's admonition about Grenada as a test case, the report took pains to declare Urgent Fury a "success" in that its principal missions were accomplished "rapidly with little loss of life" by American forces which "performed bravely and fought well." But that inoculation set the stage for an itemized examination of organizational problems cited by the invasion's critics.

The report found the largest single organizational problem of the operation was the inability of units to communicate. It traced the root cause to Pentagon procurement practices which allowed each service to purchase its own radios with insufficient regard to their compatibility with equipment used by other services. "Is it not possible to buy equipment that is compatible, rather than having to improvise and concoct cumbersome bureaucracies so that the Services can talk to one another?" the report asked rhetorically with unconcealed exasperation. Fire support was found to be another serious problem area where coordination between Army and Navy units was "poor to non-existent." This problem, and others, might have been solved if a single ground commander had been appointed for the operation, the report stated. In sum, Urgent Fury "demonstrated that there are major deficiencies in the ability of the Services to work jointly when deployed rapidly," the report concluded.

In anticipation of a strong pushback from Weinberger and the Navy hierarchy to the report findings, the committee postponed hearings for four weeks to give anti-reform forces time to prepare the rebuttal. Ten hearings were planned with Weinberger scheduled to be the first witness on Nov. 14, 1985. Weinberger initially was conciliatory, at one point stating he could go along with about half of the recommendations in the staff report. But that olive branch wilted quickly in the heat generated by sharp exchanges with Goldwater, Kennedy and Nunn. The defense secretary sparred with Nunn over the radios used on Grenada. The exchange, though brief, got media attention and was emblematic of the then-opposing views of Urgent Fury. Weinberger refused to acknowledge that radio interoperability was enough of a problem to interfere with the success of the operation.

Weinberger was in a contentious mood because he perceived the hearings, and particularly the staff report, to be a general indictment of his management of the Pentagon, and a legislative overreach into executive matters. His principal supporter on the Senate committee was John William Warner (R–Virginia), who had served in both the Marines and the Navy in his youth and had been the secretary of the Navy under Nixon. Warner believed that the proposed changes would legislatively degrade the authority of the individual service chiefs, rather than leave the relationship between the chiefs and the president up to the president. He noted that, in the case of Grenada, Reagan chose to poll the chiefs individually before proceeding with the operation. "If I look at the collection of recommendations here, it seems to me that you're relegating the chief of service to the role of honorary chairman. You are literally stripping his epaulets right in front of his troops," Warner declared at the Oct. 16 hearing.[130]

The 19-member committee was clearly not yet united behind the need for reform, but the report and the hearing generated a strategic momentum that could not be resisted by tactical argument. On the House side, the Armed Services Committee was separately advancing a more narrowly focused Pentagon reform bill. The measure was approved on Nov. 20, six days after Weinberger's Senate appearance, by an overwhelming 383–27 vote. On Dec. 2, Weinberger was convinced to sue for peace. He sent a letter to Goldwater

offering to support making the JCS chairman the president's principal adviser and establishing a vice chairman position.[131] The offer was far short of an endorsement of broader
reform, but it was interpreted by Kennedy as "the crack in the wall."[132] The committee
next heard from the uniformed leadership. The four, four-star service chiefs all testified
before the committee on Dec. 5 and supported the official Pentagon view that legislative
reform was not needed.[133] Kennedy tried to pin them down to specifics by asking them
to respond in writing to the staff report's analysis of "what went wrong in Beirut, Iran
and Grenada." But in the case of Grenada, the Army, Navy and Air Force chiefs deflected
that spear by broadly declaring Urgent Fury to have been a successful joint operation.[134]
The two top uniformed officers involved in Urgent Fury were also called to testify: Vessey,
who had retired two months before, and McDonald, who was set to retire the week after
his testimony. Vessey generally testified in support of the existing Pentagon organization
structure and cautioned against the unintended consequences of legislative reform. "So,
as we change things, we want to make sure that we do not throw out the baby with the
bathwater," he advised. He also said that scrapping the joint chief's staff and replacing it
with a body of military advisers was a "bad idea" that "will not work."[135] McDonald, however, was surprisingly supportive of the legislative reform efforts. He praised the staff
study as "a superb job" and said he agreed with many, but not all, of the recommendations.[136] His principal advice to the committee was to bring the four-year-long debate to
a resolution so that all the parties can move on. "Further study will serve no useful purpose.... If change is to be implemented, conditions appear optimum during this Congress," he said.

Crowe, the sitting JCS chairman, was the next to last witness to testify. He used his
"new guy" status to stake out a middle ground that was supportive of past military operations while open to limited reform.[137] The pro-reform forces regarded him as an ally-
in-waiting and did not press him. After the last of 27 witnesses testified on Dec. 12, 1985,
Nunn and Goldwater saw their way clear to craft a comprehensive bill based on the staff
study. As Nunn had foreshadowed, the draft bill eliminated five of the study's most
extreme recommendations, notably the recommendation to replace the Joint Chiefs with
a four-star council. As markup began on the 56-page draft bill on Feb. 4, 1986, the top
echelon at the Pentagon made a final united appeal.[138] All three civilian service secretaries
and all four uniformed service chiefs submitted formal letters of opposition to the draft
bill, with Navy secretary Lehman and Marine corps commandant Kelley the most vocif-
erous. Warner, the leader of anti-reform sentiment on the committee, proposed 13 amend-
ments to the draft bill that became the subject of markup discussions and clarifying
changes.[139]

As the markup was underway, on Feb. 28, the Packard Commission submitted an
"interim" report to the president on its independent, administration-sponsored investigation of Pentagon organization and procurement. The report found that Pentagon organizational problems were complicating weapons development, as well as the military's
combat operations. "With notable exceptions, weapons systems take too long and cost
too much to produce. Too often, they do not perform as promised or expected," the
report declared. The study also examined the recent "horror" stories of Pentagon over-
spending on simple items and found that they were only symptoms of more complex,
systemic Pentagon waste.[140] The report was released at a White House ceremony where
Reagan pledged to quickly adopt the commission's recommendations "even if they run
counter to the will of the entrenched bureaucracies and special interests."[141]

It was now clear that the Reagan administration wanted to move to regain the initiative on Pentagon reform, regardless of the embarrassment that might pose for Weinberger, Reagan's longtime friend. With anti-reform forces besieged on multiple fronts, the Senate committee convened on March 6 for a vote on the marked-up bill. The panel of 10 Republicans and nine Democrats approved the measure by a unanimous vote of 19–0. A footrace was now on between Congress and the White House, to determine which branch of government could claim credit for enacting Pentagon reform. On April 1, 1986, Reagan signed National Security Decision Directive 219, an executive order to immediately implement the Packard Commission recommendations that could be put in place solely by presidential authority.[142] On April 24, Reagan followed up on this action by submitting to Congress a short list of legislative changes he believed to be necessary, in addition to the administrative ones he had already directed. Aside from the limited law changes he proposed, he urged Congress "to show restraint in the use of legislation as a solution to our current problems."[143] But this eleventh-hour attempt to play a presidential trump was brushed aside by the reform forces. Nunn and Goldwater wanted comprehensive reform to be implemented by federal law rather than a presidential directive that could be unilaterally rescinded or amended by the present or future occupant of the Oval Office. Propelled by the unanimous committee vote and Reagan's subsequent embrace of reform, the Senate bill sailed through the full chamber in a single day and was approved 95–0 on May 7.

At that point the House was still working on its latest version of a reform bill that was more ambitious than the two it had previously passed. Nichol's Investigative Subcommittee held its own hearings in early 1986. Those hearings produced, H.R. 4370, introduced by Nichols with strong hands-on input from Aspin.[144] The new House bill passed by a vote of 406–4. The latest bill was then combined with H.R. 3622, the bill House had passed in 1985, to be considered in conference committee with the Senate bill. Though similar in subject and sweep, the final House and Senate reform bills had more than two hundred significant differences that needed to be ironed out in a conference committee chaired by Goldwater and co-chaired by Nichols.[145] It took the committee a month of work to craft a final compromise version that was approved in a voice vote by both chambers in mid–September. Reagan signed the measure into law on Oct. 1 without a signing ceremony.

The final Goldwater-Nichols bill, Public Law 99-433, is a dense legislative document that runs 88 typed pages.[146] It's a difficult read because the specific reforms are enacted piecemeal through line-by-line additions and deletions to the existing Title 10 of the U.S. Code. Title 10 is the federal law which specifies the roles, missions and organization of the Department of Defense and its four uniform services. Goldwater-Nichols is summarized in Section 3 (Policy) of the law which enumerates and espouses eight key objectives as "the intent of Congress":

1. Strengthen civilian authority over the military. For the first time, the new law expressly declared that each of the three civilian service secretaries were "subject to the authority, direction and control" of the secretary of defense, effectively weakening their independence of action. The law also sought to loosen the bounds of the individual services on the chairman of the Joint Chiefs by freeing him from the necessity of always seeking the unanimous support of the service chiefs. The service chiefs were relegated to an arm's-length advisory role to the

president and defense secretary. Their principal responsibility was to train, support and equip the personnel assigned to the unified combat commands.

2. Improve joint military advice. The act established the chairman as the principal military adviser to the president, the National Security Council and the secretary of defense. The chairman's individual power was further enhanced by assigning the chairman a four-star deputy. The deputy outranked all the individual service chiefs and was empowered to perform such duties as may be assigned to him by the chairman, with the approval of the defense secretary. The chairman would get his advice from a revitalized uniformed staff, which would be selected by the chairman from each service's mid-career officer ranks and be responsible exclusively to the chairman.

3. Assign clear mission responsibility to the military's top war-fighting commanders. The act made the commanders of geographically defined unified commands (i.e., Pacific, European, etc.) or specific-function commands (i.e., transportation) directly answerable to the president and the secretary of defense through the chain of command. Collectively these latter two officials constituted the so-called "national command authority" the top-level source of lawful military orders.

4. Ensure that the authority of the regional combat commanders was "fully commensurate" with their mission responsibility. The unified commanders were empowered to exercise "authority, direction and control" over all their subordinate units, regardless of their uniform service. This authority would notably include the selection of unit commanders and headquarters staff.

5. Focus more top-level Pentagon attention on strategic and contingency planning. This was to be achieved, in part, by requiring the president to submit to Congress an annual national security strategy plan. This plan would be a companion to the president's spending request with the implied aim of better coordinating the request for funds with the desired strategic goals. Also, the under secretary of defense was specifically charged with assisting the secretary in guiding and reviewing military contingency plans.

6. Foster more efficient use of military funds and resources. The act called on the defense secretary to provide policy guidance on the effective use of resources. It also sought to strengthen the secretary's power to supervise the individual services, review budgets and assure the combat readiness of the armed forces.

7. Better management of the joint officer staff. A joint career specialty was established for promising mid-rank officers of all services. This career path would only be open to officers who had successfully completed a training program at a joint professional military education school and then successfully completed a full tour of duty in a joint duty assignment.

8. Enhance the effectiveness of military operations and improve the management and administration of the Department of Defense. Reformers believed that the Pentagon headquarters staffs were bloated and they mandated headcount reductions to target percentages by 1988 and 1989, respectively.

The law makes no mention of Grenada, but the flaws of Urgent Fury can be read between the lines of the final bill. If Goldwater-Nichols had been in place and functioning prior to the invasion, McDonald and Metcalf would have had an easier time controlling and directing the U.S. forces that were assigned to them as the operational commanders. Instead of having mostly Navy officers with him on his Atlantic Command staff, McDonald would have had top-shelf liaison officers from other services. He would have had a role in selecting them and gotten to know them from daily dealings—rather than being strangers of unknown abilities and/or divided loyalties. Metcalf probably would have had to spend less energy settling interservice squabbles, such as the quarrel that erupted over the use of Marine helicopters for the Ranger rescue of the students at Grand Anse. Units in the field would probably still have carried different radios, but there was a better chance they would have known each other's frequencies and call signs. Army helicopters pilots might have been trained to land on Navy ships and the Navy would have had procedures in place to pay for their fuel. Schwarzkopf's role as ground commander and Metcalf's number two would have been defined from the start of the battle, not a battlefield promotion earned at the end of the first day of battle. The unit commanders would have been more familiar with the tactics, equipment, procedures and capabilities of other services than they were during Urgent Fury. Ideally, the invasion plan Metcalf was implementing would not have been a Mulligan stew cooked up on short notice with ingredients added by various cooks at various times based on their personal tastes and what was available in the cupboard. Instead, Metcalf could have been handed an off-the-shelf contingency plan that was ready for execution and had been recently vetted at the highest level of the Pentagon.

But it is also apparent that Goldwater-Nichols was no magical remedy for all the imperfections of Urgent Fury. Units still would have arrived with inadequate intelligence and vulnerable to bad weather and bad luck. The reform bill also did not directly address the friction that occurred between conventional and unconventional forces in Grenada. Special forces commanders felt their men had been mauled and misused by conventional commanders who failed to appreciate their unique capabilities—and vulnerabilities. The organizational reform of special forces came up in the course of the Goldwater-Nichols deliberations, but the reform leaders opted to tackle that issue after the main bill was passed. The act merely directed that the Defense Department give "consideration" to creation of a unified special operations command as part of general review of the geographic and functional responsibilities for all the existing unified commands. The act gave the Pentagon a year to conduct that review, but other compelling forces prompted Congress to move ahead with immediate legislation.

As was the case with Goldwater-Nichols, the House Armed Services Committee took the lead in exploring legislative solutions. One of the committee's senior members, Rep. Dan Daniel, a conservative Democratic representing a rural Virginia district, took an early interest in the secrecy-bound subject. Daniel was a World War II Navy veteran and a former national commander of the American Legion. He brought a personal commitment, but no insider knowledge, to the subject. His expertise in special operation issues was acquired through his service on the Armed Services Committee, and, later, also on the Permanent Select Committee on Intelligence.[147] He was also influenced on the subject by his personal relationship with a one of his constituents: Samuel V. Wilson, a retired Army lieutenant general. Wilson was a former OSS officer who had held high positions within the military, the CIA and Defense Intelligence Agency until he retired at the peak of his career for family reasons.[148] Daniel found kinship with an ad hoc group of reform advocates, informally known as the SOF (special operations forces) Mafia, who were concerned about the Pentagon's ability to deal with terrorism and so-called "low-intensity warfare." In August 1985, Daniel put his name to an article published in an influential military journal calling for special forces to break away from their parent organizations to form the "sixth" uniformed service, alongside the Navy, Army, Air Force, Marines and Coast Guard.[149] The article was provocatively titled "The Case for a Sixth Service," but it was more an argument for why SOF didn't "fit" in the current Pentagon scheme than a vision of how a new uniformed service would work. Daniel's basic contention was that special forces were, by their very nature, out of step with the rest of the Pentagon. Conventional forces were oriented toward warfare that involved large number of troops, massed firepower, coordinated maneuvers and standardized weapons and tactics. Special operations usually involved small units that relied on stealth and highly specialized skills and equipment. "The whole concept of their operations runs counter to the standard wisdom of how wars are fought and won," Daniel asserted.

In the Senate, Daniel's advocacy caught the attention of Sen. William S. Cohen (R–Maine), a member of the Senate Armed Services Committee who shared an interest in special forces from his own personal contacts. In January 1986 he also wrote an article for *Armed Forces Journal*, continuing the Pentagon reform conversation that the monthly magazine's owner, publisher and editor, Benjamin F. Schemmer, was then fostering. Cohen's article tied special operations reform to the findings of the Locher report and the CSIS study.[150] "Special Operations Forces, as indicated by the U.S. experience during the Grenada and Iran rescue missions, are one aspect of the defense establishment that is most assuredly broken and must be fixed," he wrote.

On May 15, 1986, Cohen introduced a special operations reform bill in the Senate, co-sponsored by Nunn. This bill, S. 2453, called for the special forces units then attached to different services to be brought together under a unified multi-service command for special operations. This command would have responsibility for coordinating planning of operations and conducting joint training of special forces units. It also called for the creation of an assistant secretary for special operations/low-intensity conflict and urged the president to establish a corresponding position within the White House national security staff. The bill was viewed as stalking horse that would prod the administration and the Pentagon to act on their own. Congressional micro-management of Pentagon affairs was contrary to the espoused spirit of the Goldwater-Nichols Act.[151]

A month after the introduction of what later came to be known as the Cohen-Nunn (or Nunn-Cohen) Act, a more radical companion bill was introduced on the House side by Daniel. The Daniel bill, H.R. 5109, mandated that the Defense Department create a whole new agency to deal with special operations.[152] The bill called for the creation of a National Special Operations Agency, headed by a civilian. Unusually, the civilian would be inserted into the chain of command between the defense secretary and the special forces assigned to the agency. The agency would have its own budget and be, in effect, a separate entity from the other uniformed services.

On Aug. 5, 1986, a pivotal hearing on the Senate bill was held before the Sea Power and Force Projection Subcommittee of the Senate Armed Services Committee. This hearing, chaired by Cohen, was called to hear testimony on a revised version of the bill that Cohen had introduced in May. Scholtes, the now-retired special operations commander during Urgent Fury, was the last of three witnesses to testify. In brief testimony in open session, Scholtes said he preferred Cohen's bill over Daniel's, but asked to withhold further comment for a closed session because it would draw on classified information.[153] By multiple accounts, the still-secret testimony that Scholtes offered next was so shocking that it radically altered the reform debate. Scholtes reportedly spoke largely on how special operations forces had been misused in Grenada. "Scholtes told the lawmakers how his forces were robbed of their unique capabilities by the conventional planners and chain of command. His forces had suffered relatively significant casualties in Grenada as a result of numerous fundamental misunderstandings of their tactics and capabilities," wrote William G. Boykin, a Delta Force veteran of the ill-fated Richmond Hill Prison attack, in a historical background paper.[154] Cohen was so moved by Scholtes' testimony that he called the retired general back to Capitol Hill the same day for a private meeting with other Senators who had not attended the hearing. That next day, Cohen introduced a new version of his original bill. The latest version made the bill's provisions binding legislation rather than "sense of the Senate" advice. He also converted the bill from stand-alone legislation into a harder-to-veto amendment to the 1987 Defense Authorization Bill.[155]

In introducing the amendment, Cohen recounted the special forces failures in Iran and Grenada. "I do not believe that this record is attributable to persistent bad luck or an inadequate caliber of men in the armed services," he declared. "In my view, we have not been effectively organized to fight the most likely battles of the present or the future."[156] A bipartisan group of 26 Senators joined him as sponsors of the amendment. Two former secretaries of the Navy, senators Warner and John Chafee (R–Rhode Island), spoke against the amendment, to no avail. The amendment was attached to the Senate version of the defense spending bill on a voice vote the same day. Days later, the more radical Daniel measure passed the House.

The two measures now went to conference committee where neither side was inclined to bend. Daniel called on his friend Wilson, a decorated Merrill's Marauders commando during World War II, to serve as a consultant to the conference negotiators. A compromise was fashioned that gave the House members the "checkbook" provision they demanded, but it organized the new special forces command along the lines the Senate bill advocated. The final bill established the U.S. Special Operations Command (USSOCOM) to be overseen by an assistant secretary of defense. Together the powers assigned to these two new entities were something more than any other unified combat command, but something less than a new uniformed service.[157] One commentator described USSOCOM as a "near-service" branch.[158] Neither the Pentagon establishment nor the White House were happy with this legislation. Reagan signed the defense spending bill into law on Nov. 14, 1986, but he declared in his signing statement that he was "extremely disappointed that Congress saw the need to legislate the reorganization of the Special Operations Forces, particularly mandating the creation of a unified command, which has heretofore been the exclusive prerogative of the President as Commander-in-Chief."[159]

The Cohen-Nunn measure got a similarly chilly reception from the Department of Defense. Bureaucratic infighting ensued over the staffing and funding of the SOF organization. Twice Congress felt compelled to pass bills to spur on implementation of key provisions. It took until the spring of 1988 for USSOCOM to be fully staffed and functioning as the bill sponsors envisioned.[160] The assistant secretary for special operations post was held by three caretakers during the Reagan administration until President George H.W. Bush took office in January 1989. Bush nominated Locher, the West Pointer who had been director of the Goldwater-Nichols staff study and principal drafter of the various versions of the Cohen-Nunn amendment, to be the first permanent occupant of that critical post. Over time, the enacting legislation came to be mostly known as the Cohen-Nunn Amendment, though some reversed the order of the names. The amendment is often misunderstood to have been a revision of the Goldwater-Nichols Defense Reorganization Act of 1986, but it was actually a rider, Section 1311, to the 1987 National Defense Authorization Act. Like Goldwater-Nichols, the Cohen-Nunn Amendment rewrote Title 10 of the U.S. Code, which preceded both measures.[161]

The first combat test of the military under Goldwater-Nichols and Cohen-Nunn came in 1989 in the invasion of Panama, code named Operation Just Cause. Like Grenada, Pentagon was planned as *coup de main* to be executed by a joint combat command, in this case U.S. Southern Command. Powell, the newly appointed chairman of the Joint Chiefs, appointed Gen. Maxwell Thurman to command a joint task force of 700 sailors, 900 marines and 3,400 airman. The mission was completed within two weeks against an enemy force of 12,000 at the cost of 26 Americans killed and 324 wounded. "If proportionally lower friendly casualties mark operational success, Just Cause was more successful than Urgent Fury," concluded a Pentagon historian who studied both campaigns. "It showed substantial improvement in joint planning and execution. Part of that stemmed from the Goldwater-Nichols Act, part from the time available and the forces already in place, and part from the close working relationship of top political and military leaders before and during the operation," wrote Ronald H. Cole, who was also the author of the official JSC history of Urgent Fury.[162]

A full-scale wartime operation test of the impact of Goldwater-Nichols and Cohen-Nunn on the military came in 1990–91 in the First Gulf War. Powell remained the chairman of the Joint Chiefs. Schwarzkopf had moved up to become the four-star commander-in-chief of Central Command. Both officers credited Goldwater-Nichols with a generous share of their military success. "Goldwater-Nichols established very, very clear lines of command authority and responsibilities for subordinate commander and that meant a much more effective fighting force," Schwarzkopf told Congress.[163] Powell gave a similarly upbeat assessment of the act's impact in a 1996 interview for a military journal. "Performance of the armed forces in joint operations has improved significantly and Goldwater-Nichols deserves a great deal of the credit," he declared.[164]

Like the American military, the government of Grenada was also transformed by Urgent Fury. The governor general was elevated from a figurehead to an autocrat, at least initially. Scoon unilaterally expelled Soviet Bloc diplomats, authorized arrests of the Coard clique, negotiated with foreign powers and restored portions of the former constitution—all without any significant legislative or judicial involvement. Scoon sought advice from the queen and the Commonwealth. He also worked closely with Gillespie, the now-resident American ambassador to Grenada, but not always in accord with him. "Grenada had to become a showcase ... then the problems began," Gillespie later recalled.[165]

Turning Grenada from a Caribbean basket case into a showcase was not a task to be accomplished quickly or cheaply. The Grenadian economy was essentially in cardiac arrest from the combined effects of the faltering economic policies of the previous regime, the chaos of the coup, the dawn-to-dusk curfew, the regional trade embargo and the effects of the war. The recovery began while American combat troops were still present. U.S. Army engineers repaired the island's electric generators and transmission lines and opened a sanitary landfill.[166] Other Army engineers repaired the Cuban-controlled rock crusher and asphalt plant and taught Grenadians how to operate them. The first civilian aid from America arrived as soon as the fighting stopped. The U.S. Agency for International Development (AID) began an airlift of $475,000 in emergency food, water and medical supplies.[167] Another $1.7 million was soon spent to further repair the island's water, electric and road infrastructure. In November, Congress provided another $15 million in economic development aid to prop up the national budget, revive commercial lending and commerce and put Grenadians back to work. In April 1984, Reagan asked Congress for an additional $40 million, two-year aid package for the island.[168] Nearly half of that money, ironically, was earmarked to finish the airport that the administration once perceived as a threat. The work began on a hurry-up schedule that allowed it to officially open to commercial passenger traffic on Oct. 28, 1984, though full completion of the $80 million project was still another year away.[169] The lavish spending on Grenada's recovery left some wondering if the aid money might have been better spent immediately after the Bishop-led coup of 1979, instead of after the Coard-led coup of 1983. "The whole thing with Bishop was completely mismanaged; we should have built the airport for them…. It was shortsighted," Metcalf, the invasion commander, later told two Reagan-era historians.[170]

Assessing the long-term impact of the intervention on Grenadian society is beyond the scope of this work. However, it is worth noting in passing that despite corruption scandals, devastating hurricanes and a lethargic economy, democracy has persevered on Grenada. Power has peacefully changed hands through a succession of prime ministers. Ironically, the quality of Grenada's democracy in 2019 was rated marginally superior to the United States', according to a rating system used by Freedom House, an independent American watchdog organization dedicated to the expansion of freedom and democracy. The organization rated the quality of American political rights and civil liberties to be 86 on a scale of 100 in an annual rating of 209 countries and territories. Grenada, by comparison, got a score of 89 from the organization; the United Kingdom rated 93 and Canada 99. (The group found the state of democracy in the United States to be mired in an eight-year slump, due to Russian interference in the U.S. elections, executive and legislative dysfunction and pressures on judicial independence and the rule of law, among other factors.)

The most intractable recovery problem that both Americans and Grenadians faced in the aftermath of the invasion was what to do with the Coard faction. This question came up briefly in pre-invasion conversations between OECS leaders and American diplomats. According to Bish, the American ambassador in Bridgetown, it was agreed that the Grenadians directly involved in the killings at Fort Rupert would be treated as criminals.[171] Rather than a Nuremberg-style show trial focused on human rights abuses, the consensus favored "bringing the criminals to justice in the normal way: arrest, trial and conviction according to the laws of the land," Bish reported to Washington. The coup leaders and full-time members of the PRA were systematically rounded up after the intervention by American soldiers for interrogation. The Coards, Austin and the top leaders of the RMC were initially held incommunicado on Navy ships or at Point Salines for up to 12 days before being turned over to the Caribbean peacekeeping force at Richmond Hill Prison.[172] Forty-eight detainees were held for an extended time at the ridgetop prison, including some Bishop supporters who were also caught up in the post-invasion dragnet. Eventually 20 prisoners were charged under Grenadian criminal law with the killings that occurred at Fort Rupert on Bloody Wednesday, Oct. 19, 1983. The charges were based in part on purported confessions made by 11 of the defendants under interrogation at the prison by police officers, mostly from Barbados. None of the prisoners were allowed to have lawyers present during their interrogation, but they were advised that they could not be compelled to give evidence against themselves.[173] The defendants subsequently claimed that their confessions were coerced by beatings or threats from their interrogators. Nonetheless, their statements were admitted into evidence against them at trial after a judicial review.

The 20 accused consisted of two groups. One group was made up of Coard's leadership cabal. Eleven defendants were either Central Committee members or top PRA officers who were allegedly present at Fort Frederick on Oct. 19 when the killings at Fort Rupert occurred. All 11 were accused of murder for having authorized the killings that occurred two miles away. The remaining group of nine was composed of officers and soldiers who were present at Fort Rupert on Oct. 19. They were accused in the death of three civilians in the bombardment of the operations center and/or the subsequent court-yard assassination of Bishop and seven others. The officers were charged with murder for giving the orders to fire; the enlisted men were charged with manslaughter for following the orders.

The preparation of these charges for trial was a fraught process that stretched over two years and involved many different proceedings before different judges. At the first proceeding, a preliminary inquiry in the summer of 1984, testimony was taken, and the defendants were represented by court-appointed Jamaican lawyers. At the end of this two-month proceeding, charges were dropped for lack of evidence against one the accused: Ian St. Bernard, a former police commissioner and a Central Committee member. The remaining 19 where arraigned in October before another judge where the murder charges against the Fort Frederick group was amended. Instead of one charge of murder of eight people in the courtyard, the Coard-led leadership group was accused of 11 different murder counts, each corresponding to a particular victim at Fort Rupert that day.

Following the arraignment, a motion was filed on behalf of the defendants challenging the legitimacy of the designated trial court to hear the case. The motion was denied by the judge hearing the case, and subsequently upheld by the Appeals Court composed of three other Grenadian judges.[174] Further delays ensued as the defendants retained lawyers to represent them at trial. The Coards hired their own legal team headed by Ian Ramsey, a Jamaican lawyer. Ramsey Clark, a former U.S. attorney general under the Kennedy administration, now in private practice, also later joined this defense team. The other 17 defendants pleaded indigence and the court appointed another Jamaican legal team to represent them. In August 1985 a motion was filed on behalf 17 defendants alleging mistreatment by their guards at Richmond Hill Prison. This resulted in a consent order being issued that stipulated the conditions of confinement for the prisoners and allowed them access to their lawyers. The pretrial proceedings now became entangled in a web of motions, denials and appeals. The continuing dispute over the legitimacy of the court ultimately resulted in all 12 defense lawyers announcing on April 11, 1986, that they were withdrawing from active participation in the trial.[175]

When the 19 accused appeared in court on April 15, 1986, to enter their final pleas to the charges, most gave no response. Coard read a lengthy statement that stretched on until the next day. At one point in the contentious proceeding, one of the defendants refused to take his seat. The judge ordered him removed and held in contempt. Most of the remaining defendants protested by chanting, clapping their hands and stamping their feet until they were also removed. This established a pattern that was followed sporadically in the ensuing seven-month trial. Defendants would collectively express their objection to that day's court proceeding. The judge would find them in contempt and order them temporarily removed. The excluded would later return to the courtroom and proceedings would resume until the next protest erupted.

Just before the first prosecution witness was called, one defendant was conditionally pardoned. Gabriel, a PRA warrant officer accused of manslaughter, was given his freedom in exchange for his agreement to testify for the prosecution. This reduced the number of defendants to 18. The trial dragged out over the course of eight months with numerous pauses and further motions over the legitimacy and fairness of the proceeding. The defendants opted not to call any witnesses in their defense or offer their own sworn testimony. Instead, some chose to make unsworn statements from the dock. These statements became part of the court record for the jury to consider, along with the contested statements the defendants gave verbally, or in writing, to police.

When the complex proceedings finally ended in December, it took the judge 11 days to give his summary and instructions to the jury. But it took the 12-person jury just three hours to reach their decision. The jurors returned unanimous guilty verdicts against 17 defendants. One Army lieutenant who was positioned outside the fort was acquitted. The Coards, eight Central Committee members, and four PRA officers were convicted of all the murder counts and sentenced to hang. Three soldiers who had participated in the firing squad were convicted of manslaughter and sentenced to 30 or more years in prison.

All the convicted returned to prison to await the outcome of appeals that dragged on for years. In 1991, all the death sentences were commuted to life. In 2000, Phyllis Coard was released to undergo treatment for colon cancer and two other life-threatening illnesses. In September 2001, Grenada created a special three-member commission to seek answers to unanswered questions about the 15-year revolutionary era. The panel was chaired by a former supreme court judge in Guyana and included an Anglican bishop and a Catholic priest. The group launched a slow-moving, fact-finding inquiry that finally produced a report in 2006 that added little new knowledge about the traumatic events of the study period. The report's principal contribution was to urge a retrial of the imprisoned and a renewed search for the burned remains of Bishop and his assassinated followers. Also in 2006, the Privy Council in London, now reestablished as Grenada's highest appeal court, ordered a review of the sentences of those who were still incarcerated. That review resulted in the release of three soldiers convicted of manslaughter for time served and a reduction in the life murder sentences for the others. In 2009, the last seven prisoners were set free after serving 26 years.

Coard gave an interview to a Jamaican newspaper after his release in which he denied giving the order to execute Bishop and the seven others, but admitted to many, unspecified errors. "We were amateurs, we were arrogant and intolerant and all our mistakes came home to roost," he declared.[176] Coard told his interviewer he had sworn off politics forever and planned to join his wife in Jamaica to start work on his memoirs. That writing project eventually produced five draft volumes covering his life and the political history of Grenada since 1951. The first of those volumes, *The Grenada Revolution: What Really Happened*, a first-person account of the rise and fall of the Grenadian revolution, was published in 2017 in Jamaica. A second volume, *Forward Ever: A Journey to a New Grenada*, a memoir of his government days, followed in 2018. The remaining three volumes, including one with Coard's account of the invasion and aftermath, are described as "forthcoming" for publication on an unspecified time frame.[177] As for the central question of his role in the death of Bishop and his followers, Coard remained equivocal. In a declaration titled "Responsibility for the Killings" at the end of his first-volume memoir, Coard wrote that "all of us in the political leadership" are "the principal culprits" in the killings that occured at Ft. Rupert on Oct. 19. "Because of my seniority in the Party, I blame myself most of all of those alive today. I should have seen where things were heading much earlier, should have taken vigorous steps to avert the crisis, and then, when it began, to end it speedily," he declared.

Chapter Notes

Chapter 1

1. Ronald H. Spector, *U.S. Marines in Grenada, 1983* (Washington, D.C.: History and Museums Division, Headquarters, U.S. Marine Corps, 1987), 1.

2. James P. Faulkner, Col. USMC (interview by Frank M. Benis, November 13, 1983, transcript, Oral History Section, History and Museums Division, USMC, Quantico, VA), 9.

3. Dean C. Kallander and James K. Matthews, "Urgent Fury: The United States Air Force and the Grenada Operation, January, 1988" (monograph, History Office, Air Mobility Command, Scott Air Force Base, IL, declassified 2010), ix.

4. Ronald H. Cole, "Operation Urgent Fury, The Planning and Execution of Joint Operations in Grenada, 12 October—2 November 1983" (monograph, Joint History Office, Office of the Chairman of the Joint Chiefs of Staff, Washington, D.C., 1997), 18. http://www.jcs.mil/Portals/36/Documents/History/Monographs/Urgent_Fury.pdf. Accessed July 15, 2018.

5. Spector, *Marines in Grenada, 1983,* 2.

6. Frank Uhlig, Jr., "Amphibious Aspects of the Grenada Episode," in Peter M. Dunn and Bruce W. Watson, eds., *American Intervention in Grenada: The Implications of Operation "Urgent Fury"* (Boulder, CO and London: Westview Press, 1985), 89.

7. Cole, "Operation Urgent Fury," 18.

8. Louis D.H. Frasché, Col. USA, "Grenada Lessons Learned" (briefing transcript, Grenada Work Group, Ft. Leavenworth, KS, Feb. 15, 1984), 5. Archived at U.S. Army Center of Military History Library, Washington, D.C.

9. Faulkner, interview, 2.

10. *Ibid.*

11. Bernard J. Dougherty, "Media Handling of Sensitive Military Information" (research project, The Industrial College of the Armed Forces, National Defense University, Fort McNair, Washington, D.C., 1992), 7.

12. Ray L. Smith, Lt. Col. USMC (handwritten journal of Grenada operations, undated, Oral History Section, History and Museums Division, USMC, Quantico, VA).

13. Richard Butler, Cmdr. USN (interview by Frank M. Benis, Nov. 4, 1983, tape recording, #10833A, Oral History Section, History and Museums Division, USMC, Quantico, VA).

14. James Adams, *Secret Armies: Inside the American, Soviet, and European Special Forces* (New York: Atlantic Monthly Press, 1988), 231.

15. Ray L. Smith, Lt. Col. USMC (interview by Frank M. Benis, Nov. 13, 1983, transcript, Oral History Section, History and Museums Division, USMC, Quantico, VA), 2.

16. "Operational Overview," *MCDEC Newsletter*, Education Center, Marine Corps Development and Education Command, Quantico, VA (Jan.–Mar. 1984), 2.

17. Faulkner, interview, 3.

18. National Security Decision Directives (NSDDs), 1/20/1981–1/20/1989. Numbered National Security Policy Papers, 1981–1989. National Archives Research Catalog, ARC #6879708t www.archives.gov. Accessed Dec. 19, 2017.

19. George P. Shultz, *Turmoil and Triumph: My Years as Secretary of State* (New York: Charles Scribner's Sons, 1993), 323.

20. Ronald Reagan, *The Reagan Diaries,* edited by Douglas Brinkley (New York: HarperCollins, 2009), 189.

21. Shultz, *Turmoil and Triumph, 341.*

22. *Ibid.,* 329.

23. Baker as quoted in Deborah H. Strober and Gerald S. Strober, *The Reagan Presidency: An Oral History of the Era* (Washington, D.C.: Brassey's, Inc., 2003), 91.

24. Shultz, *Turmoil and Triumph,* 329.

25. *Ibid.* Reagan's official White House daily diary essentially corroborates these back-to-back phone calls with a six-minute call to Bush at 5:58 a.m. followed by a seven-minute call to Weinberger at 6:08 a.m. Shultz, perhaps mistakenly, recalled the second call went to Vessey.

26. "Special Situation Group (SSG) Saturday October 22, 1983, Room 208. OEOB, 9 a.m.," top secret agenda, unclassified in CIA Reading Room. https://www.cia.gov/library/readingroom/document/cia-rdp85m00363r000200370034-7. Accessed July 8, 2018. This document lists Rear Adm. John Poindexter, the deputy NSC director, as the chairman of this top-level, multi-agency crisis response group. However, multiple other accounts say this session was conducted by the vice president.

27. Constantine Christopher Menges, *Inside the National Security Council: The True Story of the Making and Unmaking of Reagan's Foreign Policy* (New York: Simon and Schuster, 1988),73.

28. Ralph Kinney Bennett, "Anatomy of a 'Go' Decision," *The Reader's Digest*, Feb., 1984, 74–75. This detailed "inside account" of Grenada decision-making appears to come from one of the key policy participants and is generally corroborated by other official and memoir accounts.

29. *Ibid.*

30. Menges, *Inside the National Security Council*, 79.

31. Reagan, *Diaries*, 189.

32. "Britain's Grenada Shutout," *The Economist*, March 10, 1984, 22.

33. Kathleen Osbourne, personal assistant to President Reagan (interview by Stephen Knott, Apr. 26, 2003, transcript, University of Virginia—Miller Center, Presidential Oral Histories), 47. https://millercenter.org/the-presidency/presidential-oral-histories/kathleen-osborne-oral-history-personal-assistant-reagan. Accessed Dec. 19, 2017.

34. Fred Hiatt, "U.S. Says Situation Still Unclear as Naval Force Nears Grenada," *Washington Post*, Oct. 23, 1983.

35. Reagan, *Diaries*, 189.

36. John T. Carney and Benjamin F. Schemmer, *No Room for Error: The Covert Operations of America's Special Tactics Units from Iran to Afghanistan* (New York: Ballantine Books, 2002), 117. Also, Edgar F. Raines. Jr., *The Rucksack War: U.S. Army Operational Logistics in Grenada, 1983* (Washington, D.C.: Center of Military History, 2010), 89.

37. Cole, "Operation Urgent Fury," 23.

38. Caspar W. Weinberger, *Fighting for Peace: Seven Critical Years in the Pentagon* (New York: Warner Books, 1990), 111–12.

39. Jonathan M. House, *The United States Army in Joint Operations, 1950–1983.* 1992 (Washington, D.C.: U.S. Army Center of Military History, 1992), 174.

40. *Ibid.*, 180–1.

41. *Ibid.*, 172.

42. Raines, *The Rucksack War*, 100.

43. Patricia Sullivan, "Admiral led Grenada Invasion," *Washington Post*, Feb. 12, 2009.

44. House, *The Army in Joint Operations*, 175.

45. Robert Patterson, Brig. Gen. USAF (interview by Col. Robert Bruce Hinckley, Feb. 29, 1984, handwritten notes, U.S. Army Center of Military History, Washington, D.C.), 2.

46. Raines, *The Rucksack War*, 100–102, offers a detailed and authoritative account of this meeting.

47. Nathan S. Lowrey, *The Chairmanship of the Joint Chiefs of Staff 1949-201*, Office of the Chairman of the Joint Chiefs, Joint History Office, Washington, D.C., 2016, 154–55. http://www.jcs.mil/Portals/36/Documents/History/Institutional/Chairmanship_of_the_JCS.pdf. Accessed Aug. 6, 2018.

48. Richard Halloran, "A Commanding Voice for the Military," *New York Times*, July 15, 1984.

49. Kallander and Matthews, "Urgent Fury," 22.

50. Spector, *Marines in Grenada, 1983*, 3.

51. Faulkner, interview, 14–15.

52. Patrick E. Tyler, "The Making of an Invasion: Chronology of the Planning," *Washington Post*, Oct. 30, 1983.

53. Weinberger, *Fighting for Peace*, 113.

54. Lou Cannon, *President Reagan: The Role of a Lifetime* (New York: Simon & Schuster, 1991), 447.

55. Foreign Office (FCO) Sitrep, "ODEM: 1000, 24 October, 1983," confidential memorandum, Oct. 24, 1983, Margaret Thatcher Foundation Archives. https://www.margaretthatcher.org/archive.

56. Langhorne A. Motley (interview by Charles Stuart Kennedy, March 7, 1991, Manuscript/Mixed Material, Library of Congress, Washington, D.C.) https://www.loc.gov/item/mfdipbib000842. Accessed Jan. 1, 2018.

57. Duane R. Clarridge with Digby Diehl, *A Spy for All Seasons: My Life in the CIA* (New York: Scribner, 1997), 254.

58. Christopher M. Lehman, "We are going!: Reagan was right about Grenada," posted Oct. 27, 2013, philly.com. According to the White House daily diary, this meeting began at 3:57 p.m. and lasted for three hours.

59. Bennett, "Anatomy of a 'Go' Decision," 75–6.

60. John W. Vessey, Jr., General USA (ret.) (interview by Dr. Ronald H. Cole, March 25, 1987, transcript, archived at U.S. Army Center of Military History, Washington, D.C.), 4.

61. John W. Vessey, Jr., General USA (ret.) (letter to Brig. Gen, David A. Armstrong (ret.), Director for Joint History, Joint Chiefs of Staff, undated, archived at U.S. Army Center of Military History, Washington, D.C.).

62. Vessey, Cole interview, 2–3.

63. Raines, *The Rucksack War*, 106.

64. Richard L. Prillaman, Lt. Gen. USA (interview by Dr. Ronald H. Cole, Feb. 9, 1984, transcript, archived at U.S. Army Center of Military History, Washington, D.C.), 6.

65. Steven Strasser, "Reagan's Kind of Hero," *Newsweek*, Nov. 14, 1983.

66. Dale L. Thompson, "The U.S. Coast Guard in Grenada," *Proceedings Magazine*, Nov., 1984, 65.

67. Prillaman, interview, 5.

68. Raines, *The Rucksack War*, 107.

69. H. Norman Schwarzkopf and Peter Petre, *It Doesn't Take a Hero: General H. Norman Schwarzkopf, the Autobiography* (New York: Bantam Books, 1992), 244–5.

70. Roger Cohen and Claudio Gatti, *In the Eye of the Storm: The Life of General H. Norman Schwarzkopf* (Boston: G.K. Hall & Co., 1991), 156.

71. Joseph Metcalf, III, Vice Adm. USN (interview, unknown interviewer, Feb. 13, 1984, handwritten transcript, archived at U.S. Army Center of Military History, Washington, D.C.), 2.

72. Joseph Metcalf, III, "Decision Making and the Grenada Rescue Operation," in *Ambiguity and Command: Organizational Perspectives on Military Decision Making*, edited by James G. Marsh (Marshfield, Mass: Pitman Publishing, 2006), 282.

73. Prillaman, interview, 5.

74. Vessey, Cole interview, 14.

75. Matt Schudel, "Joseph Metcalf; Led Grenada Invasion," *Washington Post*, March 11, 2007, see also Dennis Hevesi, "Joseph Metcalf II Dies at 79; Led Invasion of Grenada," *New York Times*, March 13, 2007.

76. Adm. Mike Mullen, "VADM Joe Metcalf III Memorial Service Eulogy," March 8, 2007. https://www.navy.mil/navydata/cno/mullen/speeches/Metcalf_Eulogy.pdf. Accessed Jan. 18, 2019.

77. Samuel D. Ward, "The Operational Leadership of Vice Admiral Joseph P. Metcalf" (student paper, Naval War College, May 4, 2012), 17. http://www.dtic.mil/docs/citations/ADA564017. Accessed Feb. 1, 2018.

78. *Ibid.*

79. Metcalf, "Decision Making and the Grenada Rescue," 280.

80. Jack Dorsey, "Leader tells of planning invasion," *Virginia-Pilot and Ledger-Star*, Nov. 6, 1983.

81. Metcalf, "Decision Making and the Grenada Rescue," 278.

82. House, *Army in Joint Operations*, 179.

83. Cannon, *President Reagan: The Role of a Lifetime*, 448.

84. National Security Decision Directive 110A. National Security Decision Directives (NSDDs), 1/20/1981–

1/20/1989. Numbered National Security Policy Papers, 1981–1989. National Archives Research Catalog, ARC #6879709, at www.archives.gov. Accessed Dec. 19, 2017.

85. Spector, *Marines in Grenada, 1983*, 5.

86. Kallander and Matthews, "Urgent Fury," 28.

87. Forrest L. Marion, *Brothers in Berets: The Evolution of Air Force Special Tactics, 1953–2003* (Maxwell Air Force Base, AL: Air University Press, Curtis E. LeMay Center for Doctrine Development and Education, 2018), 163.

88. Carney and Schemmer, *No Room for Error*, 130–138. Marion's monograph attempted to resolve some of diverging details among the various accounts.

89. Walker as quoted in Orr Kelly, *Never Fight Fair: Navy SEALs' Stories of Combat and Adventure* (Novato, CA: Presidio Press, 1995), 284–86. Walker's account differs in some details from Carney's, including the number of SEALs (14 versus 16) who jumped from the C-130s. Marion argues that 12 is the most likely number.

90. Dennis C. Chalker and Kevin Dockery, *One Perfect Op* (New York: Morrow, 2002), 139.

91. Robert A. Gormly, *Combat Swimmer: Memoirs of a Navy SEAL* (New York: Penguin Group, 1998), 185.

92. *Ibid.*, 185 and 205. Carney and Schemmer, *No Room for Error*, 130–31 also cite the time zone difference as a key complicating factor, but both books mistakenly attribute the proximate cause to an overlooked autumn switch from daylight saving to standard time. In 1983, the "fall back" did not happen until Oct. 30 in the U.S., after the invasion had occurred. https://www.timeanddate.com/time/change/usa?year=1983. Accessed Jan. 24, 2019.

93. Carney and Schemmer, *No Room for Error*, 132.

94. Walker as quoted in Kelly, *Never Fight Fair*, 286.

95. Gormly, *Combat Swimmer*, 186.

96. The second attempt is described by Carney and Schemmer, *No Room for Error*, 137.

97. Task Force 120 to CINCLANT, Norfolk, Sitrep 08, Oct. 25, 1983, declassified, 2018, archived in "Atlantic Command, Operation Urgent Fury Records (COLL/73)," Box 15, Folder 2, Naval History and Heritage Command, Archives Branch, Washington, D.C. Declassified after formal request by author.

98. Metcalf, "Decision Making and the Grenada Rescue," 283.

99. Schwarzkopf, *Hero*, 246.

100. Raines, *Rucksack War*, 138–9.

101. Shultz, *Turmoil and Triumph*, 334.

102. Metcalf, "Decision Making and the Grenada Rescue," 296.

103. Schwarzkopf, *Hero*, 246–7.

104. Metcalf, "Decision Making and the Grenada Rescue," 284.

105. Edward L. Trobaugh, Maj. Gen. USA (interview by Major Charles R. Bishop, Nov. 30, 1983, transcript, archived at U.S. Army Center of Military History, Washington, D.C.), 8–9.

106. Schwarzkopf, *Hero*, 246.

107. Robert Patterson, Maj. Gen. USAF (interview by Dean C. Kallander, Sept. 12, 1984, transcript, archived at Air Mobility Command, Office of History, Scott Air Force Base, Ill.), 5.

108. Kallander and Matthews, "Urgent Fury," 29. See also Schwarzkopf, *Hero*, 248 and Shultz, *Turmoil and Triumph*, 334. According to Raines, *Rucksack War*, 140, the State Department representative also successfully argued for the raid on the Richmond Hill Prison as a last-minute JSOC target, over Scholtes's objection.

109. Trobaugh, interview, 8.

110. Patterson, Kallander interview, 5.

111. Kallander and Matthews, "Urgent Fury," 29.

112. Dawn (civil twilight) occurred at 0537 Grenada time on Oct. 25, followed by full sunrise at 0558. The sun is still 6 degrees below the horizon at dawn, but there is enough natural light for objects on the ground to be distinguished.

113. Patterson, Hinckley interview, 5. See also Carney and Schemmer, *No Room for Error*, 135.

114. Headquarters Air Combat Command, "History of the Tactical Air Command, 1 January—31 December, 1983," Vol. 1. Langley Air Force Base, VA, declassified, pages 269–281: 273.

115. Patterson, Kallander interview, 14–15.

116. H. Norman Schwarzkopf, Lt. Gen. USA (interview by Dr. Ronald Cole, Dec. 15, 1987, transcript, archived at U.S. Army Center of Military History, Washington, D.C.), 4–5. Also, Schwarzkopf, *Hero*, 248.

117. Kallander and Matthews, "Urgent Fury," 33.

118. Schwarzkopf, interview, Dec. 15, 1987,6.

119. Michael T. Kaufman, "50 Marines land at Barbados field," *New York Times*, Oct. 25, 1983.

120. Vessey, Cole interview, 7.

121. Kallander and Matthews, "Urgent Fury," xi.

122. Schwarzkopf, *Hero*, 249.

123. H. Norman Schwarzkopf, Maj. Gen. USA (interview by Major Charles R. Bishop, Nov. 21, 1983, transcript, archived at U.S. Army Center of Military History, Washington, D.C.), side (1–2), 3.

124. Donn-Erik Marshall, "Urgent Fury: The U.S. Military Intervention in Grenada," (master's thesis, University of Virginia, 1989), 94.

125. Schwarzkopf, *Hero*, 249.

126. Ed Magnuson, "D-Day in Grenada," *Time*, Nov. 7,1983, 28.

127. Weinberger, *Fighting for Peace*,118.

128. Robert C. McFarlane, National Security Advisor (Interview by Robert L. Pfaltzgraff, Jr., Nov. 10–11, 1988, transcript, Oral History Project, International Securities Studies Program, The Fletcher School of Law and Diplomacy, Tufts University, Medford, MA), 149.

129. Edwin Meese, *With Reagan: The inside Story* (Washington, D.C.: Regnery Gateway, 1992), 217.

130. Howard H. Baker, Jr., Senate Majority Leader (interview by Stephen Knott, Aug. 24, 2004, transcript, University of Virginia—Miller Center. Presidential Oral Histories), 12. https://millercenter.org/the-presidency/presidential-oral-histories/howard-h-baker-jr-oral-history-senate-majority-leader. Accessed Jan. 4, 2018.

131. Kenneth Adelman, Director, Arms Control and Disarmament Agency (interview by Stephen Knott, Sept. 30, 2003, transcript, University of Virginia—Miller Center, Presidential Oral Histories),50. https://millercenter.org/the-presidency/presidential-oral-histories/kenneth-adelman-oral-history-director-arms-control-and. Accessed Jan. 4, 2018.

132. Thomas P. O'Neill and William Novak, *Man of the House: The Life and Political Memoirs of Speaker Tip O'Neill with William Novak* (New York: Random House, 1987), 365.

133. James A. Baker III, chief of staff to President Reagan (interview by Jeff Chidester, Stephen F. Knott and James Sterling Young, June 15–16, 2004, transcript, University of Virginia—Miller Center, Presidential Oral Histories), 39. https://millercenter.org/the-presidency/presidential-oral-histories/james-baker-iii-oral-history-white-house-chief-staff. Accessed Dec. 9, 2018.

134. Christopher Matthews, *Tip and the Gipper: When Politics Worked* (New York: Simon and Schuster, 2013), 274.

135. Vessey, Cole interview, 15.

136. John W. Vessey, Jr., Gen. USA (interview by Prof. Robert L. Pfaltzgraff, Jr., June 14–15, 1986, transcript, International Securities Studies Program, The Fletcher School of Law and Diplomacy, Tufts University, Medford, MA), 43–44.

137. Cole, "Operation Urgent Fury," 33.

138. George T. Curtis, MSgt USMC (interview by Frank M. Benis, November 8, 1983, audio recording, #10736, Oral History Section, History and Museums Division, USMC, Quantico, VA).

139. Greg Walker, *At the Hurricane's Eye: U.S. Special Forces from Vietnam to Desert Storm* (New York: Ivy Books, 1994), 124–6.

140. Frank L. Brewer, Major USMC (interview by Frank M. Benis, November 10, 1983, audio recording. #10729, Oral History Section, History and Museums Division, USMC, Quantico, VA.)

141. Charles Dalgleish, *Recon Marine: An Account of Beirut and Grenada* (Self-published, 1995), 120–121.

142. Robert K. Dobson, Capt. USMC (interview by Frank M. Benis, November 8, 1983, transcript, Oral History Section, History and Museums Division, USMC, Quantico, VA), 4.

143. Spector, *Marines in Grenada, 1983*, 8.

144. Garret Ogle, Capt. USN (interview by Frank M. Benis, November 15, 1983, audio recording. Oral History Section, History and Museums Division, USMC, Quantico, VA).

145. "22nd MAU Preliminary After Action Report for Operation Urgent Fury," Jan. 15, 1984. Unclassified portions released to author by Marine Corps Headquarters, Manpower and Policy Division, under the Freedom of Information Act, July 1, 1988.

Chapter 2

1. Spector, *Marines in Grenada, 1983*, 7.

2. Granville R. Amos, Brig. Gen (ret) USMC (interview by Fred Allison, Apr. 8, 2009, audio recording, Oral History Section, History and Museums Division, USMC, Quantico, VA).

3. Melvin J. DeMars, Major USMC (interview by Frank M. Benis, Nov. 5, 1983, transcript, Oral History Section, History and Museums Division, USMC, Quantico, VA.), 6.

4. Smith, interview, 11.

5. "Operational Overview," *MCDEC Newsletter*, 8.

6. Smith, journal.

7. Spector, *Marines in Grenada, 1983*, 8.

8. Walker, *At the Hurricane's Eye*, 125–6.

9. Operational Overview," *MCDEC Newsletter*, 8.

10. Anthony Payne, Paul K. Sutton, and Tony Thorndike, *Grenada: Revolution and Invasion* (New York: St. Martin's Press, 1984), 31–32.

11. "Documents on the Invasion of Grenada," *Caribbean Monthly Bulletin*, October, 1983, Supplement no. 1 (statement by the Cuban party and Revolutionary Government on the Imperialist Intervention in Grenada), 46. http://iec-ics.uprrp.edu/wp-content/uploads/downloads/2013/12/Documents-on-the-Invasion-of-Grenada.pdf. Accessed Feb. 12, 2018.

12. Spector, *Marines in Grenada, 1983*, 9.

13. Raines, *Rucksack War*, 168.

14. "22nd MAU Operations Summary for Urgent Fury," Nov. 1, 1983.

15. Smith, interview, 19.

16. Wesley B. Taylor, Jr. Lt. Col USA (interview by Edgar F. Raines, Jr., Dec. 4, 1986, transcript, archived at U.S. Army Center of Military History, Washington, D.C.), 15.

17. Hall of Valor Project, *Military Times*, https://valor.militarytimes.com/hero/143982#182837. Accessed Feb. 20, 2019.

18. Sean Naylor, *Relentless Strike: The Secret History of Joint Special Operations Command* (New York: St. Martin's Press, 2015), 8.

19. Jim Roper, *Aardvarks and Rangers* (Baltimore, MD: PublishAmerica, 2004), 223.

20. Taylor, Raines interview, 13.

21. John Nix, Major USA (interview by Major Charles R. Bishop, Nov. 2, 1983, transcript, archived at U.S. Army Center of Military History, Washington, D.C.), 4–5.

22. Nix, interview, 5.

23. The 1:50,000 "Isle of Spice" tourism map was originally prepared in 1965 for the Grenada colonial government by the British Ordnance Survey's Directorate of Overseas Surveys. Edition 3, prepared in 1979, was the most recent available in 1983. Edition 6, issued in 1992, is still sold by Omni Resources, a map merchant in Burlington, NC.

24. Michael J. Couvillon, *Grenada Grinder: The Complete Story of AC-130H Spectre Gunships in Operation Urgent Fury* (Marietta, GA: Deeds Publishing, 2011), 77–8.

25. Nix, interview, 6–9.

26. *Ibid.*, 8.

27. *Ibid.*, 12.

28. Kallander and Matthews, "Urgent Fury," 38.

29. Kenneth Finlayson, "Task Force 160 in Operation Urgent Fury," *Veritas: Journal of Army Special Operations History*, vol. 2, no. 2, 2006: 37–8.

30. Couvillon, *Grenada Grinder*, 167–9.

31. *Ibid.*, 92.

32. Michael J. Couvillon, interview with author, Sept. 13, 1983. Couvillon, a retired Air Force major, was the command pilot for one of the three gunships initially assigned to Urgent Fury. He later wrote a historically valuable book about his experience that is separately cited above.

33. Nix, interview, 19–20.

34. Roper, *Aardvarks and Rangers*, 230.

35. James L. Hobson, "Operation Urgent Fury," *Air Commando Journal*, Spring, 2012: 29.

36. Henry Zeybal, "Gunships at Grenada," *National Defense*, February,1984, 53.

37. Wesley B. Taylor, Jr. Lt. Col. USA (interview by Major Charles R. Bishop, Nov. 2, 1983, transcript, archived at U.S. Army Center of Military History, Washington, D.C.), 19.

38. John D. Lock, *To Fight with Intrepidity...: The Complete History of the U.S. Army Rangers, 1622 to Present* (New York: Pocket Books, 1998) 457.

39. Roper, *Aardvarks and Rangers*, 233.

40. Mark Adkin, *Urgent Fury: The Battle for Grenada* (Lexington, MA: Lexington Books, 1989), 202.

41. Couvillon, interview with author.

42. Kallander and Matthews, "Urgent Fury," 40.

43. Couvillon, *Grenada Grinder*, 65.

44. Ralph Hagler, Lt. Col USA (interview by Major Charles R. Bishop, Oct. 30, 1983, transcript, archived at U.S. Army Center of Military History, Washington, D.C.), 6.

45. Kallander and Matthews, "Urgent Fury," 40.

46. Gordon C. Bonham, Maj. USA. *Airfield Seizure; The Modern 'Key to Country'* (monograph, School of Advanced Military Studies, Fort Leavenworth, KS, First Term, AY 90–91), 24. http://www.dtic.mil/dtic/tr/full text/u2/a233189.pdf. Accessed Nov. 1, 2017.

47. Taylor, Bishop interview, 9.

48. Kallander and Matthews, "Urgent Fury," 40–41.

49. John P. Abizaid, Capt. USA (interview by Col. Wesley Clark, Dec. 15, 1983, handwritten notes, archived at U.S. Army Center of Military History, Washington, D.C.),2.

50. Hobson, "Operation Urgent Fury," 29.

51. Roper, *Aardvarks and Rangers,* 235–6.

52. Hobson, "Operation Urgent Fury," 29.

53. Raines, *The Rucksack War,* 245.

54. Kallander and Matthews, "Urgent Fury," 43.

55. *Ibid.*

56. Metcalf, "Decision Making and the Grenada Rescue," 286.

57. Raines, *The Rucksack War,* 170.

58. Lee Russell and M. Albert Mendez, *Grenada 1983* (London: Osprey, 1985),10.

59. "Fidel Castro on the Events in Grenada" in Maurice Bishop, *Maurice Bishop Speaks: The Grenada Revolution and Its Overthrow, 1979–83,* edited by Bruce Marcus and Michael Taber (New York: Pathfinder Press, 1983), Appendix III, 329. A somewhat different English translation of this speech is archived at the Latin American Network Information Center. http://lanic.utexas.edu/project/castro/db/1983/19831114.html. Accessed Feb. 12, 2019.

60. CIA, "Grenada: A First Look at Mechanisms of Control and Foreign Involvement Aug. 20, 1984," 15. https://www.cia.gov/library/readingroom/docs/DOC_0001313328.pdf. Accessed Dec. 23, 2017. Despite its title, this "first look" assessment was actually a reappraisal of an all-agency report initially dated Dec. 19, 1983. It is more accurately described as a second look based on a more thorough review of captured Grenadian documents than the earlier document.

61. "Fidel Castro on the Events in Grenada," in *Maurice Bishop Speaks,* Appendix III, 333.

62. Jose G. Ventura, Capt. USA (interview by Major Charles R. Bishop, Oct. 30, 1983, handwritten notes, archived at U.S. Army Center of Military History, Washington, D.C.), 4.

Chapter 3

1. U.S. Library of Congress, Federal Research Division, *A History of the 160th Special Operations Aviation Regiment (Airborne),* declassified 2010, 6–7, archived at governmentattic.org. http://www.governmentattic.org/2docs/Army_160thSOAR_Histories_1991-2001.pdf. Accessed May 6, 2018.

2. Ray D. Leoni, *Black Hawk: The Story of a World Class Helicopter* (Reston, VA: American Institute of Aeronautics, 2007), 42–3, 114.

3. Finlayson, "Task Force 160 in Operation Urgent Fury," 37.

4. *A History of the 160th,* 7.

5. Finlayson, "Task Force 160 in Operation Urgent Fury," 38.

6. Patterson, Kallander interview, 6.

7. Finlayson, "Task Force 160 in Operation Urgent Fury," 38.

8. *Ibid.* and Kallander and Matthews, "Urgent Fury," 49.

9. Michael J. Durant and Steven Hartov, with Robert L. Johnson, *The Night Stalkers: Top Secret Missions of the U.S. Army's Special Operations Aviation Regiment* (New York: G.P. Putnam's Sons, 2006), 14.

10. Gormly, *Combat Swimmer,* 190.

11. Multiple published accounts incorrectly state that this mission was assigned to two Black Hawks.

12. Donald K. "Kim" Erskine, interview with author, May, 2003. The story of the assault on the radio station is also told in detail in two books by Dick Couch, a former SEAL and friend of Erskine: Dick Couch and William Doyle, *Navy SEALs: Their Untold Story* (New York: William Morrow, 2014), 121–137 and Dick Couch, *The Warrior Elite: The Forging of Seal Class 228* (New York: Crown Publishers, 2001), 23–11. The 2014 account misspells Erskine without the final e and the 2001 account identifies Erskine by a *nom de guerre,* Lt. Jason Kendall. Other versions are offered in Orr Kelly, *Brave Men... Dark Waters: The Untold Story of the Navy SEALS* (Novato, CA: Presidio Press, 1992), 208–210 and Howard E. Wasdin and Stephen Templin. *SEAL Team Six: Memoirs of an Elite Navy SEAL Sniper* (New York: St. Martin's Press, 2011, 103–5. This telling is informed by these four previously published sources and was independently reviewed for accuracy in 2018 by an enlisted member of Erskine's team.

13. Kallander and Matthews, "Urgent Fury," xii and Adkin, *Urgent Fury,* 174–75.

14. The names of six Grenadians killed at Beausejour on or around Oct. 25, 1983 are contained in a Memorial List posted in The Grenada Revolution Online. https://www.thegrenadarevolutiononline.com/index.html. Accessed July 8, 2018. The number of wounded prisoners of war (10) was mentioned in Erskine's subsequent Silver Star citation. See note below.

15. Adkin, *Urgent Fury,* 181.

16. After the invasion, Prime was one of 18 Grenadians put on trial for the deaths of Bishop and his supporters that occurred at Ft. Rupert on Oct. 19, 1983. Prime and 13 others were convicted of murder in 1986 and sentenced to hang. He spent 21 years in prison before his release in 2007.

17. Adkin, *Urgent Fury,* 181.

18. Record Group 24, Entry P 118-H, Navy Deck Logs, 1979–83, Box 78, USS *Caron,* October 1983, National Archives II, College Park, MD.

19. Task Force 120 to CINCLANT, Norfolk, Sitrep 37, Oct. 26, 1983, declassified, 2018, archived in "Atlantic Command, Operation Urgent Fury Records (COLL/73)," Box 15, Folder 2, Naval History and Heritage Command, Archives Branch, Washington, D.C. Declassified after formal request by author.

20. Hall of Valor Project, *Military Times.* https://valor.militarytimes.com/hero/55561. Accessed Sept. 27, 2018.

21. "Analysis of the Lind Report by the Joint Chiefs of Staff," in Adkin, *Urgent Fury,* Appendix A, 349.

22. *A History of the 160th,* 9.

23. William G. Boykin, *Never Surrender: A Soldier's Journey to the Crossroads of Faith and Freedom* (New York: FaithWords, 2008), 163.

24. Michael Duffy, "Grenada: Rampant Confusion," *Military Logistics Forum* July-Aug. 1985, 23.

25. Fred Pushies, *Night Stalkers: 160th Special Operations Aviation Regiment (Airborne)* (St. Paul, MN: Zenith Press, 2005), 37.

26. Adkin, *Urgent Fury,* 189. Accounts conflict on the exact Chalk number assigned to each helicopter.

27. Finlayson, "Task Force 160 in Operation Urgent Fury," 38.

28. Couvillon, *Grenada Grinder*, Table 1, 44. This table lists two ZU-23s (23 mm) and 2 DShKM-4s (12.7 mm) at Fort Frederick. It also shows 6 AAA guns allotted for Cuban defenses at Point Salines that were never deployed according to Adkin, *Urgent Fury*, 163 (Map 8) and 165–66.

29. John Burgess, "Recruits Describe Disintegration of People's Revolutionary Army," *Washington Post*, Nov. 6, 1983.

30. Durant and Hartov, *The Night Stalkers*, 22. See also Finlayson, "Task Force 160 in Operation Urgent Fury," 38.

31. Carney and Schemmer, *No Room for Error*, 141.

32. Eric L. Haney, *Inside Delta Force: The Story of America's Elite Counterterrorist Unit* (New York: Dell, 2003), 374.

33. The crash was captured on videotape by Joe Gaylord, an American expatriate who owned a home across Prickly Bay near Point Salines. Gaylord filmed 90-minutes of combat footage on the first day of the invasion. Edited portions of his video were later broadcast on CBS and NBC news programs. The Lucas helicopter crashed on the grounds of the Calabash Hotel. In 2003 the mast of the helicopter was made into a memorial to Lucas by the Garbutt family, the hotel's current owners.

34. Boykin, *Never Surrender: A Soldier's Journey to the Crossroads of Faith and Freedom*, 162–67.

35. Finlayson, "Task Force 160 in Operation Urgent Fury," 39.

36. Michael C. Potter, "Destroyers Deliver 'Urgent Fury,'" *Proceedings Magazine*, October, 1995, 97.

37. Adkin, *Urgent Fury*, 178 and 189.

38. *Neil C. Livingstone, The Cult of Counterterrorism: The "Weird World" of Spooks, Counterterrorists, Adventures, and the Non-Quite Professionals* (Lexington, Mass: Lexington Books, 1990), 330.

39. Adkin, *Urgent Fury*, 190 and Couvillon, *Grenada Grinder*, 118.

40. George Galdorisi and Tom Phillips, *Leave No Man Behind: The Saga of Combat Search and Rescue* (Minneapolis, MN: Zenith Press, 2008), 474–76.

41. *Ibid.*, 475.

42. Harvey G. Fielding, interview with author, March 25, 2018.

43. Duffy, "Rampant Confusion," 23.

44. Haney, *Inside Delta Force*, 381.

45. Hall of Valor Project, *Military Times*. https://valor.militarytimes.com/hero/34778 and https://valor.militarytimes.com/hero/301467. Accessed Sept. 27, 2018.

46. Gary Ward, "Fury on Grenada," *VFW Magazine*, November/December, 2013. http://digitaledition.qwinc.com/article/Fury+On+Grenada/1525454/0/article.html. Accessed June 11, 2018.

Chapter 4

1. Paul Scoon, *Survival for Service: My Experiences as Governor General of Grenada* (Oxford, England: Macmillan Caribbean, 2003), 68–9. Scoon died Sept. 2, 2013. This memoir is the principal primary source for Scoon's actions and state of mind prior to, during and immediately after the invasion.

2. Phil Davidson, "Sir Paul Scoon: The Queen's Governor-General during the American invasion of Grenada," *The Independent*, Sept. 10, 2013. https://www.independent.co.uk/news/obituaries/sir-paul-scoon-the-queens-governor-general-during-the-american-invasion-of-grenada-8805612.html. Accessed Oct. 10, 2018.

3. Eric Pace, "In Eye of the Grenada Storm," *New York Times*, Oct. 27, 1983.

4. Meesha Robinson, "Tribute to the Late Sir Paul Scoon," *Caribbean Today*, undated. http://caribbeantoday.com/other/lifestyle/viewpoint/item/17169-tribute-to-the-late-sir-paul-scoon.html. Accessed Sep. 29, 2018.

5. Scoon, *Survival for Service*, 67.

6. As quoted by American Bar Association Committee on Grenada, "International Law and the United States Action in Grenada: A Report," *The International Lawyer*, vol. 18, no. 2 (Spring 1984): 347. http://www.jstor.org/stable/40705519. Accessed Aug. 27, 2017.

7. Geoffrey Howe, foreign secretary, "Grenada," restricted telegram #291 to UK High Commissioner, Bridgetown, Oct. 22, 1983. Margaret Thatcher Foundation Archives.

8. Clarridge, *A Spy for All Seasons*, 250.

9. David Montgomery, Deputy High Commissioner, "Grenada: General Impressions," confidential telegram #344 to UK Foreign Office, Oct. 23, 1983. Margaret Thatcher Foundation Archives.

10. Clarridge, *A Spy for All Seasons*, 256.

11. David Montgomery, Deputy High Commissioner, "Grenada: Governor General," secret telegram #342 to UK Foreign Office, Oct. 23, 1983. Margaret Thatcher Foundation Archives.

12. Scoon, *Survival for Service*, 135.

13. *Ibid.*, 134.

14. Clarridge, *A Spy for All Seasons*, 256.

15. UK Parliament, House of Commons. Second Report from the Foreign Affairs Committee, Session 1983–4, "Grenada," March 15, 1984, Her Majesty's Stationary Office, London (statement by Jim Lester, a House member, on Feb. 1, 1984), 9.

16. Clarridge, *A Spy for All Seasons*, 256.

17. Scoon, *Survival for Service*, 137.

18. *Ibid.*

19. Clarridge, *A Spy for All Seasons*, 256.

20. Gormly, *Combat Swimmer*, 190. This remote transmission capability could have made Scoon's planned transit to the captured Beausejour radio site unnecessary.

21. Lawrence G. Rossin, State Department (interview, March 29, 1985, unknown interviewer, handwritten notes, U.S. Army Center of Military History, Washington, D.C.).

22. This account of the abortive landing is drawn from Gormly, *Combat Swimmer*, 191–95; Durant and Hartov, *Night Stalkers*, 22–26; and Lawrence R. Rossin, "Under Fire in Grenada," in *Duty & Danger; The American Foreign Service in Action*, American Foreign Service Association, 1988, 2. http://www.afsa.org/sites/default/files/Portals/0/dutydanger.pdf

23. Schwarzkopf, *Hero*, 250.

24. Finlayson, "Task Force 160 in Operation Urgent Fury," 40.

25. Kallander and Matthews, "Urgent Fury," 34 and Durant and Hartov, *The Night Stalkers*, 14.

26. Author's WIA total based on 18 Delta operators, 11 Task Force 160 airmen and 3 Navy SEALs, as further explained.

27. "Table 2—Casualties in Operation Urgent Fury," in Raines, *Rucksack War*, 532.

28. Durant and Hartov, *The Night Stalkers*, 26.

29. U.S. Total Army Personnel Agency (Provisional), "List of 108 Army battle-wounded in Grenada," Feb. 12, 1988. FOIA response to author.

30. Naval Military Personnel Command, "Listing of Personnel Wounded in Grenada." March 29, 1988. FOIA response to author.

31. Raines, *Rucksack War*, 532.

32. "25h Anniversary of Urgent Fury," BlackFive.net, blog post, Oct. 24, 2008. https://www.blackfive.net/main/2008/10/25th-anniversar.html. Accessed Jan. 23, 2019. An earlier published report attributed to another Delta officer, put the number of Delta Squadron B wounded at the prison at 17 of its 44 Delta operators. See Huchthausen, *America's Splendid Little Wars*, 82.

33. Charlie A. Beckwith and Donald Knox, *Delta Force: The Army's Elite Counterterrorist Unit* (New York: Avon Books, 2000), 129 and 334.

34. Haney, *Inside Delta Force*, 109–12.

35. See Adkin, *Urgent Fury*, 189; Livingstone, *The Cult of Counterterrorism*, 329 and Huchthausen, *America's Splendid Little Wars*, 85.

36. Other Urgent Fury historians have also noted the scrubbing of special forces casualties from the official lists. See Marshall, "Urgent Fury," 116. Marshall put the number of unreported wounded at 23. "There may be a reason for keeping the number of wounded a secret, but one would hope that the reason is important enough to deny civilians an understanding of the effectiveness of their Special Operations Forces," he wrote.

Chapter 5

1. Sgt. Bruce McGraw, interview by Joe Muccia, transcript, *Magic Kingdom Dispatch*, website blog, Dec. 15, 2015. McGraw, the second Ranger to jump onto Grenada, was a member of the 1st platoon of Bravo Company, 1st Battalion. Muccia is a Marine veteran and an Urgent Fury historian. This website was created by Stephen Trujillo, a decorated Ranger medic, who has self- published his own Urgent Fury memoir, *A Tale of the Grenada Raiders: Memories in the Idioms of Dreams*. https://www.magickingdomdispatch.com/2015_12_13_archive.html. Accessed Jan. 11, 2019.

2. "The Truth About Cuba's Role," an Oct. 25 statement by the government and Communist Party, in *Maurice Bishop Speaks*, Appendix II, 318.

3. Alma Guillermoprietro, "Havana Seeks to Turn Loss in Grenada Into a Moral Victory," *Washington Post*, Oct. 30, 1983.

4. Adkin, *Urgent Fury*, 228. According to Adkin, a Barbadian Army staff officer and an early Urgent Fury historian: "[I]t was not until the Rangers had dropped, collected themselves, and started firing that the battle was joined by the construction workers."

5. For deployment of PRA soldiers at Point Salines and elsewhere on D-Day see Adkin, *Urgent Fury*, 206, 207, 209, 217 and 228.

6. Roper, *Aardvarks and Rangers*, 238.

7. *Ibid.*, 240.

8. McGraw, Muccia interview.

9. Roper, *Aardvarks and Rangers*, 238.

10. Couvillon, *Grenada Grinder*, 122–23.

11. *Ibid.*, 67–8.

12. Henry Zeybal, "Gunships at Grenada," *National Defense*, February, 1984, 55.

13. Taylor as quoted by the author in "Grenada: Five Years Later Evidence of Snafus Grows," *Providence Sunday Journal*, Oct. 23, 1988.

14. Couvillon, *Grenada Grinder,* 42–44.

15. Clarridge, *A Spy for All Seasons*, 251–52.

16. Kallander and Matthews, "Urgent Fury," 45.

17. Cohen, *In the Eye of the Storm*, 163.

18. Roper, *Aardvarks and Rangers*, 243.

19. Adkin, *Urgent Fury*, 163 and 165.

20. Bruce R. Pirnie, "Operation Urgent Fury: The United States Army in Joint Operations" (monograph, U.S. Army Center of Military History, Washington, D.C., 1986, unclassified 1993, archived at the U.S. Army Heritage and Education Center, Carlisle, PA), 101. I believe this 247-page, typed manuscript is the only public library copy of this valuable historical document.

21. Nix, interview, 21–33.

22. Kallander and Matthews, "Urgent Fury," 45.

23. Don Hirst, "An Alert that Became All Too Real," *Army Times*, Nov. 14, 1983.

24. Betty Darby, "Ranger Endures Jump Mishap," *Savannah Morning News*, Nov. 3, 1983.

25. Taylor, Bishop interview, 41–2.

26. Darby, "Ranger Endures Jump Mishap."

27. Hagler, interview, 8.

28. Taylor, Bishop interview, 20.

29. McGraw, Muccia interview.

30. Jose G. Ventura, Capt. USA (interview by Major Charles R. Bishop, Nov. 1, 1983, handwritten notes, U.S. Army Center of Military History, Washington, D.C.), 2–3.

31. Nix, interview, 37.

32. Hagler, interview, 7.

33. Russell, *Grenada 1983*, 17.

34. Pirnie, "Operation Urgent Fury," 216.

35. Finlayson, "Task Force 160 in Operation Urgent Fury," 37.

36. Haney, *Inside Delta Force*, 380.

37. "A look back: TacAir in Grenada," *Naval Aviation News*, Nov-Dec. 1985, 6 and also Scott Minerbrook, "Grenada Invasion's Down Side," *Newsday*, Aug. 13, 1984.

38. Richard A. Gabriel, *Military Incompetence: Why the American Military Doesn't Win* (New York: Hill and Wang, 1985), 180.

39. "DIA During Operation Urgent Fury (Grenada)," DIA Office of Corporate Communications, Washington, D.C., Oct. 29, 2014. In this news release, occasioned by the 31st anniversary of the invasion, the DIA acknowledged two "significant intelligence gaps" during Urgent Fury: failure to identify the exact locations of the Grenadian Army's command and control center and the medical students.

40. William H. Acebes, 1st Sgt., USA (interview, Nov. 2, 1983, unknown interviewer, tape recording, U.S. Army Center of Military History, Washington, D.C.). Acebes was the top-ranking NCO of Charlie Company, 1st Battalion, the Ranger unit that was detached to support Delta Force on D-Day.

41. Timothy Ashby, "Grenada: Soviet Stepping Stone," *Proceedings Magazine*, December, 1983, 30.

42. "1-75 Rangers in Grenada" (working paper, Army Studies Group, archived at U.S. Army Center of Military History, undated, Washington, D.C.). See also Adkin, *Urgent Fury*, Appendix A, "Analysis of the Lind Report by the Joint Chief of Staff," 352.

43. "Fidel Castro on the Events in Grenada," in *Maurice Bishop Speaks*, Appendix III, 334.

44. McGraw, interview.

45. Ventura, interview, 3–4.

46. See Russell, *Grenada 1983*, 44–5 for a description of the typical clothing and equipment of Cuban and Grenadian combatants.

47. Kallander and Matthews, "Urgent Fury," 108.

48. Pirnie, "Operation Urgent Fury," 107.

49. Adkin, *Urgent Fury*, 217.

50. Brian C. Ivers, interview with author, Jan. 2, 2019.

51. *Ibid.*

52. Raines, *Rucksack War*, 251,.

53. Blair Donaldson, interview with author, Feb. 2, 2019.

54. Shawn Klimek, "Ranger actions rewarded," *Ranger*, Fort Lewis, Washington, Nov. 10, 1983.

55. Pirnie, "Operation Urgent Fury," 106.

56. Couvillon, *Grenada Grinder*, 118.

57. Brian C. Ivers, "Reunion brings back memories of invasion of Grenada," *Quad Cities Times*, Nov. 5, 2008. This was a letter to the editor of Ivers' hometown Iowa newspaper which was, instead, published as a personal column.

58. Pirnie, "Operation Urgent Fury," 107.

59. Abizaid, interview, 4.

60. "17 Army Rangers Decorated for Heroism During Invasion," *Savannah Morning News*, Dec. 3, 1983.

61. Abizaid went from Grenada to a distinguished 34-year Army career, rising to four-star general and command of Central Command in the Middle East in 2003. He retired from the Army in 2007 and in 2018 was appointed the U.S. Ambassador to Saudi Arabia.

62. Ivers, interview.

63. Sydney J. Freedberg, "Abizaid of Arabia," *The Atlantic*, December, 2003.

64. Pirnie, "Operation Urgent Fury," 118.

65. Spector, *Marines in Grenada, 1983*, 10.

66. *Ibid.*

67. Pirnie, "Operation Urgent Fury," 110 and Ivers, interview. Ivers was positioned about 500 yards from the jeep ambush when it occurred.

68. Joe Muccia, "Juliet-5," Facebook posting, Nov. 18, 2015 in *Bearing the Burden: Operation Urgent Fury from the Warrior's Perspective*, Book Page.

69. Pirnie, "Operation Urgent Fury," 108.

70. "1-75 Rangers in Grenada," 10.

71. Raines, *The Rucksack War*, 252.

72. Pirnie, "Operation Urgent Fury," 118–9.

73. *Ibid.*, 119.

74. "17 Army Rangers Decorated for Heroism During Invasion," *Savannah Morning News*.

75. Neil C. Lewis, Major, Jamaica Defense Force, "Combined Operations: A Commonwealth Caribbean Perspective" (master's thesis, U.S. Army Command and Staff College, 1988), 74–75. http://www.dtic.mil/dtic/tr/fulltext/u2/a198124.pdf. Accessed July 15, 2018.

76. #10 Duty Clerk to Prime Minister, "Situation in Grenada as at 1730 hours," memorandum, Oct 22, 1983, Margaret Thatcher Foundation Archives.

77. Lewis, "Combined Operations: A Commonwealth Caribbean Perspective," 68.

78. Hugh O'Shaughnessy, *Grenada: Revolution, Invasion and Aftermath* (London: Sphere Books, 1984), 9.

79. Schwarzkopf, interview, Dec. 15, 1987, 7–8.

80. Tom Scott Capt., USN, "Urgent Fury-Lessons Learned" (briefing, Summer Joint Project Review, Ft. Monroe, VA, Aug. 23, 1988), 4. Archived in "Atlantic Command, Operation Urgent Fury Records (COLL/73)," Box 18, Folder 4, Archives Branch, Naval History and Heritage Command, Washington, D.C.

81. Mark Whitaker, "The Battle for Grenada," *Newsweek*, Nov. 7, 1983, 66.

82. Kallander and Matthews, "Urgent Fury," 46.

83. *Ibid.*

84. Ed Magnuson, "D-Day in Grenada," *Time*, Nov. 7, 1983, 24.

85. Taylor as quoted by author in "Grenada: Five Years Later."

86. Kallander and Matthews, "Urgent Fury," 18.

87. Tony Nelson, DIA analyst (interview, Dec. 9, 1985, handwritten notes, unknown interviewer, U.S. Army Center of Military History, Washington, D.C.), 1.

88. *Ibid.*, 3.

Chapter 6

1. Gormly, *Combat Swimmer*, 196.

2. Scoon, *Survival for Service*, 138.

3. Scoon as quoted in Strober and Strober, *The Reagan Presidency*, 281.

4. Scoon, *Survival for Service*, 139.

5. Dennis Chalker with Kevin Dockery, *One Perfect Op* (New York: Morrow, 2002), 163. Chalker was an enlisted member of the SEAL mansion team.

6. The Memorial List posted on The Grenada Revolution Online includes the name of one Grenadian private, Keith "Rasta" Noel, who was killed outside the mansion on Oct. 25. Noel's body was not discovered until years later and then was buried on the grounds of the residence.

7. Gormly, *Combat Swimmer*, 195.

8. *Ibid.*, 197.

9. John J. Fialka, "In Battle for Grenada, Commando Missions Didn't Go as Planned," *Wall Street Journal*, Nov. 15, 1983, and Gormly, *Combat Swimmer*, 198.

10. Adkin, *Urgent Fury*, 184.

11. Gormly, *Combat Swimmer*, 197.

12. Couvillon, *Grenada Grinder*, 74–81.

13. *Ibid.*, 82.

14. Chalker, *One Perfect Op*, 169.

15. Marshall, "Urgent Fury," 114 and Raines, *Rucksack War*, 247. Calling cards were in widespread use in the mid-1980s. These wallet-size cards were issued to consumers by long distance service providers, like ATT, embossed with unique number codes. They allowed the possessor to make direct, reduced-rate, toll calls from any touch-tone phone that would be charged to the card holder's account.

16. Scoon, *Survival for Service*, 139.

17. Bobby McNabb, an enlisted SEAL, as quoted in Kelly, *Never Fight Fair*, 293. McNabb was another member of the mansion assault team.

18. Couvillon, *Grenada Grinder*, 121.

19. Metcalf, "Decision Making and the Grenada Rescue," 288.

20. Metcalf as quoted by author in "Grenada: Five Years Later."

21. Metcalf, "Decision Making and the Grenada Rescue," 281.

22. Metcalf as quoted in Strober and Strober, *The Reagan Presidency*, 276.

23. Tim Howard, Capt. USMC (interview by Benis M. Frank, Dec. 6, 1983, tape recording, #10741A, Oral History Section, History and Museums Division, USMC, Quantico, VA).

24. This narrative account of the Marine Cobras at Fort Frederick is primarily drawn from Phil Kukielski, "The Final Flight of Lt. Scharver," *Providence Journal Sunday Magazine*, Feb. 17, 1985 and Fred H. Alison,

"Operation Urgent Fury: Grenada, 1983," *Fortitude*, vol. 37, no. 3, 2012: 26–29.

25. Kallander and Matthews, *Urgent Fury*, xiii.

26. DeMars, transcript,8.

27. Kallander and Matthews, *Urgent Fury*, xiii.

28. Russell, *Grenada, 1983*, 20.

29. Borch, *Judge Advocates in Combat*, 71–2.

30. Hall of Valor Project, *Military Times*. https:// valor.militarytimes.com/hero/4094. Accessed Oct. 1, 2018.

31. Schwarzkopf, *Hero*, 250.

32. Kallander and Matthews, "Urgent Fury," xiii.

33. Borch, *Judge Advocates in Combat*, 71.

34. U.S. Congress, House, Committee on Armed Services, *Lessons Learned as a Result of the U.S. Military Operations in Grenada*, 98th Congress, 2nd Session, Jan. 24, 1984 (statement of Fred C. Iklé, Under Secretary for Policy, Department of Defense), 2.

35. Schwarzkopf, interview, Dec. 15, 1987, 11.

36. Metcalf, "Decision Making and the Grenada Rescue," 288.

37. Schwarzkopf, interview, Dec. 15, 1987, 9.

38. Metcalf later credited Schwarzkopf with the idea, but Schwarzkopf was not sure the credit was due. The idea may have originated with Scholtes, the JSOC commander. See Gormly, *Combat Swimmer*, 198.

39. Butler, interview.

40. Charles Dalgleish, *Recon Marine: An Account of Beirut and Grenada* (Charles Dalgleish, 1995), 125.

41. Smith, interview, 22.

42. Smith, journal.

43. Couvillon, *Grenada Grinder*, 64.

44. Butler, interview.

45. H. Norman Schwarzkopf, interview, Nov. 21, 1983 (side 1–2), 30 and (side 3–4), 4–6.

46. Thomas A. Bruno, Major USA (interview, Mar. 7, 1984, unknown interviewer, typewritten notes, U.S. Army Center of Military History, Washington, D.C.). Bruno was the 82nd Airborne liaison officer on Metcalf's Guam staff.

47. Schwarzkopf, interview, Nov. 21, 1983 (side 1–2), 3.

48. Metcalf, "Decision Making and the Grenada Rescue," 292.

49. Smith, interview, 29.

50. Task Force 120 to CINCLANT, Norfolk, Sitrep 32, Oct. 25, 1983, declassified, 2018, archived in "Atlantic Command, Operation Urgent Fury Records (COLL/ 73)," Box 15, Folder 2, Naval History and Heritage Command, Archives Branch, Washington, D.C. Declassified after formal request by the author.

51. Dobson, transcript,7–8.

52. Spector, *Marines in Grenada, 1983*, 14.

53. Dobson, interview,9.

54. Butler, interview.

55. Couvillon, *Grenada Grinder*, 131.

56. Scoon, *Survival for Service*, 141.

57. Smith, interview, 27.

58. Schwarzkopf, interview, Dec. 15, 1987, 4.

59. Commander in Chief, U.S. Atlantic Command, "Operation Urgent Fury Report, October 25-November 2, 1983," Feb. 6, 1984, Enclosure 2, Chronology, 3, redacted.

60. Arthur Smith, "When Medical Support Falls Short," *Proceedings Magazine*, Nov., 2001, 71.

61. Smith, interview, 29–32.

62. Dobson, interview, 12–13.

63. Chalker, *One Perfect Op*, 159.

64. *Ibid.*, 172.

65. Schwarzkopf, interview, Dec. 15, 1987, 15.

66. Scoon, *Survival for Service*, 145, also Alan George, "Did Washington ghost-write Scoon's appeal?" *New Statesman*, Nov. 11, 1983.

67. For text of Scoon's letter to Barbados, see John Norton Moore, *Law and the Grenada Mission* (Charlottesville, VA: Center for Law and National Security, University of Virginia School of Law, 1984), Appendix 1, 87; Adkin, *Urgent Fury*, Appendix D, 365 and William C. Gilmore, *The Grenada Intervention: Analysis and Documentation* (New York: Facts on File, 1984), Appendix 7, 95.

68. Rossin, interview, 2.

69. Scoon, *Survival for Service*, 145–48.

70. Rossin, interview, 3.

71. Scoon, *Survival for Service*, 149.

72. *Ibid.*, 153.

73. Metcalf as quoted by author in "Grenada: Five Years Later."

74. Charles V. Jones, *Boys of '67: From Vietnam to Iraq, the Extraordinary Story of a Few Good Men* (Mechanicsburg, PA: Stackpole Books, 2006), 225–27.

75. Dobson, interview, 16.

76. Smith, interview, 48.

77. CIA, "Grenada: A First Look," 15.

78. Dobson, interview, 17–18.

79. Schwarzkopf, interview, Nov. 21, 1983 (side 1–2), 22–23 and 32.

80. Eric Schmitt, "Tough but Politic Chief," *New York Times*, Jan. 28, 1991.

Chapter 7

1. Schwarzkopf, interview, Nov. 21, 1983 (side 1–2), 21–2.

2. Schwarzkopf, *Hero*, 254.

3. *Ibid.*

4. Jones, *Boys of '67*, 232.

5. Brewer, interview.

6. Amos, interview.

7. Hagler, interview, 18–19. Hagler knew James Griffee as "Mr. James."

8. "MASH Units at True Blue Our Finest Hour," *St. George's University School of Medicine Newsletter*, Vol. 6, No. 1, 1984–85.

9. "Army Cites Griffee for Student Rescue," *St. George's University School of Medicine Newsletter*, Vol. 8, No. 1, 1987–88.

10. Pirnie, "Operation Urgent Fury," 141.

11. "Under Fire, Ham Radio Operators Describe the Invasion," *New York Times*, Oct. 26, 1983.

12. "Back in the Day—Oct. 30, 1983: Pompton Lakes resident rescued during Grenada invasion," NorthJersey.com, posted Oct. 19, 2013, and *Newsweek*, Nov. 7, 1983, 69 and 72.

13. Couvillon, *Grenada Grinder*,99.

14. Robert L. Jordan, interview with author, Nov. 12, 2017.

15. Couvillon, *Grenada Grinder*, 96–99.

16. Butler, interview.

17. Joe Muccia, "The 26-Minute Rescue," *Tactical MilSim Magazine*, November, 2009. http://tacticalmilsim.com/issues/TacSim-11-2009.pdf. Accessed Feb. 14, 2018.

18. *Ibid.*, and Hagler, interview, 25–6.

19. Curtis, interview, tape recording #10736A.

20. DeMars, interview, 26.

21. Hagler, interview, 28.

22. Stephen Silvasy, Col. USA (briefing, Ft. Leavenworth, KS, Dec. 8, 1983, transcript, U.S. Army Center of Military History, Washington, D.C.), 30.

23. Jordan, interview. See also Marios Loukas, Sanjay Linganna and Robert Jordan, "St. George's University: An Anatomist's Experiences During Grenada's Revolution and Intervention," *Clinical Anatomy*, no. 20 (2007): 350–56. https://www.researchgate.net/publication/6689245_St_George's_University_An_anatomist's_experiences_during_Grenada's_revolution_and_intervention. Accessed Feb. 11, 2019.

24. Hagler, interview, 51–2.

25. Hall of Valor Project, *Military Times*. https://valor.militarytimes.com/hero/34741#76178. Accessed Oct. 1, 2018.

26. Mir Bahmanyar, *Shadow Warriors: A History of the U.S. Army Rangers* (New York: Osprey Publishing, 2005), 113.

27. Phil Gailey, "Administration Puts Tough Restrictions on News of Grenada," *New York Times*, Oct. 27, 1983.

28. News Conference by Secretary of Defense, Caspar W. Weinberger, General John W. Vessey, Jr., chairman, Joint Chiefs of Staff at the Pentagon, Wednesday, October 26, 1983—4:30 p.m., transcript, 8.

29. Adkin, *Urgent Fury*, 269.

30. Couvillon, *Grenada Grinder*, 132.

31. Kallender and Matthews, "Urgent Fury," xiv.

32. Charles Anthony Gillespie (interview with Charles Stuart Kennedy, Sept. 19, 1995, Manuscript/Mixed Material, Library of Congress), 497–8. https://www.loc.gov/item/mfdipbib000420/. Accessed Jan.14, 2018.

33. As quoted by author in "Grenada: Five Years Later."

34. Ward Sinclair, "Student Evacuees Return, Praising U.S. Rescue Effort," *Washington Post*, Oct. 27, 1983.

35. Schwarzkopf, *Hero*, 255.

36. Ward, "The Operational Leadership of Vice Admiral Joseph P. Metcalf," 3.

Chapter 8

1. Trobaugh, interview, 10.

2. Stephen Silvasy, Col. USA (post-briefing interview, Ft. Leavenworth, KS, Dec. 8, 1983, transcript, U.S. Army Center of Military History, Washington, D.C.),22.

3. *Ibid.*, 22.

4. Kallander and Matthews, "Urgent Fury," xiii.

5. Trobaugh, interview, 16–17.

6. Patrick O'Kelley, *Triple Canopy* (West Conshohocken, PA: Infinity Publishing, 2014), 30.

7. Raines, *Rucksack War*, 264.

8. *Ibid.*, 259.

9. Louis D.H. Fraché, Col. USA (Grenada Lessons Learned, briefing, Ft. Leavenworth, KS, transcript, Feb. 14, 1984, U.S. Army Center of Military History, Washington, D.C.), 40.

10. Pirnie, "Operation Urgent Fury," 125.

11. Silvasy, briefing, 13.

12. John Ventour, "October 1983: The Missing Link," in *The Grenada Truth and Reconciliation Commission Report on Certain Political Events Which Occurred in Grenada 1976–1991*, vol. 2 (St. George's, Grenada: Government Printery, 2006), Appendix 14: 29–30.

13. McEwan's name appears on a memorial to 13 Grenadian soldiers killed in the invasion who are buried in St. George's Cemetery. He also appears on Memorial List posted on the Grenadian Revolution Online. McEwan's name is misspelled as "McSween or McQueen" but his rank and combat role are correctly stated on the second list.

14. Jose E. G. Gordon, interview with author, June 7, 2019. See also his rgrgordo (Ranger Gordo) posts on Dec. 24, 25 and 28, 2003, to "New Grenada Raider Thread," SOCNET.com. http://www.socnet.com/showthread.php?t=44102. Accessed Jan. 5, 2019. http://www.socnet.com/showthread.php?t=44102. Accessed Jan. 5, 2019.

15. Pirnie, "Operation Urgent Fury," 123. For details of the fight see Joe Muccia, "The BTR Counterattack," Facebook posting, March 10, 2016 in *Bearing the Burden: Operation Urgent Fury from the Warrior's Perspective*, Book Page.

16. Silvasy, post-briefing interview, 48.

17. "New Grenada Raider Thread," SOCNET.com.

18. *Ibid.*, Dec. 28.

19. Trobaugh, interview, 56.

20. *Ibid.*, 18.

21. Adkin, Urgent Fury, 229.

22. This narrative of the patrol is primarily drawn from Silvasy, briefing, 24–25, and Silvasy, interview, 11–13. Some additional details, including names, come from Pirnie, "Operation Urgent Fury," 134–5 and Raines, *Rucksack War*, 339.

23. The relief effort is described in Raines, *Rucksack War*, 339 and 341.

24. Michael J. Maraccini, Capt., "Task Force 2/325 Operation Urgent Fury" (study, Fort Benning, GA, 1988), 8. http://www.benning.army.mil/library/content/Virtual/Donovanpapers/other/STUP5/MaracciniMichael%20J.%20CPT.pdf. Accessed Jan. 6, 2018.

25. Adkin, Urgent Fury, 262.

26. Silvasy, briefing, 27.

27. Raines, *Rucksack War*, 342.

28. Susan Leonard, "Not Just a Drill," *Arizona Republic*, Nov. 6, 1983. 341.

29. Mark E. Rocke, Capt. USA (interview by Major Charles R. Bishop, Nov. 10, 1983, transcript, U.S. Army Center of Military History, Washington, D.C.), 33–39.

30. Pirnie, "Operation Urgent Fury," 221 and Raines, *Rucksack War*, 242.

31. U.S. Library of Congress, Congressional Research Service, *Grenada: Issues Concerning the Use of U.S. Forces*, by Richard Cronin, IB83170, updated Dec. 13, 1983, 3.

32. Rocke, interview, 40–42.

33. Maraccini, "Task Force 2/325 Operation Urgent Fury," 9.

34. Raines, *Rucksack War*, 343.

35. O'Shaughnessy, *Grenada: Revolution, Invasion and Aftermath*, 93.

36. Smith, interview, 43–45.

37. *Ibid.*, 47.

38. "Fidel Castro on the Events in Grenada," in *Maurice Bishop Speaks*, Appendix III, 327–8.

39. Spector, *Marines in Grenada, 1983*, 21.

40. Smith, interview, 52.

41. Spector, *Marines in Grenada, 1983*, 21.

42. Smith, interview, 54.

43. Fraché, "Grenada Lessons" briefing, 36.

44. Taylor, Raines interview, 42–43.

45. Atlantic Command, "Operation Urgent Fury Report," II-12.

46. Schwarzkopf, interview, Dec. 15, 1987, 18.

47. Cole, "Operation Urgent Fury," 53 and Schwarzkopf, *Hero*, 256.

48. Hagler, interview, 58.

49. Raines, *Rucksack War,* 437.

50. Matthew G. Easley, Major USA, "Survivability on the Island of Spice: The Development of the UH-60 Blackhawk and It's Baptism of Fire in Operation Urgent Fury" (master's thesis, Army Command and General Staff College, Fort Leavenworth, KS, 2015), 43. http://www.dtic.mil/docs/citations/ADA623282. Accessed July 15, 2018.

51. Rick Atkinson, *The Long Gray Line* (Boston: Houghton Mifflin, 1989), 488.

52. *Ibid.,* 47.

53. Potter, "Destroyers Deliver 'Urgent Fury,'" 99.

54. Butler, interview.

55. Couvillon, *Grenada Grinder,* 125.

56. Wayne P. Sinibaldi, CW2 USA (interview by unidentified interviewer, Dec. 14, 1983, transcript, archived with Army Center of Military History, Washington, D.C.), 7–8.

57. Raines, Rucksack War, 439–40.

58. William C. Sears Jr., letter to Mariann Lannon, sister of Kevin Lannon, Aug. 30, 2009. Sears died in 2014.

59. Atkinson, *Long Grey Line,* 489.

60. Robert N. Seigle, Lt. Col. USA (interview, Dec. 14, 1983, unknown interviewer, transcript, U.S. Army Center of Military History, Washington, D.C.), 33. Seigle was commander of the 82nd Aviation Battalion.

61. Stephen Trujillo, *A Tale of the Grenada Raiders: Memories in the Idioms of Dreams* (Stephen Trujillo, 2017), 273–195.

62. Hall of Valor Project, *Military Times.* https://valor.militarytimes.com/recipient.php?recipientid=23974. Accessed Jan. 10, 2018.

63. Schwarzkopf, *Hero,* 256.

64. Pirnie, "Operation Urgent Fury," 158.

65. Cole, "Operation Urgent Fury," fn 76.

66. Maj. Bruce R. Pirnie (memorandum, "Interview with Major General H. Norman Schwarzkopf," Nov. 1, 1985, Army Center of Military History, Washington, D.C.).

67. Schwarzkopf, interview, Dec. 15, 1987, 20.

68. Raines, *Rucksack War,* 433.

69. George A. Crocker, Lt. Col. USA, "Grenada Remembered, A Narrative Essay on Operation Urgent Fury" (essay, March 31, 1987, Army War College, Carlisle, PA), 14.

70. Scott A. Snook, interview with author, Sept. 14, 2017.

71. Raines, *Rucksack War,* 433–34.

72. Maj. Scott R. McMichael, "Urgent Fury: Looking Back and Looking Forward," *Field Artillery Journal,* March-April, 1985, Vol. 52, No. 2: 10.

73. "All Come Tumbling Down, Urgent Fury Part III," Hardcoreharry's Blog, posted May 22, 2010. https://hardcoreharry.wordpress.com/2010/05/22/all-come-tumblin-down-urgent-fury-part-iii/. Accessed Mar. 3, 2018.

74. Pirnie, "Operation Urgent Fury," 150 and Adkin, *Urgent Fury,* 286.

75. Scott A. Snook, *Friendly Fire: The Accidental Shootdown of U.S. Black Hawks Over Northern Iraq* (Princeton: Princeton University Press, 2002), 140.

76. Adkin, *Urgent Fury,* 286.

77. Scott Minerbrook, "Victim of Friendly Fire Dies," *Newsday,* July 2, 1984.

78. "Grenada Casualties," Memorandum for Record, Office of the Secretary of the Army, Oct. 22, 1984.

79. "History of the Tactical Air Command, 1 January—31 December, 1983," 279.

80. Atkinson, *Long Grey Line,* 488.

81. "Victim of Friendly Fire Dies," *Newsday.*

82. Silvasy, briefing, 34.

83. U.S. Congress, House, Committee on Armed Services, *Lessons Learned in Grenada (*statement of Maj. Gen. Edward Trobaugh, Commanding General, 82nd Airborne Division, U.S. Army), 23, also Crocker, "Grenada Remembered," 16.

84. Crocker, "Grenada Remembered," 17.

85. Pirnie, "Operation Urgent Fury," 224.

86. Raines, *Rucksack War,* 428 and Trobaugh, interview, 56–7.

87. Russell, *Grenada 1983,* 41.

88. Raines, *Rucksack War,* 342–4 and Roche, interview, 60, and Silvasy, briefing, 45.

89. Raines, *Rucksack War,* 216, 433.

90. *Ibid.,* 365.

91. Silvasy, briefing, 33,.

92. Loren Jenkins, "Search and Destroy Patrols Under Way," *Washington Post,* Oct. 30, 1983.

93. Pirnie, "Operation Urgent Fury," 166–7.

94. Phyllis Coard, *U.S. War on One Woman: My Conditions of Imprisonment in Grenada* (London: Karia Press, 1988), 17–18.

Chapter 9

1. Joseph Metcalf III, Vice Adm. USN (ret.), "The Mother of the Mother," *Proceedings Magazine,* August, 1991, 56–58.

2. Menges, *Inside the National Security Council,* 68–74.

3. Ronald Reagan, *An American Life (*New York: Simon and Schuster, 1990), 451.

4. Vessey, Cole interview, 6.

5. *Ibid.,* 10.

6. Metcalf, "The Mother of the Mother," 56.

7. James A. Baker to William J. Casey, confidential letter, Nov. 1, 1983, unclassified in CIA FOIA Reading Room. https://www.cia.gov/library/readingroom/docs/CIA-RDP88B00443R000903770018-0.pdf. Accessed May 15, 2018.

8. Larry Speakes and Robert Pack, *Speaking Out: The Reagan Presidency from Inside the White House* (New York: Charles Scribner's Sons, 1988), 150–53.

9. Mark Hertsgaard, *On Bended Knee: The Press & the Reagan Presidency* (New York: Schocken Books, 1989), 212–13.

10. Speakes and Pack, *Speaking Out,* 153.

11. O'Shaughnessy, *Revolution, Invasion and Aftermath,* 199–204. The following account is also informed by the published dispatches of the other journalists and the author's July 31, 2019, interview with one of the seven, Morris Thompson, then a reporter for *Newsday.*

12. Bernard Diedrich, "War News: Under New Management," *Worldview,* July, 1984, Vol., 27, no. 7: 7–8. Archived at Carnegie Council, Worldview Magazine Archive, 1958–85. https://worldview.carnegiecouncil.org/archive/worldview. Accessed May 5, 2018.

13. Kallander and Matthews, "Urgent Fury," 111–12. Also, Herbert A. Friedman, "United States Psyop in Grenada," Psywarrior.com, posted June 6, 2005. http://www.psywarrior.com/GrenadaHerb.html. Accessed Jan. 13, 2018.

14. Bernard Diederich, "Images from an Unlikely War," *Time*, Nov. 7, 1983, 30.

15. Edward Cody, "The Day War Roared into St. George's Picture-Book Harbor," *Washington Post*, Oct. 28, 1983.

16. Don Bohning, "Lots of Story but No Way to File It," *Washington Post*, Oct. 28, 1983 from Knight-Ridder News Service. I found this story, and others cited in this chapter, in *Current News*, Special Edition, "The Press in Grenada," Dec. 8, 1983, a publication of the Department of Defense, archived in the National Security Archive's unpublished Grenada collection, Box 2, George Washington University, Washington, D.C.

17. Cody, "The Day War Roared into St. George's Picture-Book Harbor," *Washington Post*.

18. H. Norman Schwarzkopf, Lt. Gen. USA (roundtable discussion with Grenada Working Group, Fort Leavenworth, KS, Nov. 10, 1983, transcript, archived in U.S. Army Center of Military History, Washington, D.C.), 48.

19. Metcalf, "Mother of the Mother," 57.

20. Don Bohning, "Newsman disputes Pentagon's view of Grenada action," *Atlanta Journal*, Oct. 28, 1983, from Knight-Ridder News Service.

21. Metcalf, "Mother of the Mother," 56–57.

22. Metcalf with Greg and Alex Daniel, "Strong Fences Make Good Neighbors: An Interview with Vice Admiral Joseph Metcalf, III, *Harvard International Review*, Vol. 6, No. 5 (March 1984): 32.

23. Schwarzkopf, *Hero*, 257. See also Potter, "Destroyers Deliver 'Urgent Fury,'" 99.

24. Kernan Turner, "Admiral Fights 2 Battles: With Grenada and Press," *Washington Post*, Oct. 31, 1983.

25. Diedrich, "War News," 8.

26. Bohning, "Newsman disputes Pentagon's view."

27. O'Shaughnessy, *Revolution, Invasion and Aftermath*, 202.

28. Metcalf, "Mother of the Mother," 57.

29. Donald R. Jillisky, Maj. USMC (interview by Frank M. Benis, no date, tape recording, #10742A, Oral History Section, History and Museums Division, USMC, Quantico, VA).

30. O'Shaughnessy, *Revolution, Invasion and Aftermath*, 203.

31. Otto Friedrich, "Anybody Want to Go to Grenada," *Time*, Nov. 14, 1983, 70.

32. O'Shaughnessy, *Revolution, Invasion and Aftermath*, 203. It is unclear if this was the same jet-reporter confrontation that Schwarzkopf described in differing detail in his memoir.

33. Butler, interview.

34. Potter, "Destroyers Deliver 'Urgent Fury,'" 99.

35. Wally McNamee, "A Pocket Calculator for Grenada," Newsweek Memories, Newsweememories.org. Posted 2012. http://www.newsweekmemories.org/mcnamee.html. Accessed Jan. 13, 2018.

36. Linda R. Prout. "Let's Clean This Up," *Newsweek*, Nov. 7. 1983, 71.

37. Cole, "Operation Urgent Fury," 56.

38. Metcalf, "Mother of the Mother," 57.

39. Jaqueline E. Sharkey, *Under Fire: U.S. Military Restrictions on the Media from Grenada to the Persian Gulf* (Washington, D.C.: Center for Public Integrity, 1991), 78.

40. Stuart Taylor, Jr., "In Wake of Invasion, Much Official Misinformation by U.S. Comes to Light," *New York Times*, Nov. 6, 1983.

41. Kallander and Matthews, "Urgent Fury," 154.

42. Turner, "Admiral Fights 2 Battles."

43. Schwarzkopf, *Hero*, 257–8.

44. Metcalf, "Mother of the Mother," 58.

45. Army Regulation 600-8-22, Military Awards, Headquarters, Department of the Army, June 25, 2015. https://history.army.mil/html/forcestruc/docs/r600_8_22.pdf. Accessed Aug. 10, 2108.

46. Awards and Decorations Statistics by Conflict, The Adjutant General Directorate, U.S. Army Human Resources Command, Oct. 11, 2018. https://www.hrc.army.mil/TAGD/Awards%20and%20Decorations%20Statistics%20by%20Conflict. Accessed Dec. 11, 2018.

47. Jeffrey Record, "More Medals Than We Had Soldiers," *Washington Post*, April 15, 1984.

Chapter 10

1. Menges, *Inside the National Security Council*, 75.

2. *Ibid.*

3. Kallander and Matthews, "Urgent Fury," 32.

4. *Ibid.*, 101.

5. *Ibid.*, 98.

6. *Ibid.*, 101.

7. Vessey, Cole interview, 1.

8. Gillespie, interview, 478.

9. Noriega as quoted in Strober and Strober, *The Reagan Presidency*, 275.

10. Ron Hinckley to Richard S. Beal, "U.S.–Cuban Communications During Grenada," Nov. 14, 1983, unclassified memorandum. From the Digital National Security Archive. Accessed June 28, 2018. Hinckley was a National Security Council staffer; Beal was Senior Director of Crisis Management Support and Planning and Special Assistant to the President.

11. Pirnie, "Operation Urgent Fury," 216 and "The Truth About Cuba's Role," in Bishop, *Bishop Speaks*, Appendix II, 322. Cuban time was one hour behind Grenada and the Daylight Savings Time on the East Coast.

12. "The Truth About Cuba's Role," in *Maurice Bishop Speaks*, Appendix II, 323 and Alan Berger, "Grenada according to Castro," *Boston Globe*, Nov. 30, 1983.

13. John Quigley, "*Parachutes at Dawn: Issues of Use of Force and Status of Internees in the United States-Cuban Hostilities on Grenada, 1983*," vol. 17, #2, *U. Miami Inter-Am Law Review* (1986): 219. https://repository.law.miami.edu/umialr/vol17/iss2/2/. Accessed Jan. 15, 2018.

14. Loren Jenkins, "Search and Destroy Patrols Under Way," *Washington Post*, Oct. 30, 1983.

15. White House to Air Force Two, top secret chronological file, 5 p.m. to 9 p.m., Oct. 25, 1983, declassified, archived in U.S. Declassified Documents Online. Accessed July 16, 2018.

16. "Preliminary Assessment of Cuban and Soviet Involvement in Grenada," Director of Central Intelligence, Interagency Intelligence Assessment, Oct. 30, 1983, secret memorandum, unclassified, 5 in CIA FOIA Reading Room. https://www.cia.gov/library/readingroom/document/cia-rdp85m00364r001502590002-1. Accessed May 14, 2018. See also Marshall, "Urgent Fury," 139.

17. Philip Taubman, "Senators Suggest Administration Exaggerated Its Cuba Assessment," *New York Times*, Oct. 30, 1983.

18. DCI, "Preliminary Assessment of Cuban and Soviet Involvement," 2. This interagency assessment, requested by McFarlane, was the coordinated work of CIA, the DIA, the National Security Agency and the State Department.

19. Cole, "Operation Urgent Fury," 58.

20. *Washington Post*, Oct. 30, 1983.

21. Richard Halloran, "U.S. Won't Dispute Havana on Tally," *New York Times*, Oct. 31, 1983. See also "This Was the Cuban Personnel in Grenada," *The Black Scholar*, Vol. 15, No. 1, Jan.-Feb. 1984: 40.

22. Donigan, Henry J., Capt. USMC (interview by Frank M. Benis, Nov. 6, 1983, tape recording, #10765A, Oral History Section, History and Museums Division, USMC, Quantico, VA).

23. See Adkin, *Urgent Fury*, 300 and endnote, 372.

24. Smith, interview, 56 and 67.

25. *Ibid.*, 65–8.

26. Vessey, Cole interview, 10.

27. Pirnie, "Operation Urgent Fury," 166.

28. Uhlig, "Amphibious Aspects of the Grenada Episode," 95.

29. Smith, interview. 72–3.

30. Donigan, taped interview, #108847A.

31. Glenn Scott, HM2 USN (interview by Frank M. Benis, Nov. 6, 1983, tape recording, #10765A, Oral History Section, History and Museums Division, USMC, Quantico, VA.)

32. Raines, *Rucksack War*, 475.

33. Smith, journal.

34. Smith, interview, 78.

35. *Ibid.*, 76–80.

36. Raines, *Rucksack War*, 476.

37. *Ibid.*, 286 and 355–7.

38. Raines, *Rucksack War,* 357.

39. John F. O'Shaughnessy, "Interrogation: Grenada," *Military Intelligence*, Jan-March, 1985, 14–17.

40. Borch, *Judge Advocates in Combat*, 65–66.

41. "The Legal Basis for United States Military Action in Grenada," *The Army Lawyer*, Department of the Army Pamphlet 27–50-147, April, 1985: fn 2. (These figures are attributed to Trobaugh.)

42. Scott, Urgent Fury briefing, 27.

43. "MPs Process Detainees," *Military Police Journal*, Vol. 11, No. 1, Spring, 1984: 37.

44. Borch, *Judge Advocates in Combat*, 66–7.

45. Larry Carney and Jim Rice, "114 Women Soldiers on Grenada," *Army Times*, Nov. 28, 1983.

46. Vessey, Cole interview, 11.

47. Schwarzkopf, interview, Nov. 10, 1983, 36.

48. Steven W. Senkovich, "From Port Salines to Panama City: *The Evolution of Command and Control in Contingency Operations.* School of Advanced Military Studies," United States Army Command and General Staff College*, Second Term, 1988–89, 16–17. https://apps.dtic.mil/dtic/tr/fulltext/u2/a234002.pdf. Accessed Nov. 25, 2018.

49. Gillespie, interview, 469.

50. *Ibid.*, 471.

51. Scoon, *Survival for Service*, 158–60.

52. "Chronology of Soviet Statements and Actions in Grenada, 7 September, 1979 to 27 October, 1983," Central Intelligence Agency, secret memorandum, Oct. 30, 1983, unclassified in CIA FOIA Reading Room https://www.cia.gov/library/readingroom/docs/CIA-RDP85M00364R001502590010-2.pdf. Accessed May 14, 2018.

53. Scoon, *Survival for Service*, 75.

54. Charles Mohr, "U.S. Denies Charges," *New York Times*, Oct. 29, 1983.

55. Gillespie, interview, 473 and 489.

56. For a text of the message see Shultz to U.S. Embassy Moscow, "Message from Soviet Ambassador on Grenada," secret telegram, Nov. 2, 1983, declassified, archived in U.S. Declassified Documents Online. Accessed July 17, 2018.

57. Gillespie, interview, 473.

58. *Time*, Nov. 14, 1983, 22.

59. Raines, *Rucksack War*, 480 and 483. The distance from the embassy to the harbor at St. George's makes this theory unlikely, among other factors.

60. O'Kelley, *Triple Canopy,* 72.

61. Stephen Trujillo, *A Tale of the Grenada Raiders: Memories in the Idioms of Dreams* (Stephen Trujillo, 2017), 205.

62. This report is contradicted by Sazhenev's Nov. 2 message to Moscow (see note above), which reported that "among the embassy members everyone is all right and healthy."

63. Dusko Doder, "Soviets Charge U.S. Plane Wounded a Russian at Embassy in Grenada," *Washington Post*, Oct. 29, 1983.

64. "U.S. Denies Charge," *New York Times*, Oct. 29, 1983.

65. Jason Brady, "Helmet Saves Soldier's Life," *Fayetteville Observer-Times*, Nov. 28, 1983.

66. U.S. Congress, House, Subcommittee of the Committee on Appropriations, *Situation in Lebanon and Grenada*, 98th Congress, 1st Session (statement of Secretary of Defense Caspar Weinberger), 59.

67. *Ibid.*, 57.

68. John F. Lehman, Jr., *Command of the Seas* (New York, Scribner, 1988) 304.

69. U.S. Library of Congress, Congressional Research Service, *American War and Military Operations Casualties: Lists and Statistics,* by Nese F. DeBruyne, RL32492, 2017, 4 and Raines, *Rucksack War*, 532. The number of killed and wounded for Urgent Fury changed when Sgt. Luketina died on June 30, 1984, and his name was moved from the wounded to the killed category.

70. The Adjutant General Directorate (TAGD), "Awards and Decorations by Conflict," Jan. 2, 2019. https://www.hrc.army.mil/content/Awards%20and%20Decorations%20Statistics%20by%20Conflict. Accessed Feb. 19, 2019.

71. Pirnie, "Urgent Fury," 160 and 170.

72. In 1997, the JCS counted 25 Cubans killed and 59 wounded; see Cole, "Operation Urgent Fury," 6. Havana announced 24 killed and 60 wounded; see Richard J. Meislin, "Statement by Havana," *New York Times*, Nov. 4, 1983. Twenty-four coffins were displayed at a Cuban memorial service.

73. Cole, "Operation Urgent Fury," 6.

74. CIA, "Grenada: A First Look," 11–12.

75. *Ibid.*, 15.

76. Cole, "Operation Urgent Fury," 6. See "Joint Overview of Operation Urgent Fury," May 1, 1985, 3.

77. Iklé, testimony, *Lessons Learned*, 2.

78. "Memorial List." *Grenada Revolution Online,*.

79. "U.S. Hospitals Treating Grenadian Wounded," *New York Times*, Feb. 5, 1984. See also Department of Defense, "Casualty Figures/Grenada," Nov. 21, 1983.

80. Raines, *Rucksack War*, 532 and Cole, "Urgent Fury," 6.

81. Vijay Tiwathia, *The Grenada War: Anatomy of a Low-Intensity Conflict* (New Delhi: Lancer International, 1987), 117–19.

82. "Auditing an Invasion," *Time*, July 23, 1984.

Chapter 11

1. Frank V. Ortiz and Donald J. Usner, *Ambassador Ortiz: Lessons from a Life of Service* (Albuquerque: University of New Mexico Press, 2005), 120 and 122.

2. Reynold A. Burrowes, *Revolution and Rescue in Grenada: An Account of the U.S.-Caribbean Invasion* (New York: Greenwood Press, 1988), 28.

3. "Firearms Raid in Hyattsville," *Washington Post*, Feb. 3, 1979.

4. Timothy S. Robinson, "Two at Grenada Embassy Accused of Gun-Running," *Washington Post*, Sept. 1, 1979.

5. Secretary of State to Embassy Bridgetown, "Treasury Investigation in Grenada," confidential cable, March 8, 1979, unclassified in State Department FOIA Reading Room. https://foia.state.gov/Search/results.aspx?search Text=Treasury+Investigation+in+Grenada&beginDate =&endDate=&publishedBeginDate=&publishedEnd Date=&caseNumber. Accessed Jan. 17, 2018.

6. Ortiz and Usner, *Ambassador Ortiz*, 122.

7. Scott Davidson, *Grenada: A Study in Politics and the Limits of International Law* (Aldershot, England: Avebury, 1987), 12.

8. Coard as quoted in Wendy C. Grenade, "Retrospect: A View from Richmond Hill Prison: An Interview with Bernard Coard," *Journal of Eastern Caribbean Studies*, Sept.–Dec., 2010, Vol. 35, No. 3–4: 159–160. This interview was conducted on Oct. 17, 2008, just prior to Coard's release from prison a year later.

9. Joseph Ewart Layne, *We Move Tonight: The Making of the Grenada Revolution* (St. George's. Grenada: Grenada Revolution Memorial Foundation, 2014), 12–14. Layne wrote that Austin was also among the 12 who were trained in Cuba in December 1977. Both men were top leaders of the short-lived Revolutionary Military Council in 1983.

10. *Ibid.*, 119.

11. *Ibid.*, 95 and Gregory W. Sandford and Richard Vigilante, *Grenada: The Untold Story* (Lanham, MD: Madison Books, 1984), 48.

12. Robert Pastor, "The United States and the Grenada Revolution: Who Pushed First and Why," in *A Revolution Aborted: The Lessons of Grenada,* Jorge Heine, ed. (Pittsburgh: University of Pittsburgh Press, 1990), 186. An earlier version of this authoritative narrative of U.S.–Grenada relations during the revolutionary era from the American policy perspective was first published by Pastor as "Does the United States Push Revolutions to Cuba? The Case for Grenada," *Journal of Interamerican Studies and World Affairs*, Vol. 28, No 1 (Spring, 1986: 1–34.) Some key details only appear in one version. Pastor was the director of Latin American and Caribbean Affairs on the National Security Council from 1977 to 1981 and participated in all the key policy decisions regarding Grenada during that period. He also interviewed Coard and Bishop for a total of almost 13 hours in October, 1982.

13. Kawando M. Kinshasa, "Prime Minister Maurice Bishop Before the Storm." *The Black Scholar*, Vol. 15, No. 1, Jan.-Feb. 1984: 45.

14. "Grenada: Two Years After the Coup," National Foreign Assessment Center, CIA, secret whitepaper, May, 1981, unclassified in CIA FOIA Reading Room. https://www.cia.gov/library/readingroom/docs/CIA-RDP03T02547R000100170001-3.pdf. Accessed Feb. 11, 2019. See also Coard as quoted by Grenade in, "Retrospect: A View from Richmond Hill Prison," 156.

15. Sandford and Vigilante, *The Untold Story,* 49.

16. U.S. Embassy Bridgetown to Secretary of State, "U.S.–Grenada Relations Since the Coup: A Background Paper," Jan. 18, 1983, secret airgram, unclassified, 3. This 85-page assessment was researched and written in 1982

by Lawrence Rossin, the State Department officer later dispatched with the SEALS to secure Scoon at this residence. An airgram is a diplomatic term for a message sent in a diplomatic pouch rather than a telegram.

17. *Ibid.*, 4–5.

18. "The People's Laws 1979," *The Grenada Revolution Online* https://www.thegrenadarevolutiononline. com/peopleslaws1979.html. Accessed March 25, 2019.

19. *Ibid.*

20. Coard as quoted in Grenade, "Retrospect: A View from Richmond Hill Prison," 156 and 166.

21. Scoon, *Survival for Service*, 49.

22. For the talking points see "U.S.–Grenada Relations Since the Coup," 20–21 and Gary Williams, *U.S.-Grenada Relations: Revolution and Intervention in the Backyard* (New York: Palgrave Macmillan, 2007), Appendix 1, 179–80.

23. Frank V. Ortiz, "Grenada Before and After," *Atlantic Monthly*, June, 1984, 9.

24. Payne et al., *Revolution and Invasion,* 49.

25. Ortiz and Usner, *Ambassador Ortiz,* 122.

26. Bishop, "In Nobody's Backyard, April 13, 1979," in *Bishop Speaks*, 31.

27. "U.S.–Grenada Relations Since the Coup," 17.

28. *Ibid.*, 19.

29. Zbigniew Brzezinski to Director of Central Intelligence, "Cuban Presence on Grenada," secret memorandum, May 8, 1979, unclassified in CIA FOIA Reading Room. https://www.cia.gov/library/readingroom/ document/cia-rdp85m00364r001502590115-6. Accessed May 15, 2018.

30. Robert Michael Gates, *From the Shadows: The Ultimate Insider's Story of Five Presidents and How They Won the Cold War* (New York: Simon & Schuster, 1996), 143.

31. *Ibid.*

32. "U.S.–Grenada Relations Since the Coup," 32.

33. U.S. Congress, House, Subcommittees on International Security and Scientific Affairs and on Western Hemispheric Affairs of the Committee on Foreign Affairs, *Military Actions in Grenada: Implications for U.S. Policy in the Eastern Caribbean*, 98th Congress, First Session, Nov. 2, 1983 (statement submitted by Kenneth W. Dam, Deputy Secretary of State), 34.

34. Payne et al., *Revolution and Invasion*, 34.

35. Quigley, "Parachutes at Dawn," 243.

36. Kai P. Schoenhals and Richard A. Melanson, *Revolution and Intervention in Grenada: The New Jewel Movement, the United States, and the Caribbean* (Boulder, CO: Westview Press, 1985), 56.

37. CIA, "Grenada: A First Look," 12.

38. Drew Fetherston, "A School in Question," *Newsday*, Oct. 31, 1978.

39. Michael Arthur Leventhal, "Entrepreneurship and Nation Building: Proprietary Medical Schools and Development in the Caribbean, 1976–1990." (doctoral dissertation, University of Chicago, 1995), 74–6.

40. *Ibid.*, 521–525.

41. *Ibid.*, 75–9.

42. *Ibid.*, 106 and 108.

43. Geoffrey H. Bourne, "Revolution, Intervention & Nutrition: What Happened in Grenada," *Nutrition Today*, Jan.-Feb. 1985: 18.

44. Sally Shelton-Colby (interview with Charles Stuart Kennedy, July 22, 1991, Manuscript/Mixed Material, Library of Congress), 48. https://www.loc.gov/item/ mfdipbib001052/. Accessed Feb. 5, 2019.

45. Leventhal, "Entrepreneurship and Nation Building," 119.

46. *Ibid.*, 264.

47. *Ibid.*, 284.

48. Pastor, "The United States and the Grenada Revolution," 198.

49. Frank McNeil, *War and Peace in Central America* (New York: Scribner's, 1988), 172.

50. "Atlantic Exercise Involves 214 Countries," *All Hands*, March, 1982, 20–29.

51. Payne et al., *Revolution and Invasion*, 65–7.

52. "Chronology of Soviet Statements…," Central Intelligence Agency, Oct. 30, 1983.

53. Department of State and Department of Defense, "Grenada: A Preliminary Report," Dec. 16, 1983, Washington, D.C., 13. Hathi Trust Digital Library. https://catalog.hathitrust.org/Record/101263364 Accessed July 8, 2018.

54. W. Robert Warne (interview with Charles Stuart Kennedy, April 1, 1995, Manuscript/Mixed Material, Library of Congress) https://www.loc.gov/item/mfdipbib001234/. Accessed Jan. 18, 2018.

55. Carol Bryant, *Milan Bish: The Measure You Give*, edited by Allene Bish, R. J. Post, and Irene Abernethy (Grand Island, NE: Allene Bish, 2000), 172.

56. Stephen R. Weisman, "Reagan in the Caribbean, Links Grenada to Moscow," *New York Times*, Apr. 9, 1982.

57. Remarks at the Annual Convention of the National Association of Evangelicals in Orlando, FL, March 8, 1983. *The Public Papers of President Ronald W. Reagan.* Ronald Reagan Presidential Library. https://www.reaganlibrary.gov/research/speeches/30883b. Accessed Feb. 16, 2018.

58. Remarks on Central America and El Salvador at the Annual Meeting of the National Association of Manufacturers, *March 10, 1983. The Public Papers of President Ronald W. Reagan.* Ronald Reagan Presidential Library. https://www.reaganlibrary.gov/research/speeches/31083a. Accessed Feb. 16, 2018.

59. Address to the Nation on Defense and National Security, March 23, 1983. *The Public Papers of President Ronald W. Reagan.* Ronald Reagan Presidential Library. https://www.reaganlibrary.gov/research/speeches/32383d. Accessed Feb. 16, 2018.

60. Bishop, "An Armed Attack Against our Country Is Imminent, March 23, 1983," in *Bishop Speaks*, 279–286.

61. Address Before a Joint Session of the Congress on Central America. April 27, 1983, *The Public Papers of President Ronald W. Reagan.* Ronald Reagan Presidential Library. https://www.reaganlibrary.gov/research/speeches/42783d. Accessed Feb. 19, 2018.

62. Edward Cody, "Grenadan Tempest Bemuses Tourists," *Washington Post*, April 21, 1983.

63. "Grenada's airport 'is not military,'" *FLIGHT International*, Nov. 19, 1983. See also Plessey statement as quoted in Fitzroy Ambursley and James Dunkerley, *Whose Freedom?* (London: Latin American Bureau, 1984), 49–50.

64. CIA, Directorate of Intelligence. "Soviet Geopolitical and Military Interests in Grenada and Suriname," secret memorandum, April 21, 1983, unclassified, in CIA FOIA Reading Room. https://www.cia.gov/library/readingroom/docs/DOC_0000695789.pdf. Accessed Jan. 18, 2018.

65. *Ibid.*, 8.

66. *Ibid.*, 4.

67. interview with Yuri Pavlov, CNN.com, *Cold War*, Episode 18, Backyard, Feb. 21, 1999. Archived at the National Security Archive. https://nsarchive2.gwu.edu/coldwar/interviews/. Accessed Feb. 6, 2019.

68. W. Richard Jacobs, "Grenada-Soviet Relations: A Summary, 7/11/83" in Paul Seabury and Walter A. McDougall eds., *The Grenada Papers* (San Francisco, CA: Institute for Contemporary Studies, 1984), 198–216.

69. Gary Williams, "Brief Encounter: Grenadian Prime Minister Maurice Bishop's Visit to Washington," *Journal of Latin American Studies* 34, no. 3 (2002):660. https://www.jstor.org/stable/3875464?seq=1#page_scan_tab_contents. Accessed June 4, 2018.

70. "Minutes of the Political Bureau, 4th May, 1983," in Michael Ledeen and Herbert Romerstein, eds., *Grenada Documents: An Overview and Selection* (Washington: U.S. G.P.O., 1985), Document 93.

71. Shultz, *Turmoil and Triumph*, 324.

72. White House to Duane Clarridge and Bob Gates at CIA, "Grenada," Top Secret, unsigned message. Oct. 19, 1983, unclassified in CIA FOIA Reading Room. https://www.cia.gov/library/readingroom/docs/CIA-RDP85M00363R000200370046-4.pdf. Accessed May 15, 2018.

73. Tony Thorndike, *Grenada: Politics, Economics and Society* (Boulder, CO: Lynne Rienner Publishers, Inc., 1985), 131.

74. Unsigned, handwritten notes of Bishop-Clark meeting, archived in Grenada Documents Collection, Georgetown University Booth Family Center for Special Collections, Washington, Box 3, Component 43. These notes are also reproduced in Seabury and McDougall eds., *The Grenada Papers*, 178–180.

75. Dam to Reagan, "Meeting with Prime Minister Maurice Bishop of Grenada, June 7. 1983," confidential memorandum, Department of State, declassified, archived in U.S. Declassified Documents Online. Accessed July 16. 2018.

76. Iklé, testimony, *Lessons Learned*, 42.

77. Jacobs, "Grenada-Soviet Relations," 203–4.

78. "Background Notes for Meeting with National Security Advisor Clark," in Seabury and McDougall eds., *The Grenada Papers*, 175–76. and Thorndike, *Politics, Economics and Society*, 132.

79. CIA, "Grenada: A First Look," 28.

80. This account of the meeting is drawn from "Extraordinary Meeting of the Central Committee 9/16/83," in Seabury and McDougall eds., *The Grenada Papers*, 280–295.

81. Jo Thomas, "From a Grenadian Diplomat: How Party Wrangle Led to Premier's Death," *New York Times*, Oct. 30, 1983.

82. "Extraordinary General Meeting 9/25/83" in Seabury and McDougall eds., *The Grenada Papers,* 300–315.

83. George Louison, *George Louison and Kendrick Radix Discuss—: Internal Events Leading to the U.S. Invasion of Grenada* (New York: Grenada Foundation, 1984), 20.

84. *Ibid.*, Radix, 28.

85. Davidson, *Grenada: A Study in Politics,* 68.

86. Handwritten statement by Errol George, dated Oct. 12, 1983, archived in Grenada Documents Collection, Georgetown University Booth Family Center for Special Collections, Washington, Box 2, Component 3.

87. Burrowes, *Revolution and Rescue*, 55.

88. Radix, *George Louison and Kendrick Radix Discuss…*, 29.

89. Steven Clark, "Introduction" in *Bishop Speaks*, xxxiv–xxxv.

90. "Resolution of People's Army, 10/12/83," in Seabury and McDougall eds., *The Grenada Papers*, 325.

91. "Statement by the Cuban Government and the Cuban Communist Party," in Bishop *Speaks,* Appendix I, 313.

92. Fidel Castro, Jeffrey M. Elliot, and Mervyn M. Dymally. *Nothing Can Stop the Course of History* (New York: Pathfinder Press, 1988), 157.

93. "Report on the meeting of the PB & CC held on Oct 12," handwritten notes by unknown author, archived in Grenada Documents Collection, Georgetown University Booth Family Center for Special Collections, Washington, Box 2, Component 3.

94. Radix, *George Louison and Kendrick Radix Discuss,* 30.

95. Coard, *What Really Happened,* 202.

96. *Ibid.,* 203–4.

97. Thorndike, *Politics, Economics and Society,* 155.

98. Adkin, *Urgent Fury,* 42 and Sandford and Vigilante, *The Untold Story, 159.*

99. Sandford and Vigilante, *The Untold Story,* 160.

100. Radix. *George Louison and Kendrick Radix Discuss, 31 and* Dunn and Watson eds., *American Intervention in Grenada,* 158. Coard, *What Really Happened,* 202.

101. Ambursley and Dunkerley, *Whose Freedom?,* 71 and Sandford and Vigilante, *The Untold Story,* 160.

102. Bridgetown Embassy to Secretary of State, "Grenada: Report of 'Marxist' coup by DPM Bernard Coard," cable, Oct. 14,1983 in Bryant, *Milan Bish,* 314.

103. Coard, *What Really Happened,* 210.

104. *Ibid.,* 211.

105. O'Shaughnessy, *Revolution, Invasion and Aftermath,* 127.

106. Clark, "Introduction" in *Bishop Speaks,* xxxv.

107. Coard, *What Really Happened,* 215.

108. *Ibid.,* 216 and Ambursley and Dunkerley, *Whose Freedom?,* 72.

109. DOD and DOS, "Grenada: A Preliminary Report," 35.

110. Radix as quoted in Strober and Strober, *The Reagan Presidency,* 259.

111. Jo Thomas, "From a Grenadian Diplomat," *New York Times,* Oct. 30, 1983.

112. Coard, *What Really Happened,* 227.

113. Alister Hughes, "Top Leader of Grenada May Be Out," *Miami Herald,* Oct. 15, 1983. Hughes's Oct. 14 report for CANA is quoted in a cable to Washington sent from Bridgetown on Oct. 15, see Bryant, *Milan Bish,* 322–3.

114. Thorndike, *Politics, Economics and Society,* 157.

115. Hughes, "Top Leader of Grenada."

116. Bridgetown Embassy to Secretary of State, "Grenada Coup: Coard announced as new prime minister…," Oct. 14,1983, in Bryant, *Milan Bish,* 316–7.

117. "Grenada: Report of 'Marxist' coup by DPM Bernard Coard," *Ibid.,* 314.

118. Bryant, *Milan Bish,* 116.

119. Raines, *Rucksack War,* 90.

120. "2nd Prime Minister Tom Adams (1976–1985)," Totally Barbados.com. https://www.totallybarbados.com/articles/about-barbados/people/barbados-prime-ministers/2nd-prime-minister-tom-adams. Accessed Apr. 28, 2018.

121. "Documents on the Invasion" (full text of speech by Prime Minister Tom Adams), 35.

122. Coard, *What Really Happened,* 223.

123. *Ibid.,* 224.

124. *Ibid.,* 225–26.

125. Menges, *Inside the National Security Council,* 61.

126. James A. Baker III with Steve Fiffer, "*Work Hard, Study…and Keep Out of Politics!"* (New York: G.P. Putnam's Sons, 2006), 197–8.

127. Reagan, *An American Life,* 448 and Edmund Morris, *Dutch: A Memoir of Ronald Reagan* (New York: Random House, 1999), 499–500. Deaver believed that it was opposition to him becoming chief of staff that scuttled the package deal. See Michael K. Deaver and Mickey Herskowitz, *Behind the Scenes: In Which the Author Talks About Ronald and Nancy Reagan … and Himself* (New York: Morrow, 1988), 130.

128. F. A. Hoyos, *Tom Adams: A Biography* (London: Macmillan Caribbean, 1988), 113.

129. "Documents on the Invasion" (Adams speech), 35–6.

130. Robert J. Beck, *The Grenada Invasion: Politics, Law, and Foreign Policy Decisionmaking* (Boulder: Westview Press, 1993),96 and n118.

131. Gary Williams, "Prelude to an Intervention: Grenada 1983," *Journal of Latin American Studies,* Vol. 29, No. 1, Feb., 1997: n148.

132. *U.S. Military Actions in Grenada* (statement submitted by Dam), 51.

133. John Burgess, "U.S. Reportedly Offered to Rescue Bishop Before His Execution," *Washington Post,* Oct. 28, 1983.

134. Adkin, *Urgent Fury,* 92–3.

135. Thorndike, *Politics, Economics and Society,* 157.

136. Radix as quoted in Strober and Strober, *The Reagan Presidency,* 259.

137. Embassy Bridgetown to Secretary of State, "Grenada: Army plumps for Coard, but Bishop is not yet out…," cable, Oct. 16, 1983, quoted in Bryant, *Milan Bish,* 326. See also O'Shaughnessy, *Revolution, Invasion and Aftermath,* 194–5.

138. Bernard Diederich, "Interviewing George Louison," *Caribbean Review,* Vol. XII, No. 4, Fall, 1983: 18. Archived at Digital Library of the Caribbean. http://www.dloc.com/UF00095576/00042.

139. Coard, *What Really Happened,* 227.

140. "Documents on the Invasion" (statement of General Hudson Austin broadcast on Radio Free Grenada at approximately 12:04 p.m. on Oct. 16, 1983), 5–10.

141. Coard, *What Really Happened,* 233.

142. "Letter from Castro to Central Committee, 10/15/83," in Seabury and McDougall eds., *The Grenada Papers,* 327–8.

143. Coard, *What Really Happened,* 233.

144. Thorndike, *Politics, Economics and Society,* 159 and O'Shaughnessy, *Revolution, Invasion and Aftermath,* 131.

145. Payne et al., *Revolution and Invasion,* 133.

146. Dated and signed resignation letters for Ramdhanny, Louison, Bain and Whiteman, archived in Grenada Documents Collection, Georgetown University Booth Family Center for Special Collections, Washington, Box 2, Component 6.

147. Coard, *What Really Happened,* 246.

148. Payne et al., *Revolution and Invasion* Grenada, 133.

149. Coard, *What Really Happened,* 248.

150. O'Shaughnessy, *Revolution, Invasion and Aftermath,* 130.

151. Davidson, *Grenada: A Study in Politics,* 70–71, Ambursley and Dunkerley, *Whose Freedom?,* 72 and Thorndike, *Politics, Economics and Society,* 158–9.

152. *Lessons Learned as a Result of the U.S. Military*

Operations in Grenada, House Armed Services Committee, 98th Congress, Second Session, Jan. 24, 1984 (statement of Langhorne A. Motley, Assistant Secretary, Bureau of Inter-American Affairs, Department of State), 11.

153. John Walton Cotman, *The Gorrion Tree: Cuba and the Grenada Revolution* (New York: P. Lang, 1993), 216.

154. Coard, *What Really Happened*, 246.

155. Alister Hughes, "Island Bloodshed 'Started with Army Rockets,' Journalist Says," *Washington Post*, Oct. 30, 1983.

156. Coard, *What Really Happened*, 269.

157. *Ibid.*, 271–74.

158. Clark, "Introduction" in *Bishop Speaks*, xxxviii.

159. Statement of Christopher Stroude, Bishop Trial Report, *The Nation Newspaper of Barbados*, December, 1986 (This journalistic trial summary was relied upon by a Grenadian government commission that in 2001 conducted an independent review of Fort Rupert killings and other crimes that took place during the Bishop era. The summary was included in Volume 2 of the commission's final report, along with other collected documents.) See Grenada, Donald A. B. Trotman, Sehon S. Goodridge, and Mark Haynes, *Redeeming the Past, a Time for Healing: Report on Certain Political Events Which Occurred in Grenada 1976–1991*, Volume 2, Appendix Q (Grenada: Truth and Reconciliation Commission], 2006).

160. Schoenhals and Melanson, *Revolution and Intervention*, 76.

161. Coard, *What Really Happened*, 267.

162. Castro et al., *Nothing Can Stop the Course of History*, 159.

163. *Ibid.*

164. Coard, *What Really Happened*, 280.

165. *Ibid.*, 282.

166. "Documents on the Invasion," (statement by Gen. Hudson Austin, broadcast on Radio Free Grenada, 10 p.m. Oct. 19, 1983), 11.

167. Ewart Layne, signed statement, as quoted in Bishop Trial Report, *The Nation Newspaper of Barbados*, December, 1986.

168. Coard, *What Really Happened*, 267–8.

169. "The Maurice Bishop Murder Trial," *The Grenadian Newsletter*, May 17, 1986, vol. 14, no. 9, 10–11. Archived at Digital Library of the Caribbean (http://dloc.com/) Caribbean Newspaper collection.

170. Callistus Bernard, signed statement, as quoted in Bishop Trial Report, *The Nation Newspaper of Barbados*, December, 1986,.

171. Colville McBarnette, statement as quoted in Bishop Trial Report, *The Nation Newspaper of Barbados*, December, 1986.

172. "The Maurice Bishop Murder Trial," *The Grenadian Newsletter*, May 17, 1986, 11–13.

173. *Redeeming the Past*, Volume 1, Part 5, Section 1 (Grenada: Truth and Reconciliation Commission], 2006).

174. Radix, *George Louison and Kendrick Radix Discuss*, 13.

175. UK Embassy Bridgetown to Foreign Office, "Grenada- Revolutionary Council," confidential telegram, Oct. 24, 1983. Margaret Thatcher Foundation Archives.

176. William D. Montalbano, "Coup Began as a Debate Among Leftists," *Los Angeles Times*, Friday, Oct. 21, 1983.

177. Copy of letter from Phyllis Coard to the Central Committee, dated Nov. 5, 1981, archived in Grenada Documents Collection, Georgetown University Booth Family Center for Special Collections, Washington, Box 1, Component 26.

178. "Grenada-Revolutionary Council," telegram, Oct. 24, 1983.

179. Diederich, "Interviewing George Louison," 18.

180. Documents on the Invasion," (Austin statement), 11.

181. Beck, *The Grenada Invasion*, 17.

182. Callistus Bernard, signed statement, as quoted in Bishop Trial Report, *The Nation Newspaper of Barbados*, December, 1986.

183. Hughes, "Island Bloodshed."

184. Stephen Edward Flynn, "Grenada as a 'Reactive' and a 'Proactive' Crisis: New Models of Crisis Decision Making" (doctoral thesis, The Fletcher School of Law and Diplomacy, Medford, MA, July, 1991), 107.

185. Motley, prepared statement, *Lessons Learned*, 11.

186. Pirnie, "Operation Urgent Fury," 201.

187. Sarah Boxer, "Operation Slick Moniker: Military Name Game," *New York Times*, Oct. 13, 2001.

Chapter 12

1. Speakes and Pack, *Speaking Out*, 153.

2. Michael Kernan, "Picturing the Invasion," *Washington Post*, Oct. 26, 1983.

3. Robert J. Beck, "The 'McNeil Mission' and the Decision to Invade Grenada," *Navy War College Review*, Spring, 1991, 104–5. See also Janet Higbie, *Eugenia: The Caribbean's Iron Lady* (London: Macmillan Caribbean, 1993), 232-5.

4. Menges, *Inside the National Security Council*, 84–86.

5. Walter Shapiro, "Testing Time: Reagan was Reagan," *Newsweek*, Nov. 7, 1983, 82.

6. Times and participants for these White House meetings come from "The Daily Diary of President Reagan," March, 1983, Archival Resources, Digital Library, Ronald Reagan Library. https://www.reaganlibrary.gov/digital-library/daily-diary/. Accessed Feb. 23, 2018.

7. "Text of Reagan's Announcement of Invasion," *New York Times*, Oct. 26, 1983.

8. Stuart Taylor, Jr., "Legality of Grenada Act Disputed," *New York Times*, Oct. 26, 1983. See also U.S. Library of Congress, Congressional Research Service, *U.S. Low-Intensity Conflicts 1899–1990*, by John M. Collins with Frederick Hamerman and James P. Seevers, 1990, 195.

9. Kallander and Matthews, "Urgent Fury," xiii.

10. The first public mention of the Scoon's invitation was made by Charles in the speech the next day at the United Nations. See Payne, *Revolution and Invasion*, 157.

11. Beck, *The Grenada Invasion*, n83.

12. "U.S. Had to Act Strongly, Decisively," *Washington Post*, Oct. 26, 1983.

13. Higbie, *Eugenia*, 235.

14. DCI, "Preliminary Assessment of Cuban and Soviet Involvement," 7–8.

15. Higbie, *Eugenia*, 236.

16. Speakes and Pack, *Speaking Out*, 158.

17. Lou Cannon, "Reagan Press Aide Resigns," *Washington Post*, Nov. 1, 1983.

18. Les Janka, "Grenada, the Media, and National Security," *Armed Forces Journal International Journal*, December, 1983:9.

19. Hertsgaard, *On Bended Knee*, 236.

20. Johnathan Friendly, "Reporting the News in a Communique War," *New York Times*, Oct. 26, 1983.

21. Speakes and Pack, *Speaking Out*, 160–1.

22. Doyle McManus, "School Chief Concedes Peril," *Los Angeles Times* wire report in *Newsday*, Oct. 27, 1983. The official, Richard C. Brown, then the Deputy Director of State's Office of Caribbean Affairs, was dispatched by Shultz to "handle" Modica. See Shultz, *Turmoil and Triumph*, 334.

23. DOD and DOS, "Grenada: A Preliminary Report," 18.

24. *Ibid.*, 20.

25. Address to the Nation on Events in Lebanon and Grenada, October 27, 1983, *The Public Papers of President Ronald W. Reagan. Ronald Reagan Presidential Library.* https://www.reaganlibrary.gov/research/speeches/102783b. Accessed Apr. 12, 2018.

26. DCI, "Preliminary Assessment of Cuban and Soviet Involvement," 1.

27. Bob Woodward, *Veil: The Secret Wars of the CIA, 1981–1987* (New York: Simon and Schuster, 1987), 299.

28. *Ibid.*, 289 and Morris, *Dutch*, 500.

29. Alfonso Chardy, "Casey rejected Grenada report, former CIA analyst says," *Miami Herald*, Feb. 13, 1985.

30. Philip Taubman, "Analyst Said to Have Quit C.I.A. in Dispute," *New York Times*, Sept. 28, 1984.

31. *Newsweek*, Nov. 7, 1983, 80.

32. Adam C. Clymer, "Grenadians Welcomed Invasion, a Poll Finds," *New York Times*, Nov. 6, 1983.

33. *The Grenadian Voice*, Jan. 21, 1984.

34. Gordon K. Lewis, *Grenada: The Jewel Despoiled* (Baltimore: Johns Hopkins Univ. Press, 1987), 185.

35. "Suriname Ousts Envoy and Halts Cuba Pacts," *New York Times*, Oct. 27, 1983.

36. McNeil, *War and Peace in Central America*, 175.

37. *Ibid.*

38. Edward Cody, "Fear of Attack Seen Causing Cubans to Leave Nicaragua," *Washington Post*, Jan. 31, 1984.

39. Clarridge, *A Spy for All Seasons*, 268.

40. *Ibid.*, 269.

41. Roy Gutman, *Banana Diplomacy: The Making of American Policy in Nicaragua, 1981–1987* (New York: Simon and Schuster, 1988), 196.

42. *Ibid.*, 198–99.

43. John F. Burns, "Soviet Tells Details of Sea Blast off Nicaragua," *New York Times*, March 23, 1984.

44. "Text of Goldwater's Letter to Head of the C.I.A.," *New York Times*, April 11, 1984.

45. Gutman, *Banana Diplomacy*, 200.

46. MacFarlane as quoted in Strober and Strober, *The Reagan Presidency*, 266.

47. Oliver L. North with William Novak, *Under Fire: An American Story* (New York: HarperCollins, 1991), 185.

48. U.S. Printing Office, *Report of the Congressional Committees Investigating the Iran-Contra Affair*, 100th Congress, 1st Session, 1987, 31.

49. *Ibid.*, 374–76. Also, Office of Independent Counsel, "Fact Sheet," December,1992, in Peter Kornbluh and Malcolm Byrne, eds. *The Iran-Contra Scandal: The Declassified History* (New York: The New Press, 1993), 342–43 and White House, "Grant of Executive Clemency," Dec. 24, 1992.

50. White House, Memorandum of Telephone Conversation, Reagan and Thatcher, secret transcript, Oct. 26, 1983, declassified, archived in U.S. Declassified Documents Online. Accessed July 17, 2018.

51. Allan Gerson, *The Kirkpatrick Mission: Diplomacy Without Apology: America at the United Nations 1981–1985* (New York: Free Press, 1991), 223 and 229.

52. Richard Bernstein, "U.S. Vetoes U.N. Resolution 'Deploring' Grenada Invasion," *New York Times*, Oct. 29, 1983.

53. Pirnie, "Operation Urgent Fury," 181–2.

54. Beck, *The Grenada Invasion*, 77.

55. "International Law and The United States Action in Grenada: A Report," Edward Gordon, Richard B. Bilder, Arthur W. Rovine and Don Wallace, Jr., *The International Lawyer*, Vol. 18, No. 2, Spring 1984: 331–380. http://www.jstor.org/stable/40705519. Accessed June 2, 2018.

56. *Ibid.* The Robinson letter was included as an annex to the "Gordon Report."

57. The three "well-established legal principles" cited by Robinson were: a request by a lawful government authority for military assistance, a collective regional action "consistent with" the U.N. and OAS charters and "the right of States to use force to protect their nationals."

58. Congressional Research Service, *U.S. Low-Intensity Conflicts 1899–1999*, 55–56.

59. Arthur Schlesinger, Jr., "Grenada Again: Living Within the Law," *Wall Street Journal*, Dec. 14, 1983.

60. Alma Guillermoprieto, "Havana Welcomes Wounded Cubans with Little Pomp," *Washington Post*, Nov. 3, 1983, and Richard J. Meislin, "Cuba Assails U.S. on Casualty List," *New York Times*, Nov. 3, 1983.

61. Castro, "Fidel Castro on the Events in Grenada," in *Bishop Speaks*, Appendix III, 326–341.

62. Castro et al., *Nothing Can Stop the Course of History*, 153.

63. "Cuba Said to Court-Martial Commander in Grenada," *Washington Post*, June 19, 1984, and "Cuban Colonel in Disgrace," *Washington Post*, Oct. 25, 1984.

64. Vessey, letter to Armstrong, undated.

65. Metcalf, "The Mother of the Mother," 58.

66. Michael W. Schoenfeld, Col. USAF, "Military and the Media: Resolving the Conflict," (student paper submitted to the Naval War College, Newport, RI, June 19, 1992), 13.

67. Johnathan Friendly, "Pentagon's Panel on Press Coverage to Meet," *New York Times*, Feb. 5, 1984.

68. Statement by the Secretary of Defense, News Release, August 23, 1984, Office of the Assistant Secretary of Defense (Public Affairs), Washington, D.C.

69. Schoenfeld, "Military and the Media," 16–17.

70. Jaqueline E. Sharkey, *Under Fire: U.S. Military Restrictions on the Media from Grenada to the Persian Gulf* (Washington, D.C.: Center for Public Integrity, 1991), 91–92.

71. For Public Law 93–148 and Reagan's letter see U.S. Congress, House, Committee on Foreign Affairs, *Grenada War Powers: Full Compliance Reporting and Implementation*, 98th Congress, 1st session, Oct. 27, 1983, Appendix 1 and 2, 33–39. The letter is also found in Moore, *Law and the Grenada Mission*, Appendix 4, 95–6.

72. U.S. Library of Congress, Congressional Research Service, *The War Powers Resolution: After Thirty-Eight Years*, by Richard E. Grimmett, R42699, Sept. 24, 2012, 1.

73. Richard Whittle, "Questions, Praise Follow Grenada Invasion, *Congressional Quarterly*, Oct. 29, 1983, 2221–2224.

74. *Ibid.*

75. Richard Halloran, "1,000 Paratroopers leave Grenada," *New York Times*, Dec. 13, 1983.

76. James R. Locher III, *Victory on the Potomac: The Goldwater-Nichols Act Unifies the Pentagon* (College Station: Texas A & M University Press, 2002), 135–6. Locher was a staff member on this fact-finding trip.

77. R.R. Reid, "Senators Stirred in Policy Debate," *Washington Post*, Oct. 29, 1983.

78. Matthews, *Tip and the Gipper*, 278.

79. House, Subcommittees of Foreign Affairs, *U.S. Military Actions in Grenada* (statement by Dam), 10.

80. *Ibid.*, 13.

81. "Invasion of Grenada" in *CQ Almanac 1983* (Washington, D.C.: Congressional Quarterly, 1984), 135–36. http://library.cqpress.com/cqalmanac/document.php?id=cqal83–1198476. Accessed May 1, 2018.

82. U.S. Library of Congress, Congressional Research Service, *War Powers Litigation Initiated by Members of Congress*, by Michael John Garcia, RL30352, Feb. 17, 2012, 5–6.

83. A transcript of the closed portion this hearing is in the custody of the Center for Legislative Archives, a division of the National Archives and Records Administration in Washington, D.C. A request for declassification by the author was denied on the basis of House rules that say records related to testimony heard in executive session must remain closed for 50 years, in this case until Jan. 24, 2034.

84. "Documents on the Invasion," (report to the Congressional Military Reform Caucus), 111–115.

85. Rick Atkinson, "Study Faults U.S. Military Tactics in Grenada Invasion," *Washington Post*, Apr. 6, 1984.

86. Adkin, *Urgent Fury*, Appendix A, 343–359 and Rick Atkinson, "Pentagon Defends Grenada Invasion Troop Performance," *Washington Post*, June 21, 1984.

87. "Grenada Post-Mortem: A 'Report' That Wasn't," *Army*, June, 1984, 16.

88. High quality historical work was done by Raines and Pirnie for the Army; Kallander and Mathews for the Air Force and Spector for the Marines, among others, as previously cited.

89. Atlantic Command, "Operation Urgent Fury Report" This 1984 commander's report was posted to the DOD FOIA Reading Room in 2017, but that web address is no longer found.

90. Schwarzkopf, *Hero*, 258.

91. Caspar Weinberger, "The Uses of Military Power," remarks prepared for delivery to the National Press Club, Washington, D.C., Nov. 28, 1984. Archived at PBS Frontline http://insidethecoldwar.org/sites/default/files/documents/Statement%20by%20Secretary%20of%20Defense%20Weinberger%20at%20National%20Press%20Club,%20November%2028,%201984.pdf. Accessed May 1, 2018. See also Richard Halloran, "U.S. Will Not Drift into a Latin War, Weinberger Says," *New York Times*, Nov. 29, 1984.

92. Richard Halloran, "Shultz and Weinberger: Disputing the Use of Force," *New York Times*, Nov. 30, 1984.

93. Ronald Reagan, *An American Life*, 466–7.

94. Michael Weisskopf, "Admiral Cleared in Gun-Smuggling," *Washington Post*, July 20, 1985 and "Navy Says Admiral is Cleared by Report on War Souvenirs," *New York Times*, July 20, 1985.

95. U.S. House, Oversight and Investigations Subcommittee of the Committee on Armed Services, *Weapons Souvenirs*, 103rd Congress, 1st Session, March 18, 1983 (statement of David C. Cole, Collections Management Branch, U.S. Army Center of Military History), 2–3.

96. E. Ashley Wills, a State Department officer assigned to Metcalf's Guam battle staff, in an Oct. 17, 2018, interview with the author, speculated that the tip had come from a disaffected subordinate officer.

97. "Grenada Gun Case; Jail for 7 but Not Admiral," *New York Times*, Feb. 8, 1985.

98. Richard C. Gross, UPI, Feb. 8, 1985. Archived at UPI Archives. https://www.upi.com/Archives/1985/02/

08/The-Pentagon-launched-an-investigation-Friday-into-an-attempt/8046068446783/. Accessed Feb. 15, 2019.

99. House, Oversight and Investigations Subcommittee, *Weapons Souvenirs* (Statement of Mark L. Waple, attorney, Armed Forces Legal Center), 55.

100. Fred Hiatt and Michael Weisskopf, "Navy Defends Action in Admiral's Case," *Washington Post*, Feb. 13, 1985.

101. "U.S. Reported to Investigate Handling of Grenada Weapons Case," UPI report in *New York Times*, Feb. 9, 1985.

102. *Ibid.*

103. Richard Marcinko and James DeFelice, *Rogue Warrior* (New York: Pocket Star Books, 2006), 281.

104. Bill Keller, "Navy Investigation of Admiral Called Faulty," *New York Times*, July 24, 1985, and Michael Weisskopf, "Admiral Cleared in Gun-Smuggling," *Washington Post*, July 20, 1985.

105. Stephen Labaton, "Three Grenada-Invasion Vets Win Clemency on Gun-Smuggling Charge," *Washington Post*, June 1, 1985.

106. "Former Joint Chiefs chairman David C. Jones dies a 92," *Washington Post*, Aug 13, 2013.

107. John T. Correll, "The Campaign for Goldwater-Nichols," *Air Force Magazine*, October, 2011, 69.

108. Locher, *Victory on the Potomac*, 33–34.

109. David C. Jones, Gen. USAF, "Why the Joint Chiefs of Staff Must Change," *Armed Forces Journal*, March, 1982: 138–149.

110. Edgar F. Raines, Jr., and Major David R. Campbell, *The Army and the Joint Chiefs of Staff: Evolution of Army Ideas on the Command, Control and Coordination of the U.S. Armed Forces, 1942-1985* (U.S. Army Center of Military History, Washington, D.C., 1986), 150. http://www.dtic.mil/dtic/tr/fulltext/u2/a640665.pdf/. Accessed Apr. 2, 2018.

111. Edward C. Meyer, "The JCS—How Much Reform Is Needed?" *Armed Forces Journal International*, April, 1982: 82–90.

112. *Ibid.*, 89.

113. Locher, *Victory on the Potomac*, 67.

114. Raines and Campbell, *The Army and the Joint Chiefs of Staff*, 165.

115. Locher, *Victory on the Potomac*, 213–5.

116. Barry M. Blechman and William J. Lynn, eds., *Toward a More Effective Defense: Report of the Defense Organization Project* (Cambridge, MA: Ballinger, 1985).

117. Bill Keller, "Overhaul is Urged for Top Military," *New York Times*, Jan. 22, 1985.

118. Blechman and Lynn, *Toward a More Effective Defense*, 91 and 118.

119. Michal Weisskopf, "Presidential Panel to Assess Defense Purchasing Practices," *Washington Post*, June 8, 1985.

120. Locher, *Victory on the Potomac*, 329.

121. *Ibid.*, 305.

122. Senator Nunn of Georgia, 99th Congress, 1st session, *Congressional Record* (Oct. 2, 1985), 25541–43.

123. Locher, *Victory on the Potomac*, 345.

124. *Ibid.*, 351–3.

125. Colin L. Powell and Joseph E. Persico, *My American Journey* (New York: Random House, 1995), 292.

126. Locher, *Victory on the Potomac*, 358.

127. The staff report was published in softcover book form by the U.S. Printing Office as *Defense Organization: The Need for Change*, Staff Report to the Committee on Armed Services, United States Senate, 99th Congress, 1st Session, October 16, 1985.

128. *Ibid.*, 11–12.

129. *Ibid.*, 363–70.

130. U.S. Congress, Senate, Committee on Armed Services, *Reorganization of the Department of Defense*, 99th Congress, 1st session, Oct. 16–Dec. 12, 1985, 30.

131. Senate, Committee on Armed Services, *Reorganization of the Department of Defense* (letter from Secretary Weinberger to Senator Goldwater, dated Dec. 2, 1985), 336–8.

132. Locher, *Victory on the Potomac*, 381.

133. Senate, Committee on Armed Services, *Reorganization of the Department of Defense*, Dec. 5, 1985, 495–571.

134. *Ibid.*, Dec. 5, 1985, 572–5.

135. *Ibid.*, Dec. 4, 1985, 353–4.

136. *Ibid.*, Nov. 21, 1985, 317–21,.

137. *Ibid.*, Dec. 12, 1985, 691–737.

138. Locher, *Victory on the Potomac*, 399.

139. *Ibid.*, 404.

140. The interim report can be found in Roger R. Trask and John P. Glennon, eds. *The Department of Defense: Documents on Organization and Mission 1978–2003* (Washington, D.C.: Office of the Secretary of Defense, Historical Office, 2008), 26–36.

141. Michael Weisskopf, "Pentagon Overhaul Proposed," *Washington Post*, March 1, 1986.

142. The directive can be found in Trask and Glennon, *DOD Documents on Organization...*, 36–40 and at the Ronald Reagan Digital Library. https://www.reaganlibrary.gov/sites/default/files/archives/reference/scanned-nsdds/nsdd219.pdf/. Accessed Apr. 4, 2018.

143. A summary of the message to Congress can be found in Trask and Glennon, *DOD Documents on Organization...*, 40–41 and the full version at the Ronald Reagan Digital Library. https://www.reaganlibrary.gov/research/speeches/42486c. Accessed Apr. 4. 2018.

144. Locher, *Victory on the Potomac*, 423.

145. *Ibid.*, 425.

146. Goldwater-Nichols Act of 1986. http://history.defense.gov/Portals/70/Documents/dod_reforms/Goldwater-NicholsDoDReordAct1986.pdf. Accessed Apr. 4, 2018.

147. Dan Daniel (1914–1988), *Encyclopedia of Virginia*. https://www.encyclopediavirginia.org/Daniel_Wilbur_Clarence_Dan_1914–1988. Accessed Apr. 5, 2018.

148. William G. Boykin, Col. USA, "The Origins of the United States Special Operations Command," (historical background paper, United States Special Operations Command, USSOCOM, no date),6. https://www.afsoc.af.mil/Portals/86/documents/history/AFD-051228-009.pdf. Accessed Nov. 27, 2018.

149. Dan Daniel, "The Case for a Sixth Service," *Armed Forces Journal International*, August, 1985: 70–75. This article reportedly was ghost-written for Daniel by a House and a DOD staffer. See Susan L. Marquis. *Unconventional Warfare: Rebuilding U.S. Special Operations Forces* (Washington, D.C.: Brookings Institution, 1997), 121.

150. William S. Cohen, "A Defense Special Operations Agency: Fix for a SOF Capability that is Most Assuredly Broken," *Armed Forces Journal International*, January, 1986: 38–45.

151. James R. Locher III, "Congress to the Rescue: Statutory Creation of USSOCOM," *Air Commando Journal*, vol. 1, issue 3, Spring, 2012: 35.

152. *Ibid.*

153. A transcript of Scholtes's classified testimony is currently in the custody of the Center for Legislative Archives, a unit of the National Archives and Records Administration in Washington. The author formally requested a declassification review on Apr. 30, 2018, that is still in process. The House and the Senate have different declassification rules for closed hearings.

154. Boykin, "The Origins of the United States Special Operations Command," 13.

155. Locher, "Congress to the Rescue," 36–7.

156. Boykin, "The Origins of the United States Special Operations Command," 13.

157. *Ibid.*, 38.

158. Marquis, *Unconventional Warfare*, 147.

159. Locher, "Congress to the Rescue," 38.

160. *Ibid.*, 174.

161. *Ibid.*, 38 and *n*39.

162. Ronald H. Cole, "Grenada, Panama, and Haiti: Joint Operational Reform," *Joint Forces Quarterly*, Autumn/Winter, 1998–99, 71.

163. U.S. Congress, Senate, Committee on Armed Services, *Operation Desert Shield/Desert Storm*, 102nd Congress, 1st session, April 24; May 8, 9, 16 and 21; June 4, 12, 20, 1991, 318.

164. "The Chairman as Principal Military Advisor: An Interview with Colin L. Powell," *Joint Force Quarterly*, Autumn, 1996, 30.

165. Gillespie, interview, 512.

166. Lt. Col. Andrew H. Perkins, Jr., "Operation Urgent Fury: An Engineer's View," *The Military Engineer*, March-April, 1984, 86–90.

167. DOD and DOS, "Grenada: A Preliminary Report," 41–2.

168. "$40 Million Asked in Aid to Grenada," *New York Times*, Apr. 15, 1984.

169. Joseph B. Treaster, "New Airport, Still Unfinished, Is Open in Grenada," *New York Times*, Oct. 29, 1984.

170. Metcalf as quoted in Strober and Strober, *The Reagan Presidency*, 257.

171. Bridgetown Embassy to the Secretary of State, "Uncleared, informal minutes of meeting between Ambassadors Bish and McNeil and West Indian heads of government to discuss Grenada Situation," secret cable, Oct. 25, 1983, unclassified in State Department FOIA Reading Room. https://foia.state.gov/Search/results.aspx?searchText=Uncleared%2C+informal+minutes+of+meeting+between+Ambassadors+Bish+and+McNeil+&beginDate=&endDate=&publishedBeginDate=&publishedEndDate=&caseNumber=. Accessed Feb. 8, 2018.

172. Amnesty International, "The Grenada 17: Last of the Cold War Prisoners?" October 2003, 8. https://www.amnesty.org/en/documents/AMR32/001/2003/en/. Accessed Apr. 10, 2018.

173. *Ibid.*, 9–13.

174. Simeon C.R. McIntosh, *Kelsen in the 'Grenada Court': Essays on Revolutionary Legality* (Kingston, Jamaica: Ian Randle Publishers, 2008), 1–3.

175. This summary of the Fort Rupert case was drawn from "The Maurice Bishop Murder Trial," *The Grenadian Newsletter*, Dec. 6, 1986, Vol. 14, No. 19. Archived at the Digital Library of the Caribbean.

176. "Elated Coard: Speaks of Prison," *Jamaica Gleaner*, Sept. 13, 2009.

177. Coard, *What Really Happened*, 318.

Bibliography

Adams, James. *Secret Armies: Inside the American, Soviet, and European Special Forces.* New York: Atlantic Monthly Press, 1988.

Adkin, Mark. *Urgent Fury: The Battle for Grenada.* Lexington, MA: Lexington Books, 1989.

Ambursley, Fitzroy, and James Dunkerley. *Grenada/ Whose Freedom?* London: Latin America Bureau, 1984.

Andrew, Christopher M. *For the President's Eyes Only: Secret Intelligence and the American Presidency from Washington to Bush.* New York: HarperCollins, 1995.

Arostegui, Martin C. *Twilight Warriors: Inside the World's Special Forces.* New York: St. Martin's Press, 1997.

Ashby, Timothy. *The Bear in the Back Yard: Moscow's Caribbean Strategy.* Lexington, Mass: Lexington Books, 1987.

Atkinson, Rick. *The Long Gray Line.* Boston: Houghton Mifflin, 1989.

Bahmanyar, Mir. *Shadow Warriors: A History of the US Army Rangers.* New York: Osprey Publishing, 2005.

Baker, James Addison, and Steve Fiffer. *"Work Hard, Study—and Keep Out of Politics!"* Evanston, Ill: Northwestern University Press, 2008.

Beck, Robert J. *The Grenada Invasion: Politics, Law, and Foreign Policy Decisionmaking.* Boulder, CO: Westview Press, 1993.

Beckwith, Charlie A., and Donald Knox. *Delta Force: The Army's Elite Counterterrorist Unit.* New York: Avon Books, 2000.

Bishop, Maurice. *Maurice Bishop Speaks: The Grenada Revolution and Its Overthrow, 1979–83.* Edited by Bruce Marcus and Michael Taber. New York: Pathfinder Press, 1983.

Blechman, Barry M, and William J. Lynn, eds. *Toward a More Effective Defense: Report of the Defense Organization Project.* Cambridge, MA: Ballinger, 1985.

Bolger, Daniel P. *Americans at War: 1975–1986, an Era of Violent Peace.* Novato, CA: Presidio, 1988.

Bowden, Mark. *Black Hawk Down: A Story of Modern War.* New York: Penguin Books, 2000.

Boykin, William G. *Never Surrender: A Soldier's Journey to the Crossroads of Faith and Freedom.* New York: FaithWords, 2008.

Bradlee, Ben, Jr. *Guts and Glory: The Rise and Fall of Oliver North.* New York: Donald I. Fine, 1988.

Bryant, Carol. *Milan Bish: The Measure You Give.* Edited by Allene Bish, R. J. Post, and Irene Abernethy. Grand Island, NE: Allene Bish, 2000.

Burrowes, Reynold A. *Revolution and Rescue in Grenada: An Account of the U.S.–Caribbean Invasion.* New York: Greenwood Press, 1988.

Cannon, Lou. *President Reagan: The Role of a Lifetime.* New York: Simon & Schuster, 1991.

Carney, John T., and Benjamin F. Schemmer. *No Room for Error: The Covert Operations of America's Special Tactics Units from Iran to Afghanistan.* New York: Ballantine Books, 2002.

Castro, Fidel, Jeffrey M. Elliot, and Mervyn M. Dymally. *Nothing Can Stop the Course of History.* New York: Pathfinder Press, 1988.

Chalker, Dennis C., with Kevin Dockery. *One Perfect Op.* New York: Morrow, 2002.

Chinnery, Philip D. *Air Commando: Fifty Years of the USAF Air Commando and Special Operations Forces, 1944–1994.* New York: St. Martin's Press, 1997.

Clancy, Tom, Carl Stiner, and Tony Koltz. *Shadow Warriors: Inside the Special Forces.* New York: Berkley Books, 2003.

Clarridge, Duane R., with Digby Diehl. *A Spy for All Seasons: My Life in the CIA.* New York: Scribner's, 1997.

Coard, Bernard. *Forward Ever: Journey to a New Grenada.* Kingston, Jamaica: McDermott Publishing, 2018.

_____. *The Grenada Revolution; What Really Happened.* Kingston, Jamaica: McDermott Publishing, 2017.

Coard, Phyllis. *Unchained: A Caribbean Woman's Journey Through Invasion, Incarceration and Liberation.* Kingston, Jamaica: McDermott Publishing, 2019.

_____. *U.S. War on One Woman: My Conditions of Imprisonment in Grenada.* London: Karia Press, 1988.

Cohen, Roger, and Claudio Gatti. *In the Eye of the Storm: The Life of General H. Norman Schwarzkopf.* Boston: G.K. Hall & Co., 1991.

Collier, Peter. *Political Woman: The Big Little Life of Jeane Kirkpatrick.* New York: Encounter Books, 2012.

Cotman, John Walton. *The Gorrion Tree: Cuba and the Grenada Revolution.* New York: P. Lang, 1993.

Couch, Dick. *The Warrior Elite: The Forging of Seal Class 228.* New York: Crown Publishers, 2001.

_____, and William Doyle. *Navy SEALs: Their Untold Story.* New York: William Morrow, an Imprint of HarperCollins, 2014.

Couvillon, Michael J. *Grenada Grinder: The Complete Story of AC-130H Spectre Gunships in Operation Urgent Fury.* Marietta, GA: Deeds Publishing, 2011.

Crandall, Russell. *Gunboat democracy: U.S. interventions in the Dominican Republic, Grenada, and Panama.* New York: Rowan and Littlefield, 2008.

Dalgleish, Charles. *Recon Marine: An Account of Beirut and Grenada.* Charles Dalgleish, 1995.

Daugherty, Leo J., and Rhonda Smith-Daugherty. *Counterinsurgency and the United States Marine Corps: Volume 2, An Era of Persistent Warfare, 1945–2016.* Jefferson, NC: McFarland & Co., 2018.

Davidson, Scott. *Grenada: A Study in Politics and the Limits of International Law.* Aldershot, England: Avebury, 1987.

Deaver, Michael K., and Mickey Herskowitz. *Behind the Scenes: In Which the Author Talks About Ronald and Nancy Reagan...and Himself.* New York: Morrow, 1988.

Dockery, Kevin. *SEALs in Action.* New York: Avon Books, 1991.

Dujmović, Nicholas. *The Grenada Documents: Window on Totalitarianism.* Cambridge, MA and Washington, D.C.: Pergamon-Brassey's, 1988.

Dunn, Peter M., and Bruce W. Watson. *American Intervention in Grenada: The Implications of Operation "Urgent Fury."* Boulder, CO and London: Westview Press, 1985.

Durant, Michael J., Steven Hartov and Robert L. Johnson. *The Night Stalkers: Top Secret Missions of the U.S. Army's Special Operations Aviation Regiment.* New York: G.P. Putnam's Sons, 2006.

Emerson, Steven. *Secret warriors: Inside the Covert Military Operations of the Reagan Era.* New York: G.P. Putnam's Sons, 1988.

Fraser, Peter A. "A Revolutionary Governor General? The Grenada Crisis of 1983." In *Constitutional Heads and Political Crises: Commonwealth Episodes, 1945–85.* Edited by Donald Low. New York: St. Martin's, 1988.

Gabriel, Richard A. *Military Incompetence: Why the American Military Doesn't Win.* New York: Hill and Wang, 1985.

Galdorisi, George, and Tom Phillips. *Leave No Man Behind: The Saga of Combat Search and Rescue.* Minneapolis, MN: Zenith Press, 2008.

Gates, Robert Michael. *From the Shadows: The Ultimate Insider's Story of Five Presidents and How They Won the Cold War.* New York: Simon & Schuster, 1996.

Gerson, Allan. *The Kirkpatrick Mission: Diplomacy Without Apology: America at the United Nations 1981–1985.* New York: Free Press, 1991.

Gilmore, William C. *The Grenada Intervention: Analysis and Documentation.* New York: Facts on File, 1984.

Gormly, Robert A. *Combat Swimmer: Memoirs of a Navy SEAL.* New York: Penguin Group, 1998.

Grenada, Duffus Commission. *Report of the Duffus Commission of Inquiry into the Breakdown of Law & Order, and Police Brutality in Grenada.* Grenada: The Commission, 1975. Digitization by Florida International University Digital Collections Center (2012). http://ufdc.ufl.edu/AA00010419/00001. (Accessed May 6, 2018)

Gutman, Roy. *Banana Diplomacy: The Making of American Policy in Nicaragua, 1981–1987.* New York: Simon & Schuster, 1988.

Haney, Eric L. *Inside Delta Force: The Story of America's Elite Counterterrorist Unit.* New York: Dell, 2003.

Harding, Stephen. *Air War Grenada.* Missoula, MT: Pictorial Histories Publishing Company, 1986.

Head, William Pace. *Night Hunters: The AC-130s and Their Role in US Airpower.* College Station: Texas A&M University Press, 2014. eBook Collection (EBSCOhost). (Accessed July 17, 2018)

Heine, Jorge, ed. *A Revolution Aborted: The Lessons of Grenada.* Pittsburgh: University of Pittsburgh Press, 1990.

Hertsgaard, Mark. *On Bended Knee: The Press & the Reagan Presidency.* New York: Schocken Books, 1989.

Higbie, Janet. *Eugenia: The Caribbean's Iron Lady.* London: Macmillan Caribbean, 1993.

Howe, Geoffrey. *Conflict of Loyalty.* New York: St. Martin's Press, 1994.

Hoyos, F. A. *Tom Adams: A Biography.* London: Macmillan Caribbean, 1988.

Hoyt, Edwin P. *SEALs at War: The Story of U.S. Navy Special Warfare from the Frogmen to the SEALs.* New York: Dell, 1993.

Huchthausen, Peter A. *America's Splendid Little Wars.* New York: Viking, 2003.

Isby, David C. *Leave No Man Behind: Liberation and Capture Missions.* London: Weidenfeld & Nicolson, 2004.

Jessamy, Michael. *Forts & Coastal Batteries of Grenada.* [Grenada]: Roland's Image Productions, 1998.

Jones, Charles V. *Boys of '67: From Vietnam to Iraq, the Extraordinary Story of a Few Good Men.* Mechanicsburg, PA: Stackpole Books, 2006.

Kelly, Orr. *Brave Men...Dark Waters: The Untold Story of the Navy SEALS.* Novato, CA: Presidio Press, 1992.

_____. *From a Dark Sky: The Story of U.S. Air Force Special Operations,* Novato, CA: Presidio Press, 1996.

_____. *Never Fight Fair: Navy Seals' Stories of Combat and Adventure,* Novato, CA: Presidio Press, 1995.

Kirkpatrick, Jeane J. *Making War to Keep Peace.* New York: HarperCollins, 2007.

Kornbluh, Peter, and Malcolm Byrne, eds. *The Iran-Contra Scandal: The Declassified History.* New York: The New Press, 1993.

Layne, Joseph Ewart. *We Move Tonight: The Making of the Grenada Revolution.* St. George's, Grenada: Grenada Revolution Memorial Foundation, 2014.

Ledeen, Michael, and Herbert Romerstein, eds. *Grenada Documents: An Overview and Selection.* Washington: U.S. G.P.O., 1985.

Lehman, John F., Jr. *Command of the Seas.* New York: Charles Scribner's Sons, 1988.

Leoni, Ray D. *Black Hawk: The Story of a World Class Helicopter.* Reston, VA: American Institute of Aeronautics, 2007.

Lewis, Gordon K. *Grenada: The Jewel Despoiled.* Baltimore: Johns Hopkins Univ. Press, 1987.

Livingstone, Neil C. *The Cult of Counterterrorism: The "Weird World" of Spooks, Counterterrorists, Adventures, and the Non-Quite Professionals.* Lexington, Mass: Lexington Books, 1990.

Locher, James R. III. *Victory on the Potomac: The Goldwater-Nichols Act Unifies the Pentagon.* College Station: Texas A & M University Press, 2002.

Lock, John D. *To Fight with Intrepidity...: The Complete History of the U.S. Army Rangers, 1622 to Present.* New York: Pocket Books, 1998.

Luttwak, Edward N. *The Pentagon and the Art of War: The Question of Military Reform.* New York: Institute for Contemporary Studies/Simon & Schuster, 1984.

MacDonald, Scott B, Harald M. Sandstrom, and Paul B. Goodwin, eds. *The Caribbean After Grenada: Revolution, Conflict, and Democracy.* New York: Praeger, 1988.

Marcinko, Richard, and James DeFelice. *Rogue Warrior.* New York: Pocket Star Books, 2006.

Marquis, Susan L. *Unconventional Warfare: Rebuilding*

US Special Operations Forces. Washington, D.C.: Brookings Institution, 1997.

Martin, David C., and John Walcott. *Best Laid Plans: The Inside Story of America's War Against Terrorism.* New York: Simon & Schuster, 1988.

Matthews, Christopher. *Tip and the Gipper: When Politics Worked.* New York: Simon & Schuster, 2013.

McFarlane, Robert C., and Zofia Smardz. *Special Trust.* New York: Cadell & Davies, 1994.

Mcintosh, Simeon C. R. *Kelsen in the 'Grenada Court': Essays on Revolutionary Legality.* Kingston, Jamaica: Ian Randle Publishers, 2008.

McNeil, Frank. *War and Peace in Central America.* New York: Scribner's, 1988.

Meese, Edwin. *With Reagan: The Inside Story.* Washington, D.C.: Regnery Gateway, 1992.

Menges, Constantine Christopher. *Inside the National Security Council: The True Story of the Making and Unmaking of Reagan's Foreign Policy.* New York: Simon & Schuster, 1988.

Metcalf, Joseph P. III. "Decision Making and the Grenada Rescue Operation." In *Ambiguity and Command: Organizational Perspectives on Military Decision Making.* Edited by James G. Marsh, 227–297. Marshfield, Mass: Pitman Publishing, 2006.

Moore, Charles. *Margaret Thatcher: The Authorized Biography.* New York: Alfred A. Knopf, 2016.

Moore, John Norton. *Law and the Grenada Mission.* Charlottesville: Center for Law and National Security, University of Virginia School of Law, 1984.

Morris, Edmund. *Dutch: A Memoir of Ronald Reagan.* New York: Random House, 1999.

Naylor, Sean. *Relentless Strike: The Secret History of Joint Special Operations Command.* New York: St. Martin's Press, 2015.

North, Oliver L., with William Novak. *Under Fire: An American Story.* New York: HarperCollins, 1991.

O'Kelley, Patrick. *Triple Canopy.* West Conshohocken, PA: Infinity Publishing, 2014.

O'Neill, Thomas, with William Novak. *Man of the House: The Life and Political Memoirs of Speaker Tip O'Neill.* New York: Random House, 1987.

Ortiz, Frank V., and Donald J. Usner. *Ambassador Ortiz: Lessons from a Life of Service.* Albuquerque: University of New Mexico Press, 2005.

O'Shaughnessy, Hugh. *Grenada: Revolution, Invasion and Aftermath.* London: Sphere Books, 1984.

Pavlov, Yuri. *Soviet-Cuban Alliance: 1959–1991.* Coral Gables, FL: North-South Center, University of Miami, 1994.

Payne, Anthony, Paul K. Sutton, and Tony Thorndike. *Grenada: Revolution and Invasion.* New York: St. Martin's Press, 1984.

Perry, Mark. *Four Stars.* Boston: Houghton Mifflin, 1989.

Persico, Joseph E. *Casey: The Lives and Secrets of William J. Casey from the OSS to the CIA.* New York: Penguin Books, 1991.

Pfarrer, Chuck. *SEAL Target Geronimo: The Inside Story of the Mission to Kill Osama Bin Laden.* New York: St. Martin's Press, 2011.

Powell, Colin L., and Joseph E. Persico. *My American Journey.* New York: Random House, 1995.

Pushies, Fred. *Night Stalkers: 160th Special Operations Aviation Regiment (Airborne).* St. Paul, MN: Zenith Press, 2005.

Pyle, Richard, and H. Norman Schwarzkopf. *Schwarzkopf: The Man, the Mission, the Triumph.* New York: Signet, 1991.

Radix, Kendrick. *George Louison and Kendrick Radix Discuss—: Internal Events Leading to the U.S. Invasion of Grenada.* New York: Grenada Foundation, 1984.

Reagan, Ronald. *An American Life.* New York: Simon & Schuster, 1990.

_____. *Reagan: A Life in Letters.* Edited by Kiron K. Skinner, Annelise Graebner Anderson, and Martin Anderson. New York: Free Press, 2003.

_____. *The Reagan Diaries.* Edited by Douglas Brinkley. New York: HarperCollins, 2009.

Roper, Jim. *Aardvarks and Rangers.* Baltimore, MD: PublishAmerica, LLLP, 2004.

Rossin, Lawrence G. "Under Fire in Grenada." In *Duty & Danger: The American Foreign Service in Action,* 1–3. Washington, D.C.: American Foreign Service Association, 1988.

Russell, Lee, and M. Albert Mendez. *Grenada 1983.* MEN-AT-ARMS. London: Osprey, 1985.

Sandford, Gregory W., and Richard Vigilante. *Grenada: The Untold Story.* Lanham, MD: Madison Books, 1984.

Schoenhals, Kai P., and Richard A. Melanson. *Revolution and Intervention in Grenada: The New Jewel Movement, the United States, and the Caribbean.* Boulder, CO: Westview Press, 1985.

Schwarzkopf, H. Norman, and Peter Petre. *It Doesn't Take a Hero: General H. Norman Schwarzkopf, the Autobiography.* New York: Bantam Books, 1992.

Scoon, Paul. *Survival for Service: My Experiences as Governor General of Grenada.* Oxford, England: Macmillan Caribbean, 2003.

Seabury, Paul, and Walter A. McDougall. *The Grenada Papers.* San Francisco, CA: Institute for Contemporary Studies, 1984.

Seaga, Edward Philip George. *The Grenada Intervention: The Inside Story.* Kingston, Jamaica: The University of the West Indies, 2009.

Sharkey, Jaqueline E. *Under Fire: US Military Restrictions on the Media from Grenada to the Persian Gulf.* Washington, D.C.: Center for Public Integrity, 1991.

Shultz, George P. *Turmoil and Triumph: My Years as Secretary of State.* New York: Charles Scribner's Sons, 1993.

Smith, Geoffrey. *Reagan and Thatcher.* New York: W.W. Norton, 1991.

Snook, Scott A. *Friendly Fire: The Accidental Shootdown of U.S. Black Hawks Over Northern Iraq.* Princeton, NJ: Princeton University Press, 2002.

Speakes, Larry, and Robert Pack. *Speaking Out: The Reagan Presidency from Inside the White House.* New York: Charles Scribner's Sons, 1988.

Strober, Deborah H., and Gerald S. Strober. *The Reagan Presidency: An Oral History of the Era.* Washington, D.C.: Brassey's, Inc., 2003.

Strosser, Edward, and Michael Prince. *Stupid Wars: A Citizen's Guide to Botched Putsches, Failed Coups, Inane Invasions, and Ridiculous Revolutions.* New York: HarperCollins, 2008.

Sunshine, Catherine, ed. *Grenada: The Peaceful Revolution.* Washington, D.C.: EPICA Task Force, 1982.

Sweeney, Michael S. *The Military and the Press: An Uneasy Truce.* Evanston, IL: Medill School of Journalism, Northwestern University Press, 2006.

Thatcher, Margaret. *The Downing Street Years.* New York: HarperCollins, 1993.

Thorndike, Tony. *Grenada: Politics, Economics and Society.* Boulder, CO: Lynne Rienner Publishers, Inc., 1985.

Tiwathia, Vijay. *The Grenada War: Anatomy of a Low-Intensity Conflict.* New Delhi: Lancer International, 1987.

Trotman, Donald A. B., Sehon S. Goodridge, and Mark Haynes. *Redeeming the Past, a Time for Healing: Report on Certain Political Events Which Occurred in Grenada 1976–1991.* Grenada: Truth and Reconciliation Commission, 2006.

Trujillo, Stephen. *A Tale of the Grenada Raiders: Memories in the Idioms of Dreams.* Stephen Trujillo, 2017.

Valenta, Jiri, and Herbert J. Ellison, eds. *Grenada and Soviet/Cuban Policy: Internal Crisis and U.S./OECS Intervention.* Boulder, CO: Westview Press, 1986.

Wagner, Geoffrey. *Red Calypso.* Washington: Regnery Gateway, 1988.

Walker, Greg. *At the Hurricane's Eye: U.S. Special Forces from Vietnam to Desert Storm.* New York: Ivy Books, 1994.

Waller, Douglas C. *The Commandos: The Inside Story of America's Secret Soldiers.* New York: A Dell Book, 1994.

Walsh, Lawrence E. *Firewall: The Iran-Contra Conspiracy and Cover-up.* New York: Norton, 1997.

Wasdin, Howard E., and Stephen Templin. *SEAL Team Six: Memoirs of an Elite Navy SEAL Sniper.* New York: St. Martin's Press, 2011.

Weinberger, Caspar W. *Fighting for Peace: Seven Critical Years in the Pentagon.* New York: Warner Books, 1990.

_____, and Gretchen Roberts. *In the Arena: A Memoir of the 20th Century.* Washington, D.C.: Regnery, 2001.

Wilentz, Sean. *The Age of Reagan: A History, 1974–2008.* New York: HarperCollins, 2008.

Williams, Gary. *US–Grenada Relations: Revolution and Intervention in the Backyard.* New York: Palgrave Macmillan, 2007.

Woodward, Bob. *Veil: The Secret Wars of the CIA, 1981–1987.* New York: Simon & Schuster, 1987.

U.S. Military/Government Monographs

Bonham, Gordon C. *Airfield Seizure; 'The Modern 'Key to Country'* School of Advanced Military Studies, Fort Leavenworth, KS, First Term, AY 90–91.

Borch, Frederic L. *Judge Advocates in Combat: Army Lawyers in Military Operations from Vietnam to Haiti.* Washington, D.C.: Office of the Judge Advocate General and Center of Military History, 2001. https://history.army.mil/html/books/070/70-77/index.html. (Accessed May 6, 2018)

Cole, Ronald. *Operation Urgent Fury, Grenada. The Planning and Execution of Joint Operations in Grenada.* United States: Joint Chiefs of Staff Washington, D.C., Joint History Office, 1997. https://history.army.mil/html/bookshelves/resmat/cold_war/urgfury.pdf (Accessed May 6, 2018)

Combelles-Siegel, Pascale. *The Troubled Path to the Pentagon's Rules on Media Access to the Battlefield: Grenada to Today.* Carlisle Barracks, PA: Strategic Studies Institute, U.S. Army War College, 1996. https://ssi.armywarcollege.edu/pubs/display.cfm?pubID=325 (Accessed May 6, 2018)

Haulman, Daniel L. *Crisis in Grenada: Operation URGENT FURY.* In *Short of War: Major USAF Contingency Operations, 1947–1997,* edited by A. Timothy Warnock, 135–144. Maxwell AFB, AL: Air Force History and Museums Program/Air University Press,

2000. https://media.defense.gov/2010/Oct/27/200133 0212/-1/-1/0/AFD-101027-044.pdf (Accessed Aug. 15, 2018)

House, Jonathan M. *The United States Army in Joint Operations, 1950–1983.* U.S. Army Center of Military History, Washington, D.C., 1992.

Kallander, Dean C., and James K. Matthews. *Urgent Fury: The United States Air Force and the Grenada Operation.* Military Airlift Command, Office of History, Scott Air Force Base, IL, 1988. Declassified Aug. 23, 2010.

Lowrey, Nathan S. *The Chairmanship of the Joint Chiefs of Staff 1949–2016.* Office of the Chairman of the Joint Chiefs, Joint History Office, Washington, D.C., 2016. http://www.jcs.mil/Portals/36/Documents/History/Institutional/Chairmanship_of_the_JCS.pdf (Accessed Aug. 6, 2018)

Marion, Forrest L. *Brothers in Berets: The Evolution of Air Force Special Tactics, 1953–2003.* Maxwell Air Force Base, AL: Air University Press, Curtis E. LeMay Center for Doctrine Development and Education, 2018.

Pirnie, Bruce R. *Operation Urgent Fury: The United States Army in Joint Operations.* U.S. Army Center of Military History, Washington, D.C., 1986. Declassified Aug, 3, 1993.

Raines, Edgar F., Jr. "The Interagency Process and the Decision to Intervene in Grenada, October, 1983." In *The US Army and the Interagency Process: Historical Perspectives: The Proceedings of the Combat Studies Institute 2008 Military History Symposium.* Fort Leavenworth, Kan: Combat Studies Institute Press, 2008, 13–24.

_____. *The Rucksack War: U.S. Army Operational Logistics in Grenada, 1983.* Washington, D.C.: Center of Military History, U.S. Army, 2010. https://history.army.mil/html/books/055/55-2-1/CMH_Pub_55-2-1.pdf (Accessed March 12, 2019)

_____, and Major David R. Campbell. *The Army and the Joint Chiefs of Staff: Evolution of Army Ideas on the Command, Control and Coordination of the U.S. Armed Forces, 1942–1985.* U.S. Army Center of Military History, Washington, D.C., 1986. http://www.dtic.mil/dtic/tr/fulltext/u2/a640665.pdf/ (Accessed May 6, 2018)

Senkovich, Steven W. *From Port Salines to Panama City: The Evolution of Command and Control in Contingency Operations.* School of Advanced Military Studies, United States Army Command and General Staff College, Fort Leavenworth, KS, *Second* Term 1988–89. http://www.dtic.mil/dtic/tr/fulltext/u2/a234002.pdf (Accessed May 6, 2018)

Spector, Ronald H. *U.S. Marines in Grenada, 1983.* Washington, D.C.: History and Museums Division, Headquarters, U.S. Marine Corps, U.S.G.P.O. 1987.

Stewart, Richard W., and Edgar F. Raines, Jr. *Operation Urgent Fury: The Invasion of Grenada, October 1983.* Washington, D.C.: Center of Military History, 2008. https://history.army.mil/html/books/grenada/urgent_fury.pdf (Accessed March 12, 2019)

Thigpen, Jerry L. *The Praetorian STARShip: The Untold Story of the Combat Talon.* Maxwell Air Force Base, AL: Air University Press, 2001.

Trask, Roger R and John P. Glennon, eds. *The Department of Defense: Documents on Organization and Mission 1978–2003.* Washington, D.C.: Office of the Secretary of Defense, Historical Office, 2008.

U.S. Department of Defense. Joint Chiefs of Staff. *Joint*

Military Operations Historical Collection. Washington, D.C., July 15, 1997. https://www.webharvest.gov/peth04/20041028232726/http://www.dtic.mil/doctrine/jel/history/hist.pdf (Accessed May 6, 2018)

U.S. Department of State and Department of Defense. *Grenada: A Preliminary Report,* Washington, D.C., Dec. 16, 1983. http://insidethecoldwar.org/sites/default/files/documents/Grenada%20A%20Preliminary%20Report%20December%2016%2C%201983.pdf (Accessed May 6, 2018)

U.S. Library of Congress. Congressional Research Service. *U.S. Low-Intensity Conflicts 1899–1990,* by John M. Collins with Frederick Hamerman and James P. Seevers, 1990. https://apps.dtic.mil/dtic/tr/fulltext/u2/a533427.pdf (Accessed Apr. 9, 2019)

_____. Congressional Research Service. *Grenada: Issues Concerning the Use of U.S. Forces,* by Richard Cronin. Issue brief # IB83170. Updated Dec. 13, 1983.

_____. Congressional Research Service. *The War Powers Resolution: After Thirty-Eight Years,* by Richard E. Grimmett. R42699. Sept. 24, 2012. https://www.hsdl.org/?abstract&did=721954. (Accessed May 6, 2018)

_____. Federal Research Division. "Grenada." In *Islands of the Commonwealth Caribbean: A Regional Study* by Richard A. Haggerty and John F. Hornbeck, 1987: 345–84. http://www.memory.loc.gov/master/frd/frdcstdy/is/islandsofcommonw00medi/islandsofcommonw00medi.pdf (Accessed May 6, 2018)

_____. Federal Research Division. *A History of the 160th Special Operations Aviation Regiment (Airborne),* by Ronald E. Dolan, October, 2001. Declassified 2010. http://www.governmentattic.org/2docs/Army_160thSOAR_Histories_1991-2001.pdf (Accessed May 6, 2018)

U.S. Printing Office. *Defense Organization: The Need for Change,* Staff Report to the Committee on Armed Services, United States Senate, 99th Congress, 1st Session, October 16, 1985.

_____. *Report of the Congressional Committees Investigating the Iran-Contra Affair,* 100th Congress, 1st Session, 1987.

Vessey, John William. *Selected Works of General John W. Vessey, Jr., USA, Tenth Chairman of the Joint Chiefs of Staff, 22 June 1982—30 September 1985.* Joint History Office, Office of the Chairman of the Joint Chiefs of Staff, Washington, D.C., 2008. https://history.army.mil/html/bookshelves/resmat/cold_war/vessey_speeches.pdf (Accessed May 6, 2018)

Index

Numbers in *bold italics* indicate pages with illustrations